RESTARTING AND SUSTAINING ECONOMIC GROWTH AND DEVELOPMENT IN AFRICA

Contemporary Perspectives on Developing Societies

JOHN MUKUM MBAKU
Series Editor
Weber State University, Ogden, Utah, USA

Between 1989 and 1991, there were several changes in the global political economy that have had significant impact on policy reform in developing societies. The most important of these were the collapse of socialism in Eastern Europe, the subsequent disintegration of the Soviet Union, the cessation of superpower rivalry, and the demise of apartheid in South Africa. These events have provided scholars a new and challenging research agenda: To help the peoples of the Third World participate more effectively in the new global economy. Given existing conditions in these societies, the first line of business for researchers would be to help these countries establish and maintain transparent, accountable and participatory governance structures and, at the same time, provide themselves with more viable economic infrastructures. The *Contemporary Perspectives on Developing Societies* series was founded to serve as an outlet for such policy relevant research. It is expected that books published in this series will provide rigorous analyses of issues relevant to the peoples of the Third World and their efforts to improve their participation in the global economy.

Also in this series

Restarting and Sustaining Economic Growth and Development in Africa: The Case of Kenya

Edited by
MWANGI S. KIMENYI
The Kenya Institute for Public Policy Research and Analysis (KIPPRA)
Nairobi, Kenya

JOHN MUKUM MBAKU
Department of Economics
Weber State University
Ogden, Utah, USA

NGURE MWANIKI
M. A. Consulting Group
Nairobi, Kenya

ASHGATE

© Mwangi S. Kimenyi, John Mukum Mbaku and Ngure Mwaniki 2003

Published by
Ashgate Publishing Limited
Gower House
Croft Road
Aldershot
Hants GU11 3HR
England

Ashgate Publishing Company
Suite 420
101 Cherry Street
Burlington, VT 05401-4405
USA

Ashgate website: http://www.ashgate.com

British Library Cataloguing in Publication Data
Restarting and sustaining economic growth and development
in Africa : the case of Kenya. - (Contemporary perspectives
on developing societies)
1.Kenya - Economic policy 2.Kenya - Economic conditions -
1963-
I.Kimenyi, Mwangi S., 1956- II.Mbaku, John Mukum, 1950-
III.Mwaniki, Ngure
338.9'6762

Library of Congress Cataloging-in-Publication Data
Restarting and sustaining economic growth and development in Africa : the case of
Kenya / edited by Mwangi S. Kimenyi, John Mukum Mbaku, and Ngure Mwaniki.
     p. cm. -- (Contemporary perspectives on developing societies)
   Includes bibliographical references and index.
   ISBN 0-7546-3472-8 (alk. paper)
     1. Kenya--Economic conditions--1963- 2. Kenya--Economic policy. 3.
Africa--Economic conditions--1960- I. Kimenyi, Mwangi S., 1956- II. Mbaku, John
Mukum, 1950- III. Mwaniki, Ngure. IV. Series.

HC865 .R478 2003
338.96762--dc21

2002028146

ISBN 0 7546 3472 8

Printed and bound in Great Britain by Antony Rowe Ltd., Chippenham, Wilts.

Contents

List of Tables

List of Contributors

GEM ARGWINGS-KODHEK holds a Masters Degree in Agricultural Economics and has been working in agricultural policy analysis and advocacy for the last 12 years. He is a Senior Research Fellow at the Tegemeo Institute of Egerton University and has been involved in several long-term research projects in association with his alma maters—The University of Arizona, Stanford University and Michigan State. He has spoken and published widely on the full range of agricultural policy issues in Kenya and represented the private sector in the recent PRSP process in Kenya's Ministry of Finance.

AIDAN F. EYAKUZE is Head of Business at Capital Finance Limited in Dar-es-Salaam, Tanzania. Between 1995 and 2000, he was an economic consultant in Kenya, participating in projects supported by the World Bank, the African Development Bank, DFID, USAID and the Harvard Institute for International Development. He has reviewed the investment climate, policy and corporate constraints to private sector growth in East Africa, and assisted various companies to develop corporate strategies for improved performance. He has also carried out economic analysis of macroeconomic management, poverty reduction, globalization and national competitiveness and agricultural policy, and has advised on public sector reform, including the development of commercialization strategies for infrastructure, agriculture, training and standardization. Kenya's Institute of Economic Affairs published his research on the impact of globalization on Kenya's economy for International Development for the Kenya Scenarios Project in 2001. Mr. Eyakuze received a B.Sc. (Hons) in Economics from Trent University in Ontario, Canada and an MA (Economics) from Simon Fraser University in British Columbia, Canada.

GRAHAM GLENDAY is a Professor of the Practice in Public Policy Studies and Director of the Public Finance Group in the Duke Center for International Development at the Sanford Institute for Public Policy at Duke University. He came to Duke in July 2001 from Harvard University where he was Director of the

Public Finance Group in the Kennedy School of Government and for 15 years prior to that in the Harvard Institute for International Development. He has over 20 years of international experience in public finance, acting as an advisor in tax policy and administration reforms and other fiscal matters to over a dozen countries in Africa and Asia, including co-ordination of the Tax Modernization Program in Kenya. He served as a resident advisor in the Ministry of Finance in Kenya from 1990 to 2001, covering tax policy and related trade and capital market issues, civil service reform, and local government finance reforms. In the early 1980s, he served as Assistant Director of Tax Policy Analysis in the Department of Finance in the Government of Canada. Dr. Glenday has also published research and taught graduate courses and executive workshops in taxation and project appraisal matters. He was a Rhodes Scholar at Oxford University and has a Ph.D. in Public Policy from Harvard University.

GERRISHON K. IKIARA is a Senior Lecturer in Economics at the Institute of Diplomacy and International Studies, University of Nairobi. For the last 15 years, he has been engaged in research work on Kenya's economy with special reference to industrialization and development policy issues. He is a co-editor of two books on Kenya's industrialization process and has also published a large number of articles and chapters on a wide range of issues on African economies.

MWANGI S. KIMENYI, who holds a Ph.D. in Economics from the Center for Study of Public Choice at George Mason University, USA, is the Executive Director of the Kenya Institute for Public Policy Research and Analysis (KIPPRA). He has been Assistant Professor of Economics at the University of Mississippi (1986–1991) and Associate Professor of Economics at the University of Connecticut (1991– 1999). He is also vice-president of the African Educational Foundation for Public Policy and Market Process. Professor Kimenyi has also worked as a World Bank consultant attached to the National Institute of Statistics, Ministry of Planning, in Angola. He is the author of over 60 refereed journal articles, which have appeared in ranked journals such as the *Journal of Institutional and Theoretical Economics,* the *Yale Journal on Regulation,* the *Southern Economic Journal, Public Choice* and the *European Journal of Political Economy.* He is also author and co-author of five books. He is the co-editor (with John Mukum Mbaku) of two book series: *Public Choice and Developing Countries,* and *Contemporary Perspectives on Developing Countries,* both published by Ashgate, UK. He is the recipient of several honors and awards including the Georgescu-Roegen Prize in Economics and the co-recipient (with W. Wasike) of the 2001 Global Development Network Award for Outstanding Research. Professor Kimenyi's current research focuses on institutional and economic reforms.

JOHN MUKUM MBAKU is Willard L. Eccles Professor of Economics and John S. Hinckley Fellow at Weber State University, Ogden, Utah and Associate Editor (Africa), *Journal of Third World Studies*. He is also President of the African Educational Foundation for Public Policy and Market Process, Inc. He was born in Cameroon and received the Ph.D. degree in economics from the University of Georgia in 1985. He has previously taught at the University of Georgia and Kennesaw State University. His present research interests are in public choice, constitutional political economy, trade integration, intergroup relations, and institutional reforms in Africa. During 1994–1995, he served as the President of the Association of Third World Studies, Inc. He is the author of *Institutions and Reform in Africa: The Public Choice Perspective* (Praeger, 1997), and *Bureaucratic and Political Corruption in Africa: The Public Choice Perspective* (Krieger, 2000); editor of *Corruption and the Crisis of Institutional Reforms in Africa* (The Edwin Mellen Press, 1998), and of *Preparing Africa for the Twenty-First Century: Strategies for Peaceful Coexistence and Sustainable Development* (Ashgate, 1999); co-editor (with Julius O. Ihonvbere) of *Multiparty Democracy and Political Change: Constraints to Democratization in Africa* (Ashgate, 1998), (with Mwangi S. Kimenyi) of *Institutions and Collective Choice in Developing Countries: Applications of the Theory of Public Choice* (Ashgate, 1999); (with Pita Ogaba Agbese and Mwangi S. Kimenyi) of *Ethnicity and Governance in the Third World* (Ashgate, 2001). He is the co-editor (with Mwangi S. Kimenyi) of two book series—*Public Choice and Developing Countries*, and *Contemporary Perspectives on Developing Societies*, published by Ashgate Publishing Limited (UK).

NGURE MWANIKI is founder and Managing Director of M.A. Consulting, an African regional economics and management consulting firm based in Nairobi, Kenya. In that capacity, he has managed, directed or directly participated in numerous assignments for various clients in the region during the past 21 years. These have included the Economic Commission for Africa, The World Bank, African Development Bank, DFID, USAID, IFAD, UNDP, APDF, UNESCO, SIDA, as well as governments and private sector organizations and NGOs. He holds a B.A. degree in Economics and Government from the University of Nairobi, a Diploma in Economics from The Economics Institute of the University of Colorado at Boulder, and an MPA in Economics and Public Policy from Harvard University. He served as the Kenya Coordinator for the EAGER Research project whose results are the contents of this publication.

DAVID NDII is currently Executive Director of the Kenya Leadership Institute, and previously Economist with the World Bank, Chief Executive, Institute of Economic Affairs in Nairobi, and Lecturer, Department of Economics, University of Nairobi.

He holds B.A. and M.A. degrees from the University of Nairobi, and M.Sc. and DPhil degrees in economics from the University of Oxford. His research interests include development macroeconomics, financial economics and African political economy.

NJUGUNA S. NDUNG'U is an Associate Professor of Economics in the Department of Economics, University of Nairobi. He is currently the Regional Program Officer in IDRC's Eastern and Southern Africa Regional Office (ESARO) in Nairobi. Prior to joining IDRC (International Development Research Center), Professor Ndung'u worked in the Kenya Institute for Public Policy Research and Analysis as a Principal Analyst and Head of the Macroeconomic and Economic Modeling Division. He was also jointly lecturing at the Department of Economics, University of Nairobi. Professor Ndung'u has authored and co-authored several refereed articles in journals and chapters in books mainly focussing on macroeconomic issues, economic growth, regional integration, pro-poor growth strategies and external debt problems. He obtained his Ph.D. in economics from the University of Gothenburg in Sweden, in 1993.

BENJAMIN M. NGANDA is an Associate Professor of Economics at the University of Nairobi. He is presently the Acting Chairman, Department of Economics. He initially joined the Department in 1985 as a Tutorial Fellow after completing the MA in Economics in the same Department. He completed his Ph.D. studies in the University of York in England in 1994. His present areas of research are health and poverty issues, and industrial economics. He teaches economic statistics, applied microeconomics, econometrics and health economics. He has been a consultant to both the Kenya Government and a number of international organizations including UNDP, UNICEF and WHO. He has published works on health and poverty issues and industrial economics.

HEZRON O. NYANGITO is an Agricultural Economist and is currently a Principal Policy Analyst and Head of Productive Sector Division at The Kenya Institute for Public Policy Research and Analysis (KIPPRA). He is also a Senior Lecturer, Department of Agricultural Economics, University of Nairobi since 1995 (on leave of absence). He has 15 years experience in conducting applied research and analysis in development economics with a major emphasis on agriculture, rural development and international trade and has published many professional papers and articles on these subjects. Dr. Nyangito is also the Kenya Country Coordinator of the IFPRI 2020 Network research activities on agriculture, food security and the environment. He received his Ph.D. degree from the University of Tennessee, USA in 1992 and had graduated with a B.Sc. degree in agriculture, 1983, and M.Sc. agricultural economics degree, 1987, from the University of Nairobi, Kenya.

JAMES KARANJA NYORO is a Senior Research Fellow with Tegemeo Institute, Egerton University, Kenya. Previously, he previously worked as an agricultural economist with the Coffee Research Foundation, Ruiru, Kenya. He has a bachelor's degree in Agriculture from the University of Nairobi and a Master's degree in agricultural economics from Wye College, University of London. He has been engaged in agricultural policy analysis work on key economic issues pertaining to market reform in Kenya, monitoring of the reform process and an evaluation of the impact of reform on producers and consumers. He has specifically worked on impacts of policy changes in coffee, maize, wheat and horticulture among others, and has undertaken several consultancies with the World Bank, European Union and the USAID. He has recently been involved in the preparation of the Kenya Rural Development Strategy.

JOHN OMITI holds a Ph.D. in agricultural and natural resource economics and is currently working with the Institute of Policy Analysis and Research (IPAR, Nairobi). Dr. Omiti is a member of the Toda Institute for Global Peace and Policy Research, Hawaii. He has been involved in agricultural and policy research in a number of countries including Ethiopia, Uganda and Kenya. He has also worked with a number of national and international agricultural research centers including the International Livestock Research Institute (ILRI) and the International Crops Research Institute for the Semi-Arid Tropics (ICRISAT). He has conducted several consultancies on agricultural/livestock policy with NGOs, research institutes and international donor agencies. He has published several articles in a number of international and peer-reviewed journals.

T. C. I. RYAN is an Economic Consultant specializing in macroeconomic management in developing economies. Prior to his retirement, he served as the Economic Secretary and Director of Planning in the Ministries of Finance and of Planning in the Government of Kenya. He also taught for many years in the University of Nairobi. His undergraduate degree, in Economics and Political Science, is from Trinity College, Dublin and his doctorate in Economics is from the Massachusetts Institute of Technology. As a consultant, he has worked extensively in Africa and has written in internationally on diverse areas of macroeconomic transformations.

ECKHARD SIGGEL is Associate Professor of economics at Concordia University in Montreal, Canada. A Ph.D. graduate of the University of Toronto, he has taught and done research in the areas of Development Economics and International Trade and Finance. Most of his research has focused on various African countries. He has published over 20 articles and monographs and has completed a textbook in *Methods of Economic Policy Analysis in Developing Countries*.

MBUI WAGACHA is Director of Research, Institute of Policy Analysis and Research (IPAR), in Nairobi, Kenya. He attended Swarthmore College (USA) and did graduate work at the Graduate Institute of International Studies, University of Geneva, before serving at the UN Geneva, African Center for Monetary Studies and the African Development Bank. A researcher in Macroeconomic Policies, he co-edited the book *Kenya's Strategic Policies for the 21ˢᵗ Century*. In 2001, he was Kenya's Country Director for the World Bank Institute's course, *Public Sector Policies to Benefit the Poor.*

Acknowledgments

Research underlying the papers published in this volume was carried out under the Kenya Equity and Growth Through Economic Research (EAGER) project supported by the United Sates Agency for International Development (USAID) under Co-operative Agreement No. AOT–0546–00–5133–00 with Harvard University. The Harvard Institute for International Development (HIID) implemented the agreement on behalf of Harvard. We are particularly grateful to Dr. Clive S. Gray and Dr. Malcolm McPherson, both of HIID, who acted as Chief of Party and Project Manager, respectively, of the EAGER project. They made extensive and substantive remarks on the research papers at various stages, including at various conferences and workshops, and provided valuable guidance in the management of the two year project.

The project was managed in Kenya by the MA Consulting Group, as subcontractor to HIID, under the supervision of a local advisory committee. The committee comprised of three prominent individuals from Kenya's public and private sectors, namely Mr. Harris Mule, a renowned economist and former Permanent Secretary in the Ministry of Finance and Planning, Mr. Jimnah Mbaru, a Kenyan businessman and then Chairman of the Nairobi Stock Exchange, Dr. Graham Glenday, then HIID Fellow and advisor in Kenya's Ministry of Finance. The committee did an outstanding job in giving guidance to Kenyan researchers, and in attending many meetings, workshops and conferences which deliberated on the thematic issues of the research and commented on the research findings.

We would also like to thank all the researchers and others who worked with us on this project, particularly the authors of the papers published here. Special thanks go to Research Assistants, Aidan Eyakuze (himself one of the authors) and Fred Owegi who played a special role in coordinating the research and workshops and in writing some of the drafts. Among the office and supporting staff, Esther Metha did a sterling job serving as the secretary for the project.

Many thanks are also due to Kenyan research and academic institutions that collaborated in dissemination seminars for the research. These include the Kenya Institute for Public Research and Analysis (KIPPRA), the Institute of Policy

Analysis and Research (IPAR), and the Institute of Economic Affairs (IEA). Other Kenyan institutions that discussed the research findings include the Departments of Economics at the Universities of Nairobi and Moi, the Institute for Development Studies, and the Tegemeo Institute. The Government of Kenya played a supportive role in sending senior officials to the research workshops and the dissemination conference.

Finally, we wish to thank the Kenya Institute for Public Policy Research and Analysis, the Department of Economics, Weber State University and the MA Consulting Group (Nairobi) for making it possible for the editors to devote a considerable amount of time in preparing the book manuscript. Many thanks to Hilda Basa of KIPPRA for her support in coordinating communication between the editors and authors.

Needless to say, none of the individuals or organizations whose contributions are acknowledged here bear any responsibility for any errors or omissions in this publication.

Mwangi S. Kimenyi
John Mukum Mbaku
Ngure Mwaniki

Acronyms

ASAL	Agricultural sector adjustment lending
ASAO-1	(First) Agricultural sector adjustment operation
CBK	Central Bank of Kenya; also Coffee Board of Kenya
CEO	Chief executive officer
CMA	Capital Market Authority Act
COMESA	Common Market for Eastern and Southern Africa
CPI	Consumer Price Index
CRF	Coffee Research Foundation
DDS	Domestic debt strategy
DRC	Democratic Republic of Congo; formerly called Zaire
EAC	East African Community
EAGER	Equity and Growth through Economic Research
EEC	European Economic Community
EFF	Extended Fund Facility (of the IMF)
EPPO	Export Promotion Programs Office
EPZ	Export Processing Zones
ESAF	Enhanced Structural Adjustment Facility
ESTU	Executive Secretariat and Technical Unit
EU	European Union
FDI	Foreign Direct Investment
GATT	General Agreement on Tariffs and Trade
GDP	Gross domestic product
GDS	Gross domestic savings
GoK	Government of Kenya
HIID	Harvard Institute for International Development
ICORs	Incremental capital output ratios
IDA	International Development Agency
IMF	International Monetary Fund
IPAR	Institute of Policy Analysis and Research
IPC	Investment Promotion Center
IS	Import substitution (strategy)
KARI	Kenya Agricultural Research Institute
KCC	Kenya Cooperative Creameries
KDB	Kenya Dairy Board
KPCU	Kenya Planters Cooperative Union

KSA	Kenya Sugar Authority
KSh	Kenyan Shilling (Official currency of Kenya)
KTDA	Kenya Tea Development Authority
LIBOR	London inter-bank offer rate
MLR	Maximum Residual Levels
MTEF	Medium-Term Expenditure Framework
MUB	Manufacturing Under Bond
NBFIs	Non-bank financial institutions
NCPB	National Cereals Produce Board (of Kenya)
NIC	Newly-industrialized country
NSE	Nairobi Stock Exchange
ODA	Official Development Aid (Assistance)
OECD	Organization for Economic Cooperation and Development
PRSP	Poverty Reduction Strategy Paper (Kenya public policy instrument)
PSGE	Public Strategies for Growth and Equity (a component of the EAGER project)
PTA	Preferential Trade Area
QRs	Quantitative restrictions
RCR	Real cost reduction
RPED	Regional Program on Enterprise Development (project)
SAL	Structural adjustment loan (see SAPs)
SAPs	Structural adjustment programs; also SAP for Structural adjustment program
SDR	Special drawing rights (an asset issued by the IMF; when granted a country, they are added to the country's stock of international reserves (also SDRs)
SSA	Sub-Saharan Africa
TFP	Total factor productivity
UK	United Kingdom (of Great Britain and Northern Island)
US	United States (of America); also U.S.
USAID	United States (of America) Agency for International Development
USSR	Union of Soviet Socialist Republics, also known as the Soviet Union—now defunct
VAT	Value-added tax
VERS	Voluntary Early Retirement Scheme
WTO	World Trade Organization

1

BK Title:

General Introduction

MWANGI S. KIMENYI
JOHN MUKUM MBAKU
NGURE MWANIKI

NIA

Background to the EAGER project

The papers contained in this volume were prepared under the *Kenya Equity and Growth through Economic Research* (EAGER) project, which was commissioned by the Harvard Institute for International Development (HIID) and sponsored by the United States Agency for International Development (USAID). The Kenya EAGER project was itself part of an Africa-wide research effort involving country-specific studies in eleven countries with the goal of accelerating sustainable economic growth with equity by applying research to public policy.

The EAGER project had two components: (1) Public Strategies for Growth and Equity (PSGE); and (2) Trade Regimes and Growth, whose cross cutting themes were restarting and sustaining growth and development, and trade liberalization and growth, respectively. The twin themes had, over the two decades preceding the end of the last century, been the subjects of intense research, scores of conferences, seminars and workshops by researchers and key policymakers and advisors in many African countries. Their combined efforts to reform their economies had met with little success. Equally concerned about these themes were funding institutions, donor countries and their agencies, all of whom had collectively approved many initiatives, as well as massive foreign assistance and debt relief programs to support the growth and development of African countries.

None of the recovery programs implemented in Africa during that period, however, had been sustained long enough to induce high rates of growth. In fact, most had undergone significant reversals at one time or another. The countries continued to grow and develop at rates markedly lower than those of other developing countries, particularly those in Asia.

The primary objective of the EAGER project, therefore, was to try to understand, through a process of in-depth country research and analysis, why economic reform programs were not being sustained, and how that situation could be changed. Ultimately, the focus of the studies, which lasted approximately two years, was on what has to be done, by whom and when so as to restart and sustain economic growth and development. The project also intended to enhance local ownership of research outcomes and strengthen local capacity for policy analysis by promoting collaboration between local and international research and consulting organizations in responding to the development challenges in sub-Saharan Africa.

The Kenya EAGER research study, which drew together a wide range of academics, leading Kenyan and international researchers as well as other local private and public sector institutions representing different disciplines and backgrounds, produced a total of ten papers, eight of which are contained in this volume. Each paper reflects at least one of the two cross cutting EAGER themes while addressing in specific detail, institutional, political or economic policy issues. The issues include macroeconomic management, productivity and competitiveness, agricultural productivity, governance, trade and exchange regimes, trade liberalization, and export platforms.

These issues underpin findings of empirical studies of the differences in the rates of growth and development across countries, which point to the importance of sound policies, particularly those relating to macroeconomic management, the effectiveness of institutions, and strategies to enhance productivity and competitiveness. Unifying these papers is the appreciation that research results are highly relevant in the formulation of effective policies to promote growth with equity.

A major emphasis of the EAGER project was the dissemination of research findings, particularly within the host countries. In order, therefore, to effectively and efficiently disseminate results of the Kenya country research study locally, a *Conference on Restarting and Sustaining Growth in Kenya* was held in Nairobi on January 26, 2000. The conference drew a wide cross section of participants numbering nearly 350. Among them were senior government officials, individuals from private sector firms and industry associations, members of academic institutions in Kenya and neighboring countries, representatives of non-governmental organizations (NGOs) and Kenya's bilateral and multilateral development partners, and local representatives from several diplomatic missions. The papers in this volume are discussed below.

Chapter 2, by Mwangi S. Kimenyi and John Mukum Mbaku, focuses on the importance of institutions in restarting and sustaining economic growth. While the chapter does not specifically focus on Kenyan institutions, it is relevant in that African countries exhibit fairly similar characteristics that have generally undermined economic performance. In particular, the chapter emphasizes the importance of institutional arrangements that reduce transaction costs. It provides a brief overview of the field of institutional economics and outlines linkages between institutions and economic growth. The authors also touch on public choice theories and their relevance to economic performance. In particular, the authors discuss issues of political opportunism, corruption and rent seeking that have important negative consequences on economic growth and argue that appropriate institutions are necessary to deal with these behaviors. The chapter suggests that Africa's poor economic performance is not the result of resource constraints but rather weak institutions. To restart and sustain economic growth, it is therefore necessary to implement institutional reforms and provide economic and governance structures that enhance entrepreneurial activities and hence, economic growth.

In Chapter 3, Njuguna S. Ndung'u discusses issues of macroeconomic management in Kenya. After more than a decade's experience with reforms, Kenya's economic recovery has been unsatisfactory with economic management tending to be extremely short-term with conflicting goals and outcomes characteristic of a policy dilemma. A good example is the 1993–1997 post-liberalization phenomenon that saw short-run speculative capital flows responding to an interest rate differential. The authorities, already in a bind arising from targeting a competitive exchange rate and low inflation in a floating exchange rate regime, intervened in the market with the intention of stabilizing it. However, so as to sterilize the initial capital flows, the authorities also had to raise domestic interest rates in direct contradiction to the country's goals of increasing domestic investment and thereby, jeopardizing chances of further economic recovery.

Other issues addressed in this chapter include factors that have led to the growth and investment decline in Kenya; the determinants of, and links to growth; the degree with which policies implemented in the past have succeeded – or failed – in promoting growth, and; how current policies should be changed to return the country to a sustainable growth path. Periods are analyzed on the basis of reform processes and policies formulated during the respective years, beginning with the early 1970s, which involved controls on foreign exchange transactions, importation, domestic and retail producer prices, wage guidelines and domestic interest rates among others. Kenya's 18–year experience with structural adjustment is divided into four phases, namely: the slow start and non-compliance phase (1980–1984); the poor implementation period (1985–1991); the rapid implementation phase (1992–1995); and the reluctance phase (1996–1998). Using various indicators, Ndung'u assesses the country's performance over these periods. He points out the weaknesses in managing and adhering to the required reforms, and after reviewing selected literature to show corroborating evidence in Kenya's decline, discusses measures needed to reverse this decline. A key point to this discussion is institutional reforms needed to support growth-enhancing policies.

According to Ndung'u, Kenya's poor performance and precarious recovery may be explained, in part, by the slow response of private investment to macroeconomic stabilization and to the realignment of prices. It is also affected by the large external and domestic debt, which, because it keeps interest rates high, makes investment decisions very risky. From his analysis, the author draws lessons covering short-run macro management issues and long-run or structural issues. The former include measures needed to: streamline the country's financial sector, presently characterized by 'political' banks and the government's heavy domestic borrowing; enforce institutional structures such as legal and payment systems; overhaul the current trade regime which seems to encourage commercial activities without promoting production; reduce poverty and corruption; and improve the capacity of the government to implement and monitor reform programs.

One of the conclusions under the structural issues is that future growth can only be achieved if the current environment that discourages long-term investments is reversed. This would require policies to enhance institutional reforms and reduce social and political uncertainty in the future. Other conclusions include the importance of enhancing private investments through public sector investments, which encompass both human capital and physical infrastructure, and the importance of aligning short-run macroeconomic policies with long-run growth targets. Unless the existing political climate and issues of governance such as corruption in the public sector are addressed, future growth may not be easily realized.

As part of the country's trade liberalization and export promotion efforts in the late 1980s and early 1990s, Kenya introduced three types of export platforms. The platforms are Manufacturing Under Bond (MUB); Export Processing Zones (EPZ); and the more generalized and flexible export support program (EPPO), which provides duty exemptions for imported inputs used not only in the production of exports but also of duty-free goods for the domestic market.

In Chapter 4, G. Glenday and D. Ndii analyze the structure and performance of these three platforms as well as changes in the macroeconomic policy environment, which have affected the composition, competitiveness and direction of the country's exports. Also analyzed are initiatives which have been used to promote exports such as the development of regional markets through preferential trade arrangements, the liberalization of trade through the removal of quantitative restrictions, the reduction and rationalization of duty rates, the lifting of import licensing and the removal of foreign exchange controls. The authors trace the performance of manufactured exports in Kenya from the deterioration over the decade preceding 1987, through the surge recorded in the 1993–1995 period and eventually to the deterioration in the post-1996 period. These fluctuations are attributed mainly to macroeconomic reforms and measures other than export platforms although the argument advanced is that EPPO-like programs will continue to significantly support direct and indirect exports outside the region and remove undesirable protection from the duty free or exempt goods produced for the local market. An important characteristic of such programs is their flexibility, which arises from their ability to deal simultaneously with businesses producing both for local and foreign markets, their lack of special income tax, and the fact that they can be accessed even by producers in sectors typically excluded from export-dedicated platforms.

The authors note, however, that the use of the EPPO program has been declining due to the erosion in competitiveness of the country's exports, and the decline in the tax value of the program. At the same time, the proposal by the East African Cooperation (now the East African Community, EAC) and the Common Market for Eastern and Southern Africa (COMESA) trading partners to phase out export incentives from the region, together with the reduction in tariffs have substantially eroded the program's incentives, thereby diminishing its attractiveness. As compared to the EPPO program, the impact of MUB and EPZ platforms, which only target export-dedicated business, has been inconspicuous. Whereas MUB was dealt a major setback in 1994 when the US trade authorities revoked Kenya's quota for some items, the authors recommend that 'the excess capacity in the country's public EPZ should be privatized to save costs, and parts of it de-registered and established as regular industrial parks' in order to make them more flexible. However, increasing the flexibility of export platforms alone is not sufficient to brighten Kenya's export prospects in labor-intensive manufacture.

The authors conclude by observing that a shift in the government's fiscal policy to one of budget surpluses is equally important. This will reduce the existing heavy domestic debt load, sustain a more competitive export-promoting exchange rate and encourage export-oriented investment.

Trade liberalization and openness are advocated as a key prescription to attain high economic growth. Whereas it began in the developed world circa 1950, this process started in developing countries in the 1980s under structural adjustment programs (SAPs), with effective implementation of policies often only in the 1990s. In Chapter 5, G. Glenday and T. C. I. Ryan assess whether changes in trade policy and exchange rate regimes initiated through liberalization and price decontrols, while having major and obvious influences on Kenya's international trade patterns, have also significantly affected the country's economic growth performance.

The chapter scrutinizes specific changes in the country's market, monetary, price, interest rate and trade regimes for the periods 1962–1971, 1972–1980, 1981–1992 and the period after 1993 so as to explore the policy levers, which have shaped Kenya's international trade experience. By attempting to draw meaningful relationships between changes in international trade patterns on the one hand, and economic growth on the other, the authors seek lessons regarding trade and exchange rate policies and their relationship to policies affecting the growth performance and prospects of Kenya's economy. The analysis also includes other determinants of economic growth in Kenya.

Results of the analysis indicate that regional trade policy has had major consequences for manufacturing investment prospects, and that foreign exchange controls have negatively affected both imports and export performance, particularly in manufactured and processed goods. The most dramatic effect on aggregate trade performance was witnessed between 1983 and 1993 when the Central Bank of Kenya imposed foreign exchange allocations for all imports, a move, which severely constrained import demand during the 10–year period.

The authors could not, however, establish any direct links between Kenya's growth performance and changes in its trade policy regime or trade performance. This does not imply that trade and exchange rate policy are of no importance. The country has only experienced an open trade policy since 1993–1994, which is not sufficient time for the effects of such a policy to become apparent. Secondly, for the benefits of openness in trade, and hence of international competition, to be fully realized by the economy, other complementary factors such as provision of economic infrastructure and a competitive macroeconomic environment must exist. All these have been lacking in Kenya. Thirdly, access to regional trade does seem to have had indirect effects on growth, through the promotion of private investment, 'the strongest and most significant contributor to growth'. Private sector investment can be increased through better market incentives, particularly lower real interest rates, which can be achieved primarily through a reduction in the government's domestic debt burden. The evidence suggests that government investment generally has a weak direct effect on growth although enhancing its efficiency and expanding its volume through investments in roads, for example, could indirectly contribute to growth.

In Chapter 6, Mbui Wagacha discusses the starts and reversals of liberalization of Kenya's trade and exchange regime, and reviews the trajectory of exports of goods and services since 1980, particularly non-traditional exports. In terms of trade neutrality and trade liberality, reversals and stop-go policies have been prevalent, contributing significantly to Kenya's failure to maintain the export expansion and diversification momentum of the 1965–1980 period. Although Kenyan exports have penetrated African and developing country markets mostly with manufactures, and with primary commodity exports to industrial countries (particularly the European Union), this export structure is a strategic anomaly compounded by inappropriate implementation of export-oriented measures. Income effects could spur an export boom from diversified exports at a far higher rate in industrial countries than in developing countries. The export strategy suggested from the analyses is to penetrate industrial country markets with far more diversified export products (including expansion of horticulture products which have succeeded almost independently of a supporting government policy) and at the same time, pursue developing country markets for manufactures. Applying the Constant Market Share model to measure shifting mixes of total exports and the sources of a potential policy-induced export 'deficit' since 1980, the chapter identifies the following sources of Kenya's export growth failures: (a) failure of export commodity diversification; (b) failure to maintain competitiveness; and (c) failure to diversify markets. Ranking the failures, this study shows far greater damage attributable to failures of poor commodity diversification than failures of market diversification and pursuit of competitiveness. Furthermore, interviews of exporters, including multinational companies and potential foreign investors interested in export-oriented activity, re-confirm the barriers to production and growth.

Although agriculture makes a significant contribution to the Kenyan economy, accounting for almost one-quarter of the country's gross domestic product (GDP) and employing three quarters of its labor force, the sector's performance throughout the 1990s remained dismal. Annual agricultural GDP growth rate over the period averaged 2 percent, which is half of the growth rate recorded in the 1980s and one third of the rate in the first decade of independence. The production of most commodities was characterized by a general decline. Increased production observed in a few crops can be attributed to increases in cultivated area rather than to improvements in productivity. In Chapter 7, H. O. Nyangito, G. Argwings-Kodhek, J. Omiti and J. Nyoro summarize the causes of this decline.

The chapter begins by identifying the main constraints to agricultural development in Kenya. It then outlines actions needed to revitalize productivity in the sector. The major food crops considered in the analysis are maize and wheat while the industrial crops examined are sugar and cotton. The authors then turn to export crops such as coffee, tea and horticultural produce, as well as the livestock sub-sector, which includes dairy, meat and poultry production. In each case, past performance, current production status and future policy concerns are discussed in some detail. The final section of the chapter addresses measures required to enhance the contribution of agriculture to the success of Kenya's current major development themes among which, are industrialization by the year 2020 and poverty reduction.

Although drought is most often cited in explaining low agricultural productivity, the authors contend that the problems facing this sector are largely policy-related. They note that since the government's 1993 commitment to implement liberalized market policies, 'the agricultural sector has faced problems with respect to sequencing, timing, instability and poor adjustment to policies.' This situation is aggravated by the absence of a supportive legal framework and of a clearly defined role of the government in the development of agriculture. Other general problems are also discussed such as low investments, poor delivery of services to farmers, high input costs, marketing difficulties, weak extension and research programs, poor access to credit, an unclear land-use policy, poor export promotion, uncontrolled imports and insecurity, which leads to the loss of investor confidence. According to the analysis, only the horticultural sub-sector has recorded steady growth mainly due to the expansion of exports. However, Kenya continues to face stiff international competition in this area and if constraints hindering its further growth are not addressed, the sub-sector's performance may not be sustained.

In the wake of market liberalization and the move away from government-provided services and policy leadership, the international competitiveness and future progress of agriculture depends on a number of factors. One of these is the ability of different groups of agricultural sector stakeholders to form workable institutional arrangements for solving their common problems. Another is the ability of these groups to organize ways of gaining access to services no longer provided either by government or by the profit-motivated private sector. Finally, sector policymakers and stakeholders need to use research-based information so as to strengthen their capacities for policy analysis and also develop common visions of the directions and actions needed to revitalize agricultural productivity.

In Chapter 8, A. Eyakuze reviews four previous studies on the theoretical and empirical dimensions of productivity and competitiveness in Kenya. He begins by describing and examining links between the concepts of productivity, competitiveness and growth.

National productivity, which is defined in this chapter as the value of the goods and services produced per unit of a nation's human, capital and physical resources, is directly linked to the productivity of the nation's firms. This, in turn, depends upon the efficiency of the operations, effectiveness of the firms' strategy, the quality of the microeconomic business environment and the soundness of the legal and political structure as well as macroeconomic policies. Competitiveness is defined as the value or prices that a nation's goods and services can command in the international marketplace and the efficiency with which standard units are produced. The author points out, however, that this definition of competitiveness has been vigorously debated especially when applied to national economies. Like the discussions on comparative and competitive advantage and how these explain the economic performance of nations, it remains controversial.

After identifying some of the major factors affecting productivity and competitiveness, the chapter analyses the past performance of Kenya's economy. It assesses various macroeconomic indicators and then examines the country's microeconomic environment and firm-level behavior. Growth in inputs, growth in output and change in productivity in five sectors, namely agriculture, mining, manufacturing, wholesale and transport are analyzed in great detail. The analysis shows, among other things, that for the 30–year period beginning in 1964 and ending in 1994, Kenya registered almost zero growth rates in terms of aggregate productivity and technological advancement. A 1984 study of 78 Kenyan firms in 24 industries reveals that the country had neither a comparative nor a competitive advantage in its manufacturing sector, most likely as a result of overly capital-intensive production technologies. Another study in 1997, however, reveals industries to have gained somewhat in terms of comparative advantage.

According to the survey, only the horticultural sector has been a success story as far as international competitiveness is concerned. The sector has registered substantial increases both in the aggregate volume and value of its exports. It is now an important component of Kenya's economy, contributing a major percentage of the country's foreign exchange earnings and providing employment and farm income opportunities to many. Eyakuze uses this success to draw some lessons for African countries, not only in improving the productivity and competitiveness of their horticultural sectors, but also the industrial and other sectors.

The first lesson is that developing a competitive horticultural trade requires not just ecological, locational and cost-of-labor advantages, which many African countries already possess, but also technical, financial, infrastructural and managerial assets, most of which are still lacking. Secondly, developing a competitive horticultural trade requires foreign investments or long-term marketing contracts between domestic and foreign firms and hence the need for governments to develop the necessary incentives. Thirdly, to develop a competitive horticultural trade, prospective exporters are advised to first gain experience by developing crop procurement and distribution arrangements to supply high quality produce to local restaurants, hotels and up-market retail outlets. The chapter concludes that in encouraging new entry into this sector, attention should focus on firms that already have the necessary market contacts, an understanding of the risks involved in international trade, and the production capacities required for success.

Kenya hopes to become one of Africa's industrial 'tigers' by the year 2020 even though its industrial growth performance in recent years does not seem to warrant such a prediction. Uganda, on the other hand, has recently experienced rapid economic growth and industrialization while having a manufacturing sector which is smaller than Kenya's. Within the region, manufacturing industries in the two countries have met with increasing international competition and are therefore, likely to maintain a certain level of protection although it is not yet clear what that level ought to be.

In Chapter 9, E. Siggel, G. K. Ikiara and B. Nganda investigate the international competitiveness of manufacturing industries in Kenya and Uganda and attempt to predict future trade flows and industrial growth in the two countries. The chapter examines changes in Kenya's trade and industrial policy environment. Using data for 1984 and 1997, it compares the competitiveness of 42 firms in 16 industries to understand how these have adjusted to the various policy changes over the 13–year period. It then compares the industries' competitiveness with that experienced in 11 matching industries in Uganda during 1997. The methodology consists of the computation of competitiveness indicators and their decomposition according to the major sources of competitiveness. Finally, the authors use the results of their analysis to suggest policy options.

The analysis reveals that since the mid-1980s, very few industries in Kenya have had comparative advantage or been internationally competitive in spite of over 10 years of structural adjustment and trade policy changes. Evidence is produced attributing this scenario to two major factors: The first factor is the increase in new kinds of cost distortions – distortions due to public service deficiencies – rather than decreased protection. These costs are the result of infrastructural deterioration and inefficiencies of the financial sector, which severely prohibit borrowing for investment. The second factor is overvaluation of local currencies, which is mainly the result of unstable and poorly aligned exchange rates and which contributes to competitive weakness. One of the major conclusions of the authors is that the industrial sector in Kenya is still at an adolescent stage, and plunging it into fully, or even partially liberalized international trade is not enough to accelerate the much desired industrialization. What is needed instead, is for the country to formulate a new industrial strategy in which the government's role is to create an enabling business environment. Such a setting, the authors argue, has been lacking during recent years.

The authors make several policy recommendations as preconditions for industrial growth in Kenya. These include a reduction in interest rates and hence, in the cost of borrowing; a careful approach to currency depreciation; an improvement in infrastructure through privatization; a cautious progression of trade liberalization to give industries time to adjust to the changing environment; an effective enforcement of the trade regime, particularly through customs administration; stringent quality controls; and the promotion of intra-industry trade as a means of fostering superior competition.

Concluding remarks

All the papers contained in this volume have attempted to answer questions posed initially by the EAGER research objectives. Under the first objective of explaining inadequate sustainability of reforms and efforts necessary to reverse this trend, the papers have identified four imperatives for restarting growth in Kenya. First is the need to strengthen institutions. Second is the need for greater focus on measures to enhance productivity and competitiveness both locally and internationally. Third is the importance of identifying and utilizing opportunities arising from globalization, and dealing with problems posed by it. Fourth is the need to reduce dependence on aid, by devising appropriate aid-exit strategies together with homegrown solutions to the country's economic challenges.

Under its second objective of encouraging local ownership of research outcomes and strengthening local capacity for policy analysis, the EAGER project has highlighted the relevance of collaboration involving local and international research as well as consulting organizations in responding to the development challenges in the country and in sub-Saharan Africa.

Whilst these remain the most pertinent policy issues for Kenya's future growth and development, they are by no means the only ones. The AIDS pandemic for instance, continues to exact a heavy toll on the country's human and other resources; worsening insecurity and the resultant negative international publicity continue to plague tourism, a vital sector of the economy; the technological and digital divide separating Kenya and other countries continues to widen, implying that the country is lagging further behind the rest of the world in this area; and issues of equity in national wealth and power distribution continue to be of major concern. In the external sector, a growing debt overhang continues to limit public investment while at the same time discouraging new private investments even more. Quite obviously the policy research pipeline is full, and even with economic reform, it is unclear whether all the country's problems will find lasting solutions. The imminent task amidst all this is to keep responding to new as well as existing policy challenges through innovative and well-researched solutions. Efforts such as EAGER, in addition to producing practical outputs like this volume, also serve to stimulate the type of work needed to ensure that Kenya develops such a capacity.

In this regard, the EAGER process has been a major challenge for Kenyan researchers to take the lead in identifying the main issues and conducting research to produce relevant policy interventions. Shortly after the Conference on Restarting and Sustaining Growth of January 2000, the organizers convened another meeting: the Kenya Post-EAGER Research Workshop, whose intention was to take forward the work, which was begun through EAGER. Objectives of this workshop, which was held in Naro Moru, Kenya, between April 26–28, 2000 were threefold: to identify relevant future policy research topics arising out of the recommendations of the January conference; to identify mechanisms for disseminating the research findings to their end users (i.e., public policymakers); and to determine modalities for further co-operation among public and private sector researchers in Kenya, based on experiences and lessons from the EAGER project.

Workshop participants reviewed the debate surrounding the Government of Kenya's new development policy framework with particular reference to the formulation of the Poverty Reduction Strategy Paper (PRSP), and the Medium-Term Expenditure Framework (MTEF) for fiscal policy. Key concerns in this debate, including governance, decentralization, globalization and financial development, were analyzed in great detail and in each case, a summary of agreed-upon future research agenda produced. The workshop proposed the production of policy briefs covering themes of these papers for presentation to respective policymakers within Government as well as specific 'agents of change' who should effect the recommended policy interventions. Finally, participants agreed that subsequent meetings should focus on monitoring how far recommendations from the EAGER research had gone in terms of affecting the formulation and implementation of public policy in Kenya.

Whereas it is too early in the day to cite examples of the full breadth of this impact, the publication of this volume in itself represents an important milestone in the process of communicating the research findings to those it addresses. These include those in the policy-making environment, academicians engaged in public policy research, development organizations as well as other development support institutions and also members of the reading public who have a general interest in issues of development in Kenya, sub-Saharan Africa and the developing world. It is hoped that the papers will be of great use to all these groups.

(african

Institutions and Economic Growth

MWANGI S. KIMENYI
JOHN MUKUM MBAKU

Economists and policymakers agree that institutions are central to the growth process. This has frequently been summarized by the expression 'institutions matter.' In essence, availability of capital, labor and technological progress are necessary but are not sufficient conditions for sustainable economic and social progress in the absence of strong and viable institutions that facilitate growth. As a matter of fact, institutions can be viewed as production inputs, just as capital, labor and technology. An important implication here is that, while low-income countries can import the capital and technology that they need, they are unlikely to achieve sustainable economic growth unless they have in place pro-growth institutions. Unfortunately, unlike capital and technology, institutions cannot be imported. Sustainable institutions have to be developed by the relevant stakeholders.

During most of the 20th century, not much attention was given by economists to the study of the role of institutions in economic growth and development. However, Ronald Coase (1960) was quite instrumental in incorporating transaction costs and institutions in neo-classical economics. The increasing interest in studying how institutions shape economic growth (i.e., institutional economics) is fuelled by emerging evidence that the institutional structures of an economy cannot be simply assumed away in an examination of the determinants of economic growth. Institutions play an important role in the exchange process (i.e., production and distribution of goods and services), which is usually characterized by uncertainty, incomplete and asymmetrically held information. The above factors increase the cost of transacting and therefore prevent markets from being efficient. Institutions, therefore, serve to either increase or reduce the transaction costs of exchange. Those economies in which exchange is characterized by low cost tend to grow faster than those in which exchange involves high transaction costs. The latter include the costs of obtaining the necessary licenses for production and for the import of essential inputs from abroad; dealing with the potential for opportunistic behavior by market participants in environments characterized by significant risk; problems of adverse selection, moral hazard, shirking, free riding, and corruption; costs of securing, analyzing and utilizing information; etc. As argued by Ostrom, Schroeder and Wynne (1993, pp. 48–68), institutions can help reduce the costs of information asymmetries, limit opportunistic behaviors, and generally reduce transaction costs. In fact, unless a country has the counteracting institutions to deal effectively with certain opportunistic behaviors (such as rent seeking and corruption), many productive activities may not take place. Hence, institutions are a critical ingredient in the production and distribution of goods and services.

Studies show that countries with strong and viable institutions tend to have strong economies while those that are characterized by weak and non-viable institutions tend to have poorly performing economies (World Bank, 2002, p. 9). The available evidence suggests that institutions are an integral part of development and must be treated as a critical determinant of economic growth. For this reason, neo-classical theories that assume away property rights and transaction costs are not able to adequately explain the differences in economic growth across countries. Developments in the study of the role of institutions in economic growth have given rise to *institutional economics*, which blends neo-classical economics with private and public policies that determine and guide investments and exchange. Institutions are very critical for, they influence the nature of interactions between economic agents (individuals, households, firms) and governments, and therefore, economic performance.

In defining institutions, various authors have emphasized two elements, namely, formal and informal rules that guide, influence or shape all aspects of exchange in a society (see, e.g., North, 1997; Goldsmith, 1998). Broadly speaking, institutions are the rules (social, political and economic) that govern human interactions and thus, determine the incentive structures faced by market participants (e.g., property rights). The role of the government in the economy is important because the state is one of the most important institutions in any society. Goldsmith (1998, p. 2) defines institutions as 'stable, recurring patterns of behavior', while North (1997, p. 2) argues that institutions are 'rules of the game in a society ... the humanly devised constraints that shape human interaction'. According to the World Bank (2000, p. 22) institutions are the 'sets of formal and informal rules governing the actions of individuals and organizations and the interactions of participants in the development process'. For example, in private markets, institutions determine the behavior of profit-maximizing agents, while in the public sector, institutions serve as constraints on the behavior of self-interested bureau managers (Kimenyi, 1987, 1989; Mbaku, 1997). According to Shaffer (1995, p. 2),

> Institutions are the formal and informal rules which govern or at least influence the behavior of participants of a society as they interact in political and economic activities. The formal rules include laws and regulations as interpreted and enforced by political authority. The informal rules are the shared beliefs about acceptable and unacceptable behavior enforced by conscience, a result of socialization, based upon the actual and expected reactions of other members of society.

Although several reasons have been advanced to explain poor economic performance in African and other developing countries, the role of institutions has largely been ignored or assumed away. To a large extent, most of these studies have focused primarily on the absence of a stable macroeconomic environment. For example, during most of the last two decades, the World Bank and the International Monetary Fund (IMF) have tried to get the developing countries to adopt policies that seek to achieve macroeconomic stability as a strategy to accelerate economic growth. As a result, emphasis in the public policies of these countries has been placed on such areas as monetary stability, fiscal discipline and lower public debt. Unfortunately, these efforts have not produced the expected outcomes and instead, economic performance has either deteriorated or stagnated.

At the same time, other researchers have argued that the primary causes of underdevelopment and poverty in Africa have been (1) lack of physical and human capital; and (2) policy mistakes made by poorly educated, ill-informed, and incompetent but well-meaning post-independence policymakers. Informed by these arguments, a lot of emphasis has been placed, during the last few decades, on bringing to the public sectors of the African countries, more competent, better trained, honest, and well-disciplined individuals. The belief of this school of thought is that African countries are unable to develop because they lack physical capital (due to poor savings rates) and highly skilled manpower to direct development. As a consequence, there has been a call for the US and other developed countries, for example, to design and implement a 'Marshall Plan' for Africa, so that the continent can be provided with the capital resources (through a combination of official development aid – ODA, no-interest loans, with extended repayment periods, and private direct foreign investment) they need to undertake industrialization.

But, there seems to be little evidence that large inflows of capital to Africa would result in sustained economic growth. It is true, for example, that large amounts of capital by way of foreign aid have been transferred to Africa during the post-colonial era. Yet, there is little economic growth and development to show for these transfers. Thus, it is evident that the availability of physical capital is not sufficient to restart and sustain economic growth in Kenya or any other African country.

Recent work by public choice scholars has uncovered evidence that points to the following: (1) that political opportunism (e.g., rent seeking and corruption) is a major constraint to entrepreneurial activities, and hence wealth creation in Africa; and (2) the many 'policy mistakes' supposedly made by African policymakers were actually deliberate and purposeful programs designed and implemented by opportunistic civil servants seeking ways to enrich themselves at the expense of the rest of their societies (see, e.g., Mbaku, 1998; Kimenyi and Mbaku, 1999; Mbaku, 2000a). Opportunism, as mentioned earlier, is a problem that can be dealt with effectively with the appropriate institutional arrangements (also see, Mbaku, 1997). Granted, during the last forty years, most African countries have been plagued with relatively poor leadership, poorly developed economic infrastructures, and a severe shortage of both human and physical capital. However, it is important to recognize that the availability of skilled and well-educated individuals and significant stocks of physical capital is a necessary but not sufficient condition for wealth creation and economic development. In order for each African country to create the wealth that it needs to deal effectively and fully with poverty and deprivation and be able to promote economic and human development, it not only has to have the necessary resources, but it must provide itself with the right institutional environment. In the absence of strong and viable institutions, rent seeking and corruption are most likely to be pervasive and civil servants and politicians will use their public positions to enrich themselves at the expense of the population. Evidence from the last forty years shows that if not properly constrained (by appropriate institutional arrangements), politicians and bureaucrats will engage in opportunistic behaviors, promote perverse economic policies in an effort to generate extra-legal compensation for themselves and, in the process, stunt entrepreneurial activities and wealth creation (Mbaku, 2000b).

As argued by Brett (1995, p. 200), the primary determinants of economic failure in Africa during the last forty years:

> are clearly structural rather than contingent, since breakdown is almost universal and cannot simply be attributed to particular national circumstances. Instead, they must stem from the nature of *institutional arrangements* developed under colonialism and hastily modified during the political transition of the 1950s and 1960s (emphasis added).

According to North (1981, p. 59), 'it is the successes and failures in human organization that account for the progress and retrogression of societies.' African elites attempted to transform the institutions that they inherited from the colonial government and make them more suited to the needs of the post-colonial society. Unfortunately, such institutional transformation, often by opportunistic and reluctant leaders, failed to improve these institutions' ability to serve as effective constraints on the behavior of civil servants and politicians. As a consequence, those laws and institutions that have governed socio-political interaction in the African countries during the last forty years have actually enhanced financial mismanagement, rent seeking, rent extraction, corruption and other forms of opportunism, thus, increasing transaction costs and discouraging most forms of wealth creation. As Africans face poverty and deprivation in the new millennium, the first step to dealing with continued underdevelopment is to replace these laws and institutions with more appropriate ones – those that can force public servants to perform their jobs more efficiently and effectively, and hence minimize transaction costs, thereby encouraging engagement in productive activities (see Mbaku, 2000b, pp. 11–13).

It is now clear that what has been missing from many of the studies devoted to underdevelopment in Africa has been the critical role played by institutions in resource allocation and hence, economic performance. The neglect of the critical role played by institutions in economic growth and development by the World Bank, the IMF and other groups and organizations concerned with poverty alleviation in the developing countries is somewhat surprising given the fact that several years earlier public choice theorists (e.g., Buchanan and Tullock, 1962; Brennan and Buchanan, 1985; Olson, 1965) had recognized the role that institutions play in determining the incentives faced by participants in markets. In fact, several scholars (e.g., Kimenyi, 1987, 1989; Mbaku, 1991; Mbaku and Paul, 1989; Brough and Kimenyi, 1986; Kimenyi and Mbaku, 1999; Ayittey, 1992, 1997) have written extensively on how the absence of strong, viable and sustainable institutions has contributed significantly to poor economic performance and hence, continued underdevelopment in the continent. It was not until just a few years ago that the World Bank and other multilateral agencies began to treat institutions as critical to economic performance in developing countries. In fact, by the early 1990s, the World Bank and the IMF had made 'good governance' and laws minimizing corrupt behaviors a critical part of the reforms they had imposed on African and other developing countries as a condition for gaining access to credit from the international donor and financial communities (Baylies, 1995). Thus, today, most analysts concerned with poverty eradication and development in Africa argue that sustainable development can only be achieved within the appropriate institutional environment. Providing what has been termed or referred to as the 'enabling environment' for economic growth and poverty alleviation must start with reforms to establish the appropriate *institutional structure*.

Like those in other African countries, Kenya's institutions trace their origins to the colonial period. These institutions were designed to serve the interests of the colonialists and not those of the indigenous people of Kenya. At independence, the institutions were supposed to be transformed to reflect post-independence realities and enhance the ability of the indigenous people to govern themselves and allocate their resources in a socially equitable manner. To accomplish this task, the relevant stakeholders were supposed to have been enfranchised and provided the facilities to participate fully and effectively in the process of transforming the institutions or develop their own laws and institutions instead of adopting structures that had been created without their participation. The basic thrust of this chapter is to argue that Kenya and other African countries cannot effectively restart and sustain economic growth without first establishing for themselves, appropriate (i.e., democratic) institutions. Hence, the first line of business for Kenya and each African country that expects to achieve sustainable economic growth and development, as well as participate more effectively and gainfully in the new global economy, is to engage the people in reforms to create strong and viable institutions.

In discussing strategies for restarting and sustaining economic growth, there is need to make sure that institutions promote entrepreneurship. The most important problems for entrepreneurship in Africa today are: (1) the lack of accurate, cost-effective and reliable information about trading partners (i.e., other market participants); (2) property rights are poorly defined or not well-specified and many people do not have formal title to their land and as a consequence, cannot use the land as collateral to obtain loans from bank; and (3) perverse public policies, which are designed to constrain entrepreneurial activities – such policies usually benefits for civil servants, politicians and entrenched interest groups. Although markets can provide individuals, including the poor, with the framework to utilize their skills and resources in productive activities, this can only occur within an economy with institutions that support market activities. Such institutions can be defined as '[r]ules, enforcement mechanisms, and organizations supporting market transactions' (World Bank, 2002, p. 4). Institutions differ across countries and societies and, as argued by the World Bank (2000, p. 4) function to 'transmit information, enforce property rights and contracts, and manage competition in markets.' In performing these activities, institutions provide the appropriate incentive structures for participants in markets to engage in productive activities (e.g., wealth creation). In other words, institutions determine the incentive structures faced by traders in markets and hence, affect the way individuals behave. Whether an entrepreneur lives in a poor or rich country, his ability to engage in productive activities and use his talents and resources to create the wealth that he needs will be determined by the institutional arrangements that regulate markets in his society.

For a country to enhance entrepreneurial activities and maximize wealth creation, it must not only promote 'good' policies, but arm itself with institutions that (1) are pro-growth; (2) enhance the ability of citizens, especially the historically marginalized and deprived individuals and groups to participate in markets, empower them and provide them with the facilities to more effectively use their talents and resources to improve their quality of life; and (3) adequately constrain the state so that civil servants and politicians do not engage in opportunism (e.g., rent seeking and corruption) to redistribute income and wealth in their favor. For Kenya, and other African countries trying to restart and sustain growth, the first step is to build the institutions that would support the nation's market, enhance the ability of all citizens to engage in productive activities, adequately constrain the state and generally promote efficient and equitable allocation of resources.

Another particularly detrimental aspect of African institutions, one that has a significantly negative impact on economic growth, is the inability of these institutions to maintain law and order and preserve the peace. The evidence points to the fact that the worst performing economies are those in countries that have had prolonged internal conflicts, including civil wars, during the last several years. For African countries to be able to restart and sustain growth, they must establish institutions of governance that can adequately preserve the peace and avert wars and other destructive forms of mobilization.

Institutions and economic growth

It is quite clear that no meaningful interactions in an economy can take place unless institutions are in place that facilitate productive human interaction. According to Papandreou (1994, p. 221), 'institutions provide the structure through which individual action is channeled towards collective ends'. Institutions reduce transaction costs, for example, by enhancing the flow and quality of information, promoting competition and enforcing property rights (World Bank, 2002, p. 5). The institution of property rights determines how fairly and efficiently contracts are enforced, which in turn shapes the various ways in which economic agents or market participants interact. For example, in societies where property rights are poorly specified and/or are not well enforced, entrepreneurs are reluctant to engage in productive activities or use their resources and talents productively. The role of institutions is more critical in market economies because they determine the transaction costs of doing business. For market economies to evolve and develop, institutions must play the role of eliminating or reducing the costs of forming markets and defining and protecting private property rights. The implication of all this is that the overall performance of economies depends not just on the efficiency of alternative resource allocation mechanisms but more importantly, on how efficiently institutions perform the above functions.

It is the fact that institutions are more important in determining economic outcomes than are resource endowments. The case of sub-Saharan Africa is particularly informative – some of the poorest countries in the world in terms of well-being and quality of life of the people (e.g., Democratic Republic of Congo – DRC; Angola; and Mozambique) are also the most richly endowed in terms of natural resources. As a matter of fact, it does appear that resource-rich environment without the appropriate institutions translates into very poor outcomes in terms of economic performance. In DRC, Angola, and Mozambique, weak and non-viable institutions, all of which were not founded through democratic constitutional processes, have resulted in prolonged destructive conflicts, thereby preventing productive exchange. The implication here is that in discussing institutions, it is critical to look broadly at the rules that determine political outcomes. Thus, the lack of appropriate institutions or the existence of weak, non-viable and inefficient institutions is mostly responsible for the poor development record in Africa and other developing regions of the world (see, e.g., Olson, 1996).

The basic message of institutional economies is that economic performance is a function of a country's institutional arrangements. Thus, for any particular country, the existing formal and informal rules affect economic performance through their influence on the behavior of market participants (i.e., economic agents). As mentioned earlier, institutions can reduce transactions costs and make mutually beneficial exchange possible. However, it is important to note that while rules are critical, the issue of compliance must be considered just as important.

Each individual within a society would benefit if all members of that society behaved cooperatively (i.e., they all complied to the rules). However, uncertainty regarding whether other members of society would adhere to the rules can result in a socially-inefficient equilibrium, which is characterized by the absence of cooperation. To significantly reduce or eliminate the uncertainties that force members of society to act opportunistically, enforceable contracts are required. A set of constitutional rules forms an agreement between members of society to cooperate. It is important to note, however, that unless there is a mechanism to enforce compliance and punish post-contractual (i.e., post-constitutional) opportunism, such a social contract is not likely to endure. An economy characterized by high levels of opportunism would necessarily allocate its resources in inefficient ways and fail to create the wealth needed to meet societal needs. In fact, opportunism (e.g., corruption and rent seeking) are major constraints to entrepreneurship and hence, economic growth.

A lot has been written about how to deal with post-constitutional opportunism (see, e.g., Lowenberg, 1992; Wiseman, 1990; Mbaku, 1997). An effective way to deal with post-contractual opportunism is to make the constitution self-enforcing. The latter produces mutual gains that are easily recognizable by all parties to the contract, making it beneficial for them to cooperate. As argued by Niskanen (1990, p. 58), many self-enforcing rules have been known to evolve spontaneously, requiring no enforcement by a third party. For example, Niskanen argues that the desire by traders within a market to maintain a successful exchange relationship may be enough to minimize or completely eliminate shirking – the latter, of course, is a form of opportunism designed to benefit one party at the expense of the other. Additionally, North (1990) has determined that in repeat transactions, a trader's reputation develops or evolves into an asset whose value the trader must protect, forcing economic agents in such situations to refrain from engaging in opportunistic behaviors for fear of damaging their long-term reputations.

How then, does a society develop a self-enforcing constitution? One method is to introduce competition into both political and economic markets in the post-constitutional society. In other words, during the constitutional deliberations, participants in the process deliberately make the country's political and economic systems competitive. Part of the process should involve the constitutional guarantee of economic freedoms (i.e., the right of individuals to engage freely in exchange and contracting). In addition, the power of the central government should be reduced significantly in favor of more political autonomy for regional and local governmental jurisdictions. Introducing and sustaining competition in the political systems of African countries such as Kenya, requires that the polity be divided into as many autonomous political jurisdictions as possible and the right of citizens to migrate freely between jurisdictions be constitutionally guaranteed. To start, competitive units of collective choice can be achieved through constitutional decentralization that allows local jurisdictions to operate with a fair degree of autonomy. Such decentralization introduces competition and also reduces the monopoly power of the central government. Furthermore, such autonomy could significantly reduce conflicts among population groups. For many African countries, decentralization many not be sufficient and it may be necessary to establish some form of constitutional federalism. As argued by Wiseman (1990, pp. 121–122), a federal system with many autonomous political jurisdictions, each with a constitutionally protected level of autonomy, should effectively constrain the ability of governments, at all levels, to exploit and oppress citizens. Of course, a federalist system of the kind being described here embodies the kind of diversity and pluralism characteristic of many African countries (see, e.g., Kimenyi and Mbaku, 1999; Kimenyi, 2001).

Given the fact that individuals at the local level have greater access to relevant time-and-place information than those at the center, decentralization as described above should significantly improve government and bureaucratic efficiency. Giving more people the opportunity to participate fully and effectively in the design and implementation of policies that directly affect their lives or welfare will allow them to allocate resources in ways that are more likely to be socially-equitable. In fact, such a process should significantly reduce the extent and scope of opportunism. In addition, competition between political jurisdictions for tax-payers should force governmental units to significantly improve the quality of the fiscal packages that they offer their constituents. If the power of the central government is constitutionally constrained, then interest groups are less likely to invest in rent seeking and other forms of opportunism since such outlays are most likely to prove unprofitable. Entrenching free internal migration and political plurality within the constitution should help establish and maintain a competitive post-contractual environment, making it much more difficult for individuals and groups to engage in opportunism (see, e.g., Anderson and Hill, 1986; Congleton, 1994; Wildavsky, 1990).

It is important to note here that in order for African countries, including of course, Kenya, to successfully restart and sustain economic growth, requires minimal restrictions on economic freedom. Unfortunately, restrictions on trade or exchange have, during the last 50 years, provided significant benefits to specific groups within these economies. In the case where these groups are well organized, they are usually in a position to take control of governmental structures and effectively utilize them to plunder the economy for their own benefit. Such plundering necessarily restricts exchange, stunts entrepreneurship and generally interferes with productive activities. Examples include price controls on agriculture (Bates, 1981); financial repression; extremely high tariff rates; foreign exchange controls; high marginal tax rates; etc. (Mbaku, 1997). Although many of these well-organized interests benefit significantly from such restrictions on economic freedom, society in general suffers tremendously. To make certain that such interests do not use the legislative process to plunder the economy for their own benefit, economic freedoms should be constitutionally entrenched. As argued by Gwartney and Holcombe (1999, p. 39), an important role for the constitution is to 'constrain the government, whatever its form, and to guarantee the rights of individuals, in order to prevent the government from favoring narrow interests over the general public interest.' They further state that a '[a] constitution that promotes economic growth will (1) provide access to a stable currency, (2) ensure minimal government involvement in the economy, either through regulation or direct production, (3) protect property from takings and discriminatory taxation, and (4) allow freedom of international exchange' (Gwartney and Holcombe, 1999, p. 38; also see Grubel, 1998, pp. 287–304).

As African countries are transformed (preferably through democratic constitutionalism) and each one of them shifts away from government-led to market-centered economies, the role of institutions in economic growth and development will become more apparent and important. Why? First, well-defined property rights will become more critical to resource allocation. In order for the market to operate efficiently as a framework for the proper allocation of resources, it is necessary to have well-specified property rights regimes and an effective enforcement system. As argued by Hanna and Munasinghe (1995, p. 4), 'property rights regimes consist of *property rights*, bundles of entitlements defining the rights and duties in the use of natural resources, and *property rules*, the rules under which those rights and duties are exercised' (emphasis in original).[1] The right of ownership, implied in the property rights regime, grants the owner of record the right to use the asset; the right to obtain earnings generated by the asset; and the right to change the asset's form. The owner can transfer all his rights in the asset to someone else (i.e., sell the asset) or transfer only some of the rights to other market participants (e.g., to rent a house). The way in which property rights are defined or specified has a significant impact on the nature of market incentives and hence, affects the behavior of market participants and how they use their assets. Second, institutional arrangements (not personal relationships) are required to facilitate exchange and the availability of inputs for production. Finally, contracting arrangements and enforcement procedures must be explicitly spelled out. These structures can be established through democratic constitutionalism (see, e.g., Mbaku, 1997).

Lipsey and Chrystal (1995, p. 642) observe that 'almost all aspects of a country's institutions can foster or deter the efficient use of a society's natural and human resources.' For example, farmers require well-defined and enforced property rights in order for them to invest in land improvements, while entrepreneurs need judicial institutions that enforce contracts fairly and efficiently before they can undertake risky business ventures. Similarly, shareholders need strong and viable corporate governance institutions to serve as a check on managers and ensure that the latter not only maximize the value of the firm but also avoid opportunistic behaviors. While the latter may enrich the managers, they can severely damage the value of the firm, as well as that of the investor's stake in the firm. These few examples clearly show the gaps that institutions have to fill to make more efficient the various ways in which economic agents interact. Given the fact that interaction between economic agents within a market has a significant impact on economic performance, it is important to establish institutions which enhance that interaction and make it more efficient.

In a recent study, Ferree, Singh and Bates (1997) explore the relationship between economic growth and political institutions in 46 African countries between 1975 and 1991. The nature of political institutions is proxied by an executive scale (existence of an executive, free choice, and competitive politics) and a legislative scale (existence of a legislature and competition for seats). The results indicate that political institutions influence economic growth and that countries ruled by authoritarian regimes realize less economic growth than those with democratically elected leaders. This is consistent with the theoretical prediction by Brough and Kimenyi (1986). As argued by the World Bank (2000, p. 23), institutions influence economic growth since countries with 'stable governments, predictable methods of changing laws, secure property rights, and a strong judiciary' are likely to realize high investments and growth than those that lack these institutions.'

In explaining the role of institutions in economic growth, North (1997, pp. 3–4) notes that:

> Efficient markets are a consequence of institutions that provide the low-cost measurement and enforcement of contracts at a moment of time, but we are interested in markets with such characteristics over time. Essential to efficiency over time are institutions that provide economic and political flexibility to adopt to new opportunities. Such adaptively efficient institutions must provide incentives for the acquisition of knowledge and learning, induce innovation, and encourage risk taking and creative activity. In a world of uncertainty no one knows the correct solution to the problems we confront ... therefore, institutions should encourage trials and eliminate errors.

In short, then, institutions are critically important to economic growth because they create a framework that guides all interactions in society, whether these are between individuals or between individuals and governments. This is achieved through the enforcement of contracts, the setting of standards, as well as the coordinating of the activities of innumerable exchanges taking place between economic agents (i.e., traders in markets). A particularly important role played by institutions in exchange is to reduce uncertainty. Here are few examples that illustrate that institutions matter:

- No rational individual or economic agent is unlikely to deposit money in a bank if there are no institutions that credibly determine the relationship between the depositor and the bank. This in turn affects savings and investment behavior and therefore, economic performance.
- Banks will be unwilling to lend money if there are no clearly defined processes that set out the contractual obligations of the borrower and the procedures to recover funds in the case of default.
- Private investors will shy away from investing in countries in which institutions undermine investments either through cumbersome, inefficient and highly unpredictable arbitration procedures, corruption or other impediments related to institutional failures.
- Farmers will have no incentive to undertake long-term investment on their land in the absence of secure property rights, especially those that guarantee them claims to the future benefits of the piece of land in question. This has implications for agricultural production and employment.
- Investors, both local and foreign, will shy away from engaging in long-term investments in countries in which existing institutions do not make it possible for regime change to be undertaken through constitutionally mandated procedures.
- Social, political and economic institutions can affect the ability of individuals and firms to realize their full potential, as well as make effective use of market opportunities.

Institutions and development failures in Africa

Most of today's African countries are characterized by weak, inappropriate and non-viable institutions. As argued elsewhere (see, e.g., Mbaku, 1997; Kimenyi and Mbaku, 1999; Mbaku, 1999), part of the reason why many Africans have relatively weak and inappropriate institutions is that many of them were inherited from the colonial governments and the people were never given the opportunity, in the post-independence period, to engage in the process of transforming and restructuring their institutions. At the least, the African people should have been provided with the opportunity to engage in the reconstruction of the post-colonial state, through democratic constitutionalism, to create laws and institutions that reflected their values, ideals, interests and expectations. Through such a bottom-up, transparent, participatory and people-driven process, these inherited laws and institutions, all of which were developed by the colonialists to enhance their exploitation of Africans and their resources, should have been reconstituted to provide more effective rules, as well as structures for governing the post-independence society. Ideally, each country should have engaged in democratic constitutionalism in the immediate post-independence period to arm itself with laws and institutions that enhanced peaceful coexistence, promoted wealth creation and adequately constrained the state so that its custodians would not engage in opportunism. Unfortunately, the indigenous elites who captured the evacuated structures of colonial hegemony, engaged only in opportunistic reform efforts, producing laws and institutions that enhanced their ability to monopolize political power and the allocation of resources. Hence, many of these countries came to be governed by institutions that (1) encourage rent seeking, corruption and other forms of opportunism; (2) discourage entrepreneurial activities and wealth creation; and (3) exacerbate ethnic conflict. Thus, the emphasis in Africa today is on state reconstruction through democratic constitution making to provide each country with more appropriate institutions.

Weak institutions have had a significantly negative impact on economic growth, and hence, the creation of the wealth that African countries need to meet their rising obligations. In particular, weak institutions discourage investments, stunt or undermine entrepreneurship, and encourage and enhance economic plundering by opportunistic civil servants and politicians. Perhaps, more important, is the fact that such institutions generally increase the costs of doing business and force some entrepreneurs to exit into the underground economy. Large informal sectors usually reduce the country's legal tax base, negatively affecting public revenues and hence, the provision of essential public goods, including critical social overhead capital (e.g., roads, bridges, hospitals, and schools).

Since the 1950s, when the African colonies began to gain independence, countries in the continent have lacked strong political institutions that are capable of checking the excesses of ruling coalitions, many of which are often ethnic based. This inability of existing institutions to adequately constrain the behavior of national leaders is partly responsible for economic collapse in countries such as Zaire under the late Mobutu Sese Seko; Uganda under exiled Idi Amin; Nigeria under the late Sani Abacha; and the Central African Republic under the late Jean-Bedel Bokassa. Although some African countries with weak institutions were lucky enough not to go through such plundering as occurred in Nigeria, Zaire, Uganda and the Central African Republic, they nevertheless suffered significant social disruptions, lower rates of economic growth, political instability, destructive ethnic conflict and other problems that had a significantly negative impact on growth and development. For example, where institutions were weak, ruling elites engaged in employment practices (e.g., filling top positions in the civil service with members of their own ethnic group, regardless of qualification) that demoralized the civil service, increased levels of bureaucratic inefficiency and generally created in the people, especially the poor and marginalized groups, mistrust for government and its institutions. To see how this behavior affects economic growth, one need only examine what happens to law and order when critical positions in the judiciary, military, and police are filled by unqualified relatives of politicians. Whenever employment and promotion in the civil service are not based on merit, efficiency and productive problems arise, resulting in significant misallocation of resources. Of course, one may argue that appointing members of one's ethnic group to important positions in the civil service may not necessarily be a problem, especially if they are qualified. However, two important problems are evident: (1) politicians rarely consider qualification in their 'hiring' practices – they are more likely to base their decisions on political considerations. (2) not basing employment decisions on merit and employing an arms-length process to fill positions in the civil service can cause a lot of morale problems, even if the individuals hired through nepotism are qualified. The fact that an individual owes his job to the president or prime minister, for example, can interfere enormously with his ability to make critical decisions. Where a decision may produce enormous benefits for the society as a whole, but negatively affect the welfare (or re-election efforts) of the person who appointed him to the position, a civil servant may choose to protect his benefactor and hence, his job instead of advancing the welfare of greater society.

As mentioned briefly earlier, many reasons have been advanced to explain Africa's poverty and underdevelopment. Add to those the following: colonial exploitation; unsustainable population growth rates; bad governance; destructive ethnic conflict and civil wars; and ignorance. Based on the experiences of some countries, it is quite likely that some of these factors may have contributed to poor economic performance and hence, continued poverty. However, as this chapter has argued, the primary cause of most economic failure and/or collapse in Africa is the absence of appropriate institutions or the presence of weak ones. There is no question that some African countries have either destroyed or significantly weakened what were already very fragile institutions. The latter, as mentioned earlier, were inherited from the colonialists at independence. One of these institutions is the judiciary, which serves a very important and critical role in the economy. For one thing, a properly functioning judiciary system is critical for the *maintenance of the rule of law*. Without the latter, there would not be the enabling environment for the productive use of resources, including the talents of individuals. In fact, investors – both local and foreign, are very concerned about the quality and credibility of the judiciary and its efficiency and fairness in enforcing the law, including contracts. If, for example, prospective investors perceive the judiciary as incapable of fairly and effectively enforcing contracts, they may decide not to invest in the country and, instead take their resources to economies with more effective judiciary systems. This would not augur well for economic and development (see, e.g., World Bank, 2002).

It is true, as has been argued by several authors (see, e.g., Millikan and Rostow, 1957; Chenery and Strout, 1966), that capital (both human and physical) are very important for economic growth. In the late 1950s and early 1960s, as the European colonies gained independence, the severe shortage of capital was considered a critical constraint to the rapid economic growth that was needed to generate enough wealth for poverty alleviation. It was believed that development aid from the continent's former colonizers, as well as the US, would be used to augment meager domestic savings and allow these new economies to eventually engage in capital formation on their own (Millikan and Rostow, 1957). In fact, in countries such as Kenya, there were very few indigenous people trained in the sciences and the professions. In addition, top positions in the civil service were still held by Europeans, as a result of the paucity of trained indigenous people This situation, of course, was not unique to Kenya. Throughout the continent, the new African countries all suffered from a severe lack of highly skilled and trained individuals to manage both the private and public sectors and enhance each country's ability to develop. As has been argued elsewhere (see, e.g., Mbaku, 1997), the availability of both human and physical capital are necessary but not sufficient conditions for economic growth. In order for these resources to be employed productively and generate the wealth needed, there must exist the appropriate institutional environment. This is borne by the fact that since the 1960s, countries such as Kenya, Nigeria, Ghana, and Cameroon have managed to develop significant stocks of human capital (either locally or with the help of universities in Europe, the USSR, China, and North America) and yet, economic performance has not improved significantly. Nor has public administration improved. During the last several years, the economies of these countries have been characterized by relatively high levels of inefficiency and their bureaucracies pervaded with corruption (see, e.g., Hope and Chikulo, 2000).

Evidence from the last 50 years shows that despite significant flows of aid from the developed countries to Africa, most of the continent, especially the sub-region called sub-Saharan Africa, remains essentially underdeveloped. Apparently, such significant flows of development aid have, at best, had only a nominal impact on poverty eradication in the continent. Some researchers have gone as far as arguing that 'aid does not promote economic development for two reasons: poverty is not caused by capital shortage, and it is not optimal for politicians to adjust distortionary policies when they receive aid' (Boone, 1995, p. 33). After studying more than a hundred countries, including several in Africa, Boone went on to argue that development aid does not have a positive impact on investment and capital formation in the recipient country and that aid was unlikely to enhance the ability of many of the poor countries to escape from the poverty trap. Most of the development aid sent to these countries had been illegally appropriated by opportunistic elites for their own benefit, without any effort being made to direct the resources towards productive activities. Such misappropriation of aid resources, of course, has been made possible by the absence of strong institutions, those that adequately constrain the state and prevent its custodians from engaging in opportunism.

Another factor often cited for continued poverty and underdevelopment in Africa is the high incidence of political instability as evidenced by the large number of military coups that have taken place in the continent since 1950 and the many civil wars that continue to engulf the region (e.g., in Burundi, Rwanda, Somalia, Angola, Liberia, Sierra Leone, and Sudan). In addition, destructive ethnic conflict remains an essential part of society in Kenya, Uganda, Nigeria and several other countries. Most political violence in post-independence Africa, including violent ethnic mobilization, however, is closely tied to institutional failure (see Mbaku, 2001; Kimenyi, 2001; Agbese, 2001; Saitoti, 2002). As argued elsewhere (see, e.g., Mbaku, 1997; 2000a), few African countries have institutions that provide credible and viable procedures for ensuring peaceful regime change. Even fewer have been able to find ways to prevent the military from meddling in politics. In fact, it is only recently that some African countries (e.g., Ghana, Uganda, and Eritrea) have engaged their people in democratic constitutionalism designed to prevent the military from further intervention in politics. These countries hope to establish, through participatory, people-driven constitutionalism, institutions that can effectively constrain the military and prevent the latter's elites from assuming power through illegal means. Regarding violent ethnic mobilization, most of it comes from the fact that existing institutions have failed to provide procedures for the peaceful resolution of the conflicting interests of the various ethnic and social cleavages in each country. In fact, in many cases, the laws and institutions adopted at independence placed some ethnic groups at a competitive disadvantage and enhance the ability of others to dominate governance and the allocation of resources. Locked out groups came to realize that the only way they could productively participate in economic processes was to capture the apparatus of government. Given the fact that constitutional processes for regime change either did not exist in these countries or functioned poorly, many of these groups resorted to violent mobilization as a way to secure for themselves positions in government and minimize further marginalization (see Mbaku, 2001).

The frequent occurrence of natural disasters (e.g., droughts and floods) has also been advanced as a major contributor to poor economic performance in Africa. In recent years, for example, floods have caused massive destruction in Kenya and Mozambique. Natural disasters, however, are not unique to Africa. Many other regions of the world continue to be plagued by such things as earthquakes, heavy rains, severe snow storms, and typhoons. Yet, many of these places are highly developed and do not suffer from the levels of material deprivation common in Africa. One reason why these natural disaster-prone regions are able to develop and Africa is not, is that they have institutions that are capable of effectively managing these disasters and minimizing their impact on people, national stocks of capital and the natural environment. Existing institutions in the African countries, on the other hand, do not have the capacity to adequately manage these disasters and prevent them from having such negative impact on development. In fact, in countries such as Somalia and Ethiopia, famines throughout the years, have destroyed a significant portion of these countries' productive labor resources. Yet, even as we write, governments in these countries have yet to develop the capacity to deal effectively with such phenomenon.

Corruption, excessive population growth, unmanageable external debt, economic policies of the industrial market economies, and policy mistakes made by well-meaning but poorly educated civil servants and politicians have also been mentioned as obstacles to development in the continent. While these reasons seem highly plausible in explaining why Africa has failed to develop, it is important to note that strong and efficient institutions can check many of these problems. For example, institutional structures can serve to enhance society's ability to deal more effectively with such things as corruption and the misuse of public funds. An efficient judiciary, as well as a free press, can check venality in the civil service. Also, many of the so-called policies mistakes made by African elites have actually been deliberate programs designed and implemented by opportunistic bureaucrats and politicians seeking ways to enrich themselves. Strong and efficient institutions could have made it quite difficult for these elites to promote the perverse economic policies that allowed them to plunder national economies for their own benefit (see, e.g., Mbaku, 1997, 2000a).

This discussion bring us back to the argument made earlier, that institutions matter and they are indeed, the most important determinant of economic growth. The appropriate institutions can (1) provide structures for peaceful resolution of conflict; (2) enhance entrepreneurship and wealth creation; (3) adequately constrain the state and prevent its custodians from engaging in opportunistic behaviors; (4) provide an environment within which groups can compete for scarce resources without resorting to violence mobilization; (5) provide investors with the information they need to engage their resources, including their talents, in productive activities; (6) protect the person and property of individuals; and (7) generally promote development.

Institutions and restarting and sustaining economic growth in Kenya

The primary thrust of this chapter is that institutions are indeed central to the process of restarting and sustaining growth. By extension, this implies that institutional arrangements must have, to some degree, been responsible for the poor performance of the Kenyan economy. Clearly, issues of governance have been a primary cause of the poor economic performance encountered by the country during a significant portion of its post-independence existence. In particular, high levels of corruption in the public sector have adversely impacted on the cost of doing business in the country. Likewise, political uncertainty, policy reversals, heavy government intervention in markets, have all contributed to poor economic performance. Likewise, sporadic ethnic conflicts that have tended to escalate around political elections have also contributed to poor economic performance. This has much to do with institutions of law and order and also with the security of property rights.

To restart and sustain economic growth in Kenya, it is therefore prudent that there be important institutional reforms to accompany the economic reforms proposed in this book. For example, although there has been serious attempts to deal with corruption, these efforts have not been successful. One reason has been the fact that the three branches of government (executive, judiciary and legislative) are not independent as is necessary for effective anti-corruption efforts. In essence, prosecuting corruption cases has been quite difficult. It is therefore important that constitutional reforms include the issue of separation of powers. This should be accompanied by the strengthening of the judiciary and the legislature.

But, of course, the best way to deal with corruption is to reduce the supply and demand for corrupt activities. This can be accomplished by reducing unnecessary government intervention in markets and providing the civil service with a more efficient and merit-based compensation system (see, e.g., Mbaku, 2000a).

Economic growth in Kenya can only be restarted and sustained if peace is maintained in the country and the country is able to live peacefully with its neighbors. Recent conflicts have fairly been localized and have been of relatively short duration. However, the fact that these conflicts have resulted in the deaths of many people and in the displacement of even more people, suggests that such conflicts could, in the future, escalate into civil wars. Thus, the issue of a constitution that enhances the peaceful coexistence of all groups in Kenya is critically important.

As a far as property rights are concerned, major reforms are called for, particularly in the area of land and water. Hopefully, the Presidential Land Commission appointed recently will propose reforms that will ensure equity in land ownership and the security of ownership rights. Equally important are clear rules and procedures for formalizing *informal* property rights.

Conclusion

Currently, a lot of emphasis is being placed on the role played by institutions in economic growth and development. Until recently, economists and other development experts argued that the most important determinants of economic growth were physical and human capital, as well as the level of technology in the country. Recent research now points to the fact that although these resources (i.e., human and physical capital, and technology) are necessary, they are not sufficient conditions for economic growth and development. In order for these resources to be used efficiently to promote growth, there must exist the appropriate institutional environment. Hence, institutions are now considered a very important determinant of economic growth. Countries that aspire to achieve economic and social progress must strive to build and sustain strong social, economic and political institutions (see, Saitoti, 2002).

As argued earlier, these institutions are critical because they shape the way economic agents (individual traders, households, firms and governments) behave and thus, determine economic outcomes. There is a need to establish and maintain institutions, which enhance the efficient allocation of resources and also reduce inequities in the distribution of income and wealth. However, if the country's institutions do not protect individual liberty; do not guarantee individuals the right to engage freely in exchange; are not transparent, accountable and participatory; and do not protect property that has been legally accumulated; they will stifle economic growth and development. Institutions must also encourage and nourish entrepreneurship, promote the expansion of market opportunities and create and maintain credible and predictable conditions for market operations.

What the African countries need is to have strong and efficient political and economic institutions that guarantee economic freedoms, adequately constrain the state, enhance wealth creation, and promote the peaceful coexistence of population groups. Developing and sustaining these institutions, however, is a major challenge for most countries in Africa. Unless they are developed and sustained, the continent will continue to suffer from high levels of poverty and deprivation.

Note

1. The authors' analysis was limited to the exploitation of environmental resources, hence the reference in their definition to natural resources; the definition, however, applies to all types of assets).

References

Agbese, P. O. (2001), 'Managing Ethnic Relations in a Heterogeneous Society: The Case of Nigeria', in Mbaku, J. M., Agbese, P. O. and Kimenyi, M. S. (eds.), *Ethnicity and Governance in the Third World*, Ashgate: Aldershot, UK.

Anderson, T. L. and Hill, P. J. (1986), 'Constraining the Transfer Society: Constitutional and Moral Dimensions', *Cato Journal*, Vol., 6, No. 1, pp. 317–339.

Ayittey, G. B. N. (1992), *Africa Betrayed*, St. Martin's Press: New York.

Ayittey, G. B. N. (1997), *Africa in Chaos*, St. Martin's Press: New York.

Bates, R. H. (1981), *Markets and States in Tropical Africa*, University of California Press: Berkeley, CA.

Baylies, C. (1995), '"Political Conditionality" and Democratization', *Review of African Political Economy*, Vol. 22, No. 65, pp. 321–337.

Boone, P. (1995), *Politics and the Effectiveness of Aid*, National Bureau of Economic Research, Inc., Working Paper No. 5308.

Brennan, G. and Buchanan, J. M. (1985), *The Reason of Rules: Constitutional Political Economy*, Cambridge University Press: Cambridge.

Brett, E. A. (1995), 'Institutional Theory and Social Change in Uganda', in Harriss, J., Hunter, J. and Lewis, C. M. (eds.), *The New Institutional Economics and Third World Development*, Routledge: London.

Brough, W. T. and Kimenyi, M. S. (1986), 'On the Inefficient Extraction of Rents by Dictators', *Public Choice*, Vol. 48, No. 1, pp. 37–48.

Buchanan, J. M. and Tullock, G. (1962), *The Calculus of Consent: Logical Foundations of Constitutional Democracy*, The University of Michigan Press: Ann Arbor, MI.

Chenery, H. B. and Strout, A. M. (1966), 'Foreign Assistance and Economic Development', *American Economic Review*, Vol. 56 (September), pp. 679–733.

Coase, R. (1960), 'The Problem of Social Cost', *The Journal of Law and Economics*, Vol. 4 (October), pp. 1–44.

Congleton, R. D. (1994), 'Constitutional Federalism and Decentralization: A Second Best Solution', *Economia Delle Scelte Pubbliche* (Italy), Vol. 11, No. 1, pp. 15–29.

Ferree, K., Singh, S. and Bates, R. H. (1997), 'Political Institutions and Economic Growth in Africa', Harvard Institute for International Development, Development Discussion Paper No. 583.

Goldsmith, A. A. (1998), 'Institutions and Economic Growth in Africa', Paper written for the *Equity and Growth Through Economic Research* Project Funded by the US Agency for International Development, Division of Strategic Analysis, Office of Sustainable Development, Bureau for Africa, Activity No. 698–0546, Washington, DC: USAID.

Grubel, H. G. (1998), 'Economic Freedom and Human Welfare: Some Empirical Findings', *Cato Journal*, Vol. 18, No. 2, pp. 287–304.

Gwartney, J. D. and Holcombe, R. G. (1999), 'Economic Freedom, Constitutional Structure, and Growth in Developing Countries', in Kimenyi, M. S. and Mbaku, J. M. (eds.), *Institutions and Collective Choice in Developing Countries: Applications of the Theory of Public Choice*, Ashgate: Aldershot, UK.

Hanna, S. and Munasinghe, M. (1995), 'An Introduction to Property Rights in the Environment', in Hanna, S. and Munasinghe, M. (eds.), *Property Rights and the Environment*, The World Bank: Washington, DC.

Hope, K. R., Sr. and Chikulo, B. C. (eds.) (2000), *Corruption and Development in Africa: Lessons from Country Case Studies*, Macmillan: London.

Kimenyi, M. S. (1987), 'Bureaucratic Rents and Political Institutions', *Journal of Public Finance and Public Choice* (Italy), Vol. 3, pp. 189–199.

Kimenyi, M. S. (1989), 'Interest Groups, Transfer Seeking and Democratization', *The American Journal of Economics and Sociology*, Vol. 48, No. 3, pp. 339–349.

Kimenyi, M. S. (2001), 'Harmonizing Ethnic Claims in Africa: A Proposal for Ethnic-based Federalism', in Mbaku, J. M., Agbese, P. O. and Kimenyi, M. S. (eds.), *Ethnicity and Governance in the Third World*, Ashgate: Aldershot, UK.

Kimenyi, M. S. and Mbaku, J. M. (eds.) (1999), *Institutions and Collective Choice in Developing Countries: Applications of the Theory of Public Choice*, Ashgate: Aldershot, UK.

Lipsey, R. G. and Chrystal, K. A. (1995), *An Introduction to Positive Economics*, Oxford University Press: Oxford.

Lowenberg, A. D. (1992), 'A Post-Apartheid Constitution for South Africa: Lessons from Public Choice', *Cato Journal*, Vol. 12, No. 2, pp. 297–319.

Mbaku, J. M. (1991), 'Military Expenditures and Bureaucratic Competition for Rents', *Public Choice*, Vol. 71, Nos. 1–2, pp. 19–31.

Mbaku, J. M. (1997), *Institutions and Reform in Africa: The Public Choice Perspective*, Praeger: Westport, CT.

Mbaku, J. M. (ed.) (1998), *Corruption and the Crisis of Institutional Reforms in Africa*, The Edwin Mellen Press: Lewiston, NY.

Mbaku, J. M. (1999), 'The Relevance of the State in African Development: Preparing for the New Century', *Journal of Asian and African Studies*, Vol. 34, No. 3, pp. 298–320.

Mbaku, J. M. (2000a), *Bureaucratic and Political Corruption in Africa: The Public Choice Perspective*, Krieger: Malabar, FL.

Mbaku, J. M. (2000b), 'Appropriate Institutional Environment for Development in Twenty-First Century Africa', *Africa Quarterly* (New Delhi), Vol. 40, No. 3, pp. 7–44.

Mbaku, J. M. (2001), 'Ethnicity, Constitutionalism, and Governance in Africa', in Mbaku, J. M., Agbese, P. O. and Kimenyi, M. S. (eds.), *Ethnicity and Governance in the Third World*, Ashgate: Aldershot, UK.

Mbaku, J. and Paul, C. (1989), 'Political Instability in Africa: A Rent-Seeking Approach', *Public Choice*, Vol. 63, No. 1, pp. 63–72.

Millikan, M. F. and Rostow, W. W. (1957), *A Proposal: Key to an Effective Foreign Policy*, Harper & Brothers: New York.

Niskanen, W. A. (1990), 'Conditions Affecting the Survival of Constitutional Rules', *Constitutional Political Economy*, Vol. 1, pp. 53–62.

North, D. C. (1981), *Structure and Change in Economic History*, W. W. Norton & Company: New York.

North, D. C. (1990), *Institutions, Institutional Change and Economic Performance*, Cambridge University Press: Cambridge.

North, D. C. (1997), *The Contribution of the New Institutional Economics to an Understanding of the Transition Problem*, UNU World Institute for Development Research: Helsinki.

Olson, M., Jr. (1965), *The Logic of Collective Action*, Harvard University Press: Cambridge, MA.

Olson, M., Jr. (1996), 'Distinguished Lecture on Economics in Government – Big Bills Left on the Sidewalk: Why Some Nations are Rich, and Others Poor', *Journal of Economic Perspectives*, Vol. 10, No. 2 (Spring), pp. 3–24.

Ostrom, E., Schroeder, L. and Wynne, S. (1993), *Institutional Incentives and Sustainable Development: Infrastructure Policies in Perspective*, Westview: Boulder, CO.

Papandreou, A. (1994), *Externality and Institutions*, Clarendon Press: London.

Saitoti, G. (2002), *The Challenges of Economic and Institutional Reforms in Africa*, Ashgate: Aldershot, UK.

Shaffer, J. (1995), 'Institutions, Behavior and Economic Performance: Comments on Institutional Analysis', Staff Paper No. 95–52, Department of Agricultural Economics, Michigan State University, East Lansing, MI.

Wildavsky, A. (1990), 'A Double Security: Federalism as Competition', *Cato Journal*, Vol. 10, pp. 39–48.

Wiseman, J. (1990), 'Principles of Political Economy: An Outline Proposal, Illustrated by Application to Fiscal Federalism', *Constitutional Political Economy*, Vol. 2, No. 1, pp. 101–124.

World Bank (2000), *World Development Report, 1999/2000: Entering the 21st Century*, Oxford University Press: New York.

World Bank (2002), *World Development Report, 2002: Building Institutions for Markets*, Oxford University Press: New York.

3

Kenya Macroeconomic Management

NJUGUNA S. NDUNG'U

Introduction

The chapter discusses economic growth and its sources in Kenya. This is accomplished by borrowing from available literature that has identified the most important factors that drive growth in Kenya. Furthermore, the literature is used to allude to the pre-conditions necessary to restart and sustain growth. The questions addressed are:

- What are the factors that have led to the growth pause in Kenya, and by extension, what has led to an investment pause?
- What are the determinants of, and links to, growth from the literature, and are they applicable to the Kenyan case?
- What are the mechanisms or channels through which short-run macroeconomic management affects growth in Kenya?
- How have previously implemented policies succeeded or failed in promoting growth and what do economic performance indicators show?
- How should current policies be changed or reforms deepened to restart and sustain growth in the future?

The chapter accomplishes several objectives, and to do so, we divide it into two main sections. In the first section, we start by reviewing some background materials about the economy, specifically Kenya's history with structural adjustment policies and the weaknesses found in managing and conforming to the required reforms.

Then, we evaluate the performance indicators in an attempt to assess what has happened over the years. Next, we review the literature and show what is the corroborating evidence in Kenya's growth decline. Finally, with these 'facts' in hand, we focus the discussion on what has to be done, in order to reverse and sustain a high growth rate in the future. The key to this discussion is a highlight of the institutional reforms necessary to support growth-friendly policies.

In the second section, we examine Kenya's reform process and categorize periods in terms of the reforms and policies formulated. Next, we provide a summary of performance indicators and attempt to determine why growth has slowed down. Then, we review the literature on economic growth, in addition to looking at short-run stabilization aspects and their links to growth. Some of these short-run stabilization aspects and their links to growth require explicit modeling to show their effects, the feedback effects from growth to these variables, and to assess the strength of these links. However, we do not undertake such modeling, Instead, we borrow from estimated results and provide important insights and conclusions. First, inflation is seen as driven by monetary overhang/expansion and exchange rate movements. In addition, it is seen as a significant constraint to economic growth. All these variables have direct as well as indirect effects on growth. The inter-relationships between interest rates and investment, exchange rate, short-term capital flows, domestic debt and their feedback effects are then explored. Finally, we focus on what direction future policies should take given the evidence provided in the study, thereby providing a summary of the achievements of the chapter together with institutional underpinnings that are required to support an investment and growth-friendly environment in Kenya.

The Kenya economy and the history of reforms

As a result of macroeconomic imbalances due to distortionary effects of controls, Kenya engaged in structural adjustment programs (SAPs) in the early 1980s. Structural adjustment, as undertaken by Kenya and several other African countries, consists of making changes in macroeconomic policies so that the economy is adaptable to changing economic realities and is market oriented. These policies then aim at setting prices right, by effecting changes in the relative price structure in order to give efficient signals to economic agents. The changes in relative price structure are supposed to induce changes in both the level of real income and the productive structure, through relative sectoral profitabilities and resource allocation.

This does not seem to have been the outcome in Kenya. Several reasons may explain this outcome, some of which include policy reversals, short-run inconsistency policy problems, lack of complementarity in reforms, political uncertainty, corruption, and above all, weak institutions that have destroyed the incentive structure and returns to investment. A growing literature has argued that there is a strong relationship between incentives, growth, and private investments.

To trace Kenya's entry into SAPs, we start with the history of controls in the early 1970s, which was an easier response to deal with the repercussions of expansionary policies. Faced with macroeconomic instability in the 1970s,[1] the Government of Kenya (GoK) placed controls on foreign exchange transactions and purchase of foreign goods; regulated domestic retail and producer prices; introduced wage guidelines, ceilings on domestic rates of interest, and selective restrictions on bank borrowing. In other words, the aim was to control the demand side instead of making adjustments in the supply side. The pressure for adjustment was relieved in 1976/1977 when the country experienced a commodity boom in the form of coffee and tea. The controls were somewhat relaxed but not all were removed. This commodity boom led to a boom in the construction industry and in the financial sector. Given the fixed exchange regime, this led to a moderate overvaluation of the currency (Mwega and Ndung'u, 1996).

By 1982, it was clear that the macro policies pursued were not sustainable and drastic change was called for. Between 1980–1982, the Kenya shilling was devalued by about 20 percent in real terms against the SDR. The first policy change was the exchange rate regime from a fixed peg to a crawling peg, in effect, a real exchange rate rule. However, the capital account was still closed and selective price controls were still in existence. After the crawling peg was adopted, there was a deliberate attempt by the GoK to depreciate the shilling between 1983–1986, which improved the export sector tremendously and was complemented by a mini-coffee boom in 1986.

In addition, by 1983, various other policy measures were put in place including interest rate adjustment and a reduction in the fiscal deficit. These measures helped to stabilize the balance of payments, reduce the excess liquidity generated by the coffee boom of 1976/1977, reduce the explosive fiscal deficit as well as the rate of inflation. These and other broader measures had a successful impact in the early years of the stabilization program, but in the later half of the 1980s, there was a gradual decline and worsening of the economic environment.

To put the policy environment in Kenya into perspective, we review the structural adjustment policies and categorize the period and the inclination of the government during this period. We then review the GoK's reform efforts between 1985–1995 where tangible policies were implemented.

An overview of structural adjustment programs in Kenya: objectives and targets

Kenya was one of the first African countries to adopt SAPs in 1980 after the prolonged economic decline triggered by the two oil shocks of the 1970s, falling world commodity prices, fiscal and monetary instability, and rising levels of unemployment, which forced the country to seek assistance from the International Monetary Fund (IMF) in 1979. The country had already sought assistance from the IMF twice before: in 1974 for a loan within the Oil-Facility, and in 1975 for a loan from the Extended Fund Facility. The terms for a stand-by agreement were agreed upon by the Government of Kenya (GoK) and the IMF in 1979. However, failure by the government to reduce its domestic borrowing to the required level led to delays in disbursements by a year (Swamy, 1994). This compelled the GoK to turn to the World Bank for quick disbursing financial resources.

The country's 18 years experience with structural adjustment can be divided into five phases, which we label: (1) slow start and non-compliance 1980–1984; (2) poor implementation period 1985–1991; (3) the rapid implementation phase 1992–1995; (4) the reluctance phase 1996–1998; and (5) developments since 1999.

1980–1984 – slow start and non-compliance: The economic policies contained in *Sessional Paper No. 4 of 1980* on how to deal with the prevailing economic crisis were largely in line with the recommendations of the World Bank and the IMF, and served as the basis on which Kenya's first Structural Adjustment Loan (SAL) was agreed and signed in March 1980 between the World Bank and the Kenyan government. A second stand-by agreement was signed in October 1980.

These developments marked the beginning of SAPs in Kenya. The first phase between 1980–1984, was characterized by non-compliance with the agreed terms, due to timing and design shortcomings, as well as limited commitment by the Kenyan authorities. Failure to meet the conditions registered with the first stand-by agreement continued in subsequent years and became a persistent source of friction between the government and the multilateral donor institutions. Furthermore, success of these policies depended critically on their full implementation. Poor implementation of recommended policy measures resulted in a delay in the disbursement of the second tranche of the second SAP facility signed by the government and the World Bank for the period July 1982 to January 1984. Due to the general reluctance by the government to implement the agreed terms of the program, there was no noticeable impact of the program in the country. Poor implementation and lack of commitment continued into the second phase (1985–1991).

1985–1991 – poor implementation of agreed reforms: Between 1985–1991, there was considerable official acceptance or ownership of the reform program, especially after the publication of *Sessional Paper No. 1 of 1986 on Economic Management for Renewed Growth*. Although the pace of implementation remained poor, efforts were made to introduce economic reforms in various sectors especially in agriculture, trade and industry, finance, education, health, parastatal and foreign exchange markets, as well as the financial sector. SAPs were basically medium to long-term economic policies directed at the supply side of the economy and aimed at restructuring various economic sectors to enhance their efficiency and responsiveness to price and other market signals. In addition to the SAPs, the country undertook some macroeconomic stabilization programs, largely aimed at correcting short-term instabilities such as inflationary tendencies, budgetary and balance of payments deficits. The main objectives of the reform program were the achievement of rapid and sustained economic growth, employment creation, improvement of the general standard of living through better access to basic needs, and reduction of rural-urban imbalance.

Frustrations on the part of the World Bank and lack of success in the reforms led the World Bank to change strategies and start pursuing sectoral adjustment programs. The first World Bank sectoral credit to Kenya was approved in June 1986. This was a quick disbursing sectoral adjustment credit referred to as the first Agricultural Sector Adjustment Lending (ASAL) for the purpose of restructuring the National Cereals and Produce Board (NCPB) and a number of other parastatals. This was under the first Agricultural Sector Adjustment Operation (ASAO-1). This restructuring included implementation of agricultural reforms and the reduction of NCPBs claims on budgetary resources.

A new stand-by agreement with the IMF and a three-year structural adjustment facility, together with credits from the International Development Agency (IDA) program and other donors, was signed to support the country's stabilization and reform measures adopted in February 1988. The program was aimed at the restoration of fiscal and monetary discipline that had been eroded in the previous few years, particularly during the mini-coffee boom of 1986. The program's main objectives were to strengthen macroeconomic policies and to facilitate implementation of industrial and financial sector reforms.

The structural adjustment facility of 1988 was replaced by a 3–year (1989–1991) Enhanced Structural Adjustment Facility (ESAF) in May 1989. The performance targets attached to ESAF included rapid economic growth with a targeted rate above the country's population growth rate, deceleration of the inflation rate to the average rate of Kenya's trading partners, a reduction of the current account deficit, and the build up of the country's net official international resources. The ESAF program was, however, poorly implemented and donor frustration reached unprecedented levels. By 1991, the last year of ESAF, three out of four quantitative performance criteria, namely the ceilings on net domestic assets of the domestic banking sector, government borrowing from the banking system and net official international reserves, showed that the program had been poorly implemented and was not functioning properly. In addition, the sectoral adjustment programs had limited results due to lack of strong government commitment in terms of implementation, especially the removal of controls on the industrial and agricultural sectors, and domestic trade.

1992–1995 – rapid implementation of SAPs: Donor frustration with the slow pace of implementation and in some instances reversals of SAPs reached a climax in 1991, when quick disbursing aid was suspended during the Consultative Group Meeting held in November that year. The reasons given for this suspension were (1) poor implementation of economic reforms; (2) rising levels of corruption in the country; (3) failure to correct macroeconomic imbalances caused by fiscal indiscipline; (4) slow reforms in the civil service and in the privatization of public enterprises; (5) lack of accountability of public enterprises; (6) failure to establish a supportive environment for the growth of the private sector; and (7) a slow pace of political reforms. These, in essence, served as the conditions that needed to be satisfied before aid could be resumed.

At the beginning of 1992, a shadow program was negotiated with the IMF under which the government was required to stabilize the macroeconomic environment by reducing the budget deficit to 2 percent of GDP in 1992/1993. This was to be achieved through improved efficiency of revenue collection, reduction of government expenditures, privatization and restructuring of parastatals, tightening of monetary policy using open market operations, and improved supervision of the banking sector by the Central Bank.

In September 1992, the World Bank decided to postpone disbursement of the second tranche of the programs that were in progress, again due to poor implementation of several of the conditions attached to sectoral programs. In December of the same year the second tranche of ASAL was cancelled because the grain movement controls had been re-imposed.

Although monetary, financial and external sectors were the main areas of concern by the donors in 1992, there were no significant improvements by the beginning of 1993. The government quickly implemented some critical reforms which included floating the currency, introducing foreign exchange retention accounts, the re-introducing of retention accounts for traditional exports and service sectors, expansion of the inter-bank market, and liberalization of the coffee and tea marketing systems.

In spite of these efforts, the IMF and the World Bank were not satisfied because the government had not effectively implemented the tight monetary policies required. It is important to note that although the third phase of Kenya's reform program between 1992–1995 generally witnessed more dramatic implementation of the recommended reforms compared with the previous periods, considerable tension between donors and the Kenya government frequently emerged on specific issues.

For instance, in March 1993, disagreements with donors were high with some elements in the Kenyan political system threatening to reverse the reforms that had been introduced. This led to the abolition of retention accounts with a directive requiring remittance of all export proceeds to the Central Bank at the official rate of exchange, abandonment of the policy of floating the currency and the subsequent collapse of the market for Foreign Exchange Bearer Certificates (Forex Cs).[2] These frequent lapses in the country's policy reform effort meant that liberalization of the financial system could not proceed until some basic stability had been achieved. In addition, this destroyed the credibility of the government to effect and sustain reforms thereby discouraging prospective investors and damaging chances of an early economic recovery.

In November 1993, Kenya applied for a one-year arrangement under ESAF for a total of SDR 45.23 million. The IMF accepted the application, indicating that the loan would be disbursed in two equal installments as long as a number of conditions were fulfilled. The conditions included more effective control of the fiscal deficit, control on government borrowing from the Central Bank of Kenya, and observation of targets on the net international reserves of the Central Bank of Kenya. In addition, the arrangement required placing limits on new non-concessional external loans contracted or guaranteed by the government, and limiting the increases on short-term external debt. The second disbursement was to be released only if the government fully decontrolled pricing and marketing of maize and petroleum products; increased the proportion of foreign exchange retained by exporters to 100 percent of export earnings; and relaxed restrictions on foreign exchange transactions, imports, and the balance of payments accounts.

1996–1998 – reluctance: By the end of October 1995, the country was negotiating for a new three-year $200 million loan under ESAF. The negotiations that had started in January 1995 had stalled due to the country's poor implementation of both economic and political reforms. However, by the end of 1995, the country had reluctantly implemented the major political and economic reforms agreed upon with the multilateral and bilateral donors. Economic reforms implemented included removal of virtually all price and foreign exchange controls, liberalization of domestic marketing trade, import liberalization, reduction of the budget rationalization, financial reforms, privatization, removal of wage guidelines and other labor market reforms, and liberalization of the exchange rate. The country was set for another Consultative Group meeting with multilateral donors early in 1996 in Paris to receive new aid commitments. However, there were strong hints from the IMF that this would not be possible due to unresolved differences, especially over massive corruption and scandals involving public resources. One of the critical areas at the time was the government's lack of commitment to prosecute those involved in the Goldenberg Scandal and other financial scams. The issue of corruption in public service and a new conditionality on governance led again to the suspension of ESAF by the IMF in August 1997. Discussions in early 1999 indicated that there were still major problems in dealing with corruption. An anti-corruption body was formed and then disbanded. Towards late 1998 it was reinstalled without a director. The ESAF, under a new umbrella on poverty reduction, was concluded with the IMF early in 1999. Tensions with donors, however, were still high due to the slow process of privatization and the high level corruption in the country, especially in the public sector.

1999–present: Since 1999, the Government of Kenya has struggled with donors as the latter have continued to push for an increase in the pace of privatization. In fact, by December 2000, tensions between the government and the IMF were still very high because of what the IMF believed was Kenya's reluctance to deal effectively and decisively with high levels of venality in the public sector. By 2001, those tensions remained quite high, especially since the reform programs that Kenya had completed by this time appeared to reveal a less than strong commitment to the institutional reforms necessary to significantly improve the environment for more efficient allocation of resources. The loans approved by the international community were to be disbursed in small amounts in order to control the pace of domestic reforms. However, only the initial disbursement was successfully advanced. Others have since been delayed as a result of governance problems and the government's inability to deal effectively with high levels of corruption and financial malfeasance, at least, to the satisfaction or approval of the international financial and donor communities.

Components of SAPs, 1985–1998

The policy reform process in this decade can be summarized under two headings: those aimed at enhancing competitiveness such as trade and exchange rate liberalization; and those largely oriented towards institutional changes such as privatization and governance. Privatization has both a competitiveness angle and an institutional reform angle

Competition enhancing policy reforms

Some of the reform measures implemented by the GoK were intended to enhance the competitiveness of Kenyan products in both domestic and external markets.

Examples of the reforms in this category include trade liberalization and exchange rate reforms.

External trade liberalization: Liberalization of Kenya's external trade sector was one of the areas that received greater attention in the country's three phases of reform program. Trade liberalization has included removal of quantitative restrictions (QRs), reduction of tariff levels, and adoption of a more flexible exchange rate regime.

Import liberalization has made considerable progress since the early 1980s. Between 1980–1985, the share of items that could be imported without any restrictions rose from 24 percent to 48 percent of total value of imported items. The average tariff rate was also reduced by about 8 percent over the same period (Swamy, 1994). An improved import licensing system that had restricted and unrestricted schedules was established. In 1988, import liberalization was taken a step further when the import licensing system underwent significant improvements. The new system created five schedules with the aim of increasing strictness in licensing requirements. By July 1991, imports requiring licensing were restricted largely on health, security, or environmental grounds. By November 1993, all administrative controls in international trade, including import licensing and foreign exchange allocation, together with departments dealing with them had been abolished. Tariff reforms were also progressively implemented with tariff rates gradually lowered and tariff bands or categories reduced. Between 1989/1990 and 1991/1992 for instance, the overall production weighted tariffs had declined from 62 percent to 48 percent (Swamy, 1994).

The maximum tariff rate had been reduced from 135 percent in the 1980s to 45 percent by 1994, while the number of non-zero bands was reduced from 25 to 6 over the same period. Since 1987/1988, tariff dispersion has been lowered as the number of tariff bands was reduced. Harmonization of the tariffs is another policy that was pursued, especially from the second phase. The average tariff rate had declined significantly in the third phase. Two factors, however, disturbed the general downward trend: the first was that tariffs reached their highest level in 1989/1990 as a result of the replacement of quotas with equivalent tariffs; the second was a management crisis in 1993/1994 that raised tariffs temporarily to cater for a shortfall in government revenue collections.

Foreign exchange transactions and exchange rate policy reforms: Kenya's third phase of reform was essentially aimed at enhanced competitiveness. These reforms included the removal of foreign exchange controls, the liberalization of foreign exchange transactions, and the floating the exchange rate leading to a large depreciation of the shilling especially in the 1992–1993 period. Other reforms related to foreign exchange in the early 1990s included (1) the introduction of Foreign Exchange Bearer Certificates (Forex Cs) in October 1991; (2) the introduction of export earnings retention schemes for exporters in 1992; (3) the merging of the official exchange rate with the inter-bank foreign exchange rate; and (4) the removal of exchange controls on current and capital account transactions in 1993. These reforms had the overall effect of making the foreign exchange market freer than in the first and second phases of the reform program. In the 1994 Budget Speech, all regulations pertaining to the Exchange Control Act were suspended and parliament finally repealed the Foreign Exchange Act in December 1995. One of the latest reforms in the foreign exchange market was the move to allow legislation of foreign exchange bureaux in 1995.

Prior to the removal of foreign exchange controls and the liberalization of the exchange rate, the country's production sectors, especially manufacturing and agriculture, faced acute shortages of imported inputs due to non-availability of foreign exchange. This resulted not only in highly frequent interruptions in many firms' production schedules but also in chronic under-utilization of installed capacity. In as far as controls in foreign exchange persisted, available imported inputs were a function of available foreign exchange allocations (Mwega, 1993). However, once this constraint was removed through liberalization, the determination of import demand reverted to its fundamentals, and foreign exchange availability was no longer a significant determinant of industrial growth. Removal of the controls helped to reduce the transactions costs, which were hitherto quite prohibitive.

Reducing barriers to foreign ownership and investments: A floating exchange regime and the liberalization of foreign exchange transactions has facilitated repatriation of dividends by foreign investors. This, together with the removal of barriers to foreign commercial private borrowing, has provided a more enabling environment for foreign investors. Furthermore, the establishment of EPZs allowed unrestricted foreign ownership and employment of expatriates, firms' control over their foreign exchange earnings, in addition to extensive tax advantages.

Financial sector reforms, and in particular the amendment of the Capital Markets Authority Act (CMA), have further eased restraints on foreign ownership. The CMA established in 1990 attempted to liberalize the financial and capital markets in the country. As a result of these efforts, trading in the Nairobi Stock Exchange was opened to foreign investors in January 1995, though on a limited scale. In June 1995, the limit on portfolio investment in Kenyan companies quoted in the Nairobi Stock Exchange (NSE) by foreigners was raised from 20 percent to 40 percent for the corporate group of investors, and from 2.5 percent to 5 percent for individual portfolio holdings. The investment environment has thus undergone significant changes aimed at encouraging local and foreign investments.

Domestic trade liberalization: Price controls had extended to most of the manufactured and agricultural products by the end of 1970s. From 1986, deliberate efforts were taken to remove price controls such that by early 1995, virtually all price controls on commodities had been dismantled. Between 1983 and 1991, the number of commodities whose price was controlled under the general order dropped from 56 to 6, while those controlled under specific order fell from 87 to 29 (Swamy, 1994). By September 1993, only petroleum products and some pharmaceutical products remained under price controls under the general order, while only 3 items remained in the specific order. By July 1995, the maize market, the one that had hitherto resisted reform the most and the central focus of donors, and the petroleum/ oil sector had been completely liberalized.

Financial sector reforms: Kenya's financial sector reform program in the last decade focussed on both market and institutional reforms in an attempt to remove distortions in the credit market. Positive real interest rates, the target of the market reforms, were aimed at enhancing efficient utilization of available credit resources. Institutional reforms related to the financial sector focussed on strengthening the Central Bank to enable it to undertake its inspection and regulatory roles more effectively.

To facilitate the reforms, the Banking Act was amended in 1989. In addition to strengthening the Central Bank's regulatory and supervisory roles, other areas affected by the amendments included: introduction of stricter licensing requirements of financial institutions, raising the minimum capital requirements, the establishment of the Deposit Insurance Fund, new guidelines for granting loans and minimum disclosure requirements, and increasing penalties for non-compliance. Nevertheless, enforcement of the banking regulations even after the amendment of the Banking Act continued to be hampered by political forces, leading to a new banking crisis in 1986 when 2 banks and 20 non-bank financial institutions (NBFIs) faced liquidity problems. Financial sector reforms in the country in the latter part of 1980s and early 1990s emphasized tight credit control to suppress inflation. This was achieved through adjustments of cash ratio requirements for the commercial banks and raising of interest rates. The political factors seem to have persisted and in 1998 several banks and financial institutions were in a financial crisis and placed under statutory management while others were liquidated.

There were complaints from the business community that the tight monetary policy implemented had contractionary effects due to reduced lending by commercial banks. One of the instruments of this tight monetary stance was increased cash ratio to 20 percent in 1994. Even though it came down to 13 percent in 1998 and 9 percent in 2000, it represents a high component cost of credit to the borrower via high interest rates. The problem was aggravated by the high interest rate on treasury bills, which deprived the private sector of credit facilities as resources for investment were being increasingly put in government treasury bills at a time when there was no secondary market for these instruments. One of the disadvantages of government floating of short-term commercial paper is that it hampers the development of the financial sector and the intermediation process. Commercial banks will opt for a default-free commercial paper sometimes with a higher interest rate and relegate their financial screening role to the background. This has two effects: first lending to the private sector is unattractive due to the risk involved; and second, the process of financial intermediation is halted. Thus, financial development is checked. These factors have had contractionary effects on the economy.

Institutional change oriented policy reforms

Parastatal sector reforms: Very limited parastatal sector reforms had been implemented by the end of the second phase of the reform program. By 1990, the Kenya government owned equity in about 250 commercially oriented enterprises, 60 percent of them in manufacturing and mining, 18 percent in distribution, 15 percent in finance and the rest in transport, electricity and other services. While the parastatal enterprises accounted for a large share of public sector employment, they also became a major source of budgetary deficits, as the majority of them depended on subsides from the central government. Many of them were also overstaffed and mismanaged.

These factors provided the rationale for the parastatal reform program whose broad objective was the reduction of the financial burden placed on the Treasury by these poorly managed and inefficient enterprises, improvement of the efficiency of service delivery and enhancing opportunities for private sector investment. The program had two main components: restructuring strategic enterprises to raise their productivity and efficiency; and privatizing the non-strategic parastatals. While the parastatal reform program has been generally slow, some considerable progress was made after 1994. The main developments in this area are:

- In late 1991, the government identified 207 enterprises for divestiture, 10 of which were listed for privatization by 1995, and 33 strategic enterprises whose ownership the government intended to retain.
- The Executive Secretariat & Technical Unit (ESTU) was established in May 1992 to implement the sale of parastatal enterprises.

• By 1997, several of the non-strategic parastatals had been privatized or liquidated.

Public expenditure control and reduction: Control and reduction of public expenditures has been a major objective of most of the reform measures adopted under the SAPs, such as the budget rationalization program, civil service reform, parastatal sector reforms, and introduction of user charges.

By 1995, expenditure on most recurrent items had been reduced sharply, allocations for (O&M) had risen, while core projects received about 75 percent of the development resources. Civil service reform was a crucial area for reducing government spending especially in the third phase of the reform program. The program was instituted in April 1992 with the objectives of improving the quality of public service, reducing government spending, raising the productivity of the workforce, and rationalizing the staffing levels. The program had the target of reducing the 272,000 civil servants at an annual rate of 6 percent for 5 years, with emphasis on unskilled and semi-skilled categories of civil servants. By October 1994, the number of civil servants had been reduced from 272,000 to 248,057 mainly through the Voluntary Early Retirement Scheme (VERS). Staff reductions constituted the first stage of the civil service reform program while the second stage would lay emphasis on improvement of the performance of the service through increased training and incentives to the remaining workforce. Since the initial voluntary retirement, no other significant developments have taken place in the civil service reform program.[3]

Labor market reforms: Kenya's labor market was, for many years, highly regulated in terms of wage guidelines, approval mechanisms for redundancies by the Ministry for Labor, and government involvement in the trade union matters. There has been widespread belief by the Kenya authorities, for most of the post-independence period, that regulation of the labor market was indispensable for rapid economic development and improvement of the welfare of the workers. It was, for instance, argued that wage guidelines were essential to ensure that labor costs remained low not only to attract foreign investments but also to encourage firms to use labor-intensive technologies to help create more employment opportunities. In the same way, government intervention in fixing minimum wages was regarded as an important way of protecting the interests of the workers. It was argued that high levels of unemployment created a conducive environment for employers to exploit unskilled workers through underpayment.

The labor market has, however, undergone considerable liberalization in the 1990s. By July 1994, the Industrial Court had allowed trade unions to seek full compensation for increases in the cost of living without hindrance through wage guidelines. As a result of this liberalization, various laws have been amended to allow firms to more easily discharge redundant workers when necessary. Thus, due to relaxation of the redundancy declaration procedures in 1994, enterprises can declare workers redundant without having to seek the approval of the Minister for Labor. The enterprises are required to simply notify regional or district labor officers of their intention. The removal of wage guidelines makes it possible for firms to negotiate and change the level of wages on the basis of productivity and performance rather than on the basis of cost of living indices, as was hitherto the case.

Indicators of performance

From the overview of implementation of SAPs, it does appear that short-run control of observable policies was critical. There was emphasis on stabilization, control of fiscal spending, domestic credit, and money supply. The end results were, however, disappointing due to non-compliance with the requirements of the SAPs. This meant that the economy was constantly in disequilibrium which required further stabilization. But the long run structural issues touched on by the reform policies such as exchange rate policy; parastatal reforms and privatization; civil service reforms; sectoral adjustment operations involving agriculture, industry, education (human capital), financial sector reform; and decontrol of domestic prices, do not seem to have provided the required results or expectations. These long-run issues have a direct bearing on the success of short-run economic management and changes in observable variables.

From the overview above, it is natural to ask where Kenya's economy was by the end of the 1990s. We discuss in this section the performance of the economy in relation to growth of incomes, investment, savings, exports, inflation, real exchange rate, interest rates, and fiscal deficit as the key indicators and pointers for economic growth and the path towards development. Table 3.1 shows a summary of indicators of some of these aggregates in the 1990s. We show that first, GDP growth has at best been stochastic in the 1990s, hardly enough to show the direction or performance of economic activity. The rate of growth of private investment has improved only marginally and in fact declined in 1997 compared to 1995. National savings declined in 1997 even after recovering in 1994, while *domestic* debt to GDP stood at 4.2 percent in 1997 (not shown in Table 3.1),[4] which implies that 15 percent of government expenditure was financed by domestic borrowing. External debt stock relative to economic activity declined from a peak of 133.4 percent in 1993 to 64.8 percent in 1997. Perhaps, this was responsible for the falling external debt service ratio from a peak of 35.2 percent in 1990 to 21.4 percent in 1997.[5]

Table 3.1   Summary indicators of economic performance in Kenya in the 1990s

	DSX	DY	GDPG	PIY	GNS	DEF	GDPCAP
1990	35.20	87.0	4.2	11.0	15.8	−7.3	380.0
1991	32.40	98.3	1.4	10.6	16.1	−1.9	350.0
1992	30.90	91.3	−0.8	9.5	13.6	−3.5	330.0
1993	26.90	133.4	0.4	9.6	17.7	−6.0	270.0
1994	32.80	106.1	2.6	9.9	19.0	0.8	260.0
1995	30.10	84.8	4.4	13.5	16.4	−0.9	280.0
1996	27.60	76.8	4.1	12.3	18.2	−1.5	320.0
1997	21.40	64.8	2.1	11.3	14.7	−3.0	330.0
1998	16.94	57.7	1.8	8.0	9.8	0.9	353.0
1999	16.70	58.8	1.4	–	11.3	−0.4	318.8

Notes: DSX is the debt service to exports ratio; DY is external debt stock as a ratio to GNP; GDPG is GDP growth; PIY is private investment to GDP ratio; GNS is gross national savings; DEF is fiscal deficit to GDP ratio; and GDPCAP is GDP per capita in US dollars.

Sources: (1) Government of Kenya (various years), *Economic Survey* (various issues), Government Printer: Nairobi; (2) World Bank (1999), *World Development Report, 1998/1999*, Oxford University Press: New York.

The whole spectrum of economic performance looks stochastic. For example, overall deficit declined and produced a surplus of 0.8 percent of GDP in 1994, but built up to a deficit of 3 percent of GDP in 1997. Even with a budget surplus in 1994, per capita income fell to its lowest level of $260 and then rose to $330 with no significant change in other macro-variables. GDP growth declined to 2.1 percent in 1997 from 4.1 percent in 1996, savings and investment having fallen, and domestic borrowing increased by 1997. Furthermore, indebtedness in the country has merely shifted in composition, external debt declined while domestic debt increased. Domestic debt does not create wealth in a country, it merely transfers the purchasing power to the government with the accompanying crowding-out and distortionary arguments on both the interest rates and exchange rates.

In order to explain this outcome, the argument is that instability in the basic macro-variables are responsible for the slow response in investment and hence the poor out-turn in growth performance in Kenya and its stochastic nature. In order to build on this argument, one needs to recognize the necessity of structural adjustment in Kenya. As reviewed above, the SAPs, which started in 1985, were supposed to set prices right. The argument is that when prices are right and the environment is conducive for the private sector to thrive, then the relative price structure induces both changes in the level of real income and the productive structure through relative sectoral profitability and resource flows to the profitable sectors. This is supposed to contribute to output growth in two ways: from primary factor income claims from the production process; and second, from the dynamics of relative income multiplier effects in the economy. However, in the short run, there are structural rigidities and inherent weaknesses in the economy that have led to a recession in the adjustment process and produced 'divider' effects on primary incomes rather than the multiplier effects. Part of these effects comes through the negative shocks that tend to be dynamically severe. Droughts, for example, tend to marginalize more people and impoverish wealth and rural incomes.[6]

From the review, we can summarize several important stylized facts about Kenya's economic performance after more than a decade of experience with economic reforms:

- Economic recovery has been rather disappointing; real per capital GDP growth has improved only marginally.
- Economic management has tended to be extremely short-term with conflicting goals and outcomes characteristic of a policy dilemma. For example, in the liberalization period, 1993–1997, a phenomenon that arose is that of short-run speculative capital flows responding to the interest rate differential. During this period, the authorities encountered a policy dilemma due to their pursuance of conflicting goals and objectives in the exchange rate management and accompanying policies. The policy dilemma relates to targeting a competitive exchange rate and low inflation in a floating exchange rate regime. In order to pursue these goals, the authorities have on occasion intervened in the foreign exchange market to stabilize – and sometimes protect the exchange rate due to volatile capital flows. This would then be followed with sterilization of the capital flows in the money market, thereby raising the domestic interest rates. The result was that the exchange rate was stabilized in the short-run but at high interest rates, thus, jeopardizing the goals of increased domestic investments and chances of economic recovery. It thus followed that in order to lower the interest rate, the authorities would have to accept a relatively weak currency.
- In 1998, the government realized that its own borrowing kept interest rates artificially high. The government, through the Central Bank, decided to sell fewer Treasury Bills than demanded by the financial sector (the main dealers in T-bills)

at the auction.[7] Due to excess liquidity in the financial sector and low demand on investment, the weaker banks started suffering with their profit margins squeezed. The result was a banking crisis at the end of 1998 and early 1999. This further depressed private investments.

- One of the key factors behind this rather poor performance or precarious recovery is the slow response of private investment to macroeconomic stabilization and realignment of prices. This has further been worsened by high domestic interest rates and a shift into trading in lucrative financial instruments, government commercial paper – the treasury bills. Even when interest rates on commercial paper have fallen, alternative investments have been lacking particularly given prevailing uncertainty in the social-political environment. Investors have thus tended to hold back investment plans in fixed irreversible assets.

- Related to the above is the existence of pervasive risks that are both policy and politically induced. In this case, a coordination problem has emerged where the would-be investors exercise a waiting option until the front-loading of investment returns are sufficient to compensate them from the risk of investing or repatriating capital. Where investments have been made, they have tended to be short-term in nature, mainly on financial instruments, and in commercial activities, rather than in productive but irreversible fixed investment. The result is that the recession gripping the economy lingers on.

- The existence of a large external and domestic debt has given rise to a significant debt overhang problem, which has had adverse effects on investment and growth. This is because investors expect current and future taxes to be increased to effect the transfer of resources abroad or to pay for domestic debt. In addition, there are the usual crowding-out and liquidity arguments. The problem is that private investors exercise a waiting option in their investment decisions as argued above.

- Domestic debt has affected the domestic interest rate structure, and enlarged the fiscal deficit, thereby affecting financial development, investment and savings responses and thus negatively affecting output growth. Data seem to point to the fact that with a freeze on aid, the government has tended to borrow domestically to service its external debts. Since 1995, net loan repayments abroad have been negative, showing extensive resource transfers abroad, usually between 2–5 percent of GDP between 1995 and 2000.

The challenge of this chapter, then is to show how structural long-run factors are linked to short-run macroeconomic management, and the avenues through which growth can be re-started and sustained. The short-run macroeconomic issues relate to stabilization of basic prices necessary to give adequate signals for long-term growth. These are reviewed in relation to:

- Inflation rate, which reflects the outcome of macroeconomic management;
- Interest rate, which is the price of capital and also reflects inflationary expectations;
- Real and nominal exchange rate, which is a relative price that ensures a healthy balance of importers and exporters return. Furthermore, it is an indirect tool of monetary policy; and
- Fiscal deficit, where fiscal policy should maintain internal balance and foster investment and thus appropriate signals for investors and less crowding out effects of private loanable funds.

To show the links, we further review some economic events and indicators of liberalization and stabilization of the 1990s. This is because of the significant steps undertaken in the liberalization process and the significant weaknesses that have emerged in the economy. For example, as the process of liberalization continued, the financial market showed short-run fluctuations largely due to the volatility of the foreign exchange flows. The primary focus of the monetary and exchange rate policies shifted due to conflicting objectives and problems facing the authorities with the presence of heavy portfolio capital flows.

By 1994, the policy focus was to keep reserve money on the targeted path while at the same time intervening in the foreign exchange market to minimize the appreciation of the exchange rate. However, interventions in the foreign exchange market led to increased money supply. This in return required sterilization through the sale of Treasury bills. In order to make commercial paper attractive, the rate of interest had to be high relative to that on other financial assets. This would cushion domestic prices but also meant that the Treasury bill rate had to rise. Several effects have emanated from these policy actions:

- The high interest rates, though an instrument to meet the monetary authorities' goals, were jeopardizing chances of economic recovery and discouraging investments necessary for future economic growth;
- The high interest rate on Treasury bills implied that the domestic and foreign interest rate differential remained positive and thus tended to perpetuate the speculative private capital flows problem;
- The Treasury bills sold in the sterilization process were building government domestic debt. These short-term (91 days) bills were mainly being held by the financial sector and thus turning the financial sector to be driven by short-term lending, hardly conducive for financial sector development. In addition, short-tem debt had high roll-over risk and a temptation for the government to play a Ponzi game, that is, borrow to pay debts.

- The Treasury bills rate, due to this short-term nature of the commercial paper and government debt, was thought to be inflexible downwards, and thus not a good instrument of monetary policy. But, as has happened since April 1998, the treasury bills rate has been forced down,[8] but with devastating consequences on the financial sector. This is because it was being driven by short-tem returns from these short-term liquid assets. This explains why in 1998 and early 1999 there was a banking crisis and a further compression of private investments that checked current and future growth.

But this problem was realized earlier. For example, in 1994 the authorities realized that high interest rates were counterproductive and thus adopted a policy goal aimed at bringing the interest rates down. This was a tricky policy because lowering interest rate – with short-term bills, led to massive redemption of the Treasury bills and substantial outflows of portfolio capital. This showed that short-term capital inflows came in to take advantage of a high domestic interest rate and thus were subject to abrupt reversal. In addition, it showed that capital inflows were not being invested in irreversible fixed assets. These outflows of capital put the exchange rate under pressure to depreciate. In response, the authorities decided to protect the value of the shilling from sliding. The only way to do this was to draw down the stock of international reserves. This led to a depletion of reserves to critically low levels and, as such, this policy was not sustainable. Thus, at this stage, the unfolding policy dilemma acquired a third dimension, volatility in the exchange rate, high interest rates, and low levels of international reserves. The problem with low levels of foreign exchange reserves is that the currency could easily come under speculative attack with devaluation expectations.

To reverse the trend and protect the level of international reserves and stabilize the exchange rate, the authorities resorted to monetary policy measures. This required that the NBFIs be subjected to cash ratio requirements just like the commercial banks, the discouragement of the discount window at the central bank through high and punitive interest rates, and the raising of the short-term Treasury bills rate. These measures stabilized the exchange rate and helped in the build-up of foreign exchange reserves. The interest rates were, however, much higher and so the old problem reappeared. That is, how can economic recovery take place within an environment of high interest rates? The policy contradiction thus relates to trying to stimulate economic recovery through lower interest rates and at the same time maintain macroeconomic stability through high interest rates. But to maintain a competitive exchange rate would require accepting relatively large exchange rate fluctuations. This has been considered less feasible since it introduces wide instability in the economy.

From this review, it has been shown that the authorities in Kenya have been overly concerned with the movements of the nominal exchange rate in the face of volatile capital flows. Capital flows are a reflection of stock adjustment, reacting to either changes in asset prices or shocks or both, which is essentially part of the arbitrage process (see Goldestein, Mathieson and Lane, 1991). Furthermore, capital flows to a particular country represent the private sectors' market-based response to improvements or worsening in the risk profiles of domestic assets (Asea and Reinhart, 1996). Asea and Reinhart (1996) argue that doing nothing, that is, failure to intervene, may be an optimal policy. This is because the exchange rate would move to stabilize these short-run flows. The reaction in Kenya has, however, been to intervene in the foreign exchange market and thus defend the shilling from this pressure. An outcome of these actions is to temporarily endogenize the money supply process. This has tended to de-rail the long-term goals of raising investment growth, reducing unemployment and eradicating poverty. The outcome of economic management in Kenya has thus, been disappointing. This, however, does not mean that the appropriate policy formulation has not taken place. Several appropriate policy formulations have been presented. For example, the *Policy Framework Papers* and several *Sessional Papers* have dwelt on policy issues in the short- and medium terms and have emphasized the following:

- The economy needs to grow by not less than 7 percent per year for a sustained period (8.2 percent for 25 years, as presented in the country's Development Plans). The question is, where would this growth come from?;
- Provide an enabling environment for private sector business activity to thrive – increase investment;
- Provide an enabling environment that will promote savings;
- Reduce government domestic borrowing;
- Revitalize infrastructure and thus reduce transactions costs for the private sector; and
- Create an environment of certainty in the economy.

These policy guidelines notwithstanding, the results have been disappointing. The major question has been, what has given rise to this outcome? Recent debate on the pitfalls of economic management has centered on various factors namely:

- The financial sector has not responded effectively and appropriately to financial liberalization. It seems that the sector has moved from financial repression to liberalization, to secondary financial repression. In addition, the presence of "political banks" in the country, has increased the riskiness of the sector.[9]

Financial instruments have become more profitable to invest in. In addition, the government's heavy domestic borrowing has discouraged financial intermediation.

- Institutional structure, the legal and payments system and the enforcement of contracts have been eroded.
- Trade policies, like trade liberalization and converting QRs into tariffs, leads to the basic question of who plays by the rules of the game? Due to this, production is discouraged. The economy seems to be drifting to commercialization with quick and sure returns rather than production, which has a long gestation period and is riskier. For example, the importation of sugar discourages production and encourages illegal rent extraction through cheaper imports.
- Income distribution/poverty. As growth decelerates, poverty has become rampant and aggregate demand has fallen, checking future expansion of local industries.
- Capacity to implement and monitor the reform programs and the ability of the government to implement these programs seem to be lacking or political will has been absent.
- Degree of corruption. For example, a number of studies have tried to estimate the degree of corruption using various indices – weighted averages of these indices are used to rank countries. These studies ranked Kenya third worst in 1996 and the situation seems to have worsened since then.
- Social spending has been reduced drastically. This has devastating consequences on the development of the human capital necessary for future growth.

Growth and sources of growth

The objectives of this section are two-fold: (1) to determine from the literature the most important factors that contribute to economic growth. This will form the basis for proposing policies necessary to revive and sustain economic growth in Kenya and other African countries; and (2) to ask whether lessons found in cross-country evidence can be replicated in the case of Kenya.

What do we learn from the literature[10]

The empirical literature suggests that economic growth and other related macroeconomic targets such as exports, private investment and savings, are associated with five broad categories of variables:

- macroeconomic policy environment, mainly reflecting the extent of departure from fundamental macroeconomic balance or the degree and quality of

intermediate macroeconomic public sector policies and outcomes, such as public investment policy;
* macroeconomic instability;
* external shocks;
* human capital and regional spillover effects; and
* institutional and political uncertainty variables.

The theoretical strand of the endogenous growth literature and the recent investment-irreversibility literature, provide the rationale and base that suggests the channels of influences of the above variables, specially those in the category of nontraditional determinants such as macroeconomic uncertainty, institutional, political, and regional variables. However, it should be pointed out at the outset that only a smaller set of policy variables and other fundamentals have been shown to be robustly and significantly associated with the three macroeconomic performance variables. Moreover, the econometrics methodology of this literature, mainly based on cross-country regressions, is subject to criticism relating to the ability of the methodology to adequately identify the various individual effects and how they relate to growth.

In what follows, we discuss the mechanism through which the five categories of variables affect growth and private investments. Using these links, we review the contributions of these factors on Kenya's economic growth. The evidence is derived from panel regressions estimated for sub-Saharan African (SSA) countries. We use the results from these panel regressions to assess the relative contribution of the various factors in explaining the determinants of private investment and growth in Kenya. But first, the broad categories of determinants are reviewed.

Macroeconomic policy environment

Starting with fiscal policy, three channels of influences are identified: financing implications of fiscal deficits; the macroeconomic uncertainty of large fiscal deficits; and the degree of complementarily (or substitutability), between public and private investment. High fiscal deficits could be financed internally by domestic credit creation, which reduces real money balances and pushes up real interest rates; or through forced savings by the private sector through financial repression. Either directly or indirectly, the end result in both cases is crowding-out of private investment, and possibly a slow down in exports and overall economic growth. Furthermore, to the extent that the rate of monetary expansion is high enough to accommodate both private and public investment demands, the ensuing economic instability associated with inflation should have a negative impact on economic performance. If on the other hand, the public sector deficit is financed by external debt, increased indebtedness could be another source of economic uncertainty with similar negative consequences.

The central role attached to fiscal reforms in the context of SAPs should in principle enhance macroeconomic performance. However, the highest and most sustainable pay-offs of fiscal adjustment are usually associated with deeper and more structural reforms that go beyond reducing the overall fiscal deficits (see for example Easterly and Schmidt-Hebbel, 1991). In particular, it has been noted by many observers that fiscal consolidation often takes the form of reduced public investment, which may be complimentary to private investment (see for example Blejer and Khan, 1984; Serven and Solimano, 1993). As argued by Schmidt-Hebbel and Muller (1991), public infrastructure, communications, and transport services are often allocated through a process that involves under-pricing, excessive demand and shortages, long delays in delivery of services, and other administrative bottlenecks, all of which inhibit efficient use by the private sector and lead to sub-optimal public investment levels in these areas. This contributes to rationing of public services which has the effect of inflating urban land prices in those areas that have access to public services. Increased availability of public services through higher public investment raises the profitability of private investment (Schmidt-Hebbel and Muller, 1991, p. 12). Even though the evidence on the complementarity of public and private investment is mixed,[11] the more recent evidence seems to suggest that there are certain categories of public investment, especially in the areas of infrastructure, human capital, and law and order, that tend to strongly crowd-in private investment, as well as enhance private sector exports and overall growth. Furthermore, there appears to be lower (and upper) thresholds below (above) which public investment may not be effective (Serven, 1996). The other dimension of the macro policy environment relates to foreign exchange policies that affect real macroeconomic target variables through the real exchange rate. A major real exchange rate disequilibrium, especially real exchange rate overvaluation, could be very harmful to overall economic competitiveness and eventually investment and economic growth. In the short-run however, corrective real devaluation to eliminate real exchange rate overvaluation can have a contractionary effect on private investment in countries where prices of capital goods have been made artificially cheaper by an overvalued currency. On the other hand, real depreciation will also cause the relative domestic currency price of exportables to rise. Despite the possible contractionary effects of real exchange rate depreciation on investment and growth in the short-run, the ensuing initial positive incentive effects for exportables and the subsequent reallocation of resources towards the export sector, should eventually lead to an export-led spur on private investment and growth.

Macroeconomic uncertainty

As has been argued in the recent literature, the importance of uncertainty arises from the nature of the investment process itself, that is, that capital equipment takes time to build is partially irreversible or sector specific.[12] It has been shown that, risk-averse firms associate uncertainty with greater variability in expected profits, and may curtail their investment altogether. Risk-neutral firms, on the other hand, may prefer the 'waiting option' to undertaking physical investment and instead invest in information gathering to reduce uncertainty.

Two sources of economic policy-based risk and uncertainty affecting private investment decisions can be identified. One stems from the risk associated with economic variables that are important determinants of overall economic stability. In the literature, this has been captured by the volatility of these variables, including the terms of trade, inflation and real exchange rate. For example, high volatility in the last two variables reduces the informational content of prices as coordinators of economic activity, and hence increases the riskiness of long-term investment.

The other source of economic uncertainty is the potential of future policy reversals or lack of policy implementation. In this case, uncertainty is caused by low credibility of the current policy framework, which induces a postponement of the investment decision. This source of uncertainty is likely to dominate cases of highly indebted countries undergoing far-reaching structural reforms,[13] or cases of reforming countries with a long history of policy reversals (Collier, 1996). This, as we argued earlier, has predominated the Kenyan reform period with adverse effects on growth.

One variable used to capture this uncertainty is the ratio of external debt to GDP. High external debt affects private investment and hence growth through three additional channels: a high stock of debt signals the negative "debt overhang effect" on private investment, due to higher expected future taxes required to service foreign debt payments;[14] a high stock of debt increases the cost of new debt and therefore acts as a credit rationing mechanism in the international capital market, which reduces the rate of domestic capital accumulation; the third is a crowding-out effect, where servicing of a growing stock of debt will reduce the national savings available for investment. This later effect is reflected by the ratio of debt service to exports. Both the stock and flow effects are expected to have negative effects on private investment. In addition, a higher domestic debt has similar effects, but most importantly distorts returns on investment by affecting the interest rate structure.

Human capital

One of the critical areas required in Africa's growth process is investment in its people, that is, human capital development. The importance of human capital for creating knowledge and technology-based externalities, which could permit significant increases in the productivity of capital, is now very firmly established in the new growth literature[15] and appears to be strongly corroborated by the recent East Asian "miracle". It can be argued that in a country endowed with a high stock of human capital, and hence a highly skilled and educated labor force, expected returns from investment would in general be higher, especially in skill-intensive industries. This is because the overall cost of training would be lower, and it would be easier to introduce more advanced production technology to raise productivity and lower unit costs. This argument is consistent with the evidence from the empirical growth literature, which finds the stock of human capital to be among the major determinants explaining cross-country differences in growth, and investment.[16]

Regional effects

Economic cooperation has a potential positive impact on national policy credibility and hence investment and subsequently growth, because it could provide a mechanism for collective commitment into economic reform in a context of a reciprocal threat-making arrangement (Collier, 1991). Furthermore, deeper economic integration in a given region could permit expansion of the regional economy to generate the threshold scales necessary to trigger the much needed strategic complementarity, and to attract the adequate levels of investment required for the development of modern manufacturing cores and the transfer of technology within the region (Krugman, 1991). The empirical strand of the literature also supports the investment and growth enhancing effects of economic integration. This literature finds that spillover effects – proxied by regional investment, regional or political instability, or regional growth, are significantly and robustly linked to variations in investment and growth across countries (Chua, 1993a, 1993b; Easterly and Levine, 1996).

External shocks

External shocks can affect national economies through several channels such as terms of trade, capital flows, or international interest rates. Fluctuations in the terms of trade can affect macroeconomic performance through two possible channels, first, and as has happened in many African countries, declines in terms of trade reduce incomes and the profitability of the export sector and hence export growth. If profits are positively correlated across sectors, the fall in incomes and the profitability of the export sector will have a negative effect on overall investment and growth. Second, terms of trade deterioration may affect investment, exports and growth indirectly, through a worsening of the current account. Countries have responded to a deteriorating current account by increasing controls on imports, devaluing the exchange rate, or tightening fiscal and monetary policies. Controls on imports of intermediate or capital goods could have a direct adverse effect on private investment. Tight fiscal policies may reduce public investment, while monetary restraint would result in credit rationing, both of which could adversely affect private investment and hence current and future growth prospects. On the other hand, international interest rates will affect the economy via two channels. The first makes external borrowing and repayment expensive if it rises, while the second will affect the exchange rate via the small open economy parity conditions. This has been shown to be an important channel that triggered the African external debt crisis in the mid-1980s.

Institutional and political uncertainty

The other source of uncertainty that has similar effects on economic performance as economic uncertainty is institutional uncertainty or instability in the political environment. Political instability judged to be harmful to investment ranges from rapid government turnover, which affects policy credibility and leads to unstable incentive and policy framework thus, raising the value of the 'waiting option', to more extreme forms of social and political unrest, for example, widespread political violence or civil wars which create more fundamental aspects of uncertainty such as the collapse of institutions of government and civil society (macro insecurity) and the loss of life, physical property or property rights (micro insecurity) (Collier, 1996). The latter takes place when, for example, violent change of government involves a radical redefinition of the basic 'rules of the game' raising the risk of expropriation and nationalization.

Investors, however, would require more than formal statements in which states commit themselves to the role of *impartial* enforcers of contracts. The presence of an efficient and impartial bureaucracy to implement the declared policies is equally important. Hence, recent cross-country studies find bureaucratic or institutional, as well as political stability, to be strongly associated with investment and growth performance (Knack and Keefer, 1995).

Empirical evidence[17]

We use the literature surveyed and cross-country regressions in this sub-section to show the performance of these variables and compare Kenya to the sub-Saharan African (SSA) region. We use the estimated equations to calculate the relative contributions of each block of these variables to economic growth. The objective is to explain macroeconomic performance in Kenya by comparing Kenya's experience with that in the SSA region. This provides a long-term view explanation of growth and macroeconomic performance. In the years 1995/1996, a number of countries in SSA experienced economic recovery. Kenya's growth in this period was on average above 4 percent. The question that arises is whether this recovery was sustainable. The answer seems to have been in the negative. This is because the response to investment and savings has been slow and this in turn has slowed the expansion of productive capacity. However, this was not sustained: and growth in Kenya declined to 2.1 percent in 1997 and further to 1.8 percent in 1998. Two indicators of performance are used in this section, that is, private investment and output growth. Using these indicators and a range of their determinants, we use the means of the variables to compare Kenya's performance with that of SSA. In addition, we used the means of each variable multiplied by the estimated coefficient to run simulations in panel regressions for Kenya. The goal is to assess the relative importance of the explanatory variables in explaining Kenya's performance in relation to the variables in the model.

Private investments

A range of variables were analyzed in the investment equation as determinants of private investment. The major question asked in the panel regression equations is what has contributed to the slow investment response even after more than a decade of economic reforms? The other question asked, and which bears extreme importance in the comparative analysis, is why even when investments have been seen to increase, output growth has been falling, implying inefficiency of investment.

The first category of determinants of private investment are external factors – external debt and terms of trade. These are shown in Table 3.2. This category of variables includes measures of current external debt stock to GDP ratio and debt overhang, which is debt stock lagged and squared, respectively. The effects from debt overhang will discourage private investments as argued in the previous section. This will depend on how the respective governments are expected to raise the revenue necessary to finance external debt service obligations. Inflation tax and excessive government expenditure will contribute to increased domestic inflation, which also discourages private investment. The perception here is that a high debt service burden is viewed by potential investors as a threat to sustaining reforms and a potential for higher inflation tax to meet debt service requirements in future (Ndulu, 1991; Elbadawi, 1994, 1996).

Table 3.2   Impact of external factors on private investments

	Means of Variables		Regression Coefficient	Contribution (%)
	Kenya	SSA		
External Debt to GDP ratio (DY)	0.577	0.719	0.171	9.870
DY^2	0.387	1.074	−0.001	0.039
Debt service to exports	0.257	0.155	−0.024	−0.620
Overall effects				9.210
Terms of Trade Effects Log (TOTVAR/TOT) (terms of trade variability adjusted by the levels of TOT)	1.510	1.970	−0.125	18.880
TOTSHOCK	0.000	0.000	−0.022	−0.106
Overall effects				18.770

In addition, there is a liquidity constraint coming from debt service obligations. Thus, these three variables encompass the effects through which external debt affects investments through various channels. Terms of trade on the other hand, affects savings and hence investment. It is argued in the literature that a decline in terms of trade reduces income and profitability of the export sector. This reduces export growth and investments. In the panel regression, these effects are accounted for by not just the level of the terms of trade but also its volatility in influencing private investment (see Elbadawi, Ndulu and Ndung'u, 1997a). The average debt stock for Kenya is shown to be 57.7 percent. In computing the relative contribution, we see that external debt flows contributes to private investment positively by 9.87 percent, but the effect of external debt accumulation, the overhang effect, is to reduce private investment. The impact is minimal, 0.039 percent, but the debt service obligations reduce private investment by 0.62 percent. The overall effect of external debt on private investment is positive, at 9.21 percent. This shows that external debt flows has still a positive contribution to private investment. These results are supported by the fact that Kenya is still classified as a country with medium levels of indebtedness and she has always managed to pay her external debt obligations. This implies that external indebtedness is not a problem in Kenya, and does not negatively impact on private investment. The effect on private investment is indirect and comes through domestic debt due to interest rate effects. We have argued above that domestic debt is raised partly to raise funds to service the country's external debt (i.e., to meet external debt obligations).

The terms of trade effects, which enters both in variability adjusted by the level of terms of trade and terms of trade shock, clearly shows a positive average effect. These results are consistent with a country, which produces primary exports and that are subject to wide price fluctuations. Terms of trade affects investment through the saving channel since income levels are affected. This shows that terms of trade variability has been beneficial to Kenya's private investment but terms of trade shock has had a negative effect. The overall effect is to stimulate private investment by almost 19 percent.

The next group of variables combines institutional, political, real output growth and regional indicators. These are shown in Table 3.3. Quite surprisingly, private investments in Kenya are driven by regional per capita GDP. This seems to be related to investment opportunities in the region. For example, Kenya is only second to United Kingdom in terms of foreign direct investments flows to Uganda. This category of variables is found to be an extremely important determinant of private investment. In addition, GDP growth is found to have a minimal or insignificant effect on private investment. This, as we have argued before, is one factor that has not encouraged private investment and thus jeopardized chances of future growth via the accelerator process.

The next class of variables is related to the policy environment (see Table 3.4). Surprisingly and consistent with our prediction, the policy environment has depressed private investment performance in Kenya. Policy-induced risks are more important in explaining the slow response of investment to economic reforms. In the Kenyan case, interest rate is less volatile than in the SSA region and financial depth relatively better than in the SSA region. But even though interest rate variability is less volatile than that of the region, it contributes –4.9 percent to private investment, whereas financial depth has a positive response to investment.

Fiscal balance has a negative impact on private investment via the crowding out channel. Public investments are supposed to be complementary to private investment. This means that public investment may improve the environment that enhances profitability of private investment. The results from the table show that changes in public investment have a positive, though weak, response on private investment. The overall result of the variables in this category is to depress private investment by –3.59 percent.

Table 3.3   Growth and social-political variables

	Mean of Variables		Regression Coefficients	Contribution (%)
	Kenya	SSA		
	Institutional and Policy Variables			
Quality of Institutions	0.745	0.656	0.087	6.67
Dummy of SSA Revolutions	0.000	0.223	−0.001	0.00
Dummy for SSA Civil Wars	0.000	0.133	−0.001	0.00
Overall Effects				6.67
	Growth and Regional Conditions			
1. Regional Per	579.200	0 549	0.001	57.92
2. Capita GDP				
3. Real GDP Growth	0.050	0.033	0.102	0.51
Overall Effects				58.43

Finally, we have grouped inflation as a policy outcome variable. If inflation is unstable, it will reflect instability of the macroeconomic policies in the economy. It is shown that in Kenya over the sample period, the influence of inflation variability on private investment has been minimal. The overall results show that using this approach, the variables in the regression help to explain 89.46 percent of private investment performance in Kenya leaving only 10.54 percent unexplained. The average private investment rate in Kenya for the period is 11.7 percent compared to 9.6 percent of the SSA region.

Table 3.4   Impact of policies on private investment

	Mean of Variables		Regression Coefficient	Contribution (%)
	Kenya	SSA		
Policy Variables				
Real interest rate variability	0.886	2.164	−0.055	−4.870
Financial depth	0.351	0.293	0.028	0.980
Fiscal balance to GDP ratio	−0.046	−0.048	0.040	0.185
Change in public investment	0.012	0.001	0.393	0.487
Overall policy contribution				−3.590
Policy Outcome				
Inflation variability	0.337	0.318	−0.001	−0.034
Unexplained Residual				10.54
Investment Ratio	11.7%	9.6%		

Real output growth

We look at the factors that determine economic growth in Kenya again by using the evidence from the estimated panel regression results. Table 3.5 shows the contribution to growth by external debt and terms of trade. The most noticeable effect is the positive contribution to growth from external debt. However, equally strong negative effects come from external debt overhang.

Table 3.5   Contributions to growth from external factors

	Mean of Variables		Regression Coefficient	Contribution (%)
	Kenya	SSA		
External Debt				
External Debt to GDP ratio (DY)	0.577	0.719	0.538	31.04
$(DY_{t-1})^2$	0.387	0.783	−0.277	−10.45
Debt Service to Export	0.257	0.155	−0.057	−1.46
Ratio Overall Contribution				19.13
Terms of Trade				
Terms of trade Variability	0.0633	0.111	−0.019	−0.120

Literature on the subject argues that the link between external debt and growth is via the effect of debt on private investment and also from the liquidity constraints due to resource outflows to pay for external debt obligations. These variables and the terms of trade affect growth negatively, but the negative effect is dislodged by the positive effect on external debt flows so that the overall effects on growth from this category of variables is positive at 19.13 percent.

Table 3.6 shows the next set of the determinants of growth. These are human capital indicators and the policy environment. These variables include initial levels of schooling, level of initial income, population growth, and life expectancy. Kenya's mean values for these variables are higher than the SSA average. However, the overall effect of this category of variables is to depress growth by −1.34 percent.

The most negative influence comes from population growth, which depresses growth via the dependency problems and the re-allocation of resources to less productive social facilities. Initial income has a strong positive effect on growth. The coefficients from the panel regressions are not strong and this shows up in the relative contributions. This is perhaps due to the fact that the effects on growth are not direct but indirect via technological developments.

Table 3.6 Contribution to growth: human capital and policy variable

	Mean of Variables		Regression Coefficient	Contribution (%)
	Kenya	SSA		
Human Capital				
Log of initial schooling	1.636	0.939	0.002	0.26
Initial income	7.215	6.715	0.006	4.33
Population growth rate	3.100	0.028	-0.001	−0.31
Life Expectancy	56.200	48.608	-0.001	−5.62
Overall Contribution				−1.34
Policy Variables				
Fiscal balances to DP ratio	−0.046	−0.048	−0.312	1.44
Lagged fiscal balances GDP	−0.046	−0.048	−0.001	0.05
Public investment ratio	0.085	0.011	0.234	1.99
Financial depth	0.350	0.293	2.957	10.33
Real exchange Rate Misalignments	0.223	0.525	-0.012	−0.27
Overall contribution				13.74
Policy Outcome				
Inflation	0.147	0.522	-3.760	-5.53
Dummy for inflation >40%	0.040	0.132	-1.220	-0.48
Overall Contribution				-5.04
Per capita GDP Growth	0.049	0.051	0.102	-0.02

The large number of explanatory variables are lumped together into the category of policy variables. Not all of them are policy variables but provide a policy environment that is friendly to growth. The most notable is financial depth. This is proxied by the monetization ratio (M2/GDP) which is shown to have a strong influence on growth. Real exchange rate misalignment affects growth negatively as would be expected. The overall outcome of this category of variables is to stimulate growth.

Finally, we have policy outcome variables, inflation and hyper-inflation crisis. We have included the level of inflation and a dummy for inflation when it is above 40 percent. This dummy is justified on the basis that inflation rates, which are consistently above 40 percent entail a macro crisis. For Kenya, inflation is way below the average for SSA, but still retards growth and the few times inflation has been above 40 percent (only once in the sample period), the effect on growth, was as expected, negative. Overall, the effect of policy outcome on growth is negative. It appears that the inflation experience in the panel regressions has been to depress growth. The literature on the subject is not conclusive but it does argue that moderate inflation is good for growth. For Kenya, the level of inflation has been high and has had a negative impact on growth. The mean growth per capita is 4.9 percent compared to 5.1 percent for SSA countries.

To summarize, the literature provides a useful guide on factors that affect growth and private investment. These factors are shown to be important determinants of growth in Kenya. The factors found to be important are:

- Private investment, which affects growth via the accelerator process;
- External debt and terms of trade;
- Human capital and initial income levels; and.
- Policy environment and outcomes.

These factors, coupled with the institutional underpinnings would be the most important to turn around growth. We provide a summary of what we perceive to be the institutional underpinnings of a growth-friendly environment.

The institutional underpinnings of growth-friendly environment

The evolution of institutions needs to be influenced by the concern for establishing policy credibility. This calls for more emphasis on 'rules rather than 'discretion'. Corbo (1996, p. 1) provides a succinct description when he states that '... the new model has strengthened the role of the state in setting the rules for the development of a competitive market economy in the form of incentives, private property laws and their enforcement, and contractual law. As the government is moved out of the production of private goods, it should take an increasing role in insuring equality of opportunities in primary education, nutrition and primary health as well as in reducing extreme poverty.'

Conventional wisdom suggests that growth-friendly institutions are likely to stimulate growth if they:

- apply simple and uniform rules, rather than selective and differentiated ones;
- endow bureaucrats with few discretionary powers;
- contain safeguards against frequent, unpredictable alteration of the rules; and
- 'keep firms and other organizational interests at arm's length from the policy formulation and implementation process' (Rodrik, 1998, p. 44).

The above principles are motivated by concerns over excesses of executive authority and the surrounding institutions as well as a strong desire to establish credibility of economic policy. In terms of the institutions entrusted with the design and implementation of macroeconomic policy, the East Asian countries have adhered to some of these institutional measures that ensure macroeconomic stability, albeit in a context that allows considerable discretionary initiatives.

Short run effects on growth

The exchange rate policy

Exchange rate management increasingly became an important tool of economic management in Kenya in the 1980s and the 1990s. It was used as a means of improving the international competitiveness of Kenya's tradable goods sector and also to bring about a reduced level of expenditures in real terms. In the 1980s, the exchange rate regime was a crawling peg. The choice of this policy was justified by the need to reduce to a minimum the undesired exchange rate fluctuations in terms of the individual currencies in the SDR and to make it easier to manage the shilling exchange rate by disguising to some extent small exchange rate changes.

This system lasted up to 1990, with the introduction of a version of a dual exchange rate in that there was the official exchange rate and the foreign exchange bearer certificates (Forex-C) market. By 1993, the dual exchange rate system was operating with an inter-bank rate and an official exchange rate. These two rates were merged in October 1993 to achieve a complete float of the exchange rate. This was preceded with the abolishing of all controls on imports and foreign exchange transactions. Thus, during the 1990s, exchange rate policy appeared to have been the most successful component of structural adjustment in Kenya, in terms of implementation.

The floating exchange rate system in the 1990s was expected to have several advantages for Kenya. First, it was expected to allow a more continuous adjustment of the exchange rate to shifts in the demand for and supply of foreign exchange. Second, it was supposed to equilibrate the demand for and supply of foreign exchange through adjustments in the rate, rather than the level of reserves. Thus, the reserves would not be a policy target but would completely be exogenous to them. Third, it was expected to allow Kenya the freedom to pursue its own monetary policy without having to be concerned about balance of payments effects.

Several issues can be highlighted on the Kenyan experience with a unified floating exchange rate system. First, consequent upon the adoption of a floating exchange rate, it was expected that the inter-play of market forces of supply and demand would raise the shilling price of exportables and hence stimulate their production and boost firms' incomes. At the same time, depreciation was expected to decrease, in terms of foreign currency, the prices of exportable goods from Kenya relative to the prices of non-traded goods abroad. The ultimate objective was to stimulate foreign demand and increase foreign exchange proceeds from exports. Consistent with these expectations, Kenya experienced the recovery of exports leading to increased accumulation of foreign exchange reserves. Not surprising, however, evidence of an export diversification, that is, the scope for extending the exports of non-traditional products appears to have been limited in the short-run due to a recent appreciation of the shilling exchange rate. Even when this appreciation was reversed towards the end of the 1990s, exports did not significantly respond due to instability of the exchange rate and importantly due to a domestic policy environment that did not support competitive production.

Second, while import substitution may become evident in the longer-term – except for food and energy products, there has been little evidence of this, in part reflecting the share of uncontrollable imports or the effectiveness of exchange rate action on import demand. This perhaps reflects the thinness of the foreign exchange market, or the inability of the monetary authorities to cushion the impact of increased inflows of foreign exchange. The exchange rate has thus tended to appreciate significantly thereby nullifying the initial advantage of improved international competitiveness and dashing hopes of a stable exchange rate and successful export promotion drive. Finally, more recently, there has been a rapid increase in capital inflows that are not mediated by government or reflective of the recovery of exports. Preliminary data indicates that while the increase in capital inflows are accompanied by resurgence in economic growth and by a marked accumulation of international reserves, they are not always an unmitigated blessing. In most developing countries, capital inflows have often been associated with inflationary pressures, a real exchange rate appreciation and deterioration in the current account of the balance of payments. These are symptoms that Kenya experienced in the 1993–1999 period requiring active use of the interest rate and tight monetary policy to contain exchange rate movements and inflationary pressures. In addition, massive capital inflows have been shown to lead to excessive expansion in domestic credit, placing in jeopardy the stability of the domestic financial system. If the inflows are of a short-term nature, these problems intensify, as the probability of an abrupt and sudden reversal increases.

If these flows have undesirable macroeconomic effects – such as over-valued exchange rates and volatility, and excessive monetary expansion, what measures can be taken by the Central Bank of Kenya and the government to counteract such problematic macroeconomic effects and how effective are such measures? In addressing this policy question, it is important to bear in mind that monetary policy has a limited scope. Many institutional factors and structural rigidities limit the extent to which monetary policy could be effectively applied. There are several factors that condition this outcome, such as the existence of a non-monetized sector within the economy – in 1994, the contribution to GDP by the non-monetary sector in Kenya stood at 5.7 percent; the dominance of currency over the financial assets in the non-bank public's financial portfolio; underdeveloped nature of the money and capital markets in terms of the array of instruments and institutional structures; and, the predominance of foreign commercial and merchant banks, which can neutralize tight monetary policy of the Central Bank of Kenya through transfer of funds from the parent office.

The environment is also made difficult by a lack of proper integration between the financial and the real sectors. This is particularly due to the activities of the commercial banks that control large amounts of money within the banking system but base their banking philosophy on the traditional liquidity and profitability concepts, thereby concentrating their lending in the short term market. By and large, the above factors limit the extent to which the Central Bank of Kenya can control activities within the money market. Despite these limitations, it is crucial to determine the objective functions of monetary policy as well as the choice of monetary tools and techniques to be used by the Central Bank of Kenya in guiding the economy towards achieving both broad and specific macroeconomic objectives consistent with proper external debt and reserves management. These are the issues that are currently at the center of the reform agenda in Kenya.

Turning back to the liberalization agenda of the 1990s, we note that it was characterized by a shift in attention away from the real economy to the one in which trade in financial assets dominates with rates on secure government paper earning a premium. During this time, lending for investment or importing inputs was seen as unattractive. Exporters were benefiting from currency depreciation while depressed demand for imports, which are fundamental for a resource poor country like Kenya, was dampening growth in other sectors of the economy. But by the end of 1993, besides merging the official exchange rate with the inter-bank rate, further liberalization in the foreign exchange market had allowed individuals to hold foreign exchange. These liberalization efforts together with a shadow program negotiated by the World Bank and IMF further created credibility and assured traders of commitments to a more market driven policy. These factors are thus responsible for the general stability of macro-prices in 1994–1996 period.

Finally, with the liberalization of the capital account of the balance of payments and foreign exchange transactions, there was the emergence of capital flows contributing to a strain in exchange rate and monetary policy management. The widening gap in the interest rate differential induced capital to flow in to take advantage of the weak shilling and the high returns on the short-term treasury bills. In the process the stock of foreign exchange reserves shot up and was also aided by the sluggish demand of foreign exchange. These capital inflows in turn led to an appreciation of the shilling and the interest rate differential that came down drastically.

The effects of liberalization

The appreciation of the shilling in 1994 reflected substantial inflows, which were a result of the liberalization of foreign exchange transactions and the high yield on domestic Treasury bills. Data suggest that the interest rate differential, the exchange rate expectations and forecast on inflation and the general stability that was being achieved were such that holders of foreign exchange took advantage of the liberalized regime to profit by bringing funds back, converting them to shillings and benefiting from the high Treasury bills rate. The events in this period indicate that the market exchange rate overshot as predicted by the Dornbusch Overshooting Theory (Dornbusch, 1988), since, inflation responded to the drying up of liquidity, then as real returns on the Treasury bills rate became excessive, the interest rate started to track inflation down.

A crucial issue for policymakers is how to manage the exchange rate and conduct monetary policy in an environment with volatile capital (portfolio) flows. In order to show the effect of liberalization on foreign exchange transactions and the capital account with a floating exchange rate, an error correction model of the relationship between the real exchange rate and real interest rate differential was estimated. In this model, the exchange rate movements are explained by the real interest rate differential.

A variant of this study is that by Asea and Reinhart (1996) who use trend-cycle decomposition and impulse response functions to investigate the relationship between interest rates and the real exchange rate for a number of African countries. By limiting the analysis to this relationship, we do not, however, exclude the effects of other macroeconomic variables. This is because we believe that other effects enter indirectly into the relationship:

- Capital flows have put pressure on the real exchange rate, giving the authorities reason to intervene. Thus, the observed real exchange rate movement has an accumulation of policy actions from intervention as well as pressure from capital flows.
- Capital flows have been shown to respond to interest rate differential. The policy response of intervention and sterilizing the effects on the exchange rate and domestic money supply amounts to curing the symptoms rather than the disease and thus has perpetuated the inflows In the period of study, this shows up in the instability of the exchange rate.
- Domestic money supply reflects both a target on low inflation, fiscal policy action, as well as sterilization in the foreign exchange market. Thus, the observed rate of domestic interest rate partly reflects an accumulation of high short-term domestic debt (fiscal pressure) and monetary policy (and fiscal policy) action.

Thus, the observed exchange rate movements and real interest rate differential relationship indirectly captures the policy action and thus the policy dilemma argued earlier. It was argued that the link between the real exchange rate and the real interest rate differential was important in Kenya during this period. The model used takes the deviation from the purchasing power parity approximation to be explained by real interest rate differential. We feel that this is plausible in view of the implicit influences taken into account, like short-term capital movements, policy response, and monetary policy.

The results, which are shown in Appendix I, indicate that, first, the interest rate differential decreases with real exchange rate appreciation. This is consistent with the arguments above that when the local currency starts sliding, capital flows in to take advantage of the weak shilling and thus causes an appreciation of the currency. Returns from the interest rate differential are therefore competed away. Because interest rates are low, any further intervention to cushion domestic prices from this liquidity injection must raise the domestic interest rate through the sale of commercial paper and thus, widen the interest rate differential and the vicious circle continues. This is consistent with the argument above that stabilization of the exchange rate requires high interest rates. But, this perpetuates capital flows problem and thus affects the interest rate structure in the economy and hence private investment and growth.

Second, inflation will increase with real exchange rate depreciation and this is consistent with the theoretical prediction. Third, the influence of foreign inflation decreases with real exchange rate appreciation, which again is consistent with expectations.

Fourth, disequilibrium in the foreign exchange market will in the long run appreciate the real exchange rate.[18] What do we learn from these results then?

- The interest rate as an instrument of achieving both stability of the exchange rate and low inflation as argued earlier, is clearly inadequate. It settles at very high levels with repercussions on investment and growth. In addition, these objectives cannot be achieved without prudent fiscal policy.
- There is need to have a target on money supply when the exchange rate is either allowed to float (no-intervention) or is within a floating band (monetary policy becomes endogenous). This would limit the movements in the domestic interest rates and thus slow down the real interest rate differential. Currently, monetary policy is passive, it follows the fiscal action and the activities (and intervention reflected by dummies in the regression results) in the foreign exchange market contrary to the dictates of a floating exchange rate policy that would allow an independent (and hence exogenous) monetary policy. In addition, the observed domestic interest rate structure is influenced by domestic debt. This has two repercussions, it slows down the development of the financial sector and second, it converts private investment into short-term investments in liquid financial assets, rather than irreversible fixed investments.
- These results show a distorted picture, which does not support long-tem growth and explains why variability of policy variables is an important determinant of private investment and growth. The results further strengthen the arguments presented earlier, as well as the conclusions reached, that explain slow growth and poor response to private investment.

Inflation experience in Kenya

We have shown from the growth model that inflation contributes negatively to growth. Next, we investigate the determinants of inflation. As shown in Appendix II, growth also reduces inflation so that as growth declines, the check on inflation is minimized.

The results provide a link from inflation to growth. Inflation is an important variable because it not only shows the outcome of policies in an economy but also shows macroeconomic stability. The results show that inflation originates from both the demand and the supply side. The demand side is represented by the demand for money function. The supply side is made up of the foreign sector. This framework is consistent with a model with a non-traded and a traded good, where the price of the non-traded good responds to disequilibrium in the money market and the movements in the exchange rate and the foreign prices govern the price of the traded good.

The results confirm the determinants of inflation in Kenya, as well as the effects of liberalization on growth. The effect of liberalization has been captured in two ways. First, there is the exchange rate regime shift in 1982, which allowed the exchange rate to crawl in line with the inflation differential between Kenya and its trading partners. This implied that the authorities accepted to live with relatively high inflation because by adopting this exchange rate regime the economy lost one nominal anchor that could hold prices down (i.e., the nominal exchange rate). This effect is reflected by the dummy D821, which shows that the effect was to spur inflation and change its profile.

Second, when liberalization and SAPs were stepped up from 1985, there appears to have been single shocks that had an inflationary effect in the first quarter and disinflation in the second quarter. Finally, the most interesting case has been the step dummy for the adjustment period from 1985, multiplied by inflation (this is INFSD 1985). In effect, we include the inflation profile in the adjustment period. This variable shows that inflation increased with liberalization. This variable is highly significant and shows that liberalization has tended to be associated with inflationary forces. This is consistent with the short-run consequences of liberalization with supply constraints in the economy. Prices rise to ration the existing supply and this seems to have been the case in Kenya.

In general, the results show that with the liberalization and adoption of a floating exchange rate regime, the economy lost a nominal anchor to tie domestic prices down. There are three contributory factors; first, the crawling peg exchange rate was aimed deliberately at depreciating the shilling, thus the depreciation fed into domestic inflation, but there were also prolonged periods of disinflation. Second, shocks hitting the economy were accommodated by inflation and ratified by monetary policy, since the exchange rate regime made monetary policy endogenous. Finally, inflation inertia increased. The error correction terms as defined in Appendix II, showed a positive impact on inflation. This implies that disequilibrium in the money market and the real exchange rate affected inflation in the long run. Thus, the activities in the money market ratified inflation in the long run. These results are important since they reinforce each other because the floating exchange rate is an indirect tool of monetary policy.

One motive in this exercise was to relate the inflation model with growth and determinants of growth in Kenya. This is captured by real growth, RY, and the effects of liberalization on inflation and the fact that real income enters in the structural relationship of money demand, which has a strong positive influence on inflation. This is the long run solution to the model. We have thus shown that inflation affects growth negatively if it is high and that growth will dampen inflation surges in the economy. But one issue that arises is that given Kenya has not been a high inflation economy, we would expect that inflation could have had a positive influence on growth albeit a weak one. This is not confirmed, instead we have a weak effect running from inflation to growth and a stronger effect running from growth to inflation. Therefore, if growth is to accelerate in the future, holding other factors constant, inflation would invariably come down but excessive deflation of the economy will move the economy to a low growth trap. This has been the experience in Kenya since 1997. So, the converse is what has happened in Kenya, the growth pause has been accompanied by surges of inflation.

Other short-run effects: domestic debt, interest rate and the financial sector

So far, what has been alluded to is the influence of fiscal management on the structure of domestic debt and its effect on domestic interest rates and the growth of the financial sector. Rather than develop structural models, we bring out some general points to relate the fiscal stance to growth here. This is because, the effect of a large domestic debt is distortionary in the economy and thus difficult to capture in a single equation model and secondly the relationship between the financial sector growth and the growth of the economy does not have a firm theoretical base. It is believed that it is economic growth that takes the lead and the development of the financial sector follows. We argued earlier that the growth of the financial sector is inhibited by the interest rate structure and the presence of liquid financial assets that are short run and default-free as to discourage financial screening thus, limiting the development of financial intermediation. The link between the fiscal standards and interest rate is via the domestic debt. It has been argued that domestic debt has influenced the interest rate structure and distorted the information content of the term structure. Thus, the interest rate structure has further discouraged investment and savings. The effects are transmitted via the interest rate effect and compounded by the quantity effect, which is the crowding out story on private investment. The high short-term interest rates attract investments and a shift away from long-term investments. The problem with this type of public debt is that it is short term in nature so that its maturity cannot be easily lengthened and that it is mainly held by the financial sector, which implies that its default would lead to a financial crisis.

In summary, high domestic debt distorts the interest-rate structure and inhibits growth in the financial sector. This has been the outcome in Kenya emanating from the failure of fiscal adjustment. The point emphasized here is that an inefficient financial sector cannot mobilize resources required for investment and therefore limits the growth stimulus of the economy. In conclusion, the picture that emerges is that further deepening of reforms is not the only answer to revive growth in that there will be a need to target both policy and institutional reforms. This is because fiscal adjustment requires political will and institutional reforms.

Summarizing the lessons

The study has looked at economic growth and its determinants in Kenya. It has used estimated panel regressions to assess the factors that drive growth and private investments. It has then looked at current macro policies with regard to inflation, interest rate, exchange rate and domestic debt and linked them to the growth pause. The lessons from the analysis are that:

• To stimulate and sustain economic growth, it is necessary to substantially increase investment. This can only happen if the current environment that discourages long-term investments is reversed. To achieve this requires other complementary policies to enhance institutional reforms and create certainty in future. As argued by Rodrik (1998), an adequate and effective institutional structure should: apply simple and uniform rules, rather than selective and differentiated ones; endow bureaucrats with few discretionary powers; contain safeguards against frequent, unpredictable alteration of the rules; and keep firms and other organizational interests at arm's length from the policy formulation and implementation process.

• Investment encompasses human capital, as well as physical infrastructure that should be complementary to private investment.

• For the private investment pause to be reversed and thus stimulate growth, it is necessary to create an environment of certainty in the economy and a policy environment that helps reduce transaction costs and enhance private sector profitability.

• To achieve increased private investment, short run macro policies should be in line with long-run growth targets. For example, to achieve export-led industrialization in Kenya by the year 2020, there should be an interest rate structure that supports investment in the export sector as well as one that is in line with the exchange rate policy. The real exchange rate is a relative price that determines the profitability of exports, yet as we have shown in our analysis, it is influenced strongly by short-term capital flows responding to the interest rate differential. Thus, an appropriate policy response from capital flows is required.

• The economic management issues reviewed include reducing domestic debt, which influences domestic interest rates, inflationary expectations, short-term capital flows and the real exchange rate. Domestic debt is thus viewed as a distortionary force or factor in the economy and needs to be drastically reduced. One of the quickest remedies to accomplish this is to change the maturity profile of domestic debt instruments and to create a fund which will service the domestic debt and reduce the principal, accompanied with a reduction in government borrowing domestically in the future. This requires defining the core functions of government so that public expenditure can be effectively trimmed.

- The domestic interest rate structure currently encourages investment in short-term financial assets, primarily government commercial paper. The consequence has been to re-orient the financial sector into short-term deposits and lending and thus limiting its intermediation roles and hence financial development. These effects spill over into the exchange rate, interest rate and encourages speculative investment and commercial activities.

- For these macro policies to provide the required short-run supply response and lead to growth in the future, institutional reforms are necessary to support and complement the economic reforms so far undertaken. Political and social certainty of long-lived and credible government and government policies are crucial.

- These conclusions stem from the fact that long run growth variables are in the short run de-railed by uncertain movements in exchange rates and interest rates and the perception that the government is not long lived. Economic agents thus acquire a wait option because they are risk averse. For example, investors and exporters will observe the interest rate, inflation rate and exchange rate movements to evaluate potential returns. To the extent that these movements are distorted by economic management in the short run, due to government perception, these agents will delay investment in the export sector. This means that the long run target for an export led growth cannot materialize.

Notes

1. The instabilities resulted from expansionary fiscal and monetary policies. It was believed at the time that there was idle capacity in the economy (the economy was Keynesian) which could be put into use by using expansionary fiscal policy. The result was a balance of payments crisis in 1971/1973 and before the crisis was over an external price shock in terms of oil prices worsened the situation.
2. Foreign Exchange Bearer Certificates (Forex Cs) were purchased at the official exchange rate from the Central Bank of Kenya, in foreign exchange in a 'no questions asked basis'. The certificates that bore an interest rate were then marketable as any other paper asset.
3. Since the year 2000, a significant number of civil servants have been earmarked for retrenchment. This is going hand in hand with retrenchment in the wider public sector.
4. This may be an understatement due to the fact that the domestic debt instruments are short term, mostly 91 day Treasury bill instruments.
5 These figures are from the IFS. The figures in *Economic Survey 1998* show a decline to 15.05 percent in 1997, where interest payments on IMF drawings are excluded.
6. In some cases, government policies are to blame for severe divider effects. In most drought crisis period, the government imports food and provides food relief, which is anyhow inadequate. This is a temporary measure in such times, but what would be required is a set of activities that defend rural incomes and wealth of nomadic groups. This would be what might be called appropriate drought management program.

7. Usually this kind of situation reflects a form of financial repression or 'secondary' financial repression. The government through the central Bank determines the interest rate level by controlling the amount of treasury bills it places in the auction for sale.
8. Secondary financial repression is here used to reflect the fact that interest rates are not driven by market forces but rather driven by a key player the government through the short term financial instruments.
9. Political banks are those that are licensed to well connected individuals and thrive through the deposits of government controlled parastatals and are conduits of financial flows for rent seekers.
10. This section borrows from the work of Elbadawi, Ndulu and Ndung'u (1997a, b, c).
11. While Serven (1996a), Mlambo and Kumar (1995), Blejer and Khan (1984), Serven and Solimano (1993), Greene and Villanueva (1991), and Oshikoya (1994), found complementarity using cross country data, Balassa (1988) found that public investment crowds out private investment.
12. See, for example, Pindyck (1993), Rodrik (1990) and van Wijnbergen (1992).
13. In a recent paper, Serven (1996b) shows that even small probabilities of policy reversal in a model with entry and exit costs for capital can deter private investment by considerable amounts.
14. Several of the most recent studies find significant and negative influence of outstanding foreign debt on private investments. See, for example, Serven (1996b) Serven and Solimano (1993); Mlambo and Kumar (1995), and Schimdt-Hebbel and Muller (1991).
15. The formal theoretical rationalisation of this argument is provided by Lucas (1988).
16. For example, studies by Barro (1991), Mankiw, Romer and Weil (1992), and Khan and Kumar (1993) have found a positive effect of the initial stock of human capital on per capita GDP growth.
17. The motivation in this empirical methodology is that it is precarious to try to estimate a growth or private investment model for Kenya using annual data and the group of variables expounded above. Due to insufficient degrees of freedom this may be an exercise in futility. We thus use estimated cross country (for SSA) regressions where Kenya is in the sample and compute Kenya's performance in relation to the variables in the models.
18. We argue that interest rates were being forced down because there was no accompanying adjustment of other variables like inflation, nominal exchange rate or economic growth. First, capital flows were essentially footloose financial resources, that is, speculative capital attracted by high interest rate, then there would have been massive capital flight and this would have depreciated the currency, exports, and then growth. Second, if on the other hand the interest rate was being used as an instrument to control inflation and maintain a competitive exchange rate, then by it coming down would have depreciated the currency –assuming monetary policy would contain inflation, even though there would be some initial rise to mimic exchange rate depreciation, and thus lead to growth via the export channel, due to increased resource flows. Finally, with interest rates coming down, and with low and stable inflation, then either the currency would have to depreciate or growth to accelerate or both. But none of this took place until May 1999 when the currency started sliding, one year after interest rates started coming down. This was an artificial balance.

References

Agenor, P.-R. and Montiel, P. J. (1998), *Development Macroeconomics*, Princeton University Press: Princeton, NJ.

Agenor, P.-R. and Ucer, E. M. (1995), *Exchange Market Reform, Inflation and Fiscal Deficits*, IMF Working Paper, WP/95/78 (August), The World Bank: Washington, DC.

Asea, P. K. and Reinhart, C. M. (1995), 'Real Interest Rate Differentials and Real Exchange Rate: Evidence from Four African Countries', A paper presented at the AERC Workshop, Nairobi, May.

Asea, P. K. and Reinhart, C. M. (1996), 'Le Prix de L'argent: How (Not) to Deal With Capital Flows', *Journal of African Economies*, Vol. 5, No. 3, Part I (Supplement), pp. 231–271.

Balassa, B. (1988), 'Agricultural Policies and International Resource Allocation', *Journal of Policy Modeling*, Vol. 10, No. 2, pp. 249–263.

Barro, R. (1991), 'Economic Growth in a Cross-Section of Countries', *Quarterly Journal of Economics*, Vol. 106 (May), pp. 407–444.

Blejer, M. and Khan, M. (1984), 'Government Policy and Private Investment in Developing Countries', *IMF Staff Papers*, Vol. 31, No. 2, pp. 379–403.

Chua, H. (1993a), 'Regional Spillovers and Economic Growth', Center Discussion Paper No. 700, Economic Growth Center, Yale University: New Haven, CT.

Chua, H. (1993b), 'Regional Public Capital and Economic Growth', Unpublished Mimeo, Economic Growth Center, Yale University: New Haven, CT.

Collier, P. (1991), 'Africa's External Economic Relations, 1960–90', *African Affairs*, Vol. 90, No. 360, pp. 339–356.

Collier, P. (1995), 'The Marginalization of Africa', *International Labor Review*, Vol. 134, Nos. 4–5, pp. 541–557.

Collier, P. (1996), 'The Role of the State in Economic Development: Cross Regional Experience', Paper presented at the *AERC Bi-annual Research Workshop*, Nairobi, Kenya, December.

Corbo, V. (1996), 'Macroeconomic Adjustment to Capital Inflows: Lessons from Recent Latin American and East Asian Experience', *World Bank Research Observer*, Vol. 11, No. 1, pp. 61–85.

Cuthbertson, K., Hall, S. G. and Taylor, M. P. (1992), *Applied Econometrics Techniques*, Phillip Allan: London.

Dornbusch, R. (1988), *Exchange Rates and Inflation*, MIT Press: Cambridge, MA.

Easterly, W. (1995), 'The Mystery of Growth: Shocks, Policies and Surprises in Old and New Theories of Economic Growth', *Singapore Economic Review*, Vol. 40, No. 1, pp. 3–23.

Easterly, W. and LeVine, R. (1996), 'The Tragedy of African Growth', Policy Research Working Paper No. 1503, The World Bank: Washington, DC.

Easterly, W. and LeVine, R. (1997), 'Africa's Growth Tragedy: Policies and Ethnic Divisions', *The Quarterly Journal of Economics*, Vol. 112, No. 4 (November), pp. 1203–1250.

Easterly, W. and Schmidt-Hebbel, K. (1991), 'The Macroeconomics of Public Sector Deficits: A Synthesis', Paper presented at the World Bank Conference on Macroeconomics of Public Sector Deficits, Washington, DC.

Edison, H. J. and Pauls, B. D. (1993), 'A Re-Assessment of the Relationship Between the Real Exchange Rates and Real Interest Rates', *Journal of Monetary Economics*, Vol. 31, No. 2, pp. 165–187.

Edwards, S. (1993), 'Openness, Trade Liberalization and Growth in Developing Countries', *Journal of Economic Literature*, Vol. 31, No. 3, pp. 1358–1393.

Elbadawi, I. A. (1994), 'Estimating Long-Run Equilibrium Real Exchange Rates', in Williamson, J. (ed.), *Estimating Equilibrium Exchange Rates*, International of International Economics: Washington, DC.

Elbadawi, I. A. (1996), 'Consolidating Macroeconomic Stabilization and Restoring Growth in sub-Saharan Africa', in Ndulu, B. and van de Walle, N. (eds.), *Policy Perspectives on African Development Strategies*, Overseas Development Council: Washington, DC.

Elbadawi, I. A. and Soto, R. (1994), *Capital Flows and Long-Term Equilibrium Real Exchange Rates in Chile*, World Bank Policy Research Working Paper No. 1306 (January), The World Bank: Washington, DC.

Elbadawi, I. A., Ndulu, B. J. and Ndung'u, N. S. (1997a), 'Debt Overhang and Economic Growth in sub-Saharan Africa', in Iqbal, Z. and Kanbur, R. (eds.), *External Finance for Low Income Countries*, IMF: Washington, DC.

Elbadawi, I. A., Ndulu, B. J. and Ndung'u, N. S. (1997b), 'Risks, Uncertainties and Debt Overhang as Determinants of Private Investment in SSA', A paper presented at the Conference on Investment, Growth and Risk in Africa to mark the 10th Anniversary of CSAE, Oxford University, Oxford, UK.

Elbadawi, I. A., Ndulu, B. J. and Ndung'u, N. S. (1997c), 'Macroeconomic Performance in sub-Saharan Africa in a Comparative Setting', Mimeo, AERC: Nairobi, Kenya.

Elbadawi, I. A., Ndulu, B. J. and Ndung'u, N. S. (forthcoming), 'Risk Uncertainties and Debt Overhang as Determinants of Private Investment in SSA', *Journal of African Economies*.

Ghura, D. and Hadjimichael, M. T. (1996), 'Growth in sub-Saharan Africa', *IMF Staff Papers*, Vol. 43, No. 3 (September), pp. 605–634.

Goldstein, M., Mathieson, D. J. and Lane, T. (1991), 'Determinants of Systematic Consequences of International Capital Flows', IMF Occasional Paper No. 77 (March), IMF: Washington, DC.

Greene, J. and Villanueva, D. (1991), 'Private Investment in Developing Countries: An Empirical Analysis', *IMF Staff Papers*, Vol. 38, No. 1 (March), pp. 33–58.

Khan, M. and Kumar, M. (1993), 'Public and Private Investment and the Convergence of Per Capita Incomes in Developing Countries', IMF Working Paper No. WPS 1993/51 (June).

Knack, S. and Keefer, P. (1995), 'Institutions and Economic Performance: Cross Country Tests Using Alternative Institutional Measures', *Economics and Politics*, Vol. 7, No. 3, pp. 207–227.

Krugman, P. (1991), *Geography and Trade*, MIT Press: Cambridge, MA.

Lucas, R. (1988), 'On the Mechanics of Economic Development', *Journal of Monetary Economics*, Vol. 22, No. 1 (July), pp. 3–42.

Mankiw, N., Romer, D. and Weil, D. (1992), 'A Contribution to the Empirics of Economic Growth', *Quarterly Journal of Economics*, Vol. 107, No. 4, pp. 407–437.

McDonald, R. and Nagayasu, J. (1997), 'On the Japaneses Yen-US Dollar Exchange Rate: A Structural Econometric Model Based on Real Interest Rate Differentials', *CEPR Discussion Paper No. 1639* (April).

Mlambo, K. and Kumar, M. (1995), 'Determinants of Private Investment in sub-Saharan Africa: An Empirical Investigation', Paper presented at the World Congress of the International Economic Association, Tunis, Tunisia, December.

Montiel, P. J. (1995), 'Financial Policies and Economic Growth: Theory, Evidence and Country-Specific Experience from sub-Saharan Africa', AERC Special Paper Eighteen (April): Nairobi, Kenya.

Mullei, A. (1995), 'The Financial Sector and Economic Development', A paper presented at the Seminar for Kenya Parliamentarians, Taita Hills Lodge (August).

Mwega, F. M. (1993), 'Import Demand Elasticities and Stability During Trade Liberalization: A Case Study of Kenya', *Journal of African Economies*, Vol. 2, No. 3, pp. 381–416.

Mwega, F. M. and Ndung'u, N. S. (1996), 'Exchange Rate Management and Macroeconomic Policies in Kenya', A paper presented at the AERC Collaborative Research, Nairobi.

Ndulu, B. (1991), 'Growth and Adjustment in sub-Saharan Africa', in Chibber, A. and Fisher, S. (eds.), *Economic Reform in sub-Saharan Africa*, The World Bank: Washington, DC.

Ndulu, B. and Ndung'u, N. S. (1998), 'Trade and Growth in sub-Saharan Africa', in Iqbal, Z. and Khan, M. S. (eds.), *Trade Reform and Regional Integration in Africa*, International Monetary Fund: Washington, DC.

Ndung'u, N. S. (1997), 'Monetary and Exchange Rate Policies in Kenya', AERC Discussion Paper 94: Nairobi, Kenya.

Ndung'u, N. S. (2001), 'Liberalization of the Foreign Exchange Market in Kenya: What Lessons Can be Learnt?', *AERC Discussion Paper Series* (forthcoming).

Obsfeld, M. and Rogoff, K. (1996), *Foundations of International Macroeconomics*, The MIT Press: Cambridge, MA.

Oshikoya, T. W. (1994), 'Macroeconomic Determinants of Domestic Private Investment in Africa: An Empirical Analysis', *Economic Development and Cultural Change*, Vol. 42, No. 3, pp. 573–596.

Pindyck, R. (1993), 'A Note on Competitive Investment Under Uncertainty', *American Economic Review*, Vol. 83, No. 1 (March), pp. 273–277.

Rodrik, D. (1990), 'How Should Structural Adjustment Programs be Designed?', *World Development*, Vol. 18, No. 7 (July), pp. 933–947.

Rodrik, D. (1998), 'Trade Policy and Economic Performance in sub-Saharan Africa', Mimeo, Kennedy School of Government, Harvard University, Cambridge, MA.

Roe, A. R. and Sowa, Ndii (1994), 'From Direct to Indirect Monetary Control in sub-Saharan Africa', *AERC Plenary Paper* (December).

Sachs, J. D. and Warner, A. M. (1997), 'Sources of Slow Growth in African Economies', *Journal of African Economies*, Vol. 6, No. 3 (October), pp. 335–376.

Schmidt-Hebbel, K. and Muller, T. (1991), 'Private Investment Under Macroeconomic Adjustment in Morocco', Policy Research Paper No. 787, The World Bank: Washington, DC.

Serven, L. (1996a), 'Does Public Capital Crowd Out Private Capita?: Evidence from India', Policy Research Paper No. 1613, The World Bank: Washington, DC.

Serven, L. (1996b), 'Irreversibility, Uncertainty and Private Investment: Analytical Issues and Some Lessons for Africa', A paper presented at the AERC Research Workshop, Nairobi, Kenya, May.

Serven, L. and Solimano, A. (1993), 'Economic Adjustment and Investment Performance in Developing Countries: The Experience of the 1980s', in Serven, L. and Solimano, L. (eds.), *Economic Adjustment and Investment Performance in Developing Countries: The Experience of the 1980s*, The World Bank: Washington, DC.

Swamy, G. (1994), 'Kenya: Structural Adjustment in the 1990s', World Bank Policy Research Working Paper No. 1238, The World Bank: Washington, DC.

van Wijnbergen, S. (1992), 'Trade Reform, Policy Uncertainty and the Current Account: A Non-Expected Utility Approach', *American Economic Review*, Vol. 82, No. 3, pp. 626–633.

World Bank (1989), 'Financial Systems and Development', Policy Research Series, No. 15, The World Bank: Washington, DC.

World Bank (1992), 'Kenya Financial Sector Adjustment Project', Project Completion Report, Nairobi.

Appendix I

Real exchange rate and interest rate differential

Empirical results: Unit root tests of the variables in the analysis are shown in Table A3.1. Several unit root tests have been used due to the fact that we are dealing with high frequency data that is extremely noisy. We see that private capital flows are a stationary process, and all the other variables are non-stationary. The tests are conclusive for all the variables except money supply, where the Dickey-Fuller and Phillips-Perron tests indicate that it might be a stationary process. The Weighted Symmetric test for money supply does not support these results. It is seen that the variable is clearly non-stationary. We proceed under the assumption that the variables are all I(1) and private capital flows is I(0). This is consistent and corroborated by the graphs of these variables.

Table A3.1   Unit root tests

Test/ Variable	RER	NER	M2	TDR	RID	I	P	P^f	PVTK
WS	−2.83	−1.90	−2.77	−2.29	−1.95	−1.07	−0.48	0.93	−2.95
P-values	0.13	0.71	0.15	0.43	0.68	0.96	0.99	0.97	0.06
DF	−2.74	−1.72	−4.28	−2.08	−2.22	−1.79	−0.79	−0.81	−5.86
P-values	0.22	0.74	0.00	0.55	0.48	0.71	0.96	0.96	0.00
PP	−13.00	−6.17	−22.40	−9.51	−8.30	−2.31	−1.26	−15.90	−83.00
P-values	0.26	0.73	0.04	0.44	0.39	0.96	0.98	0.15	0.00

Notes: RER is the real exchange rate, NER is the nominal exchange rate, M2 is money supply, TDR is the Treasury discount rate, RID is the real interest rate differential, I is foreign interest rate, P is the domestic price level, P^f is the foreign price level and PVTK is short-term private capital flows. All these variables are analyzed in this table because their time series characteristics become useful in the analysis.

The next step is to analyze cointegration relationships between nominal exchange rate, domestic and foreign prices and the real interest rate differential. The results show a cointegrating vector of the form:

$$ECM_t = NER_t - 6.12 + 0.495\, P_t + 0.241\, P_t^f - 0.8395\, RID_t$$

which incorporates the purchasing power parity and the real interest rate differential. This is consistent with the arguments that the purchasing power parity may not hold all the time and may thus require the real interest rate differential to stabilize the vector. The model was thus with this cointegrating vector and the variables in first difference and estimated with six lags of each variable and the ECM lagged one step. In addition, there were dummies that reflected interventions in the foreign exchange market. These were identified as influential points (like outliers) after recursive estimation showed instabilities in the regression coefficients. The instabilities are important in that they help trace the effects of liberalization and external shocks and the process of adjustment. Without them, we could not have achieve meaningful and stable results. The results are shown in Table A3.2.

Table A3.2   The exchange rate, real interest rate differential regression results

Variable	Coefficient	Standard Error	t-Ratio
Constant	0.001	0.006	0.158
RID_t	−0.592	0.135	−4.370
P_t	−0.610	0.277	−2.200
P_t^f	1.308	1.033	1.270
ECM_{t-1}	−0.183	0.100	−1.830
D933	−0.148	0.049	−3.030
D9410	0.136	0.033	4.050
D955	−0.189	0.046	−4.060
D9612	0.069	0.032	2.110

Note: The variables are as defined in Table A3.1. Wald Test χ^2 (8) 75.675 [.0000]** This is a linear restriction test.

Appendix II

Modeling inflation in Kenya

Empirical results: From the summary unit roots test table, Table A3.3, we see that all the variables are I(1). We have used three tests and they are all consistent except for the interest rate (TDR), the Phillips-Perron test shows that it is significant at 5.2 percent. In this case we rely on the Weighted Symmetric (WS) test which is a much more powerful test. The probability values are shown in the parenthesis.

Table A3.3   Summary of unit root tests

Test	NER	P	Pf	RY	M2	TDR
WS	−1.907 [.709]	−.0940 [.978]	−0.412 [.995]	-0.887 [.999]	−1.013 [.972]	−2.587 [.242]
DF	−1.152 [.919]	−1.491 [.832]	−1.610 [.788]	−2.217 [.480]	−1.497 [.830]	−1.527 [.819]
PP	−10.02 [.431]	−1.980 [.971]	−2.721 [.948]	−6.544 [.702]	−5.090 [.815]	−21.481 [.052]

Note: RY is the log of real income and the other variables are as defined in Table A3.1.

Cointegration test is provided in Table A3.4. This is the trace test from the Johansen maximum likelihood procedure where we test the most significance eigen vector. The hypothesis that we have three cointegrating vectors ($r< = 2$) is rejected at 31.4 percent. But the probability that we have two cointegrating vectors cannot be rejected at 10 percent. So we conclude that we have two cointegrating vectors. Through identifying restrictions, the vectors are composed as formulated in equation (8). It is this equation that helps us identify the cointegrating vectors and they can thus have some structural interpretation.

Table A3.4   Johanseen trace test procedure

Null Hypothesis	Trace Test	Eigenvalues
r = 0	124.762[.001]	0.434
r < = 1	73.605[.096]	0.284
r < = 2	45.514[.313]	0.211
r < = 3	22.241[.526]	0.141
r < = 4	8.519[.602]	0.071
r < = 5	1.82 [.173]	0.020

Note: NOBS 96, Loglikelihood 706.347 AIC -13.716. These vectors are composed as: (1) NER − 1.195 P + 0.95 Pf; (2) M2 − 1.72 P − 1.422 RY + 0.32 TDR.

The first vector almost mimics the purchasing power parity and thus defines a real equilibrium exchange rate which is data based. From the way it is formulated and normalized with nominal exchange rate it shows that any disequilibrium in the foreign exchange market will impact on the rate of inflation. The second vector is a long-run money demand relationship with coefficients greater than those postulated by theory for CPI and RY. From this vector we can see that velocity is not stable since we cannot map a vector of [1 -1 -1] of M2, CPI and RY, or a similar stationary vector. This becomes critical in Kenya since the formulation and effective monetary policy is based on the assumption of stable and predictable velocity of money in the long run. From the way this vector is formulated and normalised, it shows that disequilibrium in the money market will spur the rate of inflation. Real income enters significantly in this vector an as we shall see in Table A3.5, the real income growth is a factor dampening the acceleration of inflation.

Table A3.5   Solved inflation equation

Variable	Coefficient	S.E.	t-Ratio
EX	2.082	0.461	4.516
RY	−0.835	0.264	−3.163
M2	0.199	0.103	1.932
TDR	0.053	0.004	13.94
WP	0.607	0.217	2.797
ECM1t-1	0.191	0.041	4.650
ECM2t-1	0.004	0.00016	2.500
D821	0.086	0.022	3.909
D851	0.043	0.022	2.057
D852	−0.058	0.021	−2.700
INFSD 1985	2.188	0.352	6.216
Constant	−0.549	0.128	4.289

Wald test $\chi^2(12) = 98.37[.000]$- This is a linear restrictions test. Diagnostic tests for the equation that was solved are shown here below and none of the tests has been violated. The tests are: $R^2 = .951$ $F(37,57) = 29.86$ [0.000] S.E. $= 0.0086$, AR 1–5 $F(5,52) = 1.067[0.389]$, ARCH 1–4 $F(4,49) = .2581[0.9033]$, Normality χ^2 (2) $= 1.424[0.4906]$, RESET $F(1,56) = 0.0075[0.9314]$. The tests are AR for serial correlation (autoregression structure) of the residuals, ARCH (autoregressive conditional heteroscedasticity) to test of the heteroscedasticity of residuals, normality test whether the residuals follow a normal distribution and the RESET test is a regression specification test to test whether the linear assumption of the regression equation is valid. Their probability values are attached in brackets.

4

Export Platforms in Kenya

GRAHAM GLENDAY AND DAVID NDII

Introduction

Kenya embarked on trade liberalization and export promotion programs in 1987 in response to a deterioration of export performance over the preceding decade. Merchandise export earnings as a percentage of GDP declined from 19.6 percent in the 1970s, to 16.9 percent over 1980–1984, and a further 13.6 percent over 1985–1989, reaching an all time low of 11.5 percent in 1987. Exports surged dramatically in the early nineties, particularly after 1992, following a number of policy initiatives such as the introduction of export promotion schemes or platforms whose aim was to promote labor-intensive manufactures. Three such export schemes were (1) a bonded warehouse or manufacturing-under-bond scheme (MUB); (2) Export Processing Zones (EPZs); and (3) a duty and VAT exemption scheme known as the Export Promotion Programs Office (EPPO). The first two schemes targeted new investments while the latter two targeted existing manufacturers. The result of these policy initiatives, and of the major liberalization that occurred in trade in 1993–1994, was an increase in trade earnings from 13 percent of GDP in 1992, to over 20 percent between 1993–1996.

Export platforms are often cited as critical elements of the successful entry into developed country markets for labor-intensive manufactures by the Asian Tiger economies, the Philippines, and Mauritius in Africa among others. However, research evidence has thus far not established whether export platforms have been an essential leverage for this success or merely the icing on the cake – in other words, whether a policy of outward orientation, macroeconomic stability, and labor cost competitiveness would have been sufficient for the successful entry into, and survival in, the global economy. This study evaluates the role and performance of Kenya's export platforms in this context. It is organized as follows: the rest of this section presents a synopsis of the main findings; second, we discuss export platform structure, as well as design and operational issues using a stylized analytical framework; third, we provide an overview of implementation and performance of Kenya's export platforms; fourth, we analyze this performance in the context of the macroeconomic policy environment and its impact on overall export performance, focussing on trade liberalization, the real exchange rate, labor costs and productivity; and finally, we draw conclusions from Kenya's experience on the potential for export platforms in sub-Saharan Africa and similar countries.

Summary of the main findings

Macroeconomic reforms, trade liberalization measures, and regional integration have been the key factors behind the recovery of Kenya's manufactured exports. The export surge recorded in the 1992–1994 period coincides with a sharp depreciation of the Kenya shilling – a 25 percent real depreciation of the KSh/US$ exchange rate from 1990 to 1993, an even more significant fall in the real average wage – by 39 percent over the same period, and a major shift in the trade regime following the abolition of trade licensing requirements and foreign exchange allocations and restrictions. These favorable export conditions have not been sustained as both the real KSh/US$ exchange rate and the average wage rate in US$ terms by 1997 had reverted to pre-1990 levels and then, in the case of the exchange rate, exceeded them, which in turn explains the deteriorating export performance after 1996.

The preferential regional market, led by Uganda and Tanzania – partners in the East African Co-operation trading bloc, followed by the wider Common Market for Eastern and Southern Africa (COMESA), accounts for the dominant share of the increase in Kenya's exports. In fact, the preferential regional market has absorbed over 100 percent of the cumulative increase in processed exports over the 1993–1998 period, reflecting diversion of trade from the rest of the world to the preferential regional market. Non-COMESA markets accounted for 95 percent of the increase in primary goods exports over the same period. Overall, recorded exports to COMESA increased from a 1990–1992 average of 15 percent of the total, to 34 percent in 1996–1998. Uganda's share alone increased from 6 percent of the total to 15 percent and Tanzania's from 3 percent to 12 percent, in effect, to a combined share of close to a third of Kenya's total exports. Besides the regional economic integration initiative, this trend is also a reflection of economic recovery and trade liberalization in the region. An overall increase in import demand in the region, alongside a down turn in the Kenyan economy, provided an added impetus for Kenyan firms to seek external markets.

Not surprisingly then, the impact of MUB and EPZ platforms, designed to target dedicated export processors for overseas markets, has been, by and large, inconspicuous among exports. The combined cumulative share of exports originating from MUB/EPZ enterprises between 1993–1998 amounts to just over 1 percent of total exports. By contrast, exporters using the more flexible EPPO duty/VAT exemption program have averaged 35 percent of total exports, which we estimate to be over 50 percent of the processed and packaged exports eligible for EPPO, and over 75 percent of exports of manufactures. However, utilization of the EPPO program has been declining, from a peak share of 38 percent in 1994 to 31 percent in 1998, reflecting exports declining with the erosion in competitiveness through exchange rate and real wage appreciation as well as the tax value of the program declining with lower duty rates. That said, the MUB platform did show considerable potential. The facility became an attractive platform for contract garment manufacturing for the US market, but this suffered a major setback in 1994 when the US trade authorities revoked Kenya's quota for some items (shirts, tee shirts and pillow cases), citing transhipment of garments originating from India through Kenya. By 1997, only 10 garment factories were in operation, out of over 70 in operation at the time of the quota restriction. But even if the quota had not been revoked, success might not have been sustained on account of the subsequent appreciation of both the exchange rate and the real wage, and in 1997–1998, the precipitous fall of Southeast Asian currencies and labor costs following the financial crisis.

Kenya has a relatively large skilled and semi-skilled industrial labor force that could be readily engaged to produce labor-intensive manufactures, notably garments and footwear, for the world market. A large proportion of this labor force is engaged in a dynamic and highly competitive informal sector – somewhat analogous to Asia's 'sweat shops', where earnings are significantly lower than formal sector wages. However, unlike Asia, Kenya has not been able to translate this dynamism and wage competitiveness into labor-intensive export processing. Reliance on physical, rather than accounting controls and high transactions costs imposed by excessive bureaucracy in the administration of Kenya's export platforms constitute entry barriers for informal sector participants, either as direct exporters or through subcontracting arrangements with formal sector exporters.

Theoretical framework

The core of most export promotion schemes is to provide the inputs to the production of exports at world prices. This recognizes that exports generally only earn world or border prices for the exporter. Lowering the costs of tradable inputs at least to their world or border price levels is important to gain export price competitiveness for the exporter.

Another way of expressing this objective is by stating that the export promotion schemes aim to remove any *negative* trade protection from exports. By contrast with import-competing products, which mostly receive *positive* trade protection or a *net subsidy* from import tariffs, exports typically suffer from a disincentive from trade protection through import tariffs. An explicit derivation of the net subsidy provided tradable goods by import tariffs provides a useful framework for understanding the different types of export promotion scheme. The net rents or pure profits (_) of a business venture selling quantity, Q, at a price inclusive of import tariffs of $p(1 + \tau_Q)$, after incurring labor and other non-tradable costs of wL, tradable variable input costs inclusive of import tariffs of $mM(1 + \tau_M)$, and capital rental costs, gross of taxes on the capital income or on the capital assets and inclusive of import tariffs, of $(r+\delta+t_K)K(1 + t_K)$ are given as:[1]

$$\pi_1 = pQ(1 + \tau_Q) - [wL + mM(1 + \tau_M) + (r+\delta+t_K)K(1 + t_K)] \tag{A}$$

where p, Q and τ_Q are respectively, the world price, quantity and tariff rate of the product; m, M and τ_M are the world price, quantity and tariff rate of tradable variable inputs; r, δ, t_K and K are the rental rate, depreciation rate, tax rate and capital value of capital assets, respectively. The world prices are expressed in domestic currency at the current market exchange rate.

At world prices, excluding import tariffs, the net rents from the business would be:

$$\pi_0 = pQ - [wL + mM + (r+\delta+t_K)K] \tag{B}$$

The net subsidy received by the business from the tariff protection is the difference $(\pi_1 - \pi_0)$ or

$$s = pQ\,\tau_Q - [mM\,\tau_M + (r+\delta+t_K)K\,\tau_K] \tag{C}$$

This net subsidy can be expressed relative to the value of the product sales at world prices as:

$$s = \tau_Q - [\alpha_M\,\tau_M + (\alpha_K + \alpha_t)\,\tau_K] \tag{D}$$

where the α's are essentially the cost shares of tradable variable inputs, net-of-tax capital rental cost and capital taxes, respectively.

For most import-competing goods, the net subsidy is positive with τ_Q, τ_M and τ_K. If the product is exported, or can be imported duty free, or is sold to an aid-funded project or any other buyer with duty-free privileges at a duty-free price, then the subsidy becomes *negative* with $\tau_Q = 0$ or

$$s \quad = \quad - [\alpha_M \tau_M + (\alpha_K + \alpha_t) \tau_K] \tag{E}$$

To avoid this negative subsidy or negative protection, export promotion programs or export platforms typically make τ_M on tradable variable or current cost inputs zero, and sometimes also make τ_K on tradable capital equipment zero. The removal of the cost of the import duty content is achieved through duty exemptions, or through drawbacks or some compensation payments for the duty content. In some cases, export promotion programs or platforms will also reduce the effective taxes on the capital income – hence the share of capital taxes, α_t, is reduced below that normally charged on domestic businesses. The value of the export program is reduced to the exporter by the transaction costs of complying with the program. In addition, the economy suffers the added cost of the administration of the program by the government. Each of these program elements is discussed separately below.

Alternatively, general reductions in import tariff rates can minimize the need for specific export promotion programs. General reductions in import tariffs, however, will also have different effects on the exchange rate than specific export programs. Generally, the domestic currency is expected to devalue with general import tariff reductions. This will favor the production of tradable goods, including exports. The lower the average import tariff rates in an economy, the less the justification for incurring the transaction costs associated with compliance and administration of export promotion programs. If use of the program is voluntary, then as tariff rates are lowered, some export firms may opt out of using the program if the compliance costs exceed the program benefits. As will also be further discussed below, use of a particular export program or platform may also place other restrictions on a business that result in added costs that discourage its use.

Import tariffs on tradable variable inputs

The variable τ_M can be zeroed through either import duty exemptions or drawbacks for inputs used in the production of exports, or duty free goods or goods sold to domestic persons with duty free privileges. Where the producer of the goods exports own-produced goods, the firm is referred to as a *direct exporter*. Where tradable inputs are purchased from domestic suppliers rather than imported directly by the exporter, such domestic input suppliers are referred to as *indirect exporters*. Indirect exporters also need their negative protection removed by import duty exemptions or drawbacks based on sales to exporters, if they are to sell to exporters at world or border prices. The direct exporter always has the option of importing the input duty free rather than purchasing from a domestic producer or indirect exporter. Such first-stage indirect exporters may, in turn, either import inputs directly or purchase them from domestic suppliers which could be referred to as second stage indirect exporters. Such second stage indirect exporters could be offered duty exemptions or drawbacks on imported inputs used to produce inputs to a first stage indirect exporter that supplies inputs to an exporter. In theory, this chain of indirect exporters could be lengthy. In practice, it seldom goes back more than three or four stages.

This problem of complex chains of input-output relationships in the chain of supply leads to two potential strategies for removing the price-raising effects of import tariffs on inputs. One is to remove the actual duties paid at each stage of inputs ultimately going into the production of exports. The other is to establish the estimated import tariff content in all different types of exports and compensate the final exporter for the implicit estimated tariff content. The issues involved in each approach are discussed below.

Import tariffs on capital investments

Not all export promotion programs offer to remove the cost of import tariffs on capital equipment or other capital investments – or set τ_K to zero). The reason for this is that not all of a company's output necessarily goes into exports. Where the export share of production is low and the product receives import protection, lowering the import tariffs on all capital investments merely raises the effective subsidy received from supplying the domestic market. (See expression (D) above.) As a result, unless an export program is targeted at companies producing primarily for export, a duty exemption for capital imports is often not offered, or alternatively, under some programs, import duty is charged on domestic sales of all inputs, current and capital received import duty exemptions. Alternatively, where estimated import duty contents are paid upon export of a particular class of goods, then compensation for the import duty cost of capital investments can be included in an aggregate compensation payment rate on the export. This is discussed further below. As a general alternative, countries may offer import duty exemptions on capital goods under some more general investment promotion programs, which would include investments for export production as only one of the eligible classes of investment.

Reducing effective taxes on capital income

Reductions in the effective tax rates on capital income are offered under certain export promotion programs. These income tax incentives may take the form of tax holidays, lower tax rates, exemption on export-derived income, accelerated depreciation, increased investment deductions or reduced property tax rates. In line with the considerations for exempting import duties on capital goods, these income tax incentives are typically also limited to companies producing primarily for export to avoid increasing the effective protection of domestic production. Note that if the promotion program lowered the effective tax rate from τ_K to τ_K' and correspondingly the share of capital taxes from α_t to α_t', then the effective subsidy rate in (D) becomes:

$$s \quad = \quad \tau_Q - [\alpha_M \tau_M + (\alpha_K + \alpha_t') \tau_K + (\alpha_t' - \alpha_t)] \qquad\qquad (F)$$

The subsidy rate on export producers is therefore increased by $(\alpha_t - \alpha_t')(1+\tau_K)$. Again, instead of offering special income tax incentives to export producers, these incentives may be part of a broader investment incentive program available to both export and domestic sector producers, in which case $\alpha_t = \alpha_t'$ and the bias towards export production is removed. This approach is becoming more common given that income tax incentives confined to exporters are generally considered as export subsidies prohibited under WTO/GATT rules and can generate countervailing duties in importing countries showing damage from the subsidized exports.

Value of flexibility and options in export production

While different export platforms aim to remove the effective export disincentives from import tariffs charged on production inputs, and sometimes go further to provide income tax incentives for exporters, these programs often impose added restrictions on the locational choice and the costs of non-tradable input requirements. To illustrate, an EPZ program that offers full import duty exemptions and other tax incentives, but is limited to firms producing primarily for export as well as limited in terms of the range of locations for conducting business, can result in increases in other input costs such as transport, utilities, land, buildings, or labor in addition to program and tax compliance costs. The program would also remove options to redirect sales to the domestic market in the future. This can result in lower capacity utilization of plant and equipment that raises unit costs. Restrictions on location can also affect domestic transport costs on tradables. These real input and option costs may more than offset the tax benefits of doing business in an EPZ. These issues will be important in comparing the different export platforms offered in Kenya and their success and usage.

The costs of restricting flexibility in production choices, therefore, raise the real costs of using a particular export program. This means that the real costs of labor and other inputs as well as the related costs shares – in terms of the value of the production at world prices, in the case of using the program may be higher than without the program. The costs in the case of operating within an export program are denoted with a prime mark. In addition, the costs of compliance with the program as a share of production value are given as β. With these adjustments, the net gain from participation in an export program offering $\tau_M = \tau_K = 0$ becomes:

$$\Delta = [\alpha_M \tau_M + (\alpha_K + \alpha_t) \tau_K)] + [(\alpha_L - \alpha_L') + (\alpha_M - \alpha_M') + (\alpha_K + \alpha_t - \alpha_K' - \alpha_t') - \beta] \quad (G)$$

Real exchange rate effects

The pure profits of a domestic manufacturer of tradables are given above in (A) in terms of world prices expressed in domestic currency units. These prices could alternatively be expressed in terms of world prices in foreign currency units and the exchange rate of the domestic currency per unit of foreign currency. For example, p $= p^w E$, where p^w is the world price in foreign currency units and E is the exchange rate in domestic currency per foreign currency. Only the price of non-tradables, w, does not depend directly on the exchange rate, E. Hence, if the pure profits in (A) are restated as a share of the revenues at world prices, pQ, then (A) is transformed to:

$$\pi_1/(pQ) = (1 + \tau_Q) - [\alpha_M(1 + \tau_M) + (\alpha_K + \alpha_t)(1 + \tau_K)] - wL/(p^w E Q) \quad (H)$$

It is then clear that pure profits rise with devaluation in the domestic currency (E rises) as relative cost of non-tradables in the last term of (H) falls. This expression also shows that if all the effective import duty rates decline, then pure profits will decline for manufacturers of importables, but increase for manufacturers of exportables (with $\tau_Q = \alpha$). If the average duty rate on imports declines, however, then trade will expand and the exchange rate will devalue. For manufacturers of importables, this increase in E will partially offset the decline in effective tariff, while for manufacturers of exportables, the devaluation will further enhance their profitability. General reductions in average import duty rates, therefore, can be expected to improve the prospects of producers of exportables both directly through the reduction in the import duty content of their costs, as well as indirectly through the exchange rate lowering the relative cost of non-tradable inputs. Lower average duty rates can also be expected to result in lower benefits from using export platforms that provide exemptions for import duties on inputs, and hence, fewer firms will find the benefits of export platforms exceeding the compliance and other costs of using them. Trade liberalization is expected to lead to lower usage of export platforms.

Expression (H) also illustrates that manufacturers with higher domestic value added will be more concerned by the macroeconomic market conditions, particularly wages and the exchange rate (or w/E, the foreign currency cost of domestic labor), while those with low domestic value added will focus on their effective tariff protection. Low domestic value added manufacturers will be very sensitive to the rate of output protection (τ_Q) relative to input duties (τ_M). Such manufacturers will be more sensitive to the availability of export platforms if they are to enter the export business.

Regional markets and treatment of intra-regional exports

As discussed above, the core function of an export platform is to remove the import duty costs from exports that will be sold at world prices in unprotected markets. Ideally, if a country is a member of a common market, for customs purposes, all member countries are treated as one country. The common market members have a single common tariff charged on imports from all external countries – a so-called 'common external tariff', but no duties are charged on trade within the region. The corollary is that such intra-common market exports are treated as domestic sales behind the common tariff protective wall, and hence, do not qualify as exports under any export promotion program, as they already receive the subsidization benefits of the common external tariff. This would imply that intra-regional exports would receive the same effective subsidy from tariff protection, as would production for the domestic market as given in expression (D) above.

This ideal situation, however, has not applied in the case of Kenya and other members of COMESA. Intra-regional tariffs have been systematically reduced during the 1990s, such that most trade between members of COMESA countries on goods originating from a member country by the late 1990s, only pays a duty rate of about 10 percent to 20 percent of the regular rate. While some attempt has been made to harmonize tariff schedules of member countries, these are still far from a common external tariff. In addition, trade between member countries is still generally treated as imports or exports for purposes of export promotion programs. This means that exports to other member countries may receive a *higher effective subsidy* if they are supported by an export platform than do sales to the domestic market. This arises because intra-regional exports are sold behind the wall of tariff protection, but get exemptions or drawbacks of duties on imported raw materials. If the removal of import duties from inputs is complete (τ_M and $\tau_K = \alpha$), the effective subsidy rate given by (D) rises to the import duty rate on the good exported within the region, that is, $s = \tau_Q$. This means that the export platform biases sales in favor of intra-regional exports over exports to external countries and could cause significant trade diversion within the region. If the exemption only applies to raw materials and not to capital goods, then the effective subsidy is somewhat reduced to: $s = \tau_Q - (\alpha_K + \alpha_t) \tau_K$. Exports from an EPZ can be an exception as the EPZ is typically regarded as being outside of the customs territory of the home country. EPZ exports therefore may not qualify as originating from the home country, and hence not qualify for preferential tariff treatment by the importing country.

It is difficult for any one member of a common market to withdraw unilaterally export promotion benefits for intra-regional exports in order to remove this trade diversion incentive. This normally has to be achieved by joint action. A common market usually operates with one customs code for all members – all use the same law, regulations, procedures and tariff schedule. Under this type of arrangement, the customs territory expands to include the territory of all member countries, and exports and imports are only recognized with countries external to the common market. COMESA, and more recently the East African Co-operation arrangements, has not yet reached the stage of defining a common external tariff or a common customs code, although work is proceeding in that direction.

Removing actual versus estimated import duty content in exports

Before discussing the actual export platforms provided in Kenya, it is useful to give some background on some of the choices in strategy for designing and administering mechanisms to remove the import duty content from exports. As noted above, where a domestic firm purchases tradable inputs from other domestic firms – rather than importing them directly, problems arise with identifying and removing the full import duty content in the inputs. Multiple stages of domestic production may be involved, which involve tradable inputs, but not direct imports. This makes the exemption or drawback of actual duties paid inadequate to bring input prices back to border prices. In addition, where a domestic firm both exports and sells into the domestic market, only removing the duty content in capital assets consumed in producing the exports, poses a challenge. In particular, a duty exemption on capital goods presupposes that the goods will be used to produce exports only. After the fact, this may not prove to be the case. While WTO/GATT rules in fact require only actual duties paid on inputs physically incorporated in the export to be exempted or drawn back, countries have resorted to estimated import duty contents on specified classes of exports, to compensate the exporter for the price-raising effects of import tariffs on inputs used directly or indirectly in producing the export. Detailed studies of tradable input contents of exports can be undertaken using input-output data and/ or industrial surveys of the production, costs and effective import tariffs. While in theory this approach can deal with the problems of indirect supply and partial use of capital assets in producing exports, in practice it is difficult to apply and has unintended outcomes.

Estimating the appropriate compensation rate on exports for implicit duties on input costs suffers from a number of practical problems. First, for any one class of exports, different producers vary the input mixes and have different levels of technical efficiency in using inputs, such as levels of wastage. Second, within any class of goods, there will be significant variety of products in terms of size, quality, materials employed, etc. These factors will result in a variation in the true compensation rates around the estimated rate such that both over- and under-compensation for the effects of tariffs on input prices will arise. Over-compensation is fiscally expensive and may generate countervailing action from importing countries. Under-compensation blunts the effectiveness of the program. A second problem with the approach of using estimated compensation rates by types of exports is that it requires a major up front and ongoing investment in measuring input usage requirements and effective tariff rates on all inputs for a huge number of export goods. The resource and information requirements to develop and maintain this information are considerable and costly. Without this effort, significant errors will grow over time in the compensation rates for different exports. In the extreme, the use of a single compensation rate for all manufactured exports, as used in Kenya for a number of years, avoids these administrative costs, but also risks both significant over- and under-compensation for import duty content in the inputs.

By contrast, duty exemption or paying back programs are generally based on self-assessment of the import duty content, which is then, policed by random verification exercises. This allows rapid program start up – no prior investment in industrial information on input cost content and effective tariffs are required, and much of the administrative burden is put on the program users. Only compensating actual duties paid, will not only tend to constrain the program fiscal cost, but will also tend to under compensate export producers, and seldom, if ever, over compensate them. Actual duty exemption or drawback also has difficulty in dealing with capital costs unless production is primarily for export. Exemption or drawback of duty on capital investments tends to be limited to companies primarily producing for export.

From the above, it is clear that exemption and drawback programs that focus on the actual duties paid by a direct exporter will not remove the entire import duty content from costs to the extent that tradable inputs are purchased from domestic manufacturers or to the extent that the prices of non-tradables also contain duty content. Extending the program to indirect exporters can reduce the effective duty content, but some residual effective duty is expected to remain so that effectively τ_M and τ_K are not reduced all the way to zero by the program.

Choice of export platform

While export platforms are generally designed to remove the negative protection expressed in (E), or provide the net gain given in (G), through import duty exemptions or drawbacks on raw materials, import duty exemptions on capital equipment, and through income tax incentives, it is noted above that participation in an export promotion program may result in increased real costs of inputs or added compliance costs. In addition, the removal of the import duty costs may only be partial, dampening the benefits. An exporter may therefore decide not to use an export platform. This should happen when an exporter finds that the pure profits, as given in (A), exceed the pure profits gained from using an export platform. If the pure profits are expressed as a share of the revenues at world prices, then *without* a platform, the pure profit share is:

$$\pi_1/(pQ) = (1 + \tau_Q) - [\alpha_L + \alpha_M(1 + \tau_M) + (\alpha_K + \alpha_t)(1 + k)] \tag{I}$$

while *with* a platform, the pure profit share is:

$$\pi_1'/(pQ) = (1 + \tau_Q) - [\alpha_L' + \alpha_M'(1 + \tau_M') + (\alpha_K' + \alpha_t')(1 + k) \tag{J}$$

Each component of the costs can differ when an export platform is used compared to the situation in which no platform is used. All the cost variables in (J), therefore, are marked with a prime.

An exporter will be expected to use an export platform if pure profits in (J) exceed those in (I). Taking the difference between (J) and (I) as A gives:

$$\begin{aligned} \Delta \;=\; & (\alpha_L - \alpha_L') + (\alpha_M - \alpha_M') + (\alpha_K - \alpha_K') + (\alpha_t - \alpha_t') - \beta + (\alpha_M \tau_M - \alpha_M' \tau_M') \\ & + (\alpha_K \tau_K - \alpha_K' \tau_K') + (\alpha_t \tau_K - \alpha_t' \tau_K') \end{aligned} \tag{K}$$

An exporter is expected to choose to use an export platform if Δ is positive. In the ideal case, where there are no added compliance costs or income tax effects, and where all the input duty costs are completely removed, (K) reduces to:

$$\Delta = \alpha_M \tau_M + (\alpha_K + \alpha_t)\tau_K \tag{L}$$

which clearly has a positive value as long as there are effective import duties on the inputs and, hence, exporters can be expected to use such an export platform. This, however, generally will not be the case. On the one hand, compliance costs can be reduced by lowering license fees, improving access to foreign exchange or serviced land, and increasing the speed and certainty of obtaining licenses or approvals for investment. On the other hand, costs can be increased by (1) restricting choices of location that affect costs of labor, utilities and transportation, rents, reporting and inspection requirements; and by bringing a business into the formal tax net, which may also affect tax compliance in related businesses, or restricting its flexibility in product and volume of production choices in response to market demand shifts that would lower its capacity utilization and raise its unit costs. These potentially negative aspects of export platforms, especially the less flexible export-dedicated platforms, are more likely to be outweighed when the duty reductions on capital equipment and raw materials are large and the shares of costs on imported equipment and raw materials are large. For example, footloose industries such as clothing, footwear and light assemblies, which import raw materials in order to make use of low cost (but productive) labor to make or assemble goods for export, typically have a high imported raw material share in costs and are expected to be attracted to export-dedicated platforms.

Structure of export platforms in Kenya

Export compensation

Kenya's Customs and Excise legislation has always had provision for drawing back the import duty content of manufactured exports. These provisions, however, were never effectively utilized, in part because of the demanding administrative requirements of setting up a duty drawback program. Instead, an alternative program providing for a flat rate compensation for selected manufactured exports was introduced under the Local Manufactures (Export Compensation) Act in 1974.

The main attraction of this program was its administrative simplicity. Any exporter of eligible goods could claim export compensation payment based on the customs value of the export at the applicable compensation rate, which was typically set in the 10 percent to 20 percent range. For a period, a higher compensation rate was paid for incremental exports to further encourage export growth. Payments for eligible types of manufactured exports were made against customs, shipping and banking documents showing that eligible goods had been exported and the foreign exchange earnings repatriated into Kenya. Eligible goods were generally manufactured goods expected to have a reasonably high domestic value added, but excluding all natural resources and agricultural produce.[2] Another attractive feature of an export compensation scheme was that it offset the import duty costs of both directly imported raw materials and indirectly imported inputs including capital equipment and other productive assets. To keep the program simple, one compensation rate was offered for all eligible export products.

This simplicity formed a major critique of the program and a decision to replace it with a duty exemption scheme was adopted as part of the trade reform program in the late 1980s, and it was finally phased out in September 1993, on several grounds. First, some types of exports were over-compensated, while others were significantly under-compensated, and the lowering of import duty rates particularly in the 1990s was resulting in a higher probability of over-compensation for a higher share of exports. Second, the scheme benefited a few large firms which, typically, accounted for less than 5 percent of total exports. In 1991 for instance, two firms accounted for over 50 percent of the compensation paid, five firms for over 60 percent, and ten firms for over 70 percent.[3] Third, the program was embroiled in a major export fraud in 1992–1993. Finally, its simple *ad valorem* payment structure, which did not take into account the direct relationship between compensation and the import duties actually paid on inputs physically incorporated in the exports, made it fall into the class of prohibited subsidies which could be countervailed by an importing country under WTO/GATT rules.

Manufacturing–under-bond

Manufacturing-under-bond (MUB) was established in 1988 under the structural adjustment policy regime. It provided for: (1) bonded factories that were allowed duty-free importation of plant equipment, spares, and raw materials for the manufacture of goods for export; (2) an additional investment incentive in the form of favorable income tax treatment of capital expenditures, and (3) following the introduction of a value added tax started in 1990, imports by MUBs and their domestic input purchases were zero rated.

MUB plant and equipment qualify for 100 percent write-off against taxable profit in the year they are put into use. Other enterprises in Kenya are offered tax breaks on investment on the so-called 'split system' where a proportion of investment, presently 60 percent for most plant and equipment, is expensed immediately and the remainder receives the regular depreciation allowance applicable for the particular type of asset. Initially, the special incentive for MUBs was limited to new factories, but this was later relaxed to allow bonded manufacturers the flexibility to locate in rented facilities and still get the 100 percent write off on machinery and equipment purchases. The tax break is not transferable, that is, an enterprise leaving the scheme or selling the machinery and equipment is liable for income tax on the value of the difference between the standard investment allowance and the preferential rate.

Domestic sales of outputs or raw material require approval of the Commissioner of Customs and are subject to payment of all duties and taxes applicable to similar imports. Control of MUBs requires Customs to physically verify inventories of the imported raw materials, the manufactured products, waste and scrap material – as opposed to 'off-site' accounting controls, which in turn requires the factories to meet physical specifications. There are no restrictions on location as Customs were generally able to provide officers to inspect the factory at desired locations. Even though sales into the domestic market are subject to the duties and taxes applicable to imports, they are discouraged given that duty-exempt importation of plant machinery, equipment, and spares, as well as preferential capital investment allowance confer advantage over regular domestic factories.[4]

Export processing zones

The EPZ scheme was established through the Export Processing Zones Act passed in 1990. It provided a generous incentive package, aimed towards attracting 'footloose' manufacturers and included a corporate tax holiday for the first ten years of operation, and a guarantee that the rate would not exceed 25 percent for the next ten years (the company tax rate was 42.5 percent in 1990); duty and VAT waiver on imports of plant equipment and raw materials – except for motor vehicles and vehicle parts, unless used exclusively in the zone; exemption from foreign exchange controls; and expedited licensing at reduced business license fees. EPZs are also exempt from rent and tenancy controls, but receive no waivers from labor legislation. The exemption from foreign exchange controls would have been a significant attraction to set up EPZ enterprises, especially to attract foreign direct investment, but this changed with the liberalization of the foreign exchange markets in 1993–1994. The other incentives have also been eroded over time. For example, the company tax rate has dropped through the 1990s, reaching 30 percent in 2000.

EPZs are gazetted as special purpose corporations that can only do business in a designated EPZ location, which may be a single factory or a unit in an EPZ industrial park, supervised by the EPZ Authority, which also licenses them. Although targeted primarily at new foreign direct investment, Kenyan companies are allowed to establish EPZ subsidiaries, but cannot do part of their business inside an EPZ and part outside. Specific provisions were also introduced into the Income Tax Act to prevent tax straddling between EPZ enterprises and related domestic companies through transfer pricing, such as a domestic company providing administrative services to a related EPZ company and charging the services against the taxable income of the domestic company, or shifting taxable income into the tax free EPZ company by under-invoicing for services provided to it.

For custom duty and VAT purposes, an EPZ is regarded as being outside the customs territory. Sales from Kenyan businesses into an EPZ are treated as exports, and sales from the EPZ to Kenyan businesses are treated as imports for duty and VAT purposes. There is no limit on sales into the domestic market, but such sales would be regarded as imports subject to regular duties and taxes on imports. The duty exemption on capital equipment and the income incentives, however, give the EPZ company an advantage over other domestic producers supplying the local market. To discourage abuse of the apparent unlimited access to domestic sales, a provision exists for an optional additional duty of 5 percent on domestic sales of a specified EPZ company. An EPZ being regarded as outside of the customs territory can result in importing countries not recognizing the exports as being of Kenyan origin for the purposes of trade preferences. Notably, EPZ exports do not qualify for preferential tariff rates under the rules of origin of the COMESA. COMESA tariff rates by the late 1990s were 80 percent to 90 percent below the rates levied on imports from outside COMESA countries.

Stacked up against these incentives is a range of potential additional costs that may discourage entry into an EPZ. First, the requirement of export dedication exposes the EPZ firm to the risk of excess capacity. Second, unless a firm incurs the bureaucratic costs of convincing the EPZ Authority to gazette its chosen location – which then restricts its future uses of the site as it is difficult to remove EPZ status once awarded, EPZ status restricts choice of locations, which can influence transportation costs, access to labor, rental cost of buildings, and cost of utilities. Third, involvement in an EPZ may expose the business activities of a firm both inside and outside the EPZ to greater scrutiny by tax officials and also to program compliance costs. Entry into an EPZ essentially puts a business in the formal sector, while some businesses such as light or 'sweat shop' manufacturing may be able to operate at lower costs in the informal sector.

Duty and VAT exemption scheme

This program was introduced in 1990 to provide export incentives to manufacturers primarily serving the domestic market. The program became fully operational by 1993. It offers duty and VAT exemptions to imported inputs physically incorporated in the exported product or consumed in the production of the export.[5] It excludes exemptions for plant equipment and machinery. The Export Promotion Programs Office (EPPO) in the Ministry of Finance, often referred to as the 'EPPO' program, administers the program.

Initially, any business with confirmed export orders or with a documented track record of exports could apply for duty free imports to meet these actual or expected export orders. Firms are required to provide input-output ratios to support their applications. They are required to reconcile the duty exempt imports with goods produced and exported – including sales to EPZ enterprises or MUB export businesses, after exportation or within 9 months of exemption approval, or otherwise re-export and apply for a rollover of the exemption, or pay the applicable taxes. Exemptions are granted against a performance bond (guarantee by a bank or insurance company) to the value of the duties exempted. The bond is cancelled upon verification of the reconciliation reports.

Over time, the program has been enhanced to improve its effectiveness in reducing negative protection of domestic manufacturers. To remove the bias against using domestic inputs, and also to improve backward linkages, indirect exporters can apply for duty exemptions on imports used to produce inputs for direct exporters. Such backward linkages can go back two stages of production. For example, a paperboard manufacturer will get import exemptions for imported inputs to make boards supplied to a packaging converter who then supplies packaging to a direct exporter. Exemptions for manufacturers of goods that can regularly be imported duty free – primarily pharmaceuticals, agricultural inputs, and books, as well as domestic suppliers of certain organizations with duty free import privileges – such as the armed forces, aid-funded projects, international airlines, etc., were consolidated into the program. In addition, since 1996, general provisions were added to the Income Tax Act that allow businesses undertaking large investment projects of over $5 million within two years (whether or not for export) to apply to have the import duties on capital equipment credited against future income taxes earned from the investment project.

Actual usage and performance of export platforms in Kenya

Manufacturing-under-bond

After a slow start, MUBs proved reasonably attractive in the early 1990s, particularly, as discussed below, during the period of a weak shilling and low real wage costs around 1993 and 1994. These conditions made contract manufacturing, particularly of clothing and household textiles, more competitive internationally. At its peak in 1993, there were over 70 bonded manufacturers, all but a handful of them garment manufacturers producing cotton garments for the US market. The program was set back by the reduction of Kenya's garment quota by the US trade authorities in 1994, and the subsequent appreciation of the exchange rate and wage rate. By 1997, all but 10 of the bonded manufacturers had closed down.

Export processing zones

EPZ infrastructure development has considerably outpaced EPZ enterprise investment. At the end of 1997, there were 11 gazetted industrial park EPZs and 5 single enterprise EPZs. There were 5 developed parks with a combined capacity of 70 go-downs, as compared to only 22 operational enterprises. (See Table 4.1). All but one of the parks are privately owned and developed. The Government-owned park, which is also the largest, was funded by the World Bank and is located on a 340–hectare site in Athi River, a small industrial town 25 kilometers outside of Nairobi, and is managed by the EPZ Authority. Presently, it has 12 built-up units (9 occupied) and vacant lots available for leasing to enterprises or other park developers. Space rental rates in the EPZ industrial parks in Nairobi range from US $2.80–$3.50 per square foot per year, as compared to US$ 2.00 for industrial space in the open market.

Table 4.1   Development and utilization of EPZ infrastructure, 1990–1998

EPZ Name	License Date	Location	Ownership	Capacity	Occupancy
Sameer Indust. Park	1990	Nairobi	Private	12 units	9
Athi River EPZ	1990	Athi River	Public	12 units; 62 vacant lots	9
E. A. Molasses EPZ Ltd.	1992	Nairobi	Private	N/A	2
Thomas de La Rue EPZ Ltd.	1992	Nairobi	Private	Single status	1
Birch Invest. EPZ Ltd.	1992	Mombasa	Private	Single status	1
Anicit EPZ Ltd.	1992	Nakuru	Private	Single status	NO
Transfleet EPZ Ltd.	1993	Mombasa	Private	15 units	0
Mugoya EPZ Ltd.	1993	Nairobi	Private	UD	–
Kigorani EPZ Ltd.	1993	Mombasa	Private	15 units	0
Kwa Jomvu EPZ Ltd.	1993	Mombasa	Private	NO	–
Real Indust. Park	1993	Nairobi	Private	NO	–
Bianca EPZ Ltd.	1994	Nairobi	Private	Single status	NO
Rafiki Indust. Park	1995	Nairobi	Private	7 units	3
Coast Indust. Park	1995	Mombasa	Private	9 units	0
Kipevu EPZ Ltd.	1996	Mombasa	Private	NO	–
Golden Sun EPZ Ltd.	1997	Malindi	Private	Single status	UD
Equitea EPZ Ltd.	1998	Kilifi	Private	Single status	UD

Source: Export Processing Zone Authority.
Notes: NO = Not operational; UD = under development.

Most of the EPZs (11 out of 16) were licensed by 1993, and all but one of those licensed after 1992 are either undeveloped or have no occupants. As pointed out above for MUBs, exchange rate and wage conditions were more favorable for exporting through 1993. In addition, a major attraction of EPZs prior to the foreign exchange liberalization during 1993–1994, was the allowance that EPZs operate freely in foreign exchange at a time when the latter commanded a market premium.

Unlike MUB enterprises, which have been almost exclusively, garment manufacturers, EPZ firms are engaged in a broad range of activities, although garment manufacture is still the dominant activity (8 out of 25 firms). Other activities include agro-processing, pharmaceuticals, paper and printing, computer assembly, software development, and automotive engineering. In addition, some potential garment manufacturers who had been licensed did not commence operations as a result of the quota restrictions placed on Kenya by the US trade authorities in 1994. In terms of origin of investment, 12 out of the 22 EPZ enterprises operating in 1997 were fully foreign owned, and another two with a nominal 1 percent domestic shareholding. There were only four 100 percent domestically owned enterprises. The UK is the dominant source of foreign investment into the EPZs, accounting for close to 60 percent of the total capital investment in EPZ enterprises. See Table 4.2.

Table 4.2   Ownership of EPZ enterprises, 1993–1998

Nationality of Investors	Share of Ownership				Equity Invest. US $, millions	% of Total EPZ Investment
	100%	*Majority*	*Minority*	*Equal*		
UK	4	2	1	0	53.1	68.4
Domestic	4	2	5	1	19.4	25.0
Other	6	3	1	1	5.1	6.6
Total					**77.6**	**100.0**

Source: Export Processing Zone Authority.

The contribution by EPZs to exports and employment remains far below initial expectations. (See Table 4.3). Exports reached US$ 23 million in 1997, accounting for 3.5 percent of total manufactured exports. Between 1993–1997, the average annual growth rate of EPZ exports was 25 percent, just marginally higher than that of all manufactured exports at 22 percent. Similarly in employment, EPZ firms employed 2,855 workers in 1997, accounting for barely over 1 percent of total manufacturing employment. Excluding 1994, when employment increased by 65 percent, EPZ employment growth, at 3 percent, was about half the total manufacturing employment growth rate. Domestic expenditures, including labor costs, on average account for 20 percent of turnover. Raw material imports averaged 64 percent of turnover over 1993–1997, but declined 49 percent in 1997 showing an increased domestic value contribution from EPZ enterprises. Domestic sales also dropped from 53 percent in 1993 to 25 percent in 1997 showing a greater dedication of EPZ activity to exports.

Table 4.3   Performance of EPZ enterprises, 1993–1998

	1993	**1994**	**1995**	**1996**	**1997**	**1998**
Investment (cumulative over years, US$, mill.)	44.5	52.1	87.9	96.4	101.0	N/A
Imports (machinery, US$, mill.)	22.5	2.4	2.4	1.8	0.1	N/A
Imports (raw materials, US$, mill.)	22.1	10.9	16.3	15.2	15.0	N/A
Exports (US$, mill.)	10.4	9.0	14.2	19.5	22.8	N/A
Domestic Sales (US$, mill.)	11.6	7.8	12.3	8.9	7.7	N/A
Domestic Purchases (US$, mill.)	4.9	3.4	4.2	5.3	6.5	N/A
Employment	1,594	2,632	2,718	2,950	2,855	3,645
No. of Enterprises	13	15	19	18	22	2

Source: Export Processing Zone Authority.

Factors cited for the poor investor response to EPZ incentives include ineligibility of EPZ firms for preferential treatment in the regional market, which is the main market for Kenyan manufactures. Under COMESA rules of origin, EPZ goods are treated as foreign goods. Infrastructure deficiencies, particularly transport infrastructure and unreliable power and water supply, are other factors cited for the poor investor response to EPZ incentives. Manufacturing firms responding to a 1997 survey reported estimated production losses due to frequent power and water outages at KSh 85 million (US $1.4 million) or 4.6 percent of turnover on average. The effects of other structural and macroeconomic environmental factors will be discussed below.

Duty and VAT exemption program (EPPO)

Companies utilizing the EPPO program accounted for 35 percent of total merchandise exports over the 1993–1998 period. Processed goods accounted for 53 percent of total exports over the period, which translates into the program being utilized for over two-thirds of eligible exports. Analysis of application and reconciliation administrative data against the actual export data from Customs suggests that direct exporters using the program utilized it for 60 percent to 70 percent of their exports on average – over 50 percent of the eligible processed and packaged exports, and over 75 percent of exports of manufactures.

Table 4.4, which shows the build up activity by the number of applications, indicates that the program reached a plateau in 1994. Direct export applications fluctuated within the 1,100 to 1,300 range thereafter. Activity declined in 1998 in line with the decline in exports in that year. In addition, after 1994, the average duty rate on many intermediate goods and other raw materials dropped from around 25 percent to rates of 15 percent or lower. This lowered the net gain from participating in the EPPO program, measured relative to the export values, from an average of 3 percent to 4 percent down to 2 percent to 3 percent. Hence, some firms could have dropped out if the other compliance costs of participating exceeded this lower duty gain.

Table 4.4 Application activity under EPPO, 1991–1998

Year	Direct Exporters	Indirect Exporters	Other Duty Exemptions	No. of Companies
1991	39	–	–	N/A
1991	113	–	–	N/A
1993	618	–	305	N/A
1994	1,165	15	779	191
1995	1,120	100	575	169
1996	1,113	191	100	206
1997	1,311	251	197	200
1998	1,186	198	107	168

Source: EPPO Database, Ministry of Finance.

Some 431 different direct exporters had used the program by 1998, as had 45 indirect exporters and 48 companies for the production of other duty exempt goods. (See Table 4.5).

Table 4.5   Companies using duty/VAT exemption facility, 1991–1998

Type of Use	Number of Companies
Exporters	476
Direct exporters	431
Indirect exporters	45
Duty free goods manufacturers	48
Pharmaceuticals	21
Agricultural chemicals	4
Agricultural equipment	8
Book publishers	5
Suppliers to aid-funded projects	5
Suppliers to armed forces	4
Suppliers to international airlines	1

Source: EPPO Database, Ministry of Finance.

Typically, on an annual basis, direct exporters have been getting about KSh 5 billion of duty exempt imports through EPPO to produce about KSh 28 billion in exports; indirect exporters have been importing about KSh 1.5 billion duty exempt leading to some KSh 5 billion in supplies to direct exporters; and essential goods suppliers have been getting KSh 0.5 billion in duty exempt imports to produce about KSh 3.7 billion in duty-free products. Total merchandise exports averaged about KSh 100 billion a year over 1993–1998. However, utilization of EPPO is highly concentrated amongst large exporters. The top 10 exporters using EPPO account for about 50 percent, and the top 20 for 60 percent to 70 percent of all the exports by direct exporters in the program. These top 20 exporters qualify for 40 percent to 50 percent of the duty-exempt imports and duty remissions under EPPO. (See Table 4.6). The direct exporters utilizing the program cover more or less the entire spectrum of Kenya's processed exports; for example, processed foodstuffs (canned fruits, vegetables and juices, vegetable oils, biscuits), horticultural products, beverages, cigarettes, footwear, clothing and textiles, metal and wood products, cleaning products, cement, salt, and soda ash. The major indirect exports supported by the program are packaging materials. During 1993–1998, however, over 50 percent of the exports by firms using EPPO were directed at COMESA countries. This means that the discussion of the future role of export platforms within a free trade area such as COMESA, which was broached above, has major significance for Kenyan regional customs and trade policy. A cancellation of the use of export platforms within COMESA or the East African Co-operation region would have significant impacts on exporters, import duty revenues and the volume of export business supported by EPPO.

Table 4.6   Utilization of EPPO scheme (percent share)

	1994	1995	1996	1997	1998
By Import Value (CIF)					
Top 10 firms	22	20	25	27	23
Top 20 firms	42	39	46	51	43
By Duty Remission Value					
Top 10 firms	26	27	31	27	34
Top 20 firms	41	49	52	51	51

Source: EPPO Database, Ministry of Finance.

Macroeconomic policy factors

Export trends

The dramatic change in exports that arose in 1993 shows up whether exports are measured as an export quantity index, a share of GDP, real US$ value, or in real Kenyan pounds (K£). Outside of the small coffee boom of 1986, exports showed only modest real growth through 1992. They recovered dramatically from 1993, peaked in 1996, and fell back substantially in 1997 and 1998. In evaluating the role of export platforms, it is necessary to review this recovery against changes in the macroeconomic policy environment. This is followed by a discussion of the evolution of composition and direction of exports over the period. The usage of export platforms is then revisited against this background and some conclusions drawn about their significance and future potential.

Trade liberalization

Trade liberalization started with a conversion of quantitative restrictions to tariff equivalents in 1987–1989, which initially raised the simple average tariff rate from 40 percent to 46 percent.[6] The government embarked on phased tariff reductions – particularly in the high-rate bands, and rationalization of the tariff bands in 1990. By 1997–1998, the simple average tariff rate was reduced to 16.2 percent, and the trade weighted tariff rate to 12.8 percent, down from 25.6 percent. The number of tariff bands – including duty free, were reduced from 15 in 1990–1991 to 4 in 1997–1998 and the top regular tariff rate from 100 percent to 25 percent over the same period. The duty rates on most capital equipment came down to 5 percent from the 15 percent to 25 percent range, and most raw materials and intermediate inputs to the 5 percent to 15 percent range, down from 25 percent or higher. However, the single most significant change in the trade policy regime came in May 1993 with the abolition of import licensing requirements, and more importantly, foreign exchange controls. Over 1993–1994, all current account and virtually all capital account restrictions were lifted. The impact was immediately evident in the trade flows; imports jumped by some 7 percent of GDP after averaging 24 percent from 1981 through 1992 to over 30 percent of GDP, and as already discussed above, exports surged by about 7 percent of GDP as well.

The trade liberalization process was interrupted by the onset of a stabilization crisis in 1997, largely brought about by the collapse of an IMF program, an election-spending-related budgetary crisis, and exchange rate instability accompanying the Asian crisis. Stability was restored by raising interest rates, which in turn attracted short-term capital inflows that led to a substantial appreciation of the Kenya shilling throughout 1997 and 1998. A range of suspended duties was imposed starting in mid-1997, raising the simple average tariff to 17.8 percent and the trade weighted average to 14 percent by mid-1999. Interest rates finally moderated in early 1999 leading to a sharp 12 percent real decline in the strength of the Kenya shilling, but the temporary protection remained in place. And, as tariff rates have declined, particularly from 1994–1995 onwards, the net subsidy provided by export platforms that is tax benefit less administrative compliance and other costs of using an export platform, have declined.

Real exchange rate

The real (inflation adjusted) exchange rate is a critical variable in international trade. This is clearly borne out by Kenya's recent experience. After strengthening in 1986 through 1998 in response to a minor coffee boom, crawling peg adjustments to the shilling gradually depreciated its real value through to the early 1990s as part of the export promotion strategy. While there was some growth in exports through 1992, it was the liberalization of the foreign exchange market starting in 1993 that boosted trade significantly. In addition, a monetary overhang associated with election spending in the second half of 1992 contributed to the sharp depreciation of the shilling once the foreign exchange market was liberalized. This trend was reversed by a tight monetary stance adopted thereafter to bring inflation under control causing the shilling to appreciate throughout 1995. Suspension of an IMF program in mid-1997 resulted in a sharp rise in interest rates. In addition, the next electoral cycle in late 1997 triggered another expenditure boom followed by a tight monetary stance and a high interest rate regime that strengthened the real exchange rate beyond its 1986–1988 levels. The loss of competitiveness due to this real exchange rate appreciation, alongside sharp devaluations in Asia, South America and Southern Africa, is evidenced by the worsening export performance after 1996.

Labor costs and productivity

Data on employment and wages by export facility are not available, but given the dominance of the duty exemption program over the dedicated facilities (MUB and EPZ), the latter are unlikely to have a significant impact on the labor market, hence wage and productivity for the formal manufacturing sector are analyzed as a proxy for export platform conditions. Table 4.7 shows the employment, productivity and wage rate data for the manufacturing sector for 1991–1998. Employment and wage rate data for all sectors are also given to show that the manufacturing sector experience was similar to the overall experience over the 1990s. That said, a large proportion of Kenya's urban labor force is engaged in informal "sweat shop type" enterprises – the so called 'jua kali' sector, where earnings are considerably lower than formal sector wages, and lower still in the rural areas, hence these data present only a partial picture of the labor market. Even within the formal sector, there are large wage differentials between unionizable workers – those on 'permanent' employment, and more temporary or contract employees. Typically, the former earn twice as much as the latter for comparable work.

In aggregate, effects of inflation and exchange rate volatility have dominated real wage movements in the 1990s, while output movements reflect capacity utilization driven by domestic market conditions. In other words, there is no evidence of systematic export-led productivity growth. While real wage rates were falling through 1993, the exchange rate was also weakening resulting in declining US$ costs of labor. These made for increasingly attractive conditions for exports. From 1994 onwards, however, the real shilling wage rate grew strongly, rising by 74 percent over 1994–1998. The combination of increasing real wage rates and stable nominal shilling – it depreciated nominally between 1994–1998 by less than 7 percent, resulted in the nominal US$ terms, while the real exchange rate appreciated and labor productivity remained more or less stagnant. In 1997 and 1998, non-fuel commodity prices in international trade dropped further by 3.3 percent and 14.8 percent. Over 1994–1998, these world prices had dropped by 12 percent. These conditions can be interpreted in terms of the final term of equation (H) above, which gives the cost of non-tradables (essentially labor) in terms of world prices, namely $(w/E)L/Q)/p^w$. The real wage rate (w) in shillings increased while the exchange rate (E) strengthened giving a major increase in the US$ cost of labor (w/E). Little or no improvement is noted in labor productivity (Q/L) and real international prices (p^w) fell in 1997 and 1998 with the Asian crisis. Overall, the cost of labor in Kenyan manufacturing increased by 118 percent in terms of international trade prices from 1994~1998. This combination of adverse conditions clearly contributed to the decline in exports that began in 1997 and continued in 1998. It is also important to note that these conditions are particularly deleterious for labor-intensive exports.

Regional market developments

Kenya, Uganda and Tanzania established a common market, the East African Community, in 1966, shortly after they gained independence, but ideological tension – after Tanzania adopted a socialist manifesto in 1969, and political instability in Uganda, undermined the integration effort and the Community was officially dissolved in 1977. The decline of Kenya's export performance from the mid-1970s to the mid-1980s is attributable, to a large degree, to the collapse of the Community, and the subsequent deterioration of the Ugandan and Tanzanian economies, hitherto the principal markets for Kenya's manufactures. By the late 1980s, the Ugandan and Tanzanian economies were on the road to recovery, and by 1993 formal arrangements to re-establish the East Africa common market were underway. At the same time, internal tariffs were lowered as part of an integration initiative that aimed for zero internal tariffs by mid-2000. In effect, the 1990s have offered Kenya increasingly attractive regional export opportunities as the Tanzanian and especially, the Ugandan economies grew strongly, while Kenya still had an under-utilized manufacturing capacity.

Table 4.7   Labor productivity and wage costs in Kenya manufacturing, 1991–1998

Manufacturing sector								
	1991	*1992*	*1993*	*1994*	*1995*	*1996*	*1997*	*1998*
Employment growth (%)	0.6	0.7	1.7	2.0	3.7	2.8	1.9	1.1
Output growth (quantity index) (%)	2.8	1.3	1.8	1.9	3.8	3.2	1.9	1.4
Implicit labor productivity growth (%)	2.2	0.5	0.1	-0.1	0.2	0.4	0	0.3
Wage cost/ gross output (%)	4.1	3.5	3.1	3.0	3.3	3.3	3.5	3.7
Wage cost / Value added (%)	35.7	32.1	32.2	32.3	35.4	37.5	40.5	39.4
Real wage growth (%)	–9.4	–12.8	–22.3	–8.7	–24.7	11.7	8.9	14.5
Average real wage rate (1986 KSh p/m)	8,809	7,680	5,670	5,450	6,795	7,589	8,260	9,457
Average nominal wage (US$ p/m)	120	114	70	87	121	133	156	186
Average real wage rate (1996 US$ p/m)	139	129	76	93	125	133	153	178
Economy aggregates								
Employment growth (%)	2.3	1.4	0.9	2.0	3.4	4.0	1.8	1.1
Real wage growth (%)	–8.3	–10.9	22.1	-8.3	19.8	11.7	8.5	17.3

Source: *Economic Survey*, (various years).

Infrastructure and other economic environmental conditions

Inadequate economic infrastructure (including roads, railways, ports, telecommunication services, electricity and water), has become a persistent, and increasingly binding constraint in Kenya. Relations between the Kenya government and aid agencies have soured over the last decade and as a result, there has been inadequate new public investment in economic infrastructure. Overall, public sector gross fixed capital formation dropped from 10 percent in 1990 to 6.5 percent of GDP in 1998. Manufacturers who responded to a recent survey reported average losses close to US$ 2 million per year associated with electricity and water shortages.[7] Additionally, general law enforcement, hence physical security of people and property, and judicial support for commercial contracts, have worsened over time. All these factors tend to raise the costs of doing business in Kenya, which adversely affect export competitivenes.[8]

Foreign direct investment

Foreign direct investment (FDI) is of particular interest for export platforms, particularly the export-dedicated platforms such as MUB and EPZs, as they usually target FDI, especially the so-called 'footloose' industries. Despite a strong international presence in virtually all the sectors of the Kenyan economy, there is remarkably little information on FDI activity in Kenya. Systematic monitoring of FDI began in 1988, when the Government established the Investment Promotion Center (IPC) to promote inward investment. By the end of 1997, the IPC had approved 477 FDI projects worth US$ 600 million in capital investment. Not all FDI investment goes through the IPC, however, and the IPC also does not monitor the investors it facilitates beyond the approval stage. The IPC estimates that it facilitates about one half of new FDI, and only a third or so of the projects it approves translate into actual investments. These estimates suggest cumulative inward FDI over this period (1989–1997) at about US$ 400 million or US$ 30 million per year on average, or just under 4 percent of annual gross private investment.[9] This is consistent with the very low investment activity in EPZs and MUB export platforms discussed above.

The origin of FDI inflows to Kenya is fairly diversified, but traditionally the UK has been the single most significant origin of FDI. UK firms accounted for one out of five of new foreign investment projects facilitated by the IPC in the 1989–1997 period, and 23 percent in value terms. South African trade and investment, however, has grown dramatically since the lifting of economic sanctions in 1991, and current trends indicate that it could soon become the single largest origin of FDI. South Africa has already displaced the UK as the principal origin of imports. South

African firms, however, which have invested in Kenya, tend to be targeting the domestic market as opposed to exporting out of Kenya.

Composition and direction of exports from Kenya

As discussed earlier, export platforms were put in place in Kenya in the late 1980s (MUB) and early 1990s (EPZs and duty/VAT exemption program) but it was only after the lifting of trade licensing and more importantly, foreign exchange controls in 1993–1994, that exports grew significantly. As the analysis of the direction and composition of exports that follows will show, this growth has been driven primarily by regional market development. In other words, export platforms have not enabled Kenya to gain entry into the economies of the industrialized countries to sell its labor-intensive manufactures. Thus, today, the Kenya economy is still unable to effectively penetrate such economies as those of the EU countries, the US and Canada, to profitably market its labor-intensive manufactured goods.

Table 4.8 shows that exports in US$ terms grew in 1993–1995 by 35 percent over their 1990–1992 level, and in 1996–1998 by 67 percent over their 1990–1992 level. This masks vast differences in the pattern of export growth. Exports to COMESA countries grew by 179 percent by 1993–1995 and 290 percent by 1996–1998 compared to the base period. This raised the COMESA share of exports from 14.6 percent to 34 percent. Non-COMESA exports only grew by 10 percent by 1993–1995 and 29 percent by 1996–1998. Exports to Uganda and Tanzania showed the highest growth, reaching 320 percent and 549 percent respectively, by 1996–1998 compared to the base period. This sharp increase raised their share of Kenyan exports from 9 percent to 27 percent. Hence, there was a major shift in the direction of trade following trade liberalization.

Overall, trade liberalization and export platforms have not translated to significant trade diversification. As Table 4.9 shows, the share of primary products has declined only marginally, from 50 percent to 47 percent. Tea and coffee, Kenya's main primary exports, maintained their share during this period of rapid export growth. They accounted for 45 percent and 74 percent of total and primary exports respectively in 1990 and 41 percent and 81 percent of the same in 1998. What has changed significantly, however, is the destination of processed exports. The share of processed exports to non-COMESA regions declined by 12 percentage points over the decade, from 43 percent to 31 percent, on account of a decline in absolute value of processed exports alongside an increase in the value of primary exports. The composition of exports to the COMESA region has remained more or less stable. In effect, the growth of regional exports reflects both trade creation and diversion, as is evident from the decomposition of sources of export growth in Table 4.9.

Table 4.8   Destination of Kenya's exports, 1990–1998

Destination	1990–1992	1993–1995	1996–1998
Uganda			
Value, annual average (US$m)	69	199	290
Share (%)	5.9	12.6	14.9
Growth (%)		188	320
Tanzania			
Value, annual average (US$m)	36	157	235
Share (%)	3.1	10	12
Growth (%)		335	549
Other COMESA			
Value, annual average (US$m)	65	120	139
Share (%)	5.6	7.6	7.1
Growth (%)		84	113
All COMESA			
Value, annual average (US$m)	170	476	664
Share (%)	14.6	30.2	34
Growth (%)		179	290
Non COMESA			
Value, annual average (US$m)	995	1,098	1,268
Share (%)	85.4	69.8	66
Growth (%)		10	29
Total			
Value, annual average (US$m)	1,165	1,574	1,950
Share (%)	100	100	100
Growth (%)		35	67

Source: Government of Kenya, Economic Survey, Government Printer: Nairobi, Kenya, various issues.

Processed and manufactured exports basically represent the range of goods produced for the Kenyan market. These products include cigarettes, beer, cement, paper products, refined petroleum products, corrugated iron sheeting and other rolled metal products, pharmaceuticals, vegetable oil and processed fruit and vegetable products, flour, wheat and maize, processed sugar and other confectionery products, and processed leather. Hence, exports into the region have been an extension and expansion of products, for the Kenyan market. Many are capital intensive – cement, oil and paper products, or processed agricultural products. A very small share has been in the more common labor-intensive products that are normally taken to characterize manufactures of developing countries such as Indonesia or the Philippines – footwear, clothing and assembled electronic and other household goods.

Textiles and clothing exports increased, but only from 1.3 percent of exports in 1990–1992 to 4.9 percent in 1993–1995, and then fell back to 2.1 percent again in 1996–1998. As shown earlier, the textile and clothing exports received a boost through 1993 when the Kenya shilling and wage rate conditions were the most favorable to exports and the foreign exchange markets were being decontrolled. Subsequently, however, the Kenya shilling strengthen again in real terms and labor costs in US$ terms rose sharply. These trends reversed the competitiveness of Kenyan exports dramatically. Over 1996 through 1998, Kenyan exports declined by 5.8 percent in US$ terms. When this is decomposed, exports to COMESA countries dropped by 9.3 percent, while those to non-COMESA countries dropped by only 3.7 percent. Exports of primary goods rose by 1.2 percent, while exports of processed and manufactured goods fell by 11.9 percent. Clearly, the macroeconomic conditions in 1997 and 1998 made Kenya manufactured goods less competitive in the region, which would have dampened any new interest in using export platforms in the country.

Table 4.10 shows the distribution of exports over 1993–1998 across export platforms in aggregate and by SITC classification. The direction and patterns of Kenya exports is consistent with the overall utilization of the various export platforms in Kenya. The EPPO program accounted for 35 percent of total Kenyan exports between 1993 and 1998 as compared to a share of less than 2 percent MUB and EPZ. The predominance of the EPPO duty/VAT remission facility reflects the fact that Kenya has not attracted much new investment over the last decade and, in particular, little investment (domestic or foreign) in the traditional 'footloose' labor-intensive industries primarily to supply external markets. The program is a flexible and is best suited to export business that is an extension or expansion of the supply for the domestic market, while the MUB and EPZ programs are targeted at manufacturing dedicated to exports. The main source of processed/manufactured export growth has been from utilizing exports. The main source of processed/manufactured export growth has been from utilizing existing capacity to exploit the regional market, which (1) consumes similar goods; and (2) provides preferential access under COMESA.

Table 4.9   Composition and destination of Kenya's exports, 1990–1998

Destination/ Composition	1990–1992	1993–1995	1996–1998
COMESA, value (US$m per annum)			
Primary	9	17	30
Processed/ Manufactured	161	459	634
All exports	170	476	664
COMESA, composition (%)			
Primary	5.5	3.6	4.5
Processed/ Manufactured	94.5	96.4	95.5
All exports	100	100	100
COMESA, growth contribution (%)			
Primary		4.6	6
Processed/ Manufactured		122.3	106.1
All exports		74.7	62.9
Non COMESA, value (US$m per annum)			
Primary	571	728	889
Processed/ Manufactured	424	370	397
All exports	995	1098	1286
Non COMESA, composition (%)			
Primary	57.4	66.3	69.1
Processed/ Manufactured	42.6	33.7	30.9
All exports	100	100	100
Non COMESA, growth contribution (%)			
Primary		95.4	94
Processed/ Manufactured		-22.3	-6.1
All exports		25.3	37.1
TOTAL, value (US$m per annum)			
Primary	580	745	919
Processed/ Manufactured	585	829	1031
All exports	1165	1574	1950
TOTAL, composition (%)			
Primary	49.8	47.4	47.1
Processed/ Manufactured	50.2	52.6	52.9
All exports	100	100	100
TOTAL, growth contribution (%)			
Primary		40.4	43.2
Processed/ Manufactured		59.6	56.8
All exports		100	100

Source: Government of Kenya, Economic Survey, (various issues).

Table 4.10 Export composition by export platforms, 1993–1998

SITC Classification	Share of exports by export platforms (%)				Share of Total Exports
	EPPO	*MUB*	*EPZ*	*No. of platforms*	
0. Food & live animals	22.73	0.64	0.01	76.63	51.79
1. Beverages & tobacco	70.64	0.00	0.00	29.36	2.51
2. Crude materials, inedible	30.49	0.63	0	68.87	9.43
3. Mineral fuels	30.22	0.04	0.00	69.74	7.38
4. Animal vegetables & fats	59.87	0.01	0	40.13	1.73
5. Chemicals	40.83	0.47	0.13	58.57	6.31
6. Manufactured goods	68.66	4.14	0.11	27.1	14.18
7. Machinery & transport equip.	37.07	0.25	0.1	62.66	0.9
8. Misc. manufactures	51.33	2.56	0.01	46.1	5.4
9. Goods n.e.s	0.3	0	0.01	99.7	0.34
* SITC not found	16.13	0.13	0.13	83.62	0.04
TOTAL	**35.11**	**1.15**	**0.03**	**63.72**	**100.00**

Source: Customs Database, Ministry of Finance.

The main conclusion to be drawn from this analysis is that export platforms that are primarily designed for supporting dedicated export manufacturing (EPZ and MUBs) are much less attractive than more flexible structures such as the EPPO duty exemption program that can support regional trade in the same goods that are produced for the domestic market. The duty exemption program has been extensively used by the major local manufacturing and processing companies (beer, cigarettes, cement, paper, corrugated iron sheeting, vegetable cooking oils, soaps, etc). This contrasts dramatically with the high utilization of EPZs in a country like the Philippines, which specializes in the production of electronic goods for export to the world at large.

Conclusions

Kenya's export platforms have not generated the anticipated critical mass of 'footloose' labor-intensive export processing, despite the the fact that the country has a relatively large skilled and semi-skilled industrial labor force that could be readily engaged to produce labor-intensive manufactures, notably garments and footwear, for the world market. First, the scope for building on the existing capacity to produce up-market consumer goods is limited by the low–income and small (by world standards) regional market (except perhaps for footwear and clothing. The situation is the same in most, if not all, sub-Sahara African countries.

Second, attracting significant export dedicated investment requires that the domestic investment environment be extremely attractive; have low cost and high productivity labor, dependable and cost effective transport, reliable and cost-effective utilities and other infrastructure services, and comparatively low business risk. On a wide range of these competitive factors, many African economies are not sufficiently attractive. Evidently, tax incentive-based export platforms have not sufficiently overcome these constraints in Kenya. Given the small size of the local market, African countries will only attract export-dedicated investment by offering a cost structure well below alternative locations. In light of this outlook, the dedicated platforms, the EPZ program in particular, are unlikely to make a significant impact. The excess capacity in Kenya's public EPZ should be privatized to save costs and parts of it de-registered and established as regular industrial parks. Even better would be to freeze approvals and phase out the existing users over time, while focusing on developing more flexible platforms and generalizing investment incentives.

Arguably, the more flexible EPPO duty/VAT remission program has contributed to the remarkable growth of manufactured exports to the regional market. It is noted, however that the East African Co-operation and COMESA trading partners have committed to phase out export incentives from the program substantially. The attraction of the program will continue to diminish as further tariff reductions are implemented. However, given their flexibility, such programs will continue to have a role in (1) supporting direct and indirect exports outside the region; and (2) removing negative protection from the duty free or exempt goods produced for the local market. This flexibility arises from its ability to deal with businesses producing for both local and foreign markets simultaneously, from its lack of special income tax or other capital investment incentives, and because it is accessible to producers outside the strict limits of the manufacturing sector, such as mining and agriculture, which are typically excluded from export-dedicated platforms. In the Kenyan case, packaging is a critical input in fresh horticultural produce exports, and the duty/VAT remission program has played an important role in this leading export sector for both direct imports and locally produced packaging material.

The successful stint of the MUB platforms suggests that there is scope for expansion of clothing and possibly footwear production for the international market, but only if market prices, productivity and other conditions are right. More careful consideration will also be needed in the design of export platforms to ensure that they reduce restrictions on accessing the informal sector labor market such as through contracting out work. The tendency to use physical customs rather than accounting controls, as have characterized MUBs and EPZs to date, reduces the flexibility of exploiting the large informal sector labor market and achieving international cost-competitiveness in labor market laws and institutions is also needed to explain the growing gap between formal and informal sector labor market and achieving international cost-competitiveness in labor-intensive manufactures. Given that it is the formal sector companies that access export platforms, this wage gap trend does not augur well for export platforms becoming the springboard for job creation in labor-intensive manufactures in the medium term.

To get macroeconomic conditions right will require a shift away from the high interest rates that have persisted since 1993. Over 1994–1998, inflation-adjusted lending rates by commercial banks have generally been in the range of 15 percent to 30 percent. This will require a shift in government fiscal policy to budget surpluses to lower the current heavy domestic debt load. Lower interest rates will encourage real private investment, discourage speculative foreign capital inflows, and allow a more competitive exchange rate. If the right macroeconomic environment (lower real interest rates, weaker exchange rate, and lower wages in US dollar terms) is combined with moves to increase the flexibility of export platforms and the labor markets, and efforts to strengthen economic infrastructure, then Kenya's export prospects in labor-intensive manufacture could brighten considerably.

Acknowledgments

This chapter has benefited from comments and assistance provided by N. Kirira, E. M. Githae, and E. S. Maturu, all of the Fiscal and Monetary Affairs Department of the Ministry of Finance and by Professor T. C. I Ryan. George Omolo provided invaluable database manipulation and analysis assistance. All errors and views remain the responsibility of the authors.

Notes

1. It is assumed here that all sales taxes or VATs on consumption are neutral with respect to net rents. This is achieved variously under different consumption tax structures. Under an exemption or ring- method general sales tax, it is assumed that capital equipment, raw

material and taxable services are exempt inputs into the production of taxable goods (including exports.) Similarly, under credit-method consumption VAT, it is assumed that all input VATs are deductible against output VAT, or are otherwise creditable and refundable if the input VAT exceeds the output VAT. In some export promotion programs, certain exporters may be able to purchase inputs zero-rated to avoid financing the input VAT while waiting for the refund or credit payment.

2. Eligibility of manufactured goods for being scheduled for export compensation was based on the following criteria: (i) 30 percent domestic value added; (ii) imported inputs used should be liable for at least 20 percent duty; (i) the goods should not be subject to royalties, export taxes, international quotas or other forms of restrictions, and; (iv) goods should not be raw (unprocessed) materials or intermediate inputs which are high priority inputs in short supply locally or inputs on which value added can be substantially enhanced by further local processing.

3. Bellhouse Mwangi Ernst &Young, *Export Compensation and Import Duty Remission Study*, 1988, a study for the Ministry of Finance, Government of Kenya.

4. Two other cases of manufacturing under bond are allowed under the Customs legislation in Kenya. One is the refining of crude oil and the other is the assembly of motor vehicles from kits. Where refined oil products or assembled vehicles are exported, these facilities effectively operate as MUBs. All sales into the domestic market are treated as dutiable imports.

5. Consumables include items such as testing chemicals and cleaning materials, but exclude lubricants and fuels, except for coal, coke and residual fuel oils.

6. Average of all ad valorem tariffs in customs tariff schedule. Tariffs are weighed by the number of tariff items recognized in the tariff schedule.

7. Hopcraft, P. (1998), *Comparative Advantage, Competitiveness and Supply Capacity in Kenya's Manufacturing Sector*, Draft Report for the Export Promotion Council: Nairobi, Kenya, September.

8. Surveys, such as *The African Competitiveness Report 1998*, issued by the World Economic Forum (Geneva), in 1998, also show the inadequacy of economic infrastructure in Kenya, lowering its international competitiveness.

9. World Bank data on Foreign Direct Investment in Kenya indicates an annual average investment of $34 million in the 1980s and $19 million over 1990–1996.

5

Trade Liberalization and Economic Growth in Kenya

GRAHAM GLENDAY AND T. C. I. RYAN

Introduction

Trade liberalization and openness are advocated as a key prescription to attain high economic growth (see, e.g., Sachs and Warner, 1997; WEF, 1998). The opening up of trade in the developed world has been ongoing since the 1950s under the General Agreement on Tariffs and Trade (GATT)/World Trade Organization (WTO) arrangements. By contrast, in developing countries, particularly those in Africa, this process of opening up economies came later, starting in the 1980s, often under the auspices of the International Monetary Fund (IMF) and World Bank imposed structural adjustment programs, but with effective implementation of policies mainly only in the 1990s. This chapter looks at the case of Kenya to determine whether changes in trade policy and exchange rate regime have made any significant impact on the country's macroeconomic performance, and hence, economic growth.

Trade liberalization, which refers to the removal of tariff and non-tariff barriers in international trade transactions, is one component of an open economy. It seeks not only expanded trade, but the process of adjusting internal prices to world prices through international competition to get the right internal signals for resource allocation. Expanded trade enhances the access to and adoption of new technology, particularly through technology embodied in imported capital equipment and the transfer that accompanies foreign direct investment. For trade to function efficiently and internal prices to adjust, also requires liberalization of domestic prices in the goods and services markets, as well as interest rates and exchange rates in the capital and foreign exchange markets.

Another perspective on the same process is the switch from an import-substitution to an export-oriented growth strategy. Export expansion typically means expanded exports of manufactured and processed goods. Success in the export of manufactures is highly dependent on access to competitively priced capital equipment, raw materials and other industrial intermediate inputs. Accordingly, liberalization of import markets is often linked to successful exploitation of export markets.

Since independence, the Government of Kenya (GoK) has protected and controlled the country's markets, intervening on a regular basis in private exchange in an effort to meet certain societal goals. Such government control of economic activities peaked in the early 1980s and has declined since then. In the process, the country lost most of its regional markets during the 1970s. By the early-to-mid-1980s, the Kenya economy was virtually closed to outside contact. The country, however began opening up its economy again through trade liberalization and price decontrols starting in 1987, with liberalization reaching a peak in 1993–1994. These changes in the policy regime had significant impact on Kenya's international trade. The questions to ask here are: Did the changes taken by the GoK in its policy regime affect economic growth? If yes, how?

This chapter lays out in some detail the changes that have taken place in the market policy regime in Kenya since independence, and explores which of the policy levers were critical to changing the Kenyan international trade experience. It then attempts to identify any significant relationship between these changes in trade patterns and economic growth through exploring a broad range of factors that affect growth and investment. Based on this analysis, conclusions can be reached about the relative importance of trade and exchange rate policies relative to other elements of the overall policy environment on actual macroeconomic performance in Kenya and prospects for economic growth in the years to come.

Overview of economic growth and trade in Kenya[1]

Real economic growth – measured in terms of real gross domestic product at factor cost,[2] has been through significant swings since 1965, but maintained a steady downward trend. The average growth rate in the 1960s was 6.3 percent, declining to 5.3 percent in the 1970s, further to 4.3 percent in the 1980s, and to only 2.6 percent in 1998. There is therefore some urgency to identify the factors that can help revive and sustain growth. For example, can we ascertain how important an open trade policy is to growth and economic recovery? To do this, we need a basic understanding of the actual changes in trade and trade policy in order to relate these to the growth process.

At the outset, therefore, it is useful to have a clear picture of the overall trade experience before exploring the details of trade policy developments.

Imports of goods through the 1960s and 1970s remain fairly robust, fluctuating between 25 percent and 30 percent of GDP. Then, in the early 1980s, they drop sharply to a lower plateau in the 22 percent to 25 percent range, and remain in that range through 1992. From 1993 onwards, imports increase sharply back to the higher plateau again, around 30 percent of GDP (see, e.g., Table 5.1).

The behavior of exports is somewhat different. Exports of goods as a share of GDP show a continuous downward trend from around 20 percent down to 14 percent. This figure had fallen to around 12 percent of GDP by the latter half of the 1980s, with the exception of the major coffee boom in 1976–1977 and the minor one in 1986. This steady downward trend is more evident when coffee and tea exports are excluded from the export values. Exports, like imports, also show a marked increase in 1993, when they rise sharply again to reach a higher plateau around 20 percent of GDP (see, e.g., Table 5.1).

Tourism earnings rose sharply in the late 1980s and helped sustain imports when exported goods were on the decline. Service exports in 1993 were at about double their average value through 1980–1987. Thereafter, they underwent a sharp decline back to the earlier levels. On the other hand, service imports increased steadily through the 1990s, reducing the net contribution of services to balancing the current account. This increase reflects growing interest payments on the nation's foreign debt.

Exports, in terms of both a quantity index and value in real US dollars, grew from 1965 through to the mid-1970s and then flattened out with an extended no-growth period through 1992. Thereafter, they grow rapidly till 1996 after which a modest decline set in. Slow and no real growth in exports is consistent with a slow and then more rapid decline in exports as a share of GDP. Unless exports grow as fast as GDP, then the ratio of exports relative to GDP will decline. The post-1992 rapid growth is consistent with the rising share of exports with respect to GDP during that period (see, for example, Table 5.2).

Kenyan imports, in terms of a quantity index and value in real US dollars, grew relatively well through the 1980s, but with some large swings. This is consistent with the high, but fluctuating imports-to-GDP ratio in this period. In the early 1980s, imports declined rapidly and essentially stayed in a trough through 1993 when they again grew rapidly. It is also important to notice that during the early 1970s, quantities of trade grew faster than the dollar value of trade, reflecting the fixed exchange rate regime of the times.

Economic policy regimes

The broad analysis of the trends in trade presented above suggests possible major shifts in economic policy. To date, there have been extensive studies of the Kenya liberalization process at both the descriptive and analytic levels. The two most analytic studies attempting to identify the liberalization episodes are Reinikka (1994)[3] and Mwega (1999).[4] These studies more or less concur that the dates of the 'liberalization episodes' were 1973–1974, 1976–1977, 1980–1981, 1983, 1985, 1988–1989, and 1993–1994. In the present study, however, major shifts in trade and exchange rate policy, which had persistent impacts on trade and economic performance, are sought. To do this, economic policy from independence onwards is examined in terms of legislative and institutional changes along five policy dimensions, namely, market, monetary, price, interest rate, and trade policies. This analysis identifies four major policy regime periods: 1962–1971, 1972–1980, 1981–1992, and 1993–2000. In the following subsections, these four periods are described with respect to the five policy dimensions so as to identify the key policy characteristics affecting exchange rate and trade policy in Kenya, as well as outcomes in each of the four policy regime periods. Key policy shifts are identified. In the next section, these policy shifts are related to trade performance in these periods.

First policy regime period: 1962–1971

Market regime: The period spans the collapse of the East African Common Services Organization – with the introduction of the first inter-territorial trade restrictions – and its replacement by the East African Community (EAC). Kenya was a member of the Sterling Area and, following independence and the change from colonial status, the pattern of trade changed, particularly towards the European Economic Community (EEC), as Britain no longer enjoyed preferential trade in the Kenyan market. The critical policy document, which oriented Kenya towards a mixed economy with considerable market emphasis, was presented as *Sessional Paper No. 10 of 1965: African Socialism and Its Application to Planning in Kenya*. In the private sector, the advent of work permits and trade licenses, as well as fears of civil disturbances as the country gained independence, caused an exodus of capital and of many skilled personnel of Asian and European origin.

Monetary regime: The period spans the country's movement from the East African Currency Board to the creation of the Central Bank of Kenya and the shift from a Sterling-based currency to one which was linked to the US dollar. The Exchange Control Act of 1967 replaced the Colonial Ordinance. The turbulence of the worldwide financial crisis and the Smithsonian agreement closed the period. The rate of exchange was fixed throughout the period and linked to Sterling pound or the US dollar. Kenya's relation with Uganda and Tanzania went through minor turbulence as each country introduced its own central bank.

Price regime: Inflation was below 7.5 percent throughout the period and averaged about 2.5 percent. Specific price controls on 91 items were carried forward from the colonial era and the period closed with a new Minister for Finance introducing a General Price Controls Order, controlling virtually all retail and wholesale prices, including prices of many services.

Interest rate: Treasury bills were first introduced in early 1969, but were barely marketed during 1970. Treasury bill yields gave a negative real return even though they rose sharply in December 1971.

Trade regime: The schedules of Imports, Exports and Essential Goods Act of 1962 were amended to enhance the Act's ability to protect domestic industry. The schedules were more restrictive, and licenses and higher tariffs were introduced.

In summary, this first period was characterized by a carry over from the colonial era of conservative economic management with a fixed exchange rate regime and with industrial protection through tariffs, import licensing and restrictive schedules. Trade was open within East Africa for most of the period, while UK and EEC markets were favored by treaty. Price and interest rate controls further distorted resource allocation.

Second policy regime period: 1972–1980

Market regime: The EAC collapsed in 1977. There were two oil crises (1973 and 1979) and a coffee and tea boom (1976/1977). Hence, the period was one of considerable economic turbulence. Due to the rigidities introduced at the end of the previous period, the price regimes did not adjust appropriately, the balance of payments deteriorated, and the country started negotiating with the IMF for financial relief in the form of a Stand-By Agreement. The first Stand-By was cancelled when the coffee boom relieved the balance of payments. A second Stand-By was negotiated and drawn down as a consequence of the second oil crisis. Although analysts perceived the problems of the economy and pointed them out in various papers, the country·failed to adjust policy appropriately. A number of non-citizen-owned businesses were served with quit notices early in the period.

Monetary regime: The Kenya shilling was battered along with currencies of all other countries in the course of the US dollar crisis in 1973. It changed from its dollar link, firstly to the SDR and later to a managed float or crawl. Between May 1976 and April 1978, the average month-on-month money supply growth was 35.1 percent compared with 14.9 percent for the non-coffee boom period.

Price regime: Inflation rose significantly to around 12.5 percent. This was the result of rising oil prices, international interest rates and the influx of coffee and tea proceeds. The considerable price instability was buffered by extending the Specific and General Price Control Orders, thereby giving rise to suppressed inflation. These controls were extended even to particular brands of products and to particular importers by name.

Interest rate regime: Maximum lending rates and minimum savings interest rates were introduced. The Treasury Bill rate approached zero percent with the influx of coffee money, increasing the money supply (as noted above) as the Central Bank did not sterilize this inflow. The rate later rose to around 5 percent. The real return was negative throughout the period except for a brief period from September 1972 to February 1973 when it was positive.

Trade regime: The schedules under the Imports, Exports and Essential Supplies Act of 1962 were amended and extended on three occasions. Quantitative restrictions and quotas were introduced that increased distortions in the market. In addition, an import deposit scheme was introduced to dampen the demand. With the coming of the coffee boom and the subsequent increase in the foreign exchange earnings, many economic and trade controls were relaxed. However, new controls, including the requirement that farmers could only export their crops through government marketing boards, were introduced. Because the exchange rate was still fixed, resulting in an over-valued shilling, compensation measures for taxes paid on inputs to exports were introduced to try and encourage exports.

In summary, continued industrial protection and a growing trend towards market controls characterized the second period. Concerns with the protection of the foreign exchange reserves tended to replace concerns about industrial protection. The external environment experienced major shifts as floating exchange rate regimes were introduced for major currencies. Internationally, the pound Sterling was replaced by the US dollar as the major reserve currency. Kenya lost the Tanzanian market with the collapse of the EAC, and initiated efforts to enhance exports through controlled small devaluation and foreign exchange allocations. Hence, this was a transitional period that was disrupted, and probably extended, by the coffee boom, which allowed the government to temporarily avert a foreign exchange shortage.

Third policy regime period: 1981–1992

Market regime: The period effectively began with a shock to investors rising from the coup attempt in 1982, and closed with a second, even deeper shock of the donor aid freeze in 1991. The ministerial-level Foreign Exchange Allocation Committee that was introduced in 1983 led to the tightest control of the economy to date. The period also saw the beginning of the reform process with the advent of structural adjustment programs, enhanced structural adjustment facilities and sectoral adjustment loans. Hence, both World Bank and IMF lending appeared as major components affecting markets with their policy matrices and policy framework papers, loans for the industrial sector, exports and the financial sector. But these were marginal to the institutional control, which attracted donor support and guided growth while severely curtailing trade. The Government announced, through *Sessional Paper No. 1 of 1986 on Economic Management for Renewed Growth*, its intention to move out of direct controls of the economy, but these liberalization policies really only became effective in the next regime period. On the East African front, the Preferential Trade Area (PTA) saw a return of Tanzania as a major trading partner. At the very end of the period, sanctions were lifted on South Africa.

Monetary regime: The exchange rate was gradually converted into a more flexible policy instrument. The shilling moved from around KSh 8 to the US dollar to KSh 36 over the period. The banking system also moved towards more indirect controls by open market operations and the use of the cash ratio. A banking crisis towards the end of the period led to the introduction of a deposit protection fund. Although the money supply during the period grew, on average, at a reasonably conservative rate of 14.8 percent on a month-on-month basis, two periods of monetary indiscipline arose namely, during the mini coffee boom in 1986 and the election build up in 1992 which saw the growth in money supply move to 24.9 percent.

Interest regime: By a series of steps, the interest rate was gradually raised until it presented a positive real return and then was decontrolled. From March 1983 to August 1990, real returns were positive in all but eight dispersed months. From September 1990 to the end of the period, there was only one spell of positive real returns – from November 1991 to February 1992.

Price regime: The commodities on the General and Specific Price Control Orders were gradually all removed and the *Restrictive Practices, Monopolies and Price*

Control Act replaced the *Price Control Act*. Inflation continued to climb and was over 20 percent for much of the decade.

Trade regime: The control of imports was shifted to the Ministerial Foreign Exchange Allocation Committee, which used the non-statutory, 'Red Book' rather than the Imports, Exports and Essential Supplies Act. The 'Red Book' was issued annually showing for each import class its customs tariff together with its import schedule and any ministerial import permissions required. The schedules had different degrees of restrictiveness in licensing. In order to overcome the increasingly long queues, and consequential temptations to bribery or use of black markets, ways were introduced to allow importers to acquire foreign exchange without drawing it from the Central Bank. Particularly important among these was the foreign exchange certificate or Forex-C. Towards the end of the period, retention accounts were introduced to encourage exporters to sell their foreign exchange for Forex-Cs which could then be auctioned. Furthermore, retention accounts allowed exporters to avoid queuing. A range of other reforms lowered tariffs and introduced Manufacturing Under Bond, Export Processing Zones and the duty/VAT remission program, which were operated under the Export Promotion Programs Office.

   In summary, while this third period saw the preparatory design and initial stages of implementation of market and trade liberalization and export promotion, it was also a period which contained the most effective, and extreme, control over imports through the allocation of foreign exchange.

Fourth policy regime period: 1993 to 2000

Market regime: Since all prices were now market determined, policy focussed on improving institutional arrangements of markets. Kenya went to the Paris Club for debt rescheduling and entered into ESAF agreements with the IMF. The Nairobi Stock Exchange was opened to foreign investors and Forex Bureaus were licensed. Pre-shipment inspection agencies were contracted to ensure that prices that were quoted for customs purposes were valid.

Monetary regime: The commercial banks were controlled through the cash ratio and an independent clearing house. The Central Bank was granted independence from the Treasury and the treatment of non-bank financial intermediaries was harmonized with that of commercial banks. A further bank crisis caused several banks to close.

Trade regime: A foreign exchange shortage at the close of the previous period caused a brief suspension of the reform process. This was followed by an orderly, but nevertheless extraordinary, liberalization of both the current and capital accounts of the balance of payments. Trade licensing and the Foreign Exchange Allocation Committee were discontinued. Tariff reforms continued so as to harmonize the tariff rates with those of the PTA members. The Exchange Control Act was repealed and foreign exchange licensing terminated, hence the exchange rate was fully flexible. South Africa emerged as a major competitor.

Interest rate regime: In an effort to dry up the money that had appeared in the run up to the 1992 elections, as discussed under the third monetary regime, exchange rates and interest rates became extremely unstable rising to unprecedented levels. The foreign exchange reserves were dissipated and the economy faced a danger of dollarization. Domestic debt more than trebled. The remainder of the period saw high volatility of all the macroeconomic prices. Treasury bill yields fluctuated widely, with such fluctuations usually associated with an equally unstable exchange rate. During the eighteen months from January 1993 to June 1999, it was only in the seven months from April to October 1993 that real returns were positive. They have been positive and often high since then.

Price regime: The increase in costs associated with a high interest rate and exchange rate, together with the money supply problems associated with trying to keep total interest charges from dominating the budget, caused inflation to reach unprecedented levels. Following the enactment of the Central Bank of Kenya (Amendment) Act, of 1996, the Central Bank restricted money supply and brought inflation down to less than 5 percent on a stable basis.

In summary, the fourth period is characterized by the actual implementation of the trade and foreign exchange liberalization programs, the completion of the decontrol of market prices, the continuation of the implementation of export promotion schemes, and the development of regional markets.

Relating the trade policy regime periods to Kenyan international trade performance

Tables 5.1, 5.2 and 5.3 (compiled by the authors from various sources) give three perspectives on average Kenyan trade performance during the four trade policy regime periods identified above. Table 5.1 gives imports and exports as a share of GDP for the four periods. The third period, 1981–1992, clearly stands out from the others with its lower import and export shares. In addition, when tea and coffee exports are excluded, it is clear that the drop in exports was largely in non-traditional, non-primary commodity or manufactured goods exports. Manufacturing goods for export or more generally, industrialization, requires imports of machinery and equipment, raw materials and other intermediate inputs. If imports are effectively constrained, such as through a comprehensive foreign exchange allocation mechanism, then export growth and industrialization are also effectively constrained.

Table 5.1   Trade patterns in policy regime periods: trade component as a share of GDP (percent)

Policy Regime Period	Imports of Goods and Services	Imports of Goods	Exports of Goods and Services	Exports of Goods	Exports, Excluding Tea and Coffee
1962–1971	30.9	28.0	30.6	19.8	14.0
1972–1980	33.9	30.3	29.8	19.8	13.3
1981–1992	28.1	24.7	24.9	14.4	8.2
1993–1998	36.7	30.5	32.5	20.1	13.2

Table 5.2 effectively tells the same story of declining imports and exports during 1981–1992, except that the trade patterns are expressed in terms of real US dollars and quantity indices.

Table 5.2   Trade patterns in policy regime periods: trade in terms of US dollars and quantity index

Policy Regime Period	Imports of Goods, 1985, US $, millions	Exports of Goods, 1985, US $, millions	Import Quantity Index	Export Quantity Index
1962–1971	1,152	808	119	87
1972–1980	2,220	1,430	135	111
1981–1992	1,715	986	105	110
1993–1998	1,888	1,222	159	173

Table 5.3 analyses Kenyan exports to Tanzania and Uganda in the four periods. These exports are expressed as a share of total merchandise exports and as a share of GDP. Both measures show a steady decline in exports over the first three periods and then a sharp recovery after 1993. Again 1981–1992 stands out as the extreme period with exports to Tanzania and Uganda dropping to remarkably low levels. It is important to note that the East African markets closed down before 1981 and started opening up again before 1993. It was the constraints on trade, through the foreign exchange allocation mechanisms between 1983 and 1993 that effectively constrained trade even when these markets were available.

Table 5.3   Exports to Tanzania and Uganda in policy regime periods (percent)

Policy Regime Period	As a Share of Total Exports	As a Share of GDP
1962–1971	30.9	6.1
1972–1980	15.8	4.1
1981–1992	9.8	1.6
1993–1998	21.1	5.3

In the case of exports to Tanzania and Uganda, these were mainly manufactured and processed goods, and hence, were sensitive to constraints imposed on the availability and cost of the imported inputs required to produce exports for these markets.

Determinants of economic growth in Kenya

To analyze whether changes in trade and exchange rate policy have had significant impact on growth in Kenya, requires that an explanatory model of growth be developed that brings in other factors that explain growth so that a check can be run as to whether trade and exchange rate policy changes appear to have had any independent significant impact on growth in Kenya. It is recognized that the single-country time-series approach has limitations compared to cross country studies, which allow a greater variety of country-specific factors to be included in the explanation of growth. The changes in trade policy in the Kenyan context, however, have been large enough and the impacts on trade flows also significant enough that any strong effect on growth should show up in the results.

Standard sources of growth models are estimated here that try to isolate the effects of factor supply in the public and private sectors as well as certain exogenous shocks on real economic growth from year to year. A number of shocks are investigated. These include international oil and coffee prices, the major drought in 1984 and the attempted coup in 1982.

The specification of the labor supply is constrained by the reported statistics, which only give time series data for the modern or formal public and private sectors of the economy, and not the informal sectors. Currently, for example, the formal sector has about 1.7 million employees, but the informal sector has some 3.5 million people involved in trade and small-scale manufacturing and services. This number also excludes most of the subsistence agricultural labor. Labor should also be adjusted to reflect the human capital stock through some measure of years of education per worker. These major limitations have to be recognized in interpreting labor as a growth factor. On the other hand, Kenya is a relatively labor rich economy such that outside of shortages of some specific skills, labor supply is not expected to be a major determinant of growth.

Problems also exist in interpreting the public sector investment given that market discipline and standards are not typically applied in determining these investments. This means that public sector investment often yields a below normal rate of return which implies that measured public investment expenditure over-estimate the actual increase in the value of the productive public sector capital stock. There have been growing concerns about the quality of public sector expenditures at least since the early 1980s. Public sector performance is difficult to capture as a time-series explanatory variable, particularly because expenditures upon inputs in the public sector are not necessarily correlated with the value of public sector production. In fact, high levels of corruption and inefficiency in the public sector could result in a negative rather than positive relationship between public sector inputs of labor, capital, materials and services, and the value of public sector outputs. It is known, for example, that public sector employment, which includes central and local government officers, teachers, and parastatal employees, grew from 30 percent of total formal sector employment in 1965 to a peak of 50 percent in 1989 and has subsequently declined to 42 percent in 1998 through privatization of parastatals and downsizing in the central government. At the same time, average real wage rates in the public sector dropped over the years such that by the 1990s, they were only some 41 percent of their rates in the 1960s and early 1970s. Average public sector wages dropped from being 70 percent above the average in the private sector to being 10 percent below with the cross over being in the early 1990s. Wage gaps in the professional and managerial levels of the central government have been measured in the mid-1990s to be about 300 percent below private sector levels. These data point to growing over-employment, inefficient factor mixes, shortages of professional and other high-level skilled workers, and poor management and incentives in the public sector.

A specific concern with over-employment in government is that civil servants do not have the tools and resources to perform efficiently. This is recognized as a shortage of operating and maintenance resources. In an attempt to establish an indicator of central government input inefficiency over the full time series, operating and maintenance expenditures were measured as a residual of total expenditures after subtracting out expenditures on labor, gross fixed capital, loan repayments and interest, transfers, and military construction and equipment. This residual expenditure on goods and services is then deflated by the consumer price index and expressed as a per central government employee amount (O&M/E) – in thousands of 1982 shillings per year per employee.[5] Higher values of O&M/E expenditure per employee should lead to improved public sector output to support investment and growth, given the alternative uses to which those resources could have been put as listed in the deductions above.

Ideally, it would be better to measure changes in public sector output and unit costs to capture concerns about the declining competitiveness, rather than use input expenditures. Measures of electricity capacity and supply and costs, telephone line availability and costs, lengths of roads in adequate condition, port traffic volumes and costs, transportation costs and times, etc, are required. These would also need to be contrasted with competing countries to determine whether the costs of doing business in Kenya are getting relatively worse or not. Unfortunately these types of data are not available over the same long time periods, but some further efforts could be made in this direction.

Determinants of economic growth: a theoretical model

Three types of specification are used to estimate economic growth in Kenya. The first is to estimate the real growth rate (grY) as a function of the investment rate (gross fixed capital formation as a share of GDP or GFCF/Y). The second is to estimate the logarithm of the real GDP (LnY) as a function of the logarithm of real GFCF and other factors. The third is to estimate lnY as a function of the logarithm of the net capital stock and other factors.

Table 5.4 gives estimates of grY in Kenya over the period, 1970–1998, explained by the private sector investment rate (GFCF (pvt)/Y), parastatal sector investment rate (GFCF (para)/Y), central and local government sector investment rate – GFCF (gvt)/Y), O&M/E lagged one year, and a dummy for the 1984 drought. These estimates explain some 68 percent of the variation in the growth rate. They show a dominance of private investment in explaining real economic growth in Kenya and indicate that a one percentage point increase in the private sector investment rate leads to an increase of between 0.79 percent–0.97 percent in the real growth rate. The estimates also indicate that the 1984 drought decreased growth by about 3 percent points. Raising annual O&M/E per employee by KSh 90,000 (1998 prices) raised the growth rate by 1 percent one year later. The parastatal sector investment rate shows up as being marginally significant and the government investment rate as being insignificant.

Table 5.4   Estimates of the real economic growth rate in Kenya (grY), 1970–1998

Variables	Specifications			
	(A)	(B)	(C)	(D)
Constant	−0.05 (−2.47)	−0.083 (−3.61)	−0.062 (−2.09)	−0.097 (−3.11)
GFCF(pvt)/Y	0.81 (4.64)	0.967 (5.65)	0.79 (3.91)	0.929 (4.90)
GFCF(para)/Y	–	–	0.267 (0.95)	0.282 (1.07)
GFCF(gvt)/Y	–	–	0.058 (0.173)	0.163 (0.52)
O&M(−1) ('000 82 KSh)	–	0.001 (2.09)	–	0.001 (2.18)
D1984	−0.033 (−2.80)	0.025 (−2.12)	−0.34 (−2.85)	−0.026 (−2.24)
AR(1)	0.283 (1.35)	0.239 (1.16)	0.335 (1.50)	0.339 (1.58)
ADJ. R^2	0.635	0.679	0.601	0.659
DW	1.804	1.830	1.810	1.860
N	29	28	28	28

Note: t-Statistics are given in parentheses.

A range of other variables which hypothetically were expected to be related to growth, were tested in these specifications but none showed up as being significant. These included public sector investment rate, one-year lagged investment rates, private and public employment, real coffee price, real international oil price, the

1982 coup attempt and time. To check for significant trade effects, dummy variables for the period of the opening of the East African market and for trade liberalization were entered, and the ratio of exports to Uganda and Tanzania as a share of GDP was tested. These variables were typically negative and insignificantly positive in explaining growth, indicating no significant *direct* relationship between the major trade and exchange policy events and growth.

Table 5.5 Estimates of log of real GDP at factor cost for Kenya

Variables	Specifications			
	(A)	(B)	(C)	(D)
Constant	2.123 (2.06)	1.051 (2.01)	1.997 (2.00)	1.827 (1.71)
LnGFCF(pvt)	0.050 (2.75)	0.052 (3.07)	0.053 (2.66)	0.050 (2.60)
LnGFCF(pvt)(−1)	−	0.032 (1.79)	0.039 (1.99)	0.034 (1.72)
LnGFCF(pub)	0.022 (1.56)	0.024 (1.58)	−	−
LnGFCF(pub)(−1)	−	0.025 (1.76)	−	−
LnGFCF(para)	−	−	−0.001 (−0.12)	0.003 (0.44)
LnGFCF(para)(−1)	−	−	−	0.007 (1.18)
LnGFCF(gvt)	−	−	0.015 (0.80)	0.016 (0.88)
LnGFCF(gvt)(−1)	−	−	−	0.025 (1.28)
D1984	−0.041 (−3.46)	−0.037 (3.49)	−0.039 (−3.34)	−0.034 (−2.79)
Time	−0.0011 (−2.02)	−0.0011 (−1.98)	−0.0010 (−1.96)	−0.0010 (−1.68)
AR(1)	0.459 (2.42)	0.571 (2.68)	0.418 (1.99)	0.467 (2.05)
ADJ. R^2	0.570	0.647	0.577	0.605
DW	1.72	1.91	1.76	1.93
N	29	29	28	28

Note: t-Statistics are in parentheses.

Table 5.5 determines growth estimates by estimating the log of real GDP at factor costs (1982 prices) for 1970 to 1998 in terms of first order differences. These specifications explain up to 67 percent of the variance in the differences in lnY. Again private investment shows up as the important and significant explanatory variable. An increase of 10 percent in the real private investment leads to a 0.5 percent point increase in the growth rate.

If this increase occurs for two successive years, growth increases by 0.84 percent points.[6] Public investment (GFCF (pub)), or the combined parastatal and government investment) shows up as being less significant and having about half the impact on the growth rate. When public investment is split into parastatal and government investment, the lagged government investment has the larger and more significant, but still weak effect, of the two components. The time variable suggests an annual decline in productivity of 0.1 percent. The dummy variable for the 1984 drought shows a drop in the growth rate by about 3.7 percentage points. The employment variables, coffee price and O&M/E (-1) do not show up as being significant in this type of specification. As with the estimates of grY, the trade liberalization dummy variables and exports to East Africa variable generally show up with a negative sign and are insignificant.

Estimates are also made of LnY in terms of the real net capital stock for the public and private sectors in Kenya measured from 1974 to 1997 in terms of first order differences. In these specifications, only the real net private capital stock shows up as positive and significant. A 1 percent increase in the real net private capital stock yields an increase in 0.38 percent points in the economic growth rate.[7] Public sector capital stock and private employment give negative signs. O&M/E and the trade liberalization variables are insignificant. In addition, the real public sector wage rate was tested as an indicator of public sector efficiency, but it turned insignificant as well. The 1984 drought dummy again gave a 3.7 percent point drop in the growth rate, and a one US dollar per pound increase in the coffee price is estimated to increase growth by 7.3 percent points. Overall these variables explained 48 percent of the variation in the differences in lnY.

Determinants of private investment

Given the consistent importance and significance of private investment as a determinant of growth, the determinants of private investment are investigated to check whether any significant relationship between private investment and trade and exchange rate policy or performance stands out. Trade policy is found above to have no direct effect on growth, but may well have an indirect effect on growth through affecting private investment. Table 5.6 gives estimates of the logarithm of private gross fixed capital formation (LnGFCF (pvt.) for Kenya based on 1970 to 1998, data.

Estimates explain up to 72 percent of the variation in LnGFCF (pvt) in terms of past growth, public sector investment and support, real wage rates, coffee prices, East Africa exports, O&M and the August 1982 coup attempt. Past growth generates future expectation of growth encouraging current investment, and lagged completion of already planned projects based on past growth increases current investment – an accelerator principle. The estimates indicate that a one-percent point increase in last year's economic growth increases current private investment by 2 percent to 3 percent.

Public investment and government O&M expenditures per employee are complimentary to private investment. Increases in public sector investment last year by a 1 percent point, increase current private investment by 0.27 percent points. When public investment is divided into parastatal and government investment, the one-year lagged parastatal investment has the stronger and more significant impact on private investment. A 1 percent point increase in O&M/E two years ago increases current private investment by about 0.2 percent points. Interest rates, coffee price increases, and East African exports, generally encourage private investment. A one US dollar (1985 prices) per pound increase in the price of coffee is estimated to increase investment by 3.7 percent.[8] In the 1997 coffee boom, prices increased by over $3 per pound compared to long-run average prices. By contrast, the coup attempt in August 1982 reduced investment by some 13 percent to 25 percent in 1982 and 20 percent to 46 percent in 1983. Prior to the liberalization of interest rates in 1991, commercial lending rates were capped and in real terms averaged close to zero. Credit rationing and other hidden or indirect charges had to be used by the commercial banks. Hence, pre-1991 lending rates do not reflect the full cost of borrowing. It is noted that post-1991, the real interest (IR) rates generate a significant negative impact on investment. A severe bout of monetary instability, first led to large negative interest rates in 1992 and 1993 as inflation rose more rapidly than interest rates. This was followed by high positive interest rates thereafter under a tight monetary regime, as well as growing government domestic debt arising from high interest costs and unplanned expenditures. Real interest rates peaked at over 28 percent in 1998. These high interest rates also encouraged short-term capital inflows that strengthened the shilling leading to an uncompetitive exchange rate that damaged the competitiveness of both export and import-competing industries.[9] Real wage rates in the private sector are found to have an insignificant substitution effect on private investment. Higher wage rates appear to encourage greater capital investment, but no strong or significant effect is found. Export opportunities in East Africa show up as a significant boost to Kenyan private sector investment. When exports to Tanzania and Uganda increase by 1 percent of GDP, then private investment in GFCF increases by 2.1 percent to 3.7 percent. This increased private investment leads to increased growth. Clearly, regional market development has a significant impact on investment and growth. After 1992, as shows, exports to Tanzania and Uganda increased by 3.7 percent points of GDP, which implies an increase in private investment of up to 13.7 percent. This in turn is expected to increase the growth rate by 1.2 percent points based on the estimates above.

The analysis of trade and exchange rate policy also showed clearly that removal of foreign exchange allocation control on imports was a critical factor in the expansion of Kenya's international trade, much of it being an expansion in regional trade. Accordingly, there is no significant chain of causality between trade policy and growth. Export market opportunity development encourages investment. Open trade policy is necessary to exploit such trade and investment opportunities.

Table 5.6   Estimates of log of private gross fixed capital formation (LnGFCF(pvt)) in Kenya, 1970–1998

Variables	Specifications				
	(A)	*(B)*	*(C)*	*(D)*	*(E)*
Constant	3.409 (4.06)	4.566 (8.02)	4.324 (4.23)	2.255 (2.66)	−0.117 (−0.06)
GrY(−1)	3.090 (2.39)	3.292 (2.52)	3.284 (2.44)	2.328 (2.44)	2.039 (1.82)
LnGFCF(pup)(−1)	0.266 (2.28)	–	–	–	0.499 (4.67)
LnGFCF(para)(−1)	–	0.099 (1.82)	0.098 (1.78)	0.279 (3.99)	–
LnGFCF(gvt)(−1)	–	–	0.045 (0.31)	0.197 (1.76)	–
LnO&M/E(−2)	0.101 (1.81)	–	0.089 (1.48)	0.132 (2.20)	0.262 (3.42)
LnRealWage(pvt)	–	–	–	–	0.089 (0.61)
Ln(1+IR)	–	–	–	1.082 (1.45)	2.396 (4.54)

				−1.016	−2.297
D1999 plus*LN(I+IR)				(−1.25)	(−3.43)
Exp(T&U)/GDP	2.151	2.056	2.146	2.174	3.702
	(1.48)	(1.34)	(1.36)	(1.46)	(3.80)
Coffee price (real US$/ pound)	−	−	−	0.0263	0.0373
				(0.84)	(1.81)
D1982	−0.256	−0.247	−0.249	0.249	−0.131
	(−2.42)	(−2.23)	(−2.20)	(−2.42)	(−1.45)
D1983	−0.217	−0.205	−0.207	−0.307	−0.464
	(−1.98)	(−1.81)	(−1.78)	(−3.07)	(−4.30)
AR(1)	0.355	0.368	0.359	0.045	−0.588
	(1.60)	(1.86)	(1.63)	(0.21)	(−2.66)
AdjR^2	0.544	0.507	0.484	0.683	0.717
DW	1.40	1.46	1.44	2.51	2.61
N	28	28	28	26	26

Note: t-Statistics are in parentheses.

Conclusions

This study of Kenya's trade and growth experience has generated many significant findings:

- Trade and exchange rate policy has had major impacts on the trade performance and experience of Kenya. The two major impacts on trade have been:

    (i) The loss and regaining of the East African markets for exports. Tanzania closed its border in 1977 and Ugandan import demand declined from the late 1970s through the 1980s with internal civil instability. These markets began to recover through the late 1980s and early 1990s. Access to the East African and regional markets has been extremely important for exports of manufactured and processed goods. Hence, regional trade policy has significant consequences for manufacturing investment prospects.

    (ii) The imposition of foreign exchange allocations by the Central Bank for all imports in 1983 and its removal in 1993. This had the most dramatic effect on aggregate trade performance. These comprehensive import controls effectively constrained import demand to significantly lower levels than existed either prior to their imposition or after their lifting. Imports of goods dropped by some 6 percent of GDP during 1981–1992 compared to both earlier and later performance. Aside from the imposition of other market controls, the comprehensive foreign exchange allocation mechanism for imports made the 1981–1992 period the most distinctive policy regime period in terms of its major and clear impact on restricting trade.

- The imposition of comprehensive foreign exchange controls not only adversely affected imports, but also adversely affected export performance, particularly in manufactured and processed goods. When imports dropped by some 6 percent of GDP, exports dropped over the same period by a similar share of GDP. It is also evident that the East African market was lost before 1983 and was opened again before 1993. The significant shifts in exports came, however, with the changes in foreign exchange allocation restrictions to imports, particularly in 1993 and thereafter with a dramatic increase in exports of manufactured and processed goods to Uganda, Tanzania, and other COMESA countries. Particularly in manufactures, low cost and flexible access to imported raw materials and industrial intermediate goods is critical to export success – increased imports are essential to achieve increased exports of domestic manufactures or even merely expanded re-export trade.
- Up to 1993, Kenya had used a large range of policies, including tariffs, deposit requirements, licensing, no-objection certificates, etc., to restrict imports and protect domestic industry. After 1993, effective trade protection has largely come from relatively modest tariff rates. While these import protection devices clearly caused market distortions and resource misallocation, these policies were generally partial and often ineffective such that trade could continue at reasonably high levels. It is notable that in the early period of the EAC, trade was open within the community, but not with the rest of the world.
- No *direct* link could be established between the growth performance of Kenya and the changes in trade policy regime or trade performance. This does not imply that trade and exchange rate policy are not important for three reasons:

    (i) Kenya has only experienced a truly open trade and exchange rate policy since the major liberalization of 1993–1994. The time period for the effects of an open trade policy to evidence themselves has therefore been limited. The dramatic increases in manufactured exports since liberalization point to growth potential in the manufacturing and processing sectors over the longer term.
    (ii) Kenya has had poor performance in creating all the other complementary supportive factors that would allow the economy to fully exploit the benefits of more open trade and international competition. Kenya has under

performed in the provision of economic infrastructure and a competitive macroeconomic environment. High growth generally is the result of a number of favourable factors combining in a multiplicative manner to achieve significant surplus generation. Openness in trade is not sufficient to overcome other adverse factors.

(iii) *Indirect* relationships between trade and growth are found. Access to regional trade markets does appear to promote private investment significantly by over 13 percent which is estimated to have added 1.2 percent points to growth.

- The period of low openness to trade (1981–1992) contains a period from 1985–1990, of significant economic growth at an average rate of 5 percent. This was generally driven by inward looking investments, except for a major expansion in the tourism sector. Imports increased significantly during this period while exports of goods were at their lowest levels since Independence. The foreign exchange requirements of this growth spell were financed by higher service sector earnings from tourism and a significant increase in net Official Development Assistance starting in 1987 with the various economic adjustment programs for the development of export and other markets.
- Private investment is the strongest and most significant contributor to growth. Private sector investment has been the only major engine of growth.
- Public investment by central and local government and parastatals shows up as weak contributors to growth, but positively related to private investment. Out of public investment, parastatal investment has a weak direct impact on growth, but a stronger indirect impact through supporting private sector investment. This is consistent with the economic support role of the major utilities, which, until recently, were all parastatals. Government investment has a stronger, but still weak, direct effect on growth. This effect can act through investments in roads, for example.
- Private sector investment can be increased through improved market incentives, particularly lower real interest rates which can be achieved primarily through reducing the domestic debt burden of the government. Enhancing the efficiency of public sector investments and expanding the volume of government investments will also have significant direct and indirect effects on growth.
- Measures of operating and maintenance expenditures per employee by the central government show a significant, if not large, impact on investment and growth on a lagged basis. The large drop in government real wage rates, particularly in the managerial and professional cadres, has no doubt also undermined the efficiency of the use of operating and maintenance funds in effective public sector service delivery.

- Formal sector employment (private and public) has a weak and inconsistent relationship to growth.

Acknowledgments

This chapter has benefited from comments by and the assistance of N. Kirira; E. M. Githae; and A. Okello of the Fiscal and Monetary Affairs Department of the Ministry of Finance, Government of Kenya. All errors and views, however, remain the responsibility of the authors.

Notes

1. Data sources are key to any study of economic performance over the long term. Like most studies, this one depends primarily on the macroeconomic data published by the Central Bureau of Statistics in the *Statistical Abstract* (published annually, well back into the colonial era and since independence with the exception of 1992, 1993 and 1997) and the *Economic Survey* (published annually in June before the Budget since 1960.) These data have been subject to periodic revisions, some of which have not been picked up by such publications as the IMF *International Financial Statistics* or the data appendices of World Bank reports. Three compilations have attempted to provide a compatible long time series of most of the macroeconomic data. This study makes some marginal improvements to these and extends them to 1998. Vandermoortele, J. and Gatang'i, M. N. (1984), 'Kenya Data Compendium, 1964–1982', IDS (Nairobi) Occasional Paper No. 40, March 1984. Short, C., Keyfitz, R. and Maundu, M. (1994), 'Historical Economic Data for Kenya, 1972–1992', Technical Paper 94–01, Long Range Planning Unit, Ministry of Planning and National Development, Government of Kenya, January. T.C.I. Ryan, (forthcoming), 'Kenya/World Bank Interface', in Wai, D. (ed.), *Africa and the World Bank*, forthcoming.
2. In this chapter, economic growth is measured as the growth rate in the real level of Gross Domestic Product (GDP) measured at factor costs. Unfortunately, there is no reliable price deflator series for GDP at market prices. Making year-to-year comparisons using the GDP at factor costs will not affect the measure of growth significantly as the ratio of net indirect taxes to GDP at factor cost is relatively stable on a year-to-year basis. Over the longer term, however, the ratio of net indirect taxes to GDP has increased from about 8 percent to 17 percent from 1964 to 1998. This means that on average GDP at factor costs represents an underestimate of the growth rate of some 0.21 percent per year. This, however, only reduces the gap slightly between the high growth rates of the 1960s and the low growth rates of the 1990s. When ratios of values to GDP are reported (such as export values over GDP) in this paper, the nominal GDP at market prices is used.
3. Reinikka, R. (1994), 'How to Identify Liberalization Episodes: An Empirical Study of Kenya', WPS/94.10, Centre for the Study of African Economies, Oxford.
4. Mwenga, F. (1999), 'Trade Liberalization, Credibility and Impacts: A Case study of Kenya, 1972–1994', in Oyejide, A., Ndulu, B. and Gunning, J. W. (eds.), *Regional Integration and Trade Liberalization in Sub-Sahara Africa, Vol. II: Country Case Studies*, Macmillan: London.

5. Average O&M/E in the four periods are KSh 10.5, 12.5, 12.2, and 13.7 thousand 1982 shillings per year per central government employee. In the 1993–1998 period, this translates into KShs 188.6 thousand 1998 shillings per year per employee. This measure of O & M correlates fairly closely with the classification 'other current expenditures' in the economic analysis of central government expenditures.

6. These results for the effect of private GFCF on growth are consistent with the results for an increase in private GFCF/Y. For GFCF/Y to increase, GFCF has to increase faster than Y (or GDP). If GFCF/Y is 10 percent and grY is 5 percent, then a one-percentage point increase in GFFCF/Yto 11 percent requires GFCF to increase by 15 percent. Based on the above estimates, in one year this will increase grY by 0.75 percentage points, which is slightly lower than the estimates of grY in terms of GFCF/Y.

7. Based on past trends of private GFCF and private net capital stock, 1 percent increase in the net stock requires about 9 percent to 14 percent increase in real GFCF. Based on estimates, this will generate an increase in grY of about 0.6 to 0.8 percent, which is somewhat higher than the 0.4 percent from the net capital stock estimate.

8. This estimate of the impact of coffee prices is significant and about double the magnitude found in the estimates fo grY, which were statistically insignificant at about a 4 percent increase in the growth rate per one US dollar per pound increase in the price of coffee.

9. See G. Glenday and D. Ndii, Export Platforms in Kenya chapter of this volume for a more detailed discussion of the increasingly adverse macroeconomic environment for export and import-competition from 1995 through 1998.

References

Government of Kenya (GoK) (various years), *Statistical Abstract*, Government Printer: Nairobi.

GoK (various years), *Economic Survey*, Government Printer: Nairobi.

GoK (1965), *African Socialism and Its Application to Planning in Kenya, Sessional Paper No. 10 of 1965*, Government Printer: Nairobi, Kenya.

GoK (1986), *Economic Management for Renewed Growth, Sessional Paper No. 1 of 1986*, Government Printer: Nairobi, Kenya.

Mwega, F. (1999), 'Trade Liberalization, Credibility and Impacts: A Case Study of Kenya, 1972–1994', in Oyejide, A., Ndulu, B. and Gunning, J. W. (eds.), *Regional Integration and Trade Liberalization in sub-Saharan Africa, Vol. II: Country Case Studies*, Macmillan: London.

Reinikka, R. (1994), *How to Identify Liberalization Episodes: An Empirical Study of Kenya*, WPS/94.10, Centre for the Study of African Economies: Oxford.

Ryan, T. C. I. (forthcoming), 'Kenya/World Bank Interface', in Wai, D. (ed.), *Africa and the World Bank*, The World Bank: Washington, DC.

Sachs, J. D. and Warner, A. M. (1997), 'Sources of Slow Growth in African Economies', *Journal of African Economies*, Vol. 6, No. 3, pp. 335–376.

Short, C., Keyfitz, R. and Maundu, M. (1994), 'Historical Economic Data for Kenya, 1972–1992', Technical Paper 94–01, Long Range Planning Unit, Ministry of Planning and National Development, Government of Kenya, January.

Vandermoortele, J. and Gatang'i, M. N. (1984), 'Kenya Data Compendium, 1964–1982', IDS (Nairobi) Occasional Paper No. 40 (March).

WEF (World Economic Forum) (1998), *The African Competitiveness Report, 1998*, WEF: Geneva.

6

Analysis of Liberalization of the Trade and Exchange Regime in Kenya Since 1980

MBUI WAGACHA

F13 F14
F31 F33
O24 O19

Introduction

Statement of the problem

In the past few decades, Kenya's trade and exchange regime has been marked by negative developments in commodity composition, distribution of markets, and competitiveness, which have contributed to retarded economic growth. A potential for achieving GDP growth averaging 6 percent per annum has failed to materialize but has instead been replaced by a trend decline that brought real GDP growth from a peak of 7 percent in 1977 to an estimated 1.4 percent in 1999.[1] Behind the failure are severe domestic and external policy inadequacies, particularly a long standing belief in an import substitution strategy pursued with a combination of exchange controls, protection and interventionist Keynesian-type fiscal and monetary policies.[2] Even where appropriate and corrective policies were adopted, implementation and commitment have been patchy. Policy reversals permitted at the expedience of sector interests, including 'competitive' protectionism during the import substitution era of the 1970s and 1980s, have further reduced the potential contribution of trade to economic growth. The problem underlying this study is an analysis of policy failures, their economic consequences, and possible corrective strategies.

Objectives of the study

The study has three broad objectives:

- To tabulate past starts and reversals of liberalization of Kenya's trade and exchange regime as part of the International Monetary Fund (IMF) and World Bank imposed structural adjustment program;
- To review the trajectory of Kenyan exports of goods and services since 1980, paying particular attention to the so-called non-traditional exports, shifting mixes of total exports, and identifying the sources of a potential export 'deficit' since 1980, and explaining the gap between Kenya's actual export performance and potential performance in the intervening period; and
- To interview and report the views and experiences of exporters, including multinational companies and potential foreign investors interested in export-oriented activity, paying attention to the identification of factors that diminish potentials for production and growth of non-traditional export oriented enterprises.

To meet the above objectives, this chapter is organized as follows. First, we review structural adjustment in Kenya, including the impediments to growth that arose over the past three decades. This section examines the transmission channels via which some of the policies used may have impeded the growth of exports. Second, we undertake quantitative estimates of Kenya's export market shares, and compare them to those of other countries. Later, a model of constant-market-share analysis is used to measure and explain possible sources of the 'export deficit' concept. Export 'actuals' are tested to discover how potential gains from the growth of world trade, diversification of export commodities, and competitiveness that could have played a part in promoting economic growth in Kenya were undermined by a lack of consistency in trade liberalization, export diversification, and competitiveness. Traditional least squares regression methods are also used to estimate export supply functions, analyzing the determinants of export performance from an overall standpoint, from agriculture, and from non-traditional exports. The estimates are important in indicating key determinants of export performance in the economy. Third, we provide a brief description of the results of a survey of exporters and potential exporters. Fourth, we summarize the strategic problems of Kenya's trade regime. Finally, we present our conclusions and policy recommendations.

Review of trade liberalization and structural adjustment in Kenya

Anatomy of structural impediments to growth in Kenya

In independent Kenya, a policy-based approach to economic management may be traced to *Sessional Paper No. 10 of 1965 on African Socialism and its Application to Planning in Kenya*. Thereafter, the goals and objectives of policy-making targeted economic growth to raise the overall standard of living. Specific components of the policy stance were: 'to achieve high and rapid growth, equitably distributed, so that all are free from want, disease and exploitation, while at the same time guaranteeing political equality; social justice; human dignity; and equal opportunities, but also without prejudice to remedying the inequalities inherited from the past.[3]

Early policy and economic successes of the 1963–1972 decade can be measured by the ensuing economic transformation and expansion in output and employment. Real GDP grew at more than 8 percent annually. Growth was propelled mainly by the freeing-up of factor markets, notably in agriculture. The inclusion of the African farm sector in cash crop production, particularly small and medium-scale farms, quickly led to increased output volumes and higher value-added in commodities. For the first time, the small-scale farm sector, dominated by Africans, became a key player in the production and export of leading commodities such as coffee and tea. The use of sovereign monetary and fiscal policies also propelled growth as the regulatory distortions of colonial economic activity were removed. The domestic market expanded with a burgeoning consumer goods-oriented manufacturing sector that increased domestic supply. As described in this study, this tilt towards protection–based industrialization was biased against exports and against agriculture in particular tending towards taxing and offsetting the gains made by freeing up agriculture to the small-scale sector. The development strategy in Kenya increasingly relied on protection of domestic production.

With growth, fiscal revenues expanded mainly from tax buoyancy and also from tax elasticity, whereby there were automatic increases in revenue without much resort to increases in the tax rates.[4] In expenditures, restraints yielded healthy budgetary surpluses. The public sector was thus initially a net contributor to Gross Domestic Savings (GDS).

Structural impediments to growth and development emerged early in post-independence Kenya, but were often misinterpreted or swamped by political expediencies. Growth was unstable, with a long-run declining trend. From real GDP growth rates of 4.0 percent, 3.1 percent and 2.9 percent during 1973, 1974 and 1975, respectively, the rates rose to 4.4 percent, 8.1 percent and 7.7 percent during 1976, 1977 and 1978 respectively. The major problem of open unemployment that emerged during the period was the natural consequence of the successes of post-independence expansion in primary and higher education, as well as in several training programs. It was exacerbated by labor force growth, but it was also misinterpreted in the policy/instruments framework of the time as excess capacity in the economy, amenable to Keynesian-type expansionary policies. In each crisis, expansionary policies were repeatedly targeted on structural phenomena until the open-economy consequences of internal and external financial imbalances inevitably emerged. Given a fixed exchange rate regime, import controls and tightening of foreign exchange allocation were imposed to offset external imbalances. Pent-up demand would then lead to inflation and overvaluation of the exchange rate.

The alternation of expansionary policies with controls, licensing and foreign exchange allocations bred 'rent-seeking' activities. Attempts by the Government of Kenya to invest in a highly uncompetitive import-substitution sector led to a proliferation of parastatal enterprises. While industry achieved a degree of regional trade penetration due to the common external tariff of the East African Community (EAC) during the 1970s, it never approached international competitiveness. Domestically, the strategy suppressed incomes, investment and growth among leading export earners such as coffee, tea and a burgeoning tourist industry. It further drained the foreign exchange earned and maintained a fixed and overvalued exchange rate that favored artificially low costs for imports of capital goods and services.

The earliest attempt to address structural impediments came during the 1973–1984 decade when the economy was buffeted from its conservative policy mould by three external shocks – one positive and the other two negative. The oil crisis of 1973 triggered Kenya's qualification and application for an IMF Extended Fund Facility (EFF). The era of policy experimentation and structural adjustment had started. However, the loan signed at the time was cancelled when the serendipity of a commodity boom occurred during 1976–1978. The required structural adjustment and stabilization measures were postponed while inappropriate fiscal expansionary policies were resumed.

Three decades of macropolicy performance in Kenya[5]

Below, we present a summary of policy and performance indicators for Kenya during the 1960s and 1970s.

Highlights of the 1960s: strategic emphasis was placed on growth led by manufacturing and agriculture and development of the social sector.

- Savings and investments were approximately 20 percent of GDP, and were relatively high given low per capita incomes;

- Incremental capital output ratios at 3 but rising, with negative medium to long-term effects on output growth;
- Real GDP growth high; 6.3 percent per year (1964–1974) with agriculture and manufacturing growing at 8.3 percent and 4.3 percent, respectively;
- Low tax burden as indicated by the tax revenue/GDP ratio at 12 percent 1966/1967 but rising (to 21 percent in 1979/1980);
- Inflation at about 3 percent during the 1960s;
- Government savings were high as indicated by recurrent fiscal balances of 2 percent to 4 percent of GDP annually, which contributed to investment program; public investments in infrastructure, roads, and hospitals;
- High private and public investments in human capital formation, yielding good indicators for education and health;
- Sharp impact of the redistribution of high-performance agriculture towards small farmers; small-farm share of coffee and tea production increased from about zero in 1955 to 40 percent and 70 percent, respectively, in the early 1980s;
- Between 1965 and 1975, small-farm acreage under improved maize varieties increased forty-fold; and
- Land resettlement, agricultural research and extension.

Highlights of the 1970s: strategic emphasis was placed on import-substitution buttressed with massive public sector investment.

- Recurrent surpluses evaporate as government becomes a net dis-saver;
- ICORs deteriorate from 3–4 in the 1970s to 9–15 in early 1980s, again suppressing medium to long-run output performance;
- Terms of trade decline 22 percent with 1972–1975 oil shock, increase 53 percent during the 1976–1977 coffee boom and decline 28 percent in the 1980 second oil shock;
- Import prices increase due to fixed exchange rate regime;
- Expenditure/GDP ratio moves from 24 percent in 1973/1974 to 31 percent in 1979/1980;
- Budget deficits increase from 3 percent-4 percent in the early 1970s to about 10 percent in the early 1980s, with pervasive loss-making parastatal investments that soon over-extend the public sector;
- Inflation accelerates to 22 percent by 1982;
- Current account deficit to GDP ratio moves from 4 percent in the early 1970s to 14 percent in 1980, worsening external balances;

- Policy reaction by a 'battery' of controls: foreign exchange transactions, import licensing, bans, export taxes, retail and producer price ceilings, controls on wages, interest rates and credit. Impact is massive anti-export bias; and
- Rapid increase in external public debt.

. Rigidities in the underdeveloped financial sector remained in place throughout the 1970s, choking the absorption of export earnings into new investments and undermining an intermediation process that would have spurred an investment boom. In the circumstances, the foreign exchange earnings of the coffee export boom triggered a wave of private spending and price escalation in domestic assets.[6] Maintenance of a fixed exchange rate and a temporary relaxation of import controls exacerbated other policy blunders that allowed the real exchange rate to appreciate sharply. Export competitiveness was eroded while the impressive fiscal surpluses generated by the boom in consumption and asset transfers were squandered on ineffective fiscal expansion in the capital budgets of the late 1970s. During 1979–1980, the second oil shock and a collapse in commodity prices triggered the third external shock.

Kenya successfully negotiated a structural adjustment loan with the World Bank in 1982, with the aim of reforming the industrial sector through reduced protection, liberalization of the market, devaluation of the shilling, introduction of a uniform tariff, and an export insurance and financing scheme. However, fiscal expenditures drifted uncontrollably upwards, reaching 35 percent of GDP in 1984. Increasingly, public sector projects became inefficient and glaringly poor substitutes for private investment. They incurred high operating losses with little to show in socio-economic output effects. Furthermore, the internal price control regime had acute price-increasing effects leading to production inefficiencies.[7] By the second half of the 1980s decade, import substitution and public investment had become overall policy failures as props for the capacity of public expenditures to promote development. The case for structural adjustment had become much stronger and was most succinctly met by the policy changes proposed in *Sessional Paper No. 1 of 1986 on Economic Management for Renewed Growth*. The government policy paper proposed a shift from the import substitution strategy 'towards a policy of exposing industry progressively to international competition and encouraging non-traditional exports'.

Liberalization of the trade and exchange regime since 1980

Origins of anti-export biases in Kenya

Early discussions of the weaknesses of the import substitution strategy that was prevalent in developing countries during the 1960s and 1970s, looked at ways of increasing economic openness by eliminating biases to the production and trade in exportables and import substitutes on the one hand, and non-price trade barriers on the other. Bhagwati (1978) and Krueger (1978), for example, argued for the adoption of price-incentive-based policies to replace quantitative restrictions and controls. In Kenya, an early assessment of the import substitution strategy (IS) was presented by Wagacha (1976).

In the event, many countries that used the main instruments of liberalization in the 1970s and the 1980s found that to succeed, a comprehensive framework of other complementary measures was required. The measures included physical infrastructure, human capital – especially in the technical, policy and managerial cadres as shown by the example of Southeast Asia, and strengthening of policy and implementation capacity in regulatory institutions associated with production, markets, quality, safety, and standards. In countries marked by entrenched rent seeking from the IS strategy, or where the complementary measures were lacking or weak, the main instruments of liberalization failed or were compromised.

Characterizations of trade and exchange regimes

Given the comprehensiveness of measures required to support the two primary approaches that focus on trade liberalization, the definition and measurements of the concept of trade liberalization remained ambiguous. Two main approaches have emerged.[8] One is the *trade neutrality* criterion that looks at the relative attractiveness to producers in investing in the production of exports or imports. The main purpose of studies and policy outcomes in this genre is to establish how price-incentive-based biases that discourage investment in one activity relative to the other can be narrowed. This concept pursues a price regime where incentives are equalized between the two types of economic activity, namely export production and import substitutes. However, the approach does not investigate the multiple non-price obstacles that may be engendered by official and un-official commercial policies. These are the focus of the second concept, *trade liberality,* assessing trade barriers such as non-tariff barriers to trade and the degree of restrictiveness of trade controls, regardless of the price biases.

Developments in the trade and exchange regime in Kenya are consistent with an indistinguishable mix of obstacles and policy inadequacies spanning both the *trade neutrality* and *trade liberality* concepts. Nevertheless, we discuss several dimensions of each characterization. There is considerable empirical evidence that the IS strategy in Kenya engendered a severe anti-export bias, inefficient and inward-looking economic management, and high-cost manufacturing (World Bank, 1993; Sharpley, 1988). The acutely negative consequences of the approach were concealed by the early successes of the IS strategy in capturing an EAC market for manufactures. Kenya was highly successful in producing and trading these behind the common external tariff, thus temporarily avoiding the consequences of low international competitiveness.

In all other aspects, the biases to the production and trade of exportables and import substitutes, and non-price trade barriers cited in Bhagwati (1978), Krueger (1978) and Wagacha (1976) were evident in the Kenyan economy. Until the break-up of the EAC in 1977 removed the disguised regional competitiveness for Kenya's manufactured exports, the push for exports under protection seemed to be working. While the EAC lasted, there were few compelling pressures for Kenya to change relative incentives between import substitutes and export production or to transform industry in the same way that post-independence government policies had been employed to transform agricultural exports from a central reliance on large-scale production – tea, coffee, cotton, etc. – to the dominance of small scale export oriented production.

The shock of the break up of the EAC on Kenya's manufacturing exports was severe. Export manufactures to Uganda and Tanzania constituted more than half of the output in the early 1970s, and fell to less than one-tenth in 1980.

Domestically, Kenyan prices for manufactured goods were rising faster (under protection) than import prices after the mid-1970s. These developments suggest a number of outcomes for the gains from trade within the common market and for Kenya's international competitiveness during that period: (1) regionally, Kenya's manufacturing sector was expanding sales but raising the costs of trade diversion for the EAC market; (2) Kenya's manufacturing sector was becoming more un-competitive; (3) as a sign of increased anti-export biases, the prices of exports fell both as a ratio of production costs (reducing the profitability of export production), while an overvalued exchange rate further depressed international competitiveness; and (4) with export prices falling in relation to the prices of manufactured goods in the CPI, the manufacturing sector was also contributing to inflation. By the beginning of the 1980s, Kenya's export sector had been substantially weakened by an incentives regime that was strongly biased to manufacturing and which, was also biased toward production mostly for a captive EAC market.

When liberalization became inevitable, following the combination of EAC collapse and increasing pressures of structural impediments, Kenya faced two parallel dimensions of policy analyses. One was how to enhance competitiveness by lowering export biases, removing quantitative restrictions, lowering of tariff levels, and promoting exports. The second was reform of key indicators on external balances: exchange rate policies, the easing of controls on foreign exchange transactions, and relaxation of the capital accounts. We discuss the two channels of reforms in terms of *trade neutrality* and *trade liberality*.

Policies towards trade neutrality

Trade neutrality in Kenya may be identified from policies that have affected relative price incentives towards production for export or import substitutes. The main policies consistent with trade neutrality relate to three categories of policy instruments: (1) reform of the exchange rate regime; (2) harmonization and reduction of import taxation; and (3) liberalization of export policies. The exchange rate regime in Kenya has undergone remarkable changes since the colonial regime of the East African Currency Board. As early as 1980, the key problem was how to manage exchange rate movements around the SDR to which the shilling was pegged. The peg was abandoned in 1982, in favor of a composite of currencies representative of Kenya's main trading partners. The effect of the peg was to remove the fluctuations of currencies in the SDR unrelated to Kenya's trade flows, and maintain a measure of competitiveness. However, the peg retained the technical capability of transmitting and maintaining inflation to and in Kenya at the levels obtained by the major trading partners.

As a first step in engendering flexible exchange rates, Kenya adopted a dual exchange rate in 1990 by operating the official rate alongside the rate available in the market for those who purchased interest-bearing and marketable foreign exchange bearer certificates (the so-called Forex Cs). The monetary authorities were thus able to monitor the market performance of the paper and adjust the official rates accordingly. In 1993, following elimination of controls on imports and most foreign exchange transactions, the exchange rate attained a full float.

On balance, statistical evaluations suggest that the exchange rate movements of the 1980s could have contributed to a worsening of trade neutrality by negatively affecting the incentives for the production of tradable goods exports and import-competing goods (World Bank, 1993). Estimates of alternative measures of the real exchange rate during the 1980s show two key results: (1) the real exchange rate had a greater *appreciation* in 1989 than in 1981, having acted to reduce Kenya's international competitiveness; and (2) measures of the real exchange rate show great variability, implying exchange rate *instability*.[9] Other studies that report reversals and instability in the exchange rate (and impact on real wages) show that following a sharp depreciation of the Kenya shilling during 1990–1993, there was a surge in exports during 1993–1995.[10] The 2.5 percent real depreciation in the Ksh./US$ rate coincided with a 39 percent fall in the real wage. While this suggests that relative prices and the real wage are important determinants of export performance (as shown by the regressions of this study), by 1997, the exchange rate had re-appreciated to above the 1990 level, while the real wage, in US dollars in manufacturing had risen by 92 percent over the 1994–1998 period. At the same time, world trade prices dropped by 12 percent contributing to a fall in Kenya's export performance from 22.4

percent of GDP (1996) to 17.1 percent (1998). Proven effects of the positive impact of real exchange rate depreciation in the promotion of export performance in Kenya have thus not been pursued as a sustained policy.

In regard to harmonization and reduction of tariff levels, Kenya's experience has taken two directions. First, tariff reductions proper and second, the gradual dismantling of import restrictions involving the *tariffication* of a wide range of restricted imports. The process has exhibited a stop-go approach since it first featured in the Budget Proposals of June 1980. In that budget, which was announced under the impact of the second oil shock and a global collapse in commodity prices, import bans were converted to high tariff rates. Two schedules of imports were retained: Schedule I for unrestricted licensed goods and Schedule II for quota-restricted imports. A fledgling and ineffective compensation scheme set up earlier was simplified and increased from 10 percent to 20 percent. Subsequent to the budget, the reforms were rolled back due to balance of payments pressures and fiscal deficits induced by external shocks. Support of a fixed exchange rate also drained foreign exchange reserves. In a system-wide reversal of policies, import restrictions were restored, where undeniably, adequate devaluation of the shilling could have restored external balances. The authorities nevertheless chose to re-impose restrictions.

The next round of reforms came in 1987 with a substantial shifting of import items from Schedule II to Schedule I, and support for exports. Subsequent changes in the structure of tariffs have been dramatic. In 1987/1988, tariff bands stood at 24, with a weighted average tariff rate of 39.9 percent. The bands were brought down to 16 and 11 in 1988/1989 and 1989/1990, respectively. Furthermore, the upper rate, which stood at 170 percent in 1988, was gradually brought down. Duty rates on most capital equipment and intermediate imports came down in three steps: to 5 percent; to 15 percent; and to 25 percent.

Since the late 1980s, two strands of actions in Kenya's tariff reforms may be identified. On one hand, tariffs have been reduced substantially, staying nominally within regional trends. As of 1996/1997, tariff bands numbered six each in Kenya and Tanzania and ranged from 0 to 40 percent, compared to five bands for Uganda, ranging between 0 to 30 percent.[11] By 1998/1999, Kenya had reduced its bands to 4, ranging between 0 to 25 percent, compared to five bands for Tanzania, ranging between 0 to 30 percent and three bands in Uganda, ranging from 0 to 15 percent. On the other hand, the rates in Kenya do not reflect proportionate reductions in the escalation of tariffs that remains relatively high by world standards.[12] Overall, the period of tariff rationalization and reduction since the 1980s has left production weighted average tariffs and effective rates that are highly dispersed and with high effective rates of protection. Production is biased against exports and in favor of production for the domestic market.

More importantly, the tariff and trade liberalization reforms, in Kenya as in the rest of the EAC, do not represent the actual reductions in levels of protection. Substantial reversals have been achieved by the use of suspended duties in Kenya and partner countries. Increases in tariffs on a wide range of goods have brought an additional 5 to 20 percent.[13] Uganda has resorted to import licensing for a wide range of goods while Tanzania, like Kenya, imposes suspended duties and operates an exclusion list of imports that do not attract COMESA tariff preferences. Table 6.1 shows recent developments in reductions and harmonization of tariffs as well as the widespread offsetting impositions of suspended duties, excise taxes and (in the case of Uganda) preferential tariff rates.

An important link in Kenya's anti-export bias and reversals of trade liberalization is their close affinity to early developments within the EAC. During the 1970s, the EAC provided an easy market for Kenya's manufactures and there was little effort to promote non-traditional exports. The collapse of the EAC in 1977 was a 'wake-up' call that triggered policies for export promotion. The external shock of the collapse was such that while half of Kenya's exports of manufactured output were directed to Uganda and Tanzania in the early 1970s, only one-tenth was being exported to the two countries by 1979. Kenya responded to the shock with the development of the so-called export platforms. First, the Export Compensation Act of 1974 (ECA) established reimbursement procedures for exporters for duties paid on imported intermediate inputs. Firms qualified for the benefits if they had at least 30 percent domestic value added. Second, ten years later, in 1984, manufacturing-under-bond (MUB) facilities were established. Third, the Export Processing Zone (EPZ) scheme was set up by Act of Parliament in 1990. It advanced a generous incentive package to 'foot loose' manufacturers, including a corporate tax holiday for ten years. Fourth, the Export Promotion Programs Office (EPPO) in the Ministry of Finance offers export incentives to manufacturers primarily serving the domestic market. All the measures were aimed at enhancing export incentives and to spearhead a widening of export products and markets. All have worked poorly in penetrating alternative markets and they have been poorly complemented by other policies.

The potential impact of the ECA was undermined by the accumulated escalation of the tariff structure in Kenya that was left more or less intact after the collapse of the EAC. The structure perpetuated the domestic supply of protected inputs to the manufacturing sector disregarding imports of cheaper or better quality inputs. The requirements were strengthened by moribund 'domestic content' requirements as well as widespread import licensing requirements. Set at the flat 20 percent rebate rate while tariffs on intermediate inputs ranged between 0 percent-80 percent, the ECA distorted both the levels of incentives and the structure of investment in exports by over-compensating some exporters and under-compensating others. As of 1997, the scheme was using a positive list of 1,250 items to determine eligibility.

This ensured that potential non-traditional exports outside the list were excluded from the policy. The MUB facility proved even more restrictive. Eligible firms had to specialize in export production, pay onerous charges in license fees, bonding and customs costs, and were restricted from domestic sales even of rejects. The facility fuelled substantial contract garment manufacturing for the US market but after 1994, a trade dispute regarding trans-shipment of Indian goods through Kenya led to the decline of operating enterprises from 70 to 10. On the other hand, a very wide variation in the *levels* of applicable tariffs is observed in Kenya over the period under review.

Until its dissolution in 1977, the EAC provided a benchmark for protection in Kenya through the common external tariff. The EAC influenced Kenya's choices of policy tools for *further* protection as well as responses to external shocks at the national level. Since common external tariffs served to limit unilateral increases, quantitative restrictions and licensing of imports were the only options to ease or tighten external trade. Kenya frequently used the options depending on the authorities' objectives to counter negative developments on the balance of payments. They, thus, functioned as a crude counter cyclical tool to tighten or ease imports in response to the balance of payments. As an example, during 1972–1975, Kenya experienced a terms of trade decline of 22 percent due to the oil shock. Quantitative restrictions and licensing of imports were intensified. An increase in the terms of trade by 53 percent during 1976–1977 – associated with the coffee boom, led to a relaxation of quantitative controls and import licensing. When payments problems re-emerged, and the terms of trade declined by 28 percent in the run up to the second oil shock in 1980, the restrictions and licensing were intensified again. Analysis of the combined protection from tariffs, quantitative restrictions, and licensing of imports have demonstrated two key distortions in the Kenyan economy during the era of IS strategies in the 1970s and 1980s. First, protection in the form of tariffs, quantitative restrictions, and import licenses was skewed against imported inputs and raw materials for industrial production and agriculture. Supply of imported consumer goods was restricted and taxed heavily. When domestic investment and manufacturing of intermediate goods emerged under the IS strategy, it was encouraged with protection as well.

Table 6.1   Trade neutralizing import tax changes in Kenya, Tanzania and Uganda

(6.1a) Uganda

	1995/1996	1996/1997	1997/1998	1998/1999
Tariff Structure	0	0	0	0
	5	5	5	7
	10	10	10	15
	20	20	20	
	30	30		
	12.1			
Weighted Average Tariff	60% I.L	60% I.L	30% I.L	30% I.L
Additional Tariffs	P.T.R			0% 4% 6%
COMESA Preferential tariff		10% surcharge	10% surcharge	10% surcharge
Pref. Offsetting Measures		9.9		n.a.

(6.1b) Kenya

	1995/1996	1996/1997	1997/1998	1998/1999
Tariff Structure	0	0	0	0
	5	5	5	5
	10	15	15	15
	15	25	25	25
	25	35		
	40			
	16.1	14.1	12.3	n.a.
Weighted Average Tariff	S.D	S.D	S.D	S.D
Pref. Offsetting Measures	14.5	15.3	13.8	n.a.

(6.1c) Tanzania	1995/1996	1996/1997	1997/1998	1998/1999
Tariff Structure	0	0	0	0
	5	5	5	5
	10	10	10	10
	20	20	20	20
	30	25	30	30
	40	30		
		40		
Weighted Average Tariff	E.T	E.T	E.T	E.T
Additional Tariffs			Not provided	I.R
Pref. Offsetting Measures	27.1	28.5		n.a.

Notes: (i) (I.L) Until April 1998, Uganda maintained an import licensing regime for cigarettes, beer, soda, car batteries, and second-hand tires. In addition, tobacco imports were subject to a 60 percent tariff. Restrictions on import of these items (excluding cigarettes) were lifted in April 1998 and replaced by import surcharges (30 percent on beer, and 15 percent on sodas and car batteries). The tariff on tobacco was reduced to 30 percent in 1997/98. (ii) P.T.R: Uganda administered a complex 22–rate preferential tariff regime in 1995–1996 with 80 percent of items subject to a tariff below 10 percent. (iii) S.D.: Kenya increasingly employs 'suspended duties' which largely involve an additional tariff of 5–20 percent on a wide range of goods. (iv) E.T. The tariff-like effect of discriminatory domestic excise taxes used by Tanzania adds to the tariff on imports. (v) S.D.: Tanzania introduced a 20 percent 'suspended duty' on selected imports in 1998/1999. (vi) I.R.: The re-introduction of the COMESA preference is subject to a number of restrictions, which limit its availability. It is not provided to imports of cigarettes, beer, spirits and cement. Further, there is a requirement that to obtain the preference, an exporter to Tanzania must have a resident sales agent who is registered with the Tanzania Revenue Authority.

Source: Rajaram, A., Yeats, A., Ng'eno, N. K. Musonda, F. and Mwau, G. (1999), *Putting the Horse Before the Cart: On the Appropriate Transition to an East African Customs Union*, A Report Prepared for the East African Community (EAC) Secretariat, Arusha, April.

The trade regime that ensued in Kenya during the two decades was that of 'competitive protection' where investors and manufacturers of virtually all articles in the industrial sector sought and received some form of protection. In particular, producers of final goods and services on the one hand and producers of intermediate goods and inputs on the other hand were accorded protection. The result was a sharp overall tariff escalation in the economy. The overall cost structure that emerged harmed exports relative to protected import-substituting activities. In turn, this led to high levels of effective protection for domestic production, including protected inputs. The overall bias against exports deepened through the gradual erosion of international competitiveness made inevitable by the implicit taxation of exports. Furthermore, the erosion was deepened by the appreciation of the real exchange rate as shown above. Tariff escalation has thus played havoc with the development of exports by creating high costs and uncertainly of supplies for inputs. The persisting anti-export bias maintained during the 1970s and 1980s was marked by tariff levels spanning thirty rates in the Customs Schedule, ranging from zero to 300 percent.

Trade liberality

Trade liberality in Kenya may be identified mainly from the degree of intensity of trade barriers. There are several dimensions to trade barriers in Kenya since the 1980s. It might be argued that the distortions of the IS strategy regime itself provided the key trade barrier of speculative expectations built on the link between investment and competitive protection. With highly protected manufacturing and protection of domestic inputs in tandem, and with the addition of the system of import licensing and exchange controls, the operating conditions were set for uncertainty of access and costs of inputs. The IS strategy regime made no exceptions for exporters in the allocation of foreign exchange, import licensing or a special rate of exchange to offset overvaluation of the Kenya shilling. The choice between high-cost domestic inputs and imported inputs was highly skewed by the trade regime in favor of the former. For example, when exporters needed inputs that happened to be produced domestically under protection, import licenses were almost never granted even where imported inputs were cheaper and of better quality. In cases where inputs were available solely from import sources, import licenses were time consuming to obtain and foreign exchange allocations were limited.

During the period when liberalization was being implemented to reduce anti-export biases, an overall stance toward the sector was that restrictions on exporters remained significant, generally exceeding the export compensation scheme of the 1970s such as the manufacturing-under-bond (MUB) facility set up in 1984. Exporters required a general trading license renewable annually. Each export consignment required separate licenses. Thirty-eight items required specific export licenses renewable annually. Horticulture, which had grown rapidly since 1980, required three sets of licenses – one renewable annually and one for each shipment, before the first shipment could be made.

In the financial sector, a major supply-side impediment to export development has been the impact of government fiscal deficits on the credit markets. The simultaneous failure to curb fiscal deficits and finance them with external inflows of loans and foreign direct investment (FDI) has produced what has been termed the domestic debt strategy (DDS).[14] In this strategy, government has been forced to rely disproportionately on financing the fiscal deficit with short-term domestic debt, massively crowding out private sector credit. In addition, public investment complementary to export production has fallen.

In another dimension of financial sector weaknesses toward export production, Kenya suffers from inadequate trade financing for the purchase of domestic and imported inputs. Pre- and post-shipment facilities to exporters are limited both by costs and the inexperienced banking system in according financing based on export documentation rather than commodity exports. Nevertheless, *trade liberality* provides some of the most outstanding successes in the transformation of the trade regime. Significant policy changes and positive effects were achieved by the lifting of comprehensive import licensing and foreign exchange allocation system in May 1993.

Measuring the consequences of anti-export biases since 1980: dimensions of export 'deficit'

Growth and structure of Kenya's export markets

The real growth rates of Kenya's export volumes have been declining since 1971. The trend decline also demonstrates the starts and reversals that mark Kenya's international trade. Table 6.2 shows estimated export figures. From the rate of 6.55 percent for 1965–1971, growth of exports had declined to a negative 2.13 percent by 1976–1984. A recovery during 1984–1990 saw the growth rate improve to 4.01 percent, only to tumble in recent years. During the decade 1980–1990, only the Food and Beverages category showed significant export performance.

The structure of Kenya's exports can be viewed from at least three dimensions. They reflect a number of trends observable from the categorizations. First, viewed in terms of fuel and non-fuel categories to reflect Kenya's fuel re-exports to regional member countries, the importance and proportion of fuel re-exports in total exports is seen to have been declining sharply since 1970. On the other hand, in terms of the manufactures and primary exports categorization (of the non-fuel exports) export performance reveals the stagnation of manufactures at 15 percent for the past two decades, while primary exports rose sharply. Finally, when non-fuel exports are partitioned into traditional and non-traditional exports, as demonstrated in Table 6.3, the dramatic performance of horticulture is revealed to have partially offset the decline in manufacturing exports. Horticulture has become the lone success story in Kenya's export performance for the last two decades.[15] Since manufacturing has stagnated, it is clear that growth of the non-traditional exports category has depended on horticulture exports rather than manufactures. Were manufacturing to be revived, and horticultural development supported, export performance from non-traditional categories could improve.

Table 6.2   Annual growth rates of Kenya's exports

Period	Total	Manufacturers	Food and Beverages	Other Primary
1965–1971	6.55	17.94	5.85	4.24
1971–1976	4.85	10.45	2.55	3.26
1976–1984	–2.13	2.83	0.66	–3.39
1984–1990	4.01	4.28	1.85	–3.55
1965–1980	0.30	10.38	2.89	–3.24
1980–1990	0.06	0.24	3.03	–5.55

Note: Computed from log trend estimates using export figures in constant 1980 dollars.
Source: World Bank (1993), *Kenya's Development Challenge and the Reform Agenda Ahead*, The World: Washington, DC.

Table 6.3   Structure of merchandise exports in Kenya, 1965–1989 (percent of total exports)

Year	Fuel	Non-fuel	Manufactures	Primary	Traditional	Non-traditional
1965–1969	47	53	5	48	45	8
1970–1974	42	58	9	49	45	13
1975–1979	32	68	16	53	46	22
1980–1984	24	76	15	61	53	23
1985–1989	19	81	15	66	55	26

Note: Non-traditional exports in the table, but not in the regression report in this study, consist of manufactures and horticulture exports, so subtracting manufactures from non-traditional export yields the share of horticulture.
Source: World Bank (1993), *Kenya's Development Challenge and the Reform Agenda Ahead*, The World: Washington, DC.

Trends in all three categorizations are in turn influenced by the level of support (or lack of it) in the macroeconomic environment. Primary exports make up about 66 percent of Kenya's total merchandise exports but the ratio rises to 85 percent when fuel re-exports are included. Fuel re-exports, 47 percent of the total in 1965–1969, had fallen to 19 percent in 1985–1989. The starts and reversals in policies supposed to propel diversification have had little impact in positively influencing the trends. Given the rising share of non-fuel exports and the slow pace of diversification from traditional to non-traditional merchandise exports for example, the share of primary exports has increased. To support the growth of non-traditional exports, the stagnation in manufactures needed to be addressed simultaneously with support for horticulture where exports were growing strongly and improving the overall pace of growth in non-traditional exports.

In terms of markets, Kenya's performance reveals a number of imbalances in regional and international dimensions. A snapshot of a recent year, 1996, shown in Table 6.4, reveals the imbalances. Kenya had generally balanced trade on the trade account with the industrialized countries. Japan was the exception, running a significant trade surplus that was in turn significantly higher with Kenya than with Uganda. By far, the strongest trade ties of Kenya with the industrial countries are with the European Union (EU) compared to USA and Japan. In contrast, Kenya's significant trade deficit originates with the developing countries, concentrated mainly on Asia (outside Japan), and the Middle East. Tanzania runs a large trade surplus with Asia (outside Japan) while Uganda's trade deficit with the same region is only marginally lower than Kenya's. While Kenya's trade deficits with Asia (outside Japan) and the Middle East are high, they are moderated by trade surpluses in trade with Africa. Other African countries account for two thirds of Kenya's exports to the developing world while Kenya's imports from the group accounts for only one-fifth. Kenya's trade surpluses are concentrated on COMESA and the EAC, which account for three-quarters and one-half, respectively of Kenya's exports to the Africa region. After the lifting of trade embargoes on South Africa in the 1990s, its trade with Kenya has grown steadily and was already showing an acute deficit by 1996. In a regional context, South Africa had substantially increased its trade surplus with the EAC, especially with Kenya and Tanzania. Over 80 percent of Kenya's imports from the Africa region are accounted for by South Africa, while the latter accounts for only less than one-sixteenth of Kenya's exports to the region. Kenya's main export market for primary commodities is the developed world. Thus, although the EU is Kenya's leading export market for total exports, this reflects a predominance of primary commodities in the trade. In turn, the primary commodity trade has been driven strongly by the growth of horticulture exports to Europe. In contrast, the main markets for Kenyan exports of manufactures are in the developing countries, with 90 percent of the market being in Africa and the Middle East. The trends reflect an opportunity in the regional market for exports of manufactures, but also a failure to penetrate the lucrative and fast growing markets of the developed world. Kenya's second leading export market is Africa, with a predominant share going to COMESA. Within COMESA, the EAC partners, Uganda and Tanzania, are the leading export markets. The USA and the Middle East follow, but at a substantial distance. The poor state of Kenya's export development towards the vast United States market contrasts sharply with the successful experiences of developing countries in the Asia, Pacific and Caribbean regions. Recently, the export performance of countries such as Jamaica and Mauritius has gained export momentum from penetrating the US market.

Export performance and international comparisons

The preliminary data show that Kenya's export performance has declined since 1980, not from worsening conditions externally, but from muddled policies that produced an anti-export bias. Two periods are compared in this chapter: 1965–1980 and 1980–1989.

From a position of lead performer in exports during the first period and in relation to comparable country groupings, it is shown that over the two decades, Kenya under-performed in all groupings and in all commodity categories. Table 6.5 shows the export growth rates of non-fuel exports, food and beverages and manufacturing. During 1965–1980, growth of Kenya's exports surpassed export growth rates of all other country groupings and in the three commodity categories shown. During the 1980–1989 period, growth rate performance had gone to the bottom in manufacturing. In all categories except food and beverages, Kenya was largely outpaced by other countries in sub-Saharan Africa. It was next to the bottom in non-fuel exports. In the food and beverages category where only one country group, the low-income countries, had surpassed Kenya's performance during the period 1980–1989, the sustained performance was attributable to the emergence of a key non-traditional export, horticulture. Horticulture exports enjoyed a world price increase while export volume doubled between 1980 and 1989.

Table 6.1 Kenya's international trade imbalances and direction of trade in regional perspective, 1996

Category and region	Kenya		Uganda		Tansania		Region Means	
	Exports	*Imports*	*Exports*	*Imports*	*Exports*	*Imports*	*Exports*	*Imports*
Total Value (US$ million)	2,026.0	3,263.0	622.0	1,231.0	721.0	1,338.0	1,123.0	1,944.0
Industrialized countries (%)	46.3	46.0	82.1	46.1	38.9	34.0	55.8	42.0
Of which: European Union	38.5	34.1	72.6	34.5	27.8	24.2	46.3	30.9
USA	4.6	3.2	2.7	2.6	2.2	3.1	3.2	3.0
Japan	1.1	5.5	7.3	6.0	–	4.8	2.8	5.4
Developing countries (%)	48.3	53.9	17.9	53.9	52.7	62.5	39.6	56.8
Of which: Asia (excluding Japan)	8.9	25.9	2.9	13.4	30.3	20.0	14.0	19.8
Middle East	6.5	14.8	2.0	3.0	5.0	12.5	4.5	10.1
Europe	0.6	1.1	10.7	0.5	2.6	0.7	4.6	0.8
Africa (Of which)	32.1	11.0	2.3	36.8	14.8	28.7	16.4	25.5
COMESA	25.8	1.7	2.2	32.6	12.0	14.8	13.3	16.4
Kenya	–	–	1.6	29.4	1.6	9.9	3.0	13.1
Uganda	9.0	0.3	–	–	1.2	0.1	3.4	0.1
Tanzania	7.3	0.4	0.4	1.5	–	–	2.6	0.6
South Africa	1.6	9.3	0.2	4.2	0.6	12.6	0.8	8.7
Trade share in GNP (%, 1997)	22.0	35.0	9.0	19.0	11.0	25.0	14.0	26.3

Source: Rajaram, A., Yeats, A., Ng'eno, N. K. Musonda, F. and Mwau, G. (1999), *Putting the Horse Before the Cart: On the Appropriate Transition to an East African Customs Union*, A Report Prepared for the East African Community (EAC) Secretariat, Arusha, April.

Table 6.5   Export growth rates for Kenya and comparative country groupings, 1965–1980 and 1980–1989

	Non-fuel		Food and Beverages		Manufacturing	
Kenya	2.90	1.39	2.89	3.03	10.4	0.2
Low-income developing countries	2.70	6.97	1.62	3.66	4.1	10.6
Low-income Sub Sahara Africa	1.40	−0.32	0.51	0.41	2.0	2.3
Sub-Sahara Africa	1.51	1.44	0.43	1.07	5.5	5.5

Note: The growth rates are least square estimates of log trend using export data in constant 1980 dollars.
Source: World Bank (1993), *Kenya's Development Challenge and the Reform Agenda Ahead*, The World: Washington, DC.

While Kenya had thus outpaced all other country groups in the growth of manufactured exports during 1965–1980, the lead position was largely taken over by low-income developing countries during 1980–1989. Growth of non-traditional exports was largely supported by the emergence of horticulture in the food and beverages category.

The decline in Kenya's export performance takes on an added dimension when analyzed against the comparative performance of individual developing countries during 1965–1989. Table 6.6 uses a sample of between 13 and 17 countries, to present two dimensions of comparative changes: the relative performance in growth rates of manufactured exports, and internal changes in composition of export products reflected in the changing shares of manufactures in exports, including rankings against other developing countries.

Among thirteen selected countries, a general decline is reflected in the real growth rates of exports of manufactures from the period 1965–1980 to 1980–1989. Indonesia is notable because it tripled its growth rate of exports of manufactures. Mauritius, Philippines and Tanzania suffered substantial declines although the former two countries had enjoyed initial growth rates in the first period that were perhaps too high to be sustained in the second period. This early head start was erased over the period 1980–1989. Kenya's rate fell next to the bottom for the sample while countries which had been behind, such as Madagascar, India, Zimbabwe, Bangladesh and Pakistan, surged ahead.

Table 6.6   Change in shares of manufactured exports for selected countries, 1965–1980 and 1980–1988 (percent shares and changes in rankings)

Country	1965–1980	Ranking	1980–1989	Ranking
Turkey	2	12	64	1
Mauritius	0	17	62	2
Thailand	4	8	52	3
Morocco	5	5	50	4
Uruguay	5	5	47	5
Malaysia	6	1	45	6
Sri Lanka	1	15	43	7
Trinidad and Tobago	6	1	32	8
Mali	3	10	30	9
Indonesia	4	8	29	10
Benin	5	5	26	11
Dominican Republic	2	12	26	11
Colombia	6	1	25	13
Senegal	3	10	24	14
Panama	2	12	21	15
Kenya	6	1	17	17
Malawi	1	15	17	17

Note: The growth rates are obtained from a log trend using export data in constant 1980 dollars.

Source: World Bank (1993), *Kenya's Development Challenge and the Reform Agenda Ahead*, The World Bank: Washington, DC.

In Table 6.6, 7 countries are ranked for the periods 1965–1980 and 1980–1989 in terms of the shares of manufactures in their exports. In the first period, Kenya was tied in the first position with Malaysia, Trinidad and Tobago, and Colombia. During 1980–1989, Turkey, which had held twelfth place during 1965–1980, had taken the first position. Kenya was placed seventeenth, a position previously occupied by Mauritius, which took the second position. Other countries, which improved the shares of manufactures in total exports, were Thailand, Sri Lanka, Morocco, and Mali.

Explaining the sources of export 'deficit': a constant market share model of Kenya's export growth, 1980–1997

Theoretical framework

This section lays the theoretical framework for testing the development and sources of Kenya's export 'deficit'. Given two countries, 1 and 2, demand for each country's exports in a given market, for the two competing sources of supply may be described by the following relationship:

$$Q_1/Q_2 = f(P_1/P_2) \tag{1}$$

where Q_1 and Q_2, and P_1 and P_2 are the quantities and prices sold of commodities from the respective countries. The relationship is the basic form of the elasticity of substitution.[16] By manipulation, relation (1) may be written as:

$$P_1Q_1/P_2Q_2 = (P_1/P_2)*f(P_1/P_2) \tag{2}$$

Further manipulation yields:

$$(P_1Q_1)/[P_1Q_1 + P_2Q_2] = [1 + (P_2Q_2/P_1Q_1)]^{-1}$$
$$= \{1 + ([P_1f(P_1/P_2)]/P_2)^{-1}\}^{-1} = g(P_1/P_2) \tag{3}$$

The last statement indicates that country 1's share of the market will remain constant except as the price ratios vary. The above relation establishes that export growth implied by the constant market-share norm may be attributed to price changes. However, in the application of the analysis of changes in Kenya's exports, we use three levels or 'sources of change'. The analysis below focuses on a period of intensity in trade liberalization in Kenya (1980–1997) on the justification that policy implementation and reforms would presumably have had strong export growth-promoting effects if they had been sustained and complimentary. The period also saw a substantial expansion of world trade which could have provided markets for Kenya's exports if they had been promoted so as to take up the opportunities.

A constant market share model of changes in Kenyan exports, 1980–1997

The analysis of the last section reveals measures of failure in Kenya's export drive since 1980, analyzed in several dimensions. The theoretical framework demonstrates how the failures can arise. Our purpose is to identify areas of negative policies that could have undermined export performance even if world trade has expanded dramatically in the interim, propelling growth in many developing economies. Possible policy failures could arise from (a) the failure to promote and diversify export commodity composition towards non-traditional exports; (b) the failure to shift exports to markets that were growing relatively faster; and (c) the failure to promote competitiveness, including marketing, trade financing, etc.

This section undertakes analyses and empirical tests to determine the trajectory of Kenya's exports using the above categories of sources of poor performance. Although traditional least squares analyses are used in the next section to examine supply-side determinants of Kenya's exports, an attempt is first made in this section to capture a dis-aggregated picture of the above categorizations of failure for export performance in Kenya since 1980. We have utilized the constant market share model. It is an interesting method of analysis for testing export performance (Leamer and Stern, 1970) based on world demand for a country's exports.[17] It is assumed that a country's exports may fail to grow as rapidly as the world's average for many reasons. The method permits detection of the above four key sources of success or failure of exports to grow rapidly. We have selected two periods, 1980 (period 1) and 1997 (period 2) and examined the intervening developments in Kenya's exports for the four categories of effects described in further detail below:

- With exports viewed as undifferentiated regarding commodity and region of destination, if a country maintained its share of the percentage increase in world exports of each of its commodity exports in each of its markets from period 1 to period 2, its exports behave as a single good fully benefiting from growth in world demand and trade. But a country could also expand its benefits beyond these gains by expanding its shares from period 1 to period 2. This measure gives rise to the *world trade growth effect* to a country's export performance;
- Concentration in commodity exports whose growth rates of demand is more favorable than the world average would increase gains from trade, but concentration in commodity exports that are relatively slow-growing, would reduce benefits. This measure gives rise to the *commodity composition effect* on a country's export performance;
- Concentration in commodity exports and access to relatively rapidly growing regions increases benefits relative to concentration in exports to slow-growing neighbors or stagnant regions. The objective norm for maintaining shares is to

retain a constant share of exports of a particular commodity class to a particular region. This measure gives rise to the *market distribution effect* on a country's export performance; and

- Finally a country may fail to maintain its competitiveness in relation to other world sources of supply of its exports. This failure could arise from different sources: (a) a rise in a country's relative prices of exports; (b) differential rates of price inflation, differential rates of commodity quality improvements, and development of new exports; (c) differential impacts of improvements in marketing, export support and access to trade financing; and (d) differential rates of change in the culture of export promptness of fulfillment of orders. The residual effect is termed the *competitiveness effect*.

This section is an analysis based on the above concepts to disentangle Kenya's failures and shortcomings in export performance during the past two decades, in terms of the above decomposition. The model assumes that as the world economy grows, a country's share in the world market should remain unchanged over time. The objective of the application of the model is to assign deviations between the constant shares norm and the actual export performance to the above categories of effects. Given world trade growth, the deviation is attributed to three dimensions: competitiveness, commodity composition, and market distribution. The model and its theoretical considerations are examined in Leamer and Stern (1970). In terms of the decomposition of sources of slow export growth, decomposition in the four areas identified, yields interesting findings that are amenable to strategic policy changes in Kenya. Table 6.7 presents the 1980 and 1997 databases on which an application of the model and the desegregation of sources of export failures are evaluated. The starting point is to assemble data on actual world exports and also the county's exports. Data was assembled for the two periods, 1980 and 1997. Next the exports are assigned to regions of destination and to SITC categories. The hypothetical 'constant share' of country in world exports is computed on the basis of the rate of world growth of exports and the 'constant' SITC shares that a country has to maintain in order not to slide.

Measuring the size and sources of Kenya's export deficit

As a consistency check for data, Kenya's exports tabulated for the various market destinations or by SITC commodity classification are equal in each of the two periods. Exports grew from 1,386 million US dollars in 1980 to 2,116 million US dollars in 1997, a growth of a mere 730 million US dollars. This was equivalent to KShs 53 billion at the February 2000 exchange rate, or an increase of 52.7 percent.[19] This compares poorly with the percentage growth of total world exports at 159

Table 6.7   Constant market share analysis of changes in the growth of Kenya's exports, 1980–1997 (millions of U.S. $)

	1	2	3	4	5	6	7	8
	Actual World Exports		Actual Kenyan Exports		Growth of World Trade	C.S. Norm Growth of Trade in Respective Markets		
	1980	1997	(V.j) 1980	(V'.j) 1997	$\{(2)/(1)\}-1$ (rj)	(5)*(3) (rj V.j)	(r)*(3) (rV.j)	Sum(rijVij18)
(A) Market Analysis								
Industrialized Countries	1,280,500	3,307,400	604	1,004	1.583	956.07	958.40	521.92
Africa	74,662	96,960	365	690	0.299	109.01	579.17	59.51
Asia	157,663	922,363	165	209	4.850	800.29	261.82	436.88
Europe	69,340	240,680	15	8	2.471	37.07	23.80	20.23
Middle East	113,636	151,175	67	110	0.330	22.13	106.31	12.08
Western Hemisphere	120,515	271,683	1	3	1.254	1.25	1.59	0.68
All other*	142,802	77,505	169	92	−0.457	(77.28)	268.16	−42.19
Total	1,959,118	5,067,766	1,386	2,116	1.587	1,849	2,199	1009.11

	1	2	3	4	5	6	7	8
	Actual World Exports		**Actual Kenyan Exports**					
	1980	1997	1980	1997	(ri)	$(ri\,Vi.)$	$(rVi.)$	$Sum(rijVij)$
			$(Vi.)$	$(V'I)$				
(B) Commodity Analysis								
1. SITC 0 & 1	201,109	429,896	589	1,134	1.138	670.06	934.60	563.21
2. SITC 2 & 4	136,789	234,230	142	243	0.712	101.15	225.32	85.02
3. SITC 3	477,362	427,443	445	136	−0.105	(46.53)	706.11	−39.11
4. SITC 5	147,392	486,402	48	182	2.300	110.40	76.16	92.80
5. SITC 7	511,448	2,015,924	39	15	2.942	114.72	61.88	96.43
6. SITC 6 & 8	485,018	1,473,871	123	406	2.039	250.77	195.17	210.78
TOTAL	**1,959,118**	**5,067,766**	**1,386**	**2,116**	**1.587**	**1,200.58**	**2,199.25**	**1009.13**

Sources: IMF, *Statistical Abstracts*, Various Years.
Notations:
$Vi.$ = Value of Kenya's exports of commodity j in 1980
$V'i.$ = Value of Kenya's exports of commodity i in 1997
$V.j$ = Value of Kenya's exports to country j in period 1
$V^1.j$ = Value of Kenya's exports of commodity i to country j in period 1
r = percentage increase in total world exports from period 1 to period 2.

percent between 1980 and 1997 as estimated from the model. Even then, the sole factor among the four desegregated sources of growth of exports in world trade that has driven Kenya's exports even at that low level since 1980 is the expansion of world trade. Exports could have done far better if other factors of the model, diversification of exports, market diversification and competitiveness, had matched global trends.

Increased world trade alone would have had the effect of increasing Kenya's exports by 2,199 million US dollars between 1980 and 1997, had Kenya maintained its share of the increase attributable to the expansion by a factor of 1.587. This would have been equivalent to KShs 158 billion at the February 2000 exchange rates. Instead, by capturing only KShs 53 billion from trade expansion, Kenya was enjoying a mere one-third of the achievable increase from the expansion.

The three other sources of export growth that could have further increased the export performance, if their effects had been positive – namely commodity composition, market distribution, and competitiveness, were instead negative as shown in 8. If the other negative effects discussed below had been offset, the increased world trade effect would have yielded Kenya an export growth performance at a rate 301.3 percent of the actual increase of 730 million US dollars.

The three effects are seen to be significantly negative, and are quantified in the model. These are: at the rate of commodity diversification towards non-traditional exports, market diversification, and competitiveness in the world markets.[20]

Commodity Diversification: Kenya's failure to diversify its exports towards non-traditional exports in line with changes in world market demand for various commodities cost it the loss of 999 million US dollars – equivalent to KShs 72 billion the February 2000 exchange rate.

Market Diversification: The failure to change markets and diversify in tandem with market opportunities led to a further loss of 191 million US dollars – equivalent to Ksh.14 billion at the February 2000 exchange rate.

Competitiveness: Finally, the failure to pay attention to competitiveness led to a further loss of 279 million US dollars –equivalent to KShs 20 billion at the February 2000 exchange rate.

In sum, KShs 106 billion of the KShs 158 billion hypothetically capturable through the growth of world trade were offset by failures in commodity composition, market distribution, and lack of competitiveness. Table 6.8 gives a summary of the findings from the *Constant Market Shares Model*.

Table 6.8   Summary of findings from constant market share model (millions of U.S. $ and percentages)

Analysis	Millions of U.S. $	Percent
Kenyan exports in 1980	1386	
Kenyan exports in 1997	2116	
Change in exports	730	100
Analysis of Sources of Export Performance		
1. Due to increase in world trade:	2199	301.3
2. Due to commodity composition:	−999	−136.8
3. Due to market distribution	−191	−26.2
4. Due to increased competitiveness:	−279	−38.2
Net Export Performance	*730*	*100*
Estimated 'Export Deficit' since 1980	*1469*	*201.3*

In terms of rankings, the failure to develop non-traditional exports has been far more costly to Kenya's export performance (by a factor greater than 1:3), than the negative effects of un-competitiveness. In turn, lack of competitiveness has exerted a greater negative effect than market distribution.

The results obtained above should be taken as an order of magnitude given the theoretical and statistical observations on the elasticity of substitution concept. The appropriate analysis should also reflect the markets where the elasticity of substitution concept is thought to hold. The model takes the world market to be the competing market, which produces q2 exports, and we have used world growth rates of exports as the standard to judge growth of Kenya's exports. In particular, the world versus Kenya competition in the different SITC classes may be quite restricted particularly in the upper levels where Kenya effectively produces or exports little.

An alternative scenario of export growth under the CMS model: the 8 percent annual export growth scenario

This section of the analysis of the sources of Kenya's export 'deficit' hypothesises the outcomes that would have been achieved in the CMS model if exports had grown annually by 8 percent through greater competitiveness while maintaining the

Table 6.9 CMS scenario: analysis of changes in Kenya's exports, 1980–1997 at 8 percent annual growth rate (millions of U.S. $)

	1	2	3	4	5	6	7	8
	Actual World Exports		Kenya Actual 1980 Exp.	8% annual growth to 1997				
					$\{(2)/(1)\}-1$	$(5)*(3)$	$(r)*(3)$	Sum(rijVij)
			(V.j)	(V'.j)	(rj)	(rj V.j)	(rV.j)	Sum(rijVij)
	1980	1997	1980	1997				
(A) Market Analysis								
Industrialized Countries	1,280,500	3,307,400	604	2,234.80	1.583	956.07	958.40	521.92
Africa	74,662	96,960	365	1,350.50	0.299	109.01	579.17	59.51
Asia	157,663	922,363	165	610.50	4.850	800.29	261.82	436.88
Europe	69,340	240,680	15	55.50	2.471	37.07	23.80	20.23
Middle East	113,636	151,175	67	247.90	0.330	22.13	106.31	12.08
Western Hemisphere	120,515	271,683	1	3.70	1.254	1.25	1.59	0.68
All other*	142,802	77,505	169	625.30	-0.457	(77.28)	268.16	-42.19
Total	**1,959,118**	**5,067,766**	**1,386**	**5,128.20**	**1.587**	**1,849**	**2,199**	**1009.11**

	1	2	3	4	5	6	7	8
	Actual World exports		Kenya actural exp.	8% annual growth				
	1980	1997	1980	1997				
			$(Vi.)$	$(V'i)$	(ri)	$(ri\,Vi.)$	$(rVi.)$	$Sum(rijVij)$
(B) Commodity Analysis								
1. SITC 0 & 1	201,109	429,896	589	2,179.30	1.138	670.06	934.60	563.21
2. SITC 2 & 4	136,789	234,230	142	525.40	0.712	101.15	225.32	85.02
3. SITC 3	477,362	427,443	445	1,646.50	-0.105	(46.53)	706.11	-39.11
4. SITC 5	147,392	486,402	48	177.60	2.300	110.40	76.16	92.80
5. SITC 7	511,448	2,015,924	39	144.30	2.942	114.72	61.88	96.43
6. SITC 6 & 8	485,018	1,473,871	123	455.10	2.039	250.77	195.17	210.78
TOTAL	1,959,118	5,067,766	1,386	5,128.20	1.587	1,200.58	2,199.25	1009.13

Sources: IMF, *Statistical Abstract* (Various Years).
Notations:

$Vi.$ = Value of Kenya's exports of commodity j in 1980
$V'i.$ = Value of Kenya's exports of commodity i in 1997
$V.j$ = Value of Kenya's exports to country j in period 1
$V^1.j$ = Value of Kenya's exports of commodity i to country j in period 1
r = percentage increase in total world exports from period 1 to period 2
ri = percentage increase in total world export of commodity i from period 1 to period 2
rij = percentage increase in total world export of commodity i to country j from period 1 to period 2.

same markets and commodity composition. Greater penetration of world markets without either commodity or market diversification would still have yielded positive results. The analysis in Table 6.9 shows that exports would have grown from 1,386 million US dollars in 1980 to 5,128 million US dollars in 1997 (nearly four fold compared to less than double the volume that was actually achieved as per Table 6.8).[21] With world trade having grown by a factor of 1.587, Kenya's expansion would have increased sharply in the industrial countries and Africa where it would have more than doubled the actual performance. Exports to Asia would have tripled while exports to all other destinations would similarly have more than tripled.

Much more significant, an annual growth rate of exports at 8 percent would have turned the *export deficit* to an *export surplus*. The CMS results presented in Table 6.10 show that this surplus would have reached 41 percent of the export performance achieved with an annual growth rate of 8 percent. The expansion would have represented 70 percent over actual world trade expansion.

Similarly, there would have appeared some inter-category changes in the SITC concentrations of commodities though not in the total exports. SITC 0 and 1 would have doubled while SITC 3 would have yielded the fastest growth rate, rising from 136 million US dollars to 1,646.50 million US dollars. SITC 5 would actually have declined.

Table 6.10 CMS results under the 8 percent annual growth rate scenario

Analysis	Millions, US $	Percent
Kenyan exports in 1980	1,386	
Kenyan exports in 1997	5,128.2	
Change in exports	*3,742.2*	*100%*
1. Due to increase in world trade:	2,199	58.8
2. Due to commodity composition	−999	−26.7
3. Due to market distribution	−191	−5.1
4. Due to increased competitiveness	2,733	73.0
Net Export Performance	*3,742.2*	*100%*
Estimated Export Surplus with 8 percent annual expansion	*1,543*	*41.2%*

In summary, with an 8 percent annual growth rate of exports, growth of world trade would still have contributed 2,199 million US dollars over 1980 to 1997. Of the three other sources of export growth, commodity composition, market distribution and increased competitiveness, only the contribution of competitiveness – from greater but undiversified penetration, would have turned sharply positive. As shown in Table 6.10, the contribution from competitiveness would rise from 279 million US dollars to 2,733 million US dollars. The relative contributions of other sources would also change. The overall change in exports would be 3,742.2 million US dollars (an increase of over five times compared to the actual achievement of 730 million US dollars). A far greater contribution (73 percent) would be explained by competitiveness than by the growth of world trade (58.8 percent) while lack of commodity diversification would be a greater obstacle (-27 percent) than market diversification. Compared to the actual performance of Kenya's exports as analyzed in Table 6.8, the results re-affirm that lack of commodity diversification is a far more serious problem than lack of market diversification.

Determinants of export performance and the role of relative prices

To begin to develop policies that can deal with the export performance obstacles (discussed above), it is important to understand the determinants of export supply. Traditional regressions of surplus functions were estimated. Estimates of export performance at several levels of aggregation are presented bellow in three categories as follows:

- Total exports;
- Agricultural sector exports; and
- Non-traditional exports.

Total exports   The results of the regression analysis indicate that Kenya's total exports respond to three key explanatory variables with significant coefficients. Relative export prices (the ratio or total export price index to non-tradable price index, which is proxied by the price index of non-oil exports to the average weighed CPI) show a coefficient value of 0.69. A one percent increase in relative price increases exports by 0.7 of one percent. This is indicative of a high degree of price responsiveness. A policy to eliminate price distortions between export production and import substitutes would thus help in promoting exports. The remaining two variables exert similar magnitudes of influence save that an increase in real wages depresses export performance.

Agricultural exports   The results of regression analysis suggest that agricultural exports respond with significantly positive coefficients to relative export prices (log of average relative price over two-year periods) and lagged relative price. The relative price was defined as the price index of non-oil exports deflated by the average weighted CPI. The respective coefficient values are 0.07 and 0.9. On average a one percent increase in the relative price of agricultural exports relative to non-tradable prices is likely to raise the value of agricultural exports by roughly 0.5 percent. This also indicates a high degree of price responsiveness, while growth of real wages in agriculture almost offset growth of exports.

Non-traditional exports   The regression results on non-traditional exports show that all the coefficients are significant and correctly signed. Positive relative price changes that favor non-traditional exports elicit positive export performance responses. On average, a one percent change in relative prices will raise the value of non-traditional export production by 0.5 percent. Lagged relative price changes exert similar magnitudes of export performance. As expected, changes in real wages are negatively correlated with export performance. A one percent change in real wages strongly depresses export performance by 0.7 percent.

In summary, Kenya's exports at all levels of aggregation are highly responsive to changes in relative prices. On the other hand, increases in real wages uniformly depress all categories of exports by between 0.7 percent and 0.8 percent for every one percent change.[22]

Survey of exporters

A limited survey of Kenyan exporters was undertaken as part of the study to assess the difficulties of export expansion. The survey focused on broad areas of the export sector such as a profile of exporting firms and their location; the workings of government facilitative services towards the sector; the degree support of infrastructure services to export performance; the leading market for export; and the backward linkages of Kenya's trade regime.

A summary of Kenya's trade strategies and problems

This section summarizes the strategic problems of Kenya's trade regime as analyzed in this study.

Trade neutrality and trade liberality

Trade neutrality is associated with attempted reforms to reduce divergences between price incentives towards the production of exports and import substitutes. This study examines progress in the reform of the exchange rate, the harmonization of import taxation and the liberalization of export policies. Taking two periods, 1980 and 1989, Kenya's exchange rate had been progressively liberalized from a fixed regime to a relatively flexible rate, but with little benefit to international competitiveness. The real exchange rate was more appreciated in 1989 relatively to 1981 and measures of variability referred to in this study indicate that there was increasing exchange rate instability. In the liberalization of exports, Kenya has had tasks on two fronts: to reduce levels of tariffs, which were high across-the-board as of 1980, and to convert trade restrictions and administrative controls into equivalent tariffs. The experience of the period indicates repeated policy reversals and overall 'replacement' of tariff reductions and removal of controls with equivalent instruments such as suspended duties. Finally, export oriented policies were undertaken in recent decades not as pre-planned strategies but as reactions to the shock of the collapse of the EAC. The vehicles used for export promotion, namely the Export Compensation Act of 1974 and the Manufacturing Under Bond (MUB) facility of 1984 have been unwieldy and they have been corruptly abused.

In trade liberality, associated with the intensity of trade barriers, Kenyan policies have fared no better. The protection regime that had emerged by 1980, favored manufacturing-based import substitution that found lucrative markets in the EAC and COMESA countries, and that took advantage of the anti-apartheid trade ban of South Africa, as well as domestically produced inputs. Added to import controls and foreign exchange allocation requirements, the situation was rife for a highly escalated tariff regime as well as high input costs and shortages. Restrictions on exporters remained into the 1990s, and the export promotion agencies for incentivizing exports (the ECA and the MUB) were both unwieldy and retrograde in promoting exports let alone export diversification.

Kenya's anti-export biases and the slide into global under-performance

Real growth of export volumes in Kenya has declined since the period 1965–1971. Viewed from several dimensions of exports structure – fuel versus non-fuel, manufactures and primary export, and traditional versus non-traditional exports, different features of the decline emerge. Fuel exports have relatively declined. Manufacturing, relative to primary exports, has stagnated at 15 percent of total exports since the period 1980–1984. Finally, horticulture exports have been the lone success story in non-traditional exports while the key category, manufacturing, declined. Compared to earlier episodes of development experience, the slide in manufacturing is as uncharacteristic of Kenya's trade regime as the upsurge in horticulture exports. Kenya outpaced low-income developing countries, low-income sub-Saharan Africa and sub-Saharan Africa by far in growth of manufacturing exports during 1965–1980. By 1980–1989, it was outstripped in manufacturing growth by all three-country groupings by far. The decline can be shown against the groupings and by individual performance of selected developing countries. In terms of export markets, 38.5 percent of Kenya's exports go to the European Union. Africa is the leading destination among developing countries with two thirds of Kenya's exports to the developing world. On the other hand, Europe (34.1 percent) and Asia (25.9 percent) supply the bulk of Kenya's imports.

Measurements of Kenya's export failures

A model of constant market shares was used to capture the extent of export failures in the Kenyan trade regime. Regression estimates and results were also analyzed to reveal key determinants of export performance in Kenya. The results show that world trade growth could have contributed 2,199 million US dollars to trade expansion in Kenya from 1980–1997. Overall change in exports would have been higher if at the same time, trade policies had been geared to export diversification, market diversification and increased competitiveness. Instead, negative effects from the policies and results led to loss of export potentials amounting to 999, 191 and 279 million US dollars in each case. The overall effect was to reduce even the potential gains from world trade expansion from 2199 million US dollars to 730 million US dollars. The regression analyses of export supply functions show substantial relative price responsiveness for total agricultural and non-traditional exports. They also indicate the importance of keeping the levels of real wages from squeezing export performance.

Investor sentiment in Kenya's export sector

Exporting firms in Kenya appear to be predominantly locally owned companies (two-thirds in our survey) or joint ventures with foreign firms (nearly one third of the firms). Firms that have invested in export activities are predominantly located in urban areas or industrial estates. Food and beverages, and paper and paper products are leading exports.

Leading obstacles to exporting firms

The leading obstacles to exporting firms are transport and delivery difficulties with customs and export procedures, problems with central government procedures and official export authorizations. Difficulties with export procedures and customs in the countries to which the goods were being exported were cited far less frequently than counterpart obstacles in Kenya. The relatively high cost and prices of Kenya's exports were also cited in only 45.5 percent of the cases. Other key obstacles cited in Kenya's export production and potential were: high borrowing costs and the high cost of domestic inputs. Confirming earlier analyses, Uganda and Tanzania were cited predominantly as the leading or second leading export markets. Companies predominantly use their representatives in export market search and spend substantial amounts in the activity.

Conclusions and policy recommendations

An outline of the conclusions and recommendations of the study is presented below:

- In terms of trade neutrality and trade liberality, reversals and stop-go policies have been prevalent since 1980 and have contributed significantly to Kenya's failure to maintain the export expansion and diversification momentum of the 1965–1980 period. Trade neutrality should be pursued with greater predictability and barriers to trade should be eliminated. Where protection is called for, it should be justified and predictable for investors in the export sector.
- In export performance, Kenya has penetrated African and developing country markets mostly with manufacturers while it has penetrated industrial countries (particularly the EU) with primary commodity exports. This structure of exports is a strategic anomaly given that the income effects that can spur an export boom from Kenya through diversified exports are far higher in industrial countries than in the African market. The export strategy suggested from the analyses is to penetrate industrial country markets with far more diversified export products (including expansion of horticulture products which have succeeded almost independently of a supporting government policy) and at the same time, retain African markets for manufactures. In imports, regional trade integration would call for an increase in regional sources of imports and for a reduction in the trade deficit with Asian countries that import little from Kenya.
- Measurements of the sources of Kenya's export growth failures indicate the sources of the decline in the following order, (a) failure of export diversification; (b) failure to maintain competitiveness and; (c) failure to diversify markets.

Policies should urgently be addressed by government in consultation with the export sector, to alleviate the problems highlighted.

• In ranking the relative damage that has been caused by inappropriate export-oriented measures, this study shows that far more damage to exports has originated from failures to promote non-traditional exports than from failures to diversify markets and pursue the benefits of competitiveness.

• Investors point to an important array of issues that should be addressed to improve the environment for export activity: transport and delivery problems; difficulties with local customs and export procedures; problems with government procedures and official export authorizations; high local borrowing costs; and high-cost of domestic inputs. These issues should be addressed urgently to rebuild the export orientation of the economy.

Acknowledgments

This chapter benefited from comments made by staff members of the Institute of Policy Analysis and Research at a 'Brown Bag' session held to review the draft on March 29, 2000. The author acknowledges written comments from Professor Clive S. Gray and Dr. Malcolm McPherson, both of the Harvard Institute for International Development (HIID). Comments were received from participants at the EAGER research workshop held at Naro Moru River Lodge, Kenya during April 26–28, 2000. All errors remain the responsibility of the author.

Notes

1. *IPAR Policy Quarterly*, No. 1, April 1999. The forecast was first issued by the Institute of Policy Analysis and Research (IPAR).
2. The import substitution strategy (IS) was stated clearly in the 1966–1970 national development plan – *National Development Plan, 1966–1970*, p. 236, where the government committed itself to protecting infant industries and supporting import substitution.
3. Government of Kenya, *National Development Plan 1966–1970*. Preface by the Minister for Economic Planning and Development, Paragraph 3. The same objectives are outlined in Government of Kenya's *Sessional Paper No. 10 of 1965*, pp. 1–2. As of 2000, policies seem to have come full circle to this basic policy stance. See *Interim Policy Reduction Strategy Paper*, (IPRSP) 2000–2003, prepared by the Government of Kenya, March 2000.
4. Tax buoyancy is the ratio of the percent change in the actual tax revenue to the percent change in the tax base resulting from a tax change. The tax elasticity is the ratio of the percent change in revenue to the percent change in the tax base, assuming those tax rates are not changed.

5. See, Wagacha, M. and Ngugi, R. (1999), 'Macroeconomic Structure and Outlook', in Kimuyu, P., Wagacha, M. and Abagi, O. (eds.), *Kenya Strategic Policies for the 21st Century*, IPAR: Nairobi.
6. Economists identify this as the Dutch disease phenomenon of price and factor movements. A spending effect promotes demand for non-traded goods relative to traded goods, bidding up prices of the former and leading to an appreciation of the real exchange rate (RER). This spending effect increases the prices of domestic goods such as housing, household goods, capital, and consumer goods, moving investment in the same direction and further depressing the traded goods sector. Further, in a resource movement effect triggered by higher profitability in the *boom* sector, factor costs rise in tradable goods sector depressing it further. Inflows of foreign aid during the 1980s could have sustained the phenomenon by postponing the need to reform the exchange rate and remove controls on interest rates.
7. Price controls that set ceiling prices on a wide range of goods became sources of 'rent seeking' by control officials who selectively permitted companies to adjust their cost increases justified by increases in the prices of raw materials, including import prices.
8. See, Metzel, J. and Phillips, L. C. (1998), *Bringing Down the Barriers to Trade: The Experience of Trade Policy Reform*, African Economic Policy Discussion Paper No. 5, for the AEGR/PSGE Project: 'Restarting and Sustaining Economic Growth and Development in Africa'.
9. See, *Kenya: The Challenge of Promoting Exports*, Policy Research Division, World Bank: Washington DC, 1993.
10. See, Glenday, G. and Ndii, D. (1999), 'Export Platforms in Kenya', AEGER/TRADE Regimes Research Paper, HIID, September.
11. The information below is generated from: Rajaram, A., et al (1999), *Putting the Horse Before the Cart: On the Appropriate Transition to an East African Customs Union*, A Report prepared for the EAC, April.
12. See, *Kenya: The Challenge of Promoting Exports*, Policy Research Division, World Bank: Washington DC, 1993.
13. Imports may also face *ad valorem* and specific excise duties, which have been applied in Kenya mainly for revenue purposes. In fiscal 1996/1997, 92 items faced the duties. Many of the excise duties are non-discriminatory in terms of domestic prices because they are charged equally on domestically produced goods as well as imports. Nevertheless, the taxes exert an excess burden and reduce investment in and the competitiveness of exports. See *Putting the Horse Before the Cart: On the Appropriate Transitions to an East African Customs Union*, A report prepared for the EAC, April 1999.
14. See, *IPAR Policy Quarterly*, Vol. 1, No. 1 (April 1999).
15. An interesting research question is how the sub-sector succeeded phenomenally in penetrating the export market while the rest of the export sector was negatively affected by the stop-and-go policy reforms.
16. Although the concept has had problems of theory and measurement in international trade, it still provides a useful measure of the workings of the international price mechanism.
17. The model in no way deals with the dynamics of progress of exports in accordance with comparative advantage. Growth and its links to export growth is also not considered. In using world export growth as a standard, it is understood that competition may be quite limited between Kenya and other groups of countries (e.g., the industrial countries) in some categories of commodities. The analysis in this segment of the study is thus a first approximation and the scope does not permit identification of products that Kenya could have exported, in what volumes, if good policies had been taken and sustained.
18. Rij was first computed from the cross classification of actual world exports by market destinations and commodity groups and then multiplied by Vij, the cross classification of changes in actual Kenyan exports by market destination and commodity groups from 1980.

19. A rate of KShs 72.5 per US$ was used. The US$ based analysis assumes that a common inflation rate applies to world and Kenyan exports, so that deflating to obtain real values is redundant.
20. See the study titled, *Revealed Comparative Advantage and Export Propensity in Kenya* by Eluid Moyi and Peter Kimuyu, Discussion Paper No. 015/99, Institute of Policy Research and Analysis, March 1999. These findings are reconfirmed in an independent analysis.
21. The 8 percent annual expansion of Kenyan exports would have increased world trade expansion marginally. By the law of large numbers, this analysis ignores that impact and uses actual world trade expansion as tabulated in Table 6.7.
22. Nevertheless, this might say more about stagnation of productivity than the 'level' of wages. Hence the need to address questions of productivity as a probity. Real wage impact seems to negatively affect formal sector firms, which are predominant in export activity. Informal sector real wage does not seem to have matched formal sector wages, implying that the growth of export and wages employment will crucially depend on keeping narrow the gap between formal and informal wages. See Glenday and Ndii (1999), op. cit.

References

Bhagwati, J. (1978), *Foreign Trade Regimes and Economic Development: Anatomy and Consequences of Exchange Control Regimes*, Ballinger: Lexington, MA.

Glenday, G. and Ndii, D. (1999), 'Export Platforms in Kenya', EAGER/Trade Regimes Research Paper, Harvard Institute for International Development: Cambridge, MA.

GoK (1966), *National Development Plan, 1966–1970*, Government Printer: Nairobi.

GoK (1986), *Economic Management for Renewed Growth*, Government Printer: Nairobi.

Kimuyu, P., Wagacha, M. and Abagi, O. (eds.) (1999), *Kenya's Strategic Policies for the 21st Century*, Institute of Policy Analysis and Research (IPAR): Nairobi.

Krueger, A. O. (1978), *Foreign Trade Regimes and Economic Development: Liberalization Attempts and Consequences*, Ballinger: Lexington, MA.

Leamer, E. E. and Stern, R. M. (1970), *Quantitative International Economics*, Allyn and Bacon: Boston, MA.

Metzel, J. and Phillips, L. C. (1998), 'Bringing Down Barriers to Trade: The Experience of Trade Policy Reform', African Economic Discussion Paper No. 5.

Moyi, E. and Kimuyu, P. (1999), 'Revealed Comparative Advantage and Export Propensity in Kenya', Discussion Paper No. 015/99.

Rajaram, A., Yeats, A., Ng'eno, N. K. Musonda, F. and Mwau, G. (1999), *Putting the Horse Before the Cart: On the Appropriate Transition to an East African Customs Union*, A Report Prepared for the East African Community (EAC) Secretariat, Arusha, April.

Sharpley, E. (1988), 'Kenya's Industrialization 1964–84', IDS Discussion Paper No. 242, Institute of Development Studies: Sussex.

Wagacha, B. M. (1976), 'An Analysis of the Trade Regime in Kenya', Working Paper No. 281, Institute of Development Studies, University of Nairobi: Nairobi.

Wagacha, B. M. and Ngugi, R. (1999), 'Macroeconomic Structure and Outlook', in Kimuyu, P., Wagacha, B. M. and Abagi, O. (eds.), *Kenya's Strategic Policies for the 21st Century*, Institute of Policy Analysis and Research (IPAR): Nairobi.

World Bank (1993), *Kenya's Development Challenge and the Reform Agenda Ahead*, The World Bank: Washington, DC.

Appendix

Estimations of export performance

Total exports. In the regression equation for total exports, the following notation was used:

Tx = value of total real exports in millions of Kenya pounds 1972–1998. (proxied by the value of total exports in millions of Kenya pounds deflated by the average weighted CPI (AWCPI)

TOTEXRELPR = Price index of non-oil exports as a ratio of the index of non-tradable prices (proxied by average weighted CPI (AWCPI)

TRW = index of real wage, (proxied by total real wage earnings as a ratio of total employment). The equation fitted is

$\text{Log Tx} = a + b\text{Log TOTEXPRELPR} + c\text{Log TOTEXPRELPR}_{-1} + d\text{Log TRW}_{-1}$

The regression results are presented below. They are consistent with the determinations of total export performance. All three explanatory variables have highly significant coefficients. The results suggest that the co-efficient of change in relative prices significantly and positively influence real exports. The significance is the one percent level and the value at 0.69 implies that on average, a one percent increase in the price of exports relative to non-tradable prices is likely to raise the volume of total exports by 0.7 percent. Lagged relative price movements show slightly smaller magnitude of positive impact. Real wage increases depress export performance, such that a one percent increase in real wages should depress real exports by about 0.7 percent. This suggests that real wage increases can exert offsetting effects one-to-one with relative price increases.

Dependent Variable: LOG (TOTTEXTPT/AWCPI
Regression Methods: Least Squares
Sample (Adjusted): 1973–1998
Included observations: 26 after adjusting endpoints

Variable	Coefficient	Std. Error	t-Statistic	Prob.
DLOG(TOTEXPTRELPR)	0.687876	0.127029	5.415101	0.0000
LOG(TOTEXPTRELPR(-1))	0.626375	0.125740	4.981507	0.0001
LOG(TOTRW(-1))	−0.675862	0.126221	−5.354592	0.0000
C	10.41235	0.265049	39.28458	0.0000
R-squared	0.668458	Mean dependent var		9.035860
Adjusted R-squared	0.623248	S.D. dependent var		0.164609
S.E. of regression	0.101037	Akaike info criterion		−1.606014
Sum squared resid	0.224588	Schwarz criterion		−1.412461
Log likelihood	24.87819	F-statistic		14.78556
DW	1.732495	Prob(F-statistic)		0.000017

The equation shows satisfactory levels of serial correlation and the Akaike criterion is low.

Agricultural Exports

In the agriculture exports regression, the following definitions were used:
X = Value of agricultural exports in millions of Kenyan pounds 1972–1998
AWPI = Average weighted Consumer Price index
AGRW = Agricultural real wage per employee (calculated as real agricultural earnings divided by employees in agriculture, 1972 – 1998
AGRELPR = Price index of non-oil exports as a ratio of AWPI
LogX = Log (AGREPR – AGRELPR (-1)) + Log (AGRELPR (-1)) + Log (AGRW)
The first independent term is a proxy for the ratio of the index of agricultural export prices to the index of non-tradable prices.

The results are provided below:
Dependent Variable: LOG(AGEXPORT/AWCPI)
Method: Least Squares
Sample(adjusted): 1973–1997
Included observations: 11
Excluded observations: 14 after adjusting endpoints

Variable	Coefficient	Std. Error	t-Statistic	Prob.
LOG(AGRELPR-AGRELPR(-1))	0.065190	0.028844	2.260131	0.0583
LOG(AGRELPR(-1))	0.862256	0.247072	3.489902	0.0101
LOG(AGRW)	–0.787739	0.289324	–2.722688	0.0297
C	9.446070	0.352048	26.83174	0.0000
R-squared	0.721212	Mean dependent var		8.441291
Adjusted R-squared	0.601731	S.D. dependent var		0.234020
S.E. of regression	0.147686	Akaike info criterion		–0.712164
Sum squared resid	0.152679	Schwarz criterion		–0.567474
Log likelihood	7.916900	F-statistic		6.036229

All the coefficients are significant and are correctly signed. On average, a one percent increase in the relative price of agricultural exports relative to non-tradables is likely to raise the value of agricultural exports by roughly a half a percent, showing a substantial degree of price responsiveness to price changes. On the other hand, increases in agricultural real wages can almost nullify the price effects. A one percent increase in real agricultural wages leads to nearly a one percent decrease in agricultural exports.

Non-traditional exports

In the agriculture exports regression, the following definitions were used:
X = Value of agricultural exports in millions of Kenyan pounds 1972–1998
AWPI = Average weighted Consumer Price index
AGRW = Agricultural real wage per employee (calculated as real agricultural earnings divided by employees in agriculture, 1972–1998
AGRELPR = Price index of non-oil exports as a ratio of AWPI

LogX = Log (AGREPR – AGRELPR (-1)) + Log (AGRELPR (-1)) + Log (AGRW)
The first independent term is a proxy for the ratio of the index of agricultural export prices to the index of non-tradable prices.

The results are provided below:

Dependent Variable: LOG(NONTRADITEXPT/AWCPI)
Method: Least Squares
Sample(adjusted): 1973 1998
Included observations: 26 after adjusting endpoints

Variable	Coefficient	Std. Error	t-Statistic	Prob.
DLOG(TOTEXPTRELPR)	0.527791	0.233465	2.260681	0.0340
LOG(TOTEXPTRELPR(-1))	0.462803	0.231096	2.002642	0.0577
LOG(TOTRW(-1))	–0.708424	0.231980	–3.053817	0.0058
C	9.911066	0.487131	20.34581	0.0000
R-squared	0.358498	Mean dependent var		8.406248
Adjusted R-squared	0.271020	S.D. dependent var		0.217492
S.E. of regression	0.185695	Akaike info criterion		–0.388782
Sum squared resid	0.758620	Schwarz criterion		–0.195228
Log likelihood	9.054160	F-statistic		4.098163
DW	0.645784	Prob(F-statistic)		0.018768

The results show that all the coefficients are significant and correctly signed. A relative price change in favor of non-traditional exports by one percent elicits a half a percent change in the value of non-traditional exports. Lagged relative price changes show similar magnitudes of changes. As in the other equations changes in real wages depress export performance. A one percent change in real wages in the non-traditional export sector exerts a 0.7 percent reduction in the value of non-traditional exports.

7

Revitalizing Agricultural Productivity in Kenya

HEZRON O. NYANGITO, GEM ARGWINGS-KODHEK, JOHN OMITI
AND JAMES KARANJA NYORO

Introduction

Agriculture plays a leading role in Kenya's economic development. It directly contributes about 25 percent of the gross domestic product (GDP), employs about 75 percent of the labor force, is the major foreign exchange earner for the country, and provides most of the food requirements for the nation (Kenya, 1998a). The sector is dominated by the primary production of a few commodities, 6 of which account for 68 percent of the agricultural GDP, and 17.5 percent of total GDP. Agricultural related activities such as transportation, trading, and processing are responsible for another 20–30 percent of GDP, meaning that agriculture and related activities account for up to half of all economic activity in the country.

Indeed, the success of Kenya's current major development goals, namely, achieving the status of a newly industrialized country by the year 2020 (GoK, 1997), poverty alleviation as outlined in the *Poverty Eradication Plan* (GoK, 1999), and the *Poverty Reduction Strategy Paper* (GoK, 2000), largely depend on the development of the agricultural sector. Unfortunately, the sector is not given the prominence it deserves in the documents that outline the country's policies for industrialization and poverty alleviation. This is a reflection of the marginalization of the sector policy-wise even though it is expected to play a leading role in economic development.

Table 7.1   Production of major commodities in Kenya: 1980–1998 (in thousands of tons)

Year	Maize	Wheat	S. cane	Coffee	Tea	Cotton	Milk
1980	1,888	189.0	3,972	91.3	89.9	38.1	179.5
1981	2,560	225.0	3,822	90.7	90.0	25.5	191.0
1982	2,450	244.0	3,107	88.4	95.6	24.4	232.1
1983	1,500	251.3	3,188	95.3	119.3	25.8	284.4
1984	2,440	144.4	3,611	118.5	116.2	22.8	236.0
1985	2,870	201.0	3,463	96.6	147.1	38.0	216.1
1986	2,400	252.0	3,551	114.9	143.3	25.4	322.6
1987	3,140	207.0	3,698	104.9	155.8	23.8	347.3
1988	3,030	234.0	3,835	125.0	164.0	10.9	357.1
1989	2,890	244.0	4,261	116.9	180.6	13.8	348.1
1990	2,544	190.0	4,200	111.9	197.9	18.8	392.0
1991	2,205	195.0	4,343	87.1	203.6	8.4	359.0
1992	2,340	125.0	4,047	88.4	188.1	15.1	220.0
1993	1,773	76.9	3,839	77.8	211.1	2.5	249.0
1994	2,363	107.8	3,308	81.5	209.4	1.8	258.0
1995	2,060	128.6	4,000	95.8	244.5	0.2	350.0
1996	1,908	135.0	4,100	97.0	257.2	0.5	257.0
1997	2,046	125.8	4,278	68.0	220.7	0.5	197.0
1998	2,180	177.1	4,661	53.4	294.2	0.5	126.0

Note: The data for milk are in million liters based on recorded deliveries to processors by Kenya Dairy Board but this represents only 40 percent of total production in the country. S. cane = sugar cane.

Source: GoK, (1985, 1990, 1995 and 1999).

Despite the importance of the sector, its performance in the 1990s was dismal. Annual growth in agricultural GDP averaged 2 percent compared to an average of 4 percent in the 1980s and 6 percent in the first decade of independence. Production of most commodities declined in the 1990s, the worst affected being coffee, cereals (maize and wheat), industrial crops particularly, cotton and milk production (see Table 7.1.)

The horticulture export sub-sector has performed fairly well and continues to do so today. There was a general increasing trend of export earnings in nominal terms over the years but there was a decline in the volume of exports as from 1997. The decline in volume is attributed to a shift to higher value unit products such as pre-packs for vegetables and flowers rather than fruits and bulk French beans. Nevertheless, there are indications that the good performance may not be sustained unless the constraints hindering growth are removed.

While it is in fact true that climatic factors such as drought are important in explaining Kenya's agricultural performance, the major culprits are policy related. Further, although some commodities like tea show a general increasing trend in production, this is largely attributed to an increase in hectares under cultivation rather than an increase in productivity. In all cases, productivity for all the commodities is low, and in some cases declining.

A number of factors are responsible for the decline in production and low productivity. In this chapter, we discuss these factors. First, the broad categories of policy related factors, which can be used to explain the poor performance of the agricultural sector are examined. The performance of food and industrial crops, export crops and livestock and the factors that explain the performance of each sub sector are discussed next. Finally, in the concluding section, we make suggestions that can be used to revitalize Kenya's critically important agricultural sector.

Constraints to agricultural development in Kenya

A wide range of factors explains the poor performance of the agricultural sector in Kenya. The major factors constraining agricultural growth are examined below.

Policy direction

Until the 1990s, the major policies for agricultural development were based on government controls and direct involvement in production and marketing activities. Excessive involvement by the Government of Kenya resulted in poor delivery of services to agriculture, wastage of public funds, and stifling of the role of individuals and the private sector in agricultural development. A shift in policy towards liberalized market policies started in the 1980s but it was not until 1993 that there was some commitment to the implementation of these policies (Ikiara, Juma and Amadi, 1993; Nyangito, 1998a). This was a welcome move but unfortunately, liberalization has not borne fruits because of the following:

* Illogical sequencing of liberalized market policies;
* Improper timing of policies that kept them out of pace with the available institutional capacity;
* Policy instability which reduces investor confidence;
* Privatization of public institutions which was not gradual enough to allow for adjustments; and
* Lack of harmony and co-ordination in implementation of the policies.

Policy implementation weaknesses

Although the liberalized market policies have been accepted in principle, the legal framework to support the operation of the emerging policies has not been put in place. For example, liberalized market policies for production, processing and marketing of most agricultural commodities, such as maize, milk, coffee, and tea, have been implemented but the laws that previously gave powers of monopoly and control of the sector to public institutions have not been repealed.

In essence, most of the notices that have been gazetted to allow liberalized production and marketing of agricultural commodities are technically illegal because they are not supported by legislation (Nyangito, 1999). Thus, the enforcement of the laws that govern the sector is weak and this has hindered efficient development of institutions that serve the sector. Besides, clear roles of the government in regulating, as opposed to controlling the sector, have not been developed. These roles should include:

* Formulation and enforcement of laws that define property rights and resolve disputes;
* Provision of effective incentive structures and safety nets (e.g., taxation, contracting out delivery services, tariffs, financing, etc.);
* Investment in development of infrastructure;
* Inspectorate for quality and standards;
* Creation of functional markets and protection against rent-seeking tendencies and monopolization; and
* Development of mechanisms for disaster/crisis management (e.g., provision of early warning systems for droughts, floods, locusts, ect.).

Low investments in agricultural sector

Funding of agricultural development programs by the government has decreased drastically with the adoption of tight fiscal and monetary policies in recent years. Total expenditure on agriculture is about 4 percent of the total government expenditure compared to 10 percent in the 1980s (Nyangito, 1999). Worse still, most of the money is spent on recurrent expenditure rather than development programs. Although the government espouses the policy of privatizing investments in the agricultural sector and the wider economy, this has yet to happen in a large scale in the agricultural sector. For example, the delivery of services to farmers is still dominated by public sector organizations partly because most of the services, such as livestock disease control, are public goods. For such goods, more benefits accrue to the larger society and are therefore not financially attractive to private investors. In most cases, such investments will require special incentive packages such as tax rebates to attract private sector investors.

The use of inputs such as fertilizers, pesticides, improved seed and machinery contribute significantly to increased agricultural output. The costs of these inputs, including working capital, make up the largest component of the costs of agricultural production. For example, in commercial maize production, the cost of these inputs can be as high as 70 percent of the total costs of production while the remainder are made up of the costs of land and labor (Nyoro, 1996; Nyangito and Ndirangu, 1997). Limited use of these improved inputs in crop production leads to low yields. The high costs of inputs are due to high transportation costs, poorly developed marketing systems and tariffs on imports (Mose, Nyangito and Mugumieri, 1997; Mugumieri, Nyangito and Mose, 1997; Mose, 1998).

Marketing problems

Abrupt withdrawal of public agencies from marketing arrangements for producers and lack of appropriate regulations for new institutions coupled with slow development of the private sector and farmer based institutions has left marketing of most commodities in disarray. Marketing problems are particularly found in the maize, coffee, tea, and cotton sectors. The new maize marketing system has many competitive structures which are very fluid with evidence of barriers to expansion of marketing activities that include lack of market information on sources and outlets, price, and the costs of marketing (Nyoro, Kiiru and Jayne, 1999). For tea and coffee, marketing conflicts have arisen among the various stakeholders. This has come about because of lack of clear regulations for the operation of the new marketing systems following liberalization of the public organizations previously involved in marketing (Nyangito, 2000; Nyangito and Kimura, 1999). In the cotton sector, a poor government privatization program that restricts ownership of ginneries has led to the collapse of the industry because of the limited financial base to support cotton farmers (Argwings-Kodhek, 1995). Thus, enhancing the workings of free markets and development of adequate regulatory frameworks and institutions for the operations of the markets are the major concerns in enhancing agricultural productivity.

Weak extension and research services

Farmer access to information and new technologies is poor due to weak research and extension services. Furthermore, the link between research and extension has weakened particularly with the recent funding crisis implying that effective transmission of information from research centers to the wider rural community has been seriously compromised (World Bank, 1998). As a result, farmers, smallholders in particular, use poor production techniques. This is an unfortunate situation given the fact that agricultural extension in Kenya has been found to have a significant positive impact on yields (Evenson and Mwabu, 1998; Gautam and Anderson, 1998).

Poor access to credit

The public lending institutions such as the Agricultural Finance Corporation and Co-operative Societies, which provided the bulk of credit to the agricultural sector in the 1960s to the 1980s, collapsed in the 1990s as a result of management inefficiencies and poor recovery of loaned funds. Access to credit by farmers has also been made worse by the high interest rates charged for loans by commercial banks, coupled with the reluctance of commercial banks to lend to smallholders. Lack of credit or poor access to credit has led to low use of capital goods and services, which has led to low land and labor productivity.

Limited value adding activities

Investment opportunities for value adding activities for agricultural commodities have not been exploited to increase farm incomes and off-farm employment. Most agricultural commodities such as tea, coffee, and livestock, are exported as unfinished raw commodities. However, the commodities could fetch higher prices when processed or packaged before exporting them. For example, packaged tea exports fetch a value six times higher than unpacked tea (Nyangito and Kimura, 1999). Thus, opportunities exist to raise the value of tea, horticulture and livestock products through processing and/or packaging.

Poor development and promotion of exports

The markets for agricultural exports are the traditional European Union countries dominated by Great Britain and Germany, as well as the Middle East countries. Potential markets exist in the Americas, Asia, and the Far East for tea and horticulture but deliberate efforts to increase exports to these markets are lacking. Even within the traditional export markets, opportunities for increasing exports of livestock and livestock products, sugar, textiles and horticulture have not been exploited adequately.

Land policy and insecurity in rural areas

Land tenure policy is based on freehold individual ownership. However, less than 10 million hectares of land have been adjudicated and individual titles issued (GoK, 1998). Thus, the vast amount of land in Kenya is governed by various tenure systems, which include group ranches, customary tenure, and trust land. This restricts the development of the land market for commercial use. Furthermore, there is no clear legal framework on economical subdivision and holding of land. Another problem affecting land utilization is the lack of broad-based incentives such as improved infrastructure to encourage investment in remote areas. In addition, recent ethnic/regional violence and frequent livestock rustling in pastoral areas has hampered agricultural development.

Uncontrolled imports

Liberalization has led to an increase of imports, particularly of maize, wheat, rice, sugar, and dairy products. The country has always imported wheat and rice over the years but large imports of all commodities in recent years may have led to depressed domestic production. Cheap imports dampen producer prices and create competition for domestic supplies. However, on the other hand, imports can enhance availability of the commodities or products to the majority of the consumers cheaper than would otherwise be possible. Thus, because of the conflicting roles of imports on producer and consumer welfare, appropriate planning and regulatory mechanisms are required. Unfortunately, there are no clear regulations on importation of agricultural commodities and in some cases laxity occurs in control of imports leading to the creation of unfair competition with domestic products.

Revitalizing productivity of food crops

Maize

Maize is the primary food staple and provides between 60–80 percent of calories in different parts of the country. No part of the country produces more than 60 percent of the maize consumed by households in that region. Consequently, national production of maize is lagging behind demand meaning that even in normal production years the country must import. This dichotomy between the need to import, and the landed cost of imports versus domestically produced maize sets the policy agenda for the commodity. International agreements like the Common Market for Eastern and Southern Africa (COMESA), East African Community (EAC), and World Trade Organization (WTO), mean that Kenya will eventually have to lower import tariffs. Kenya must choose whether it will continue to grow maize behind high protective tariffs leaving consumer prices in Kenya higher than in the rest of the world, or make domestic production competitive with imports.

Costs of production.   The cost of producing maize in Kenya for most surplus producers in the North Rift is between KShs 600 and 800 per bag. Costs vary but few surplus producers can justify production costs of over KShs 1,000 per bag in spite of well-orchestrated efforts to demand up to KShs 1,800 per bag. Imports on the other hand can be landed at prices that Kenyan producers cannot compete with. Taxes and transportation costs mean that imports are landed in Nairobi at Kshs 1,500 per bag, giving a North-Rift buying price of over KShs 1,200 per bag.

Farm sizes.   Producers demand higher prices year after year because their farms are relatively small and the profits they make per bag of maize are not adequate to meet all their financial needs. Small-scale farmers, whose farm sizes are less than 20 acres, dominate maize production. These farms are, however, becoming smaller and smaller because of sub-divisions due to increased population density in the maize growing areas. Farm sizes in Kenya can only be radically changed through land reform of a type that would be hard to sell politically. Short of a policy preventing sub-divisions, there is much that can be done to improve the incomes of maize producers without punishing maize consumers. Some of the options available are outlined below.

Taxes on imports.   Kenyan maize producers are protected by taxes on imports, but at the same time, are taxed by a number of government policies. Kenyan agriculture is heavily taxed. Tariffs and excise duties on diesel, tires, and spare parts, raise the cost of transportation and in turn the cost of producing maize above that of importing countries.

Cost of fertilizer and machinery. The cost of fertilizer and farm machinery are higher than in neighboring countries and the highest in the region, even though the government has waived all duties on farm inputs suggesting the existence of some price raising market power. Transportation costs are high in Kenya due to high taxes on transport equipment and vehicles, as well as their spare parts, but also due to the poor state of all categories of roads.

Use of new technologies. Kenyan farmers do not use much of the available cost reducing technologies. The seed industry is not fully free and competitive, giving rise to frequent complaints about the availability, quality, and price of the seed available from the limited number of domestic suppliers. Fertilizer use is low by global standards, which translates into low productivity. Research and extension systems have not been very successful in generating, and getting farmers to adopt, new technologies. The limited availability of agricultural credit is partly responsible for this, as are deficiencies in the organization, funding, and management of both research and extension arising out of their public sector character.

Efficiency in production. Efficient production systems exist alongside inefficient ones with the best farmers producing a bag of maize at half the cost of inefficient farmers. For example, cost of maize production ranges from a low of KShs 500 per bag in the high potential areas to over KShs 1,500 per bag in the more marginal areas. Even within the most productive zones, significant cost differences among farmers exist depending on the timing, quality and quantity of land preparation, seed and fertilizer use, weeding, and post-harvest practices. As long as Kenya fails to differentiate between efficient and less efficient producers, imposing duties high enough to protect even the most inefficient producers, then producers have limited incentives to try and minimize per unit production costs. The more efficient producers gain from the high protection far more than do the resource constrained poorer farmers whose protection may be the goal of an import ban or high tariff policy. Only the consumer loses from a high tariff policy.

Policy bias. Kenyan maize producers have the ear and sympathy of policymakers. Duties benefit domestic producers at the expense of domestic consumers some of whom have in recent years faced famine, the result of which has been requests for food relief. A government policy that imposes high tariffs while simultaneously undertaking an expensive famine relief program, is hard to understand.

Policy concerns. Kenya can make efforts to become a low cost producer of maize. The mechanisms of doing this are known but call for radical rethinking of the policy instruments chosen. Some changes that can be made in the policy instruments are:

- Funding and delivery of services such as research, extension, credit, and marketing functions like storage. The previous dominant role of the public sector is diminishing and the private sector will have to play a leading role in this area.
- The government's use of taxes and duties on imported maize to raise revenue leading to higher domestic producer prices will have to change to avoid protecting inefficient producers.
- Input supply and output marketing will need to be competitive through the provision of infrastructure services.
- Policy on maize imports and trade policy will have to be managed efficiently to avoid distortions in the maize market. A vision of a low cost, efficient, and globally competitive agricultural sector must accompany moves toward more open borders if these arrangements are not to kill agricultural industries. Protection through high tariffs cannot make this happen.

Wheat

Domestic production of wheat meets less than 40 percent of domestic needs. Kenya produces mainly soft wheat and must depend on imports of both soft and hard wheat to meet the shortfall. Kenya cannot meet her wheat needs from domestic production due to stagnating production and an annual increase in demand estimated at a rate of 7.5 percent. Policy has consistently come down on the side of protecting a small number of producers rather than the millions of consumers. Import tariffs are used to raise domestic prices and keep some of the more inefficient producers in business, while earning excess profits for some of the large-scale producers.

Cost of production. The cost of wheat production varies between different production scales and environments. Kenya's most efficient wheat production systems are the large-scale systems in Narok, Uasin Gishu, and Nakuru, where costs of production are lower than in the corresponding small-scale systems mainly due to higher yields. Higher yields are mainly a function, of weather and the timeliness of operations (Nyoro, 1996). Timeliness of operations depends on access to, or ownership of, machinery. Some of the small-scale systems suffer greatly from delayed operations due to lack of machinery, particularly combined harvesters. However, the purchase and maintenance of machinery is extremely costly, particularly as the interest costs associated with such purchases are high, and government taxes raise the cost of spare parts and diesel.

Quality of seed. The quality of certified seed available to wheat producers has been a cause of concern. This has forced the majority of producers to use retained seed. A number of large producers are investing in dryers and seed preparation equipment and a market is developing in uncertified, but treated, seed. Improvements in seed quality could help make the Kenyan wheat systems more competitive. Wheat producers have demonstrated a willingness to contribute funds towards research programs at the KARI wheat research station at Njoro in return for some control over the research agenda. However, administrative obstacles have made this difficult to get off the ground.

The problems of high cost domestic production, and protection through prohibitive tariffs applying to maize also apply to the wheat and rice industries. The policy concerns are therefore similar for the different food crops.

Revitalizing productivity of industrial crops

Sugar

Kenya consumes over 600,000 tons of white sugar, but the country can barely produce 400,000 tons in a good year. Production increases during the post-independence period came through large government investments in Muhoroni (1966), Chemilil (1968), Mumias (1971), Nzoia (1975), and Sony (1978) – where the numbers in parentheses indicate year of construction of each sugar production unit.

Cost overruns. Severe cost overruns and other problems have forced the government not to invest in new production capacity apart from efforts to improve throughput at existing schemes. For the foreseeable future, Kenya will import sugar as investments in new production schemes, such as those proposed for Busia and Siaya, lag behind growing domestic demand. A four year freeze in cane prices that ended with a minimal 11 percent increase in March 1998 did not help matters, as did persistent delays in harvesting and payments.

Diversion of imports. Import volumes are higher than the official figures because of diversion of sugar imports purportedly to neighboring countries. Tax evasion on sugar importation is widely acknowledged, even by government, and is mainly done through diverting supposedly Uganda bound transit sugar into the local market. The level of imports is expected to rise in the future as demand continues to grow, likely faster than reflected in the official figures. This is likely to depress domestic production even more

Efficiency in production. Mumias can make money selling sugar at up to KShs 20,000 per ton less than the most inefficient factories. If the relative efficiency of the western production zone also were taken into account, then the bulk of Kenyan sugar production can be competitive with imports. Mumias, Sony, Nzoia (if more efficiently run), and the relatively well run Chemilil, that together produce over 85 percent of domestic production can compete if a number of efficiency enhancing measures are taken.

Policy concerns

- Efficiency on the farm can be increased through investments in research into high sucrose content cane varieties. Recent moves by the sugar industry to take over the running and financing of sugar research are a step in the right direction.
- Sugar farmers need strong out grower organizations. Optimal input use, combined with timely harvesting can do much to make Kenya's rain fed cane production among the most efficient in the world.
- Farmers need to be able to enforce contracts with factories with regard to date of harvesting. Currently only the farmer looses when his crop is harvested late.
- Post farm efficiency can be enhanced most directly if:
    - cane were to be purchased on the basis of sucrose content; and
    - factories are privatized. This will eliminate some of the inefficiencies associated with the parastatal run factories, particularly in the purchasing function. However, privatization already is proving to be difficult as government struggles to make the process transparent, and politically acceptable.

Long run policy. Kenya can have a large sugar industry providing income and employment to thousands of people in the western part of the country through investing in improving the efficiency of farm production and post-farm processing. The industry provides direct employment to 35,000 workers, and is a major income source to over 100,000 small-scale farmers, and supports over 2 million people. But Kenya has not yet made clear its long-run policy with regard to import competition, nor explained to the sugar industry the implications of the WTO agreement that will reduce maximum levels of duty that can be charged on import. Investment in cost reducing efficiency measures and research will be key to keeping the sugar industry alive as will effective policing of transit sugar.

Cotton

The cotton industry had all but collapsed when the government began to liberalize it in 1991. Over the 30 years since independence, the massive increases in acreage and production in eastern and central Kenya are a credit to Government and Cotton Board efforts to achieve self-sufficiency. Free seed, inputs on credit and administered prices were the tools used in this effort with legislative backing for this high degree of government control coming from the Cotton Act of 1955.

The area devoted to cotton growing and the production of cotton peaked in 1980 at 140,000 ha and 7,700 tons (42,000 bales) respectively. Both have been on a downward trend ever since. Payments for all stages of cotton handling on behalf of the board were inadequate. Yet, these payment rates were not increased throughout the 1980s. Currently, the area under cultivation is 20,000 ha while lint production from domestically grown cotton is barely 2,500 tons per year.

Cash flow problems. Cash flow problems in the industry delayed payments that led to reduced throughput and capacity utilization in co-operative societies and ginneries further exacerbating the problems of losses and negative cash flow. By 1990, liberalization was seen as the only way to save the industry from total collapse. Private buyers now compete for farmers' cotton, imports have been liberalized and the government is selling the ginneries in which it has a stake. The process of liberalization has, however, been fraught with problems both on and off the farm that have kept the industry from making a significant recovery.

Farm level constraints. Cotton is grown in fairly marginal environments where no other cash crops will grow. Cotton today does not compete favorably with other commodities due to a variety of issues, some of which are discussed below.

Poor seed quality is the biggest problem affecting the cotton industry. The purity of the different varieties has been compromised as ginneries have been mixing seed cotton from different regions. Seed varieties also have reduced genetic vigor due to repeated replanting. The problems of varietal degradation and varietal mixing are compounded by the distribution of untreated seed with low germination rates. The poor quality seed currently available to farmers is not conducive to input intensive and profitable seed cotton production.

The poorly funded National Fiber Research Stations at Kibos and Mwea had developed new higher yielding and disease resistant varieties as far back as 10 years ago. Farmers are aware that the improved planting material exists and travel long distances (to the stations) in search of it but the material is in short supply. The multiplication program was estimated, in 1995, to require about KShs 5 million. These funds have not been available and the budget for the research centers pays little apart from staff salaries, leaving little for research operations or for seed multiplication.

Extension services that are able to reach cotton farmers are minimal. The impact of delayed planting, untreated seed, inter-cropping, relay cropping, and low insecticide use, are messages that should be reaching farmers, and should form the basis of dialogue between research and extension. This is not happening. Few farmers interviewed for a cotton study had received extension advice or visits in recent years. This reflects problems in the extension service affecting all commodities. Extension workers also point to difficulties they have faced in the past after having been encouraged by the government to plant cotton. Neither seed for planting nor buyers for the cotton produced were forthcoming.

Cotton ginning.   The privatization of government owned ginneries has consumed an inordinate amount of government energy and political will. Government policy is to assist local communities to acquire these ginneries, but politicization of the privatization process is economically risky. It is questionable whether these groups will be able to run the assets profitably, especially if they have large loan obligations, little cotton available to buy, local private sector competitors, and international competition. Non-functioning, cash-strapped ginneries and societies are part of how the problems of the cotton industry began in the first place.

Given that Kenya has excess ginning capacity, the cash strapped public-owned ginneries cannot survive. This is why the privatization of ginneries is irrelevant to revitalizing the cotton industry. That money and effort would be better spent on a seed multiplication and certification system.

Policy concerns.   For the Kenyan cotton industry to survive, it must compete internationally in both price and quality. The only way in which Kenyan cotton can be made competitive is through investment in seed bulking and multiplication that makes extra insecticide spraying worthwhile on current varieties, or on new varieties. Whether the revival of the industry is to come about through better seed of currently available varieties, or through new varieties, the seed multiplication and certification system is the first step.

The lesson to be learnt from the cotton industry is that liberalization does not eliminate the role of the government, but rather that the public and private sectors be left free to undertake what each can do best. Some issues of priority in the cotton industry that need to be addressed are discussed below.

- As a matter of urgency, the public sector needs to play a more active role in seed quality assurance and certification. Kenya Agricultural Research Institute (KARI) and the Ministry of Agriculture must get improved seed out to farmers. A more active role by stakeholders and oversight by an industry body might bring a sense of urgency to this;
- The private sector should be encouraged to multiply and distribute certified seed;
- Seed cotton marketing and ginning should be left to market forces;
- The Cotton Act (Cap. 355, No 3 of 1988, Revised 1990) needs to be repealed. This will legitimize the currently free marketing system that technically is illegal; and

- The Cotton Board needs to be disbanded once and for all and be replaced by a small organization with a private sector majority and chairman where producers, ginners and lint consumers are represented. This body can look for ways of generating funds for badly needed seed multiplication and seed certification in the short run, and general cotton research in the longer run. This body can decide whether investments in a cotton extension service are viable or even necessary. Government may need to take a lead in getting such a group off the ground.

Revitalizing agricultural productivity of export crops

Coffee, tea and horticultural crops are major sources of foreign exchange, employment and income growth to many large and small-scale farmers in Kenya. These three commodities jointly contribute about 34 percent of agricultural GDP, employ over 40 percent of the agriculture labor force, and jointly contribute to over 60 percent of foreign exchange earnings in the country (GoK, 1999). Increased productivity of coffee, tea and horticulture is thus vital for the resuscitation of the economy.

Coffee production declined by more than 50 percent between 1988 and 1998 with this decline being more pronounced in the cooperatives. Coffee prices are one fourth of what they were one year ago, probably the lowest in the last ten years. In addition, Kenyan coffee has also lost the premium prices enjoyed in the world market due to its superior quality.

Although tea production has increased, this increase has caused congestion in factories thus affecting processing efficiency, which is a threat to tea quality. Kenya is now the biggest exporter of black tea in the world and is projected to account for 20–23 percent of world exports in the next five years. With a stagnating or declining demand in traditional markets, significant increases in production might negatively affect prices.

Although the volume of production remains high in the horticultural sector, Kenya continues to face increased competition from other countries like Morocco for French beans, and Israel for fruits and flowers. This has had the effect of reducing the demand for Kenyan horticultural products.

Thus, revitalization of the economy, alleviation of poverty and accelerating economic growth cannot be realized unless the current trend in production and marketing of these export crops are addressed appropriately. This section identifies the performance of each of these commodities and the challenges facing them and suggests strategies that could revitalize their production.

Coffee

Coffee production declined from about 130,000 tons in 1988 to a mere 50,000 tons in 1998, a decline of more than 50 percent. The production decline in the cooperatives has been more pronounced, falling from 80,000 tons to only 30,000 tons within the same period. Coffee quality has also been adversely affected such that the proportion of coffee in the prime classes of 1–3 has declined while the proportion of inferior qualities in the classes 7–10 and *Mbuni* has increased.

Average coffee prices have declined from about US$ 1.6 per kilogram of clean coffee in 1987/1988 to just below US$ 1.2 in 1998. This represents a decline of 25 percent, with the 1998 price most likely the lowest price for clean coffee during the last ten years. In addition, Kenyan coffee has also lost the premium prices it enjoyed in the past in the international market.

Coffee production costs in Kenya are among the highest in the world at about US$ 1.5–US$ 2 per kilogram of coffee. The average cost of production for Arabica coffee in the world is US$ 1.3 per kilogram of clean coffee. Countries like Ethiopia can produce the crop at about US$ 0.9 per kilogram, about half what it takes to produce the same in Kenya. Thus, unless world coffee prices improve to levels above the production costs, production of coffee in Kenya is likely to be unprofitable forcing farmers to exit from the business. Currently, coffee prices are about US$ 2.5 per kilogram, which leaves the farmer with a very thin margin and with the projected decline in world coffee prices, Kenyan farmers are already beginning to feel the pinch. Kenya therefore needs to devise technological and other strategies that could reduce coffee production costs and thus improve competitiveness. The high cost of production is attributed to the costs of controlling coffee berry and leaf rust diseases, which are prevalent in Kenya. Control of these diseases accounts for about 30 percent of the production cost. Kenyan coffee is also wet processed, an activity that adds value by enhancing quality but also raises the production costs.

The high costs of production are exacerbated by the significant increases to transaction costs by coffee handling, processing, and marketing institutions. Costs incurred by institutions such as the cooperative societies, millers, and the Coffee Board of Kenya (CBK), have remained high despite the decline in production and prices. In addition, these institutions are also characterized by poor management. They suffer from widespread mismanagement, corruption, lack of transparency and accountability to their members, and high political patronage. Handling and marketing costs have increased while production continues to decline. The high handling and processing costs, poor management, and lack of transparency have eroded coffee payments such that farmers only receive at best 56 percent of the final price in the best managed coffee factories and some as low as 40 percent of the world prices.

The liberalization of the industry was mistaken to mean total disengagement of government from involvement in the sector, but the self-regulatory system of the coffee industry by the CBK after liberalization has failed. Further, the combination of the commercial and regulatory functions by CBK compromised its regulatory functions thereby causing conflict of interests in the board. The liberalization process was also poorly timed, wrongly sequenced, not well monitored, and lacked preparation of the stakeholders. Cooperative societies, unions, marketing and input agents, that offered services like credit, farm inputs, and extension services were thus adversely affected. To overcome these failures, the government has tended to respond to the situation without consulting the stakeholders, leading to further discontent.

Policy concerns

- The government has important and critical roles to play in the coffee industry in enforcing the law, ensuring security, facilitating investment by the private sector, and securing external funding for the industry. However, stakeholders have always led the industry and this is provided for in the Coffee Act. This position should be upheld so that changes made in the coffee industry are done with full participation of the stakeholders. This will ensure that decisions made involve full participation of stakeholders ensuring that the decisions will be acceptable by all and are thus sustainable and easily implemented. Different stakeholders should thus be facilitated to freely discuss alternative strategies for coffee production, processing, and marketing.

- In order to accelerate the recovery of coffee production, revamp, and turn around the industry from its current depressed state, there is a need to inject capital in the form of credit into the industry to meet the recurrent and capital expenditure for coffee rehabilitation. It is unlikely that the funds will be available from the existing financial markets. There, therefore, is a need to find ways to access working capital either through government organized credit programs or by creating an institutional environment that enhances the ability of the private sector to provide the required financial resources.

- The Coffee Research Foundation (CRF) should intensify research in technologies that could reduce the costs of production such as intensified production of Ruiru 11 variety in particular, which has high yields and low cost of production.

- The CBK, CRF, and Kenya Planters Co-operative Union (KPCU) should undertake a staff rationalization and retrenchment program in order to downsize their operations so as to reduce costs and ensure efficient financial management.

- The commercial and regulatory functions of the CBK should be separated to avoid conflict of interests. Government should also be involved in the regulatory role. These functions should be carried out fairly and effectively and all stakeholders violating aspects of the law must be prosecuted.

- The Coffee Act and all legislation should also be reviewed in order to conform to reforms and policies that have been affected since the onset of the liberalization of the coffee industry. However, the review of the Act must be done with the involvement and participation of the coffee farmers and other stakeholders and should not be done exclusively by government or Parliament.

- Stakeholders need to find the best way to market coffee. Whereas the majority of large and small-scale farmers have expressed preference over the Central Auction due to its advantage in ensuring that it provides best returns to farmers, is transparent, and accountable, a few of them would prefer an alternative coffee marketing window. A consensus needs to be reached on the merits of each one so as to find the way forward.

- The other dilemma in the coffee industry is whether the co-operative societies should be allowed to split in order to meet the shareholders' aspirations. This should be facilitated rather than hindered. Providing the management of cooperatives with technical information will enable them to make informed decisions.

Tea

Tea production has expanded tremendously to over 200 million kilograms and is projected to reach 310 million kilograms by 2005 at the present growth rate. It is the most important export commodity in Kenya in terms of foreign exchange inflows in the economy. This tremendous increase in production has however provided challenges in congestion of factories which in turn affect processing efficiency. Kenya is the biggest black tea exporter in the world and is projected to account for 20–23 percent of world exports in the next 5 years. With stagnating or declining demand in traditional markets, significant increases in production might negatively affect prices.

Markets for Kenyan tea are heavily concentrated. Currently, the United Kingdom, Pakistan and Egypt account for 83 percent of Kenya's export market. With a stagnating or declining demand in traditional markets, significant increases in production might negatively affect prices. Furthermore, the tremendous increase in production has provided challenges in congestion of factories, thus, affecting processing efficiency. The quality of tea is being threatened by major congestion problems at the Kenya Tea Development Authority (KTDA) run tea factories. The congestion problem is expected to get worse as farmers improve crop husbandry and tea yields improve.

Poor management, corruption, and government interference in the running of KTDA have resulted in high transaction costs by the organization thus reducing payments to farmers. Provision of services to farmers by KTDA has also been inadequate and expensive.

In addition, many of the roads used to transport tea are impassable, a situation that has been exacerbated by the last El Nino rains. The poor condition of the roads adversely affects green leaf collection but despite the poor state of roads, farmers continue to pay less for roads improvement.

Policy concerns

Tea marketing in Kenya needs to be streamlined through the adoption of the following strategies.

- Shifting the policy thrust to market expansion from production planning.
- Implementing policies that encourage value adding and also offer opportunities for enhancing competition.
- Diversifying markets in order to reduce market and price risks. Other potential markets exist in the Middle East, Africa, and some parts of the Pacific Rim and these should be explored.
- The private sector and the cooperatives should also be encouraged to participate in putting up new factories. Policy should be geared towards encouraging such investment as opposed to the strategy that favors KTDA and discourages other possible investors. A regulatory framework needs to be put in place in anticipation of the emergence of new management agents. The proposed structure requires KTDA to pay corporate tax although it remains a farmer's organization.

Horticulture

The horticultural sub-sector has grown considerably mainly due to the expansion of exports. Export volumes grew from 57,363 tons valued at KShs 2,516 million in 1992 to a total of 84,143 tons valued at KShs 8,810 billion in 1998. These exports are dominated by cut flowers that accounts for 52 percent of the total value of exports. However, the sub-sector faces several challenges including competition from producers in Morocco and Israel.

A European Union (EU) requirement on the levels of maximum residual levels (MLR) allowed on imports has been continually changing. The MRL restricts the levels of chemical pesticides that can be used on horticultural crops. In July 2000, the EU was expected to implement the zero analytical level. The difficulties in implementing this requirement are likely to sideline most small-scale producers and exporters.

Additional constraints to growth of the horticultural sector include: lack of policies that nurture legal foundations of marketing systems, for example, those that strengthen mechanisms of specifying and enforcing contracts and raising the costs of contract non-compliance; poor infrastructure which makes production areas inaccessible leading to a loss of produce and deterioration in quality. It also reduces the usage of refrigerated trucks on these roads. This has adversely affected small-scale producers in remote areas.

Policy concerns

As stated above, horticultural production is generally constrained by: lack of policies that nurture legal foundations of marketing systems, for example, those that strengthen mechanisms of specifying and enforcing contracts and raising the costs of contract non-compliance; poor infrastructure which makes production areas inaccessible leading to a loss of produce and deterioration in quality as well as reducing the usage of refrigerated trucks on the roads, which has adversely affected the small-scale producers in remote areas; lack of adequate public research; high airfreight charges that reduce overall profits of exporters; lack of marketing information leading to asymmetrical information flows that undermine prices, particularly to producers; limited access to planting materials due to payment of royalties to breeders, thus favoring some large-scale producers who are able to pay royalties and able to limit uncontrolled multiplication of planting materials; and inadequate cargo capacity.

Some of the strategies that can be used to revitalize the horticulture industry are mentioned below.

- Improve rural infrastructure through partnership between communities and the government. Imposing a cess on horticultural exports can help the government's ability to fund the development of roads in horticultural growing areas. However, the cess should be used exclusively for the purpose of roads development.
- Review taxes on jet fuel to reduce freight costs. The current taxes are said to be responsible for high freight costs and their reduction would help alleviate this problem.
- The private sector and other stakeholders should be involved in development of pre-cooling facilities at strategic locations. This can only be possible if the roads are improved to allow for easy access to the locations of production.
- Formulate and implement policies that could nurture legal foundations of marketing such as those for enforcing contracts.

- Develop stronger partnerships between the private sector, the public sector, and the farmers in observing MRL requirements. This will require provision of technical information by the government to exporters and producers on appropriate types and levels of use of pesticides on horticultural crops production.

Revitalizing productivity of the livestock sector

Available statistics underestimate or ignore the multipurpose role that livestock plays in agricultural production and in the social life of Kenyan households. If non-monetized livestock output, for example, traction and manure, were valued and included in GDP estimates, the value of livestock output would probably account for up to 35 percent of agricultural GDP. There are various often complex, physical, socio-economic, and agro-biological attributes of livestock production that include provision and use of animal traction, manure, food products, crop residues, improvement of farm cash income, and accumulation of farm capital.

On average, animal traction accounts for 40 percent of total livestock output, meat output accounts for 35 percent, milk accounts for about 20 percent, and manure accounts for about 5 percent of total livestock output. Livestock earns the country foreign exchange through export of hides and skins, dairy products, live animals, and meat products. Socio-economic factors, demographic variables, infrastructure, farming practices, factor markets, biotechnology, and policy, are among the important factors affecting livestock production and agricultural intensification and transformation.

In Kenya, annual per capita consumption of livestock products is estimated at 9–10 kg beef, 2 kg sheep/goat meat, 1.2 kg poultry meat and 0.3 kg pork (Omiti, 2000). Beef accounts for over 70 percent of all meat consumed. Annual per capita milk consumption is estimated at 125 kg in urban areas (which is quite high compared to per capita consumption levels in Eastern and sub-Saharan Africa) and 19 kg in rural areas. There is considerable potential in the livestock sector in terms of increased employment and income generation if commercialization is intensified through appropriate technologies, improved management, and appropriate policy.

Current production status

Since the liberalization of the sector as from the mid-1980s – meat in 1987, feeds in 1988, dairy in 1992, many aspects of livestock production, processing and marketing have continued to change. However, the effects of liberalization have had mixed results. Currently, there is generally surplus production of pig, poultry, and rabbit products. Dairy production is on the balance while meat production shows a net deficit, despite considerable cross-border trade in livestock animals and products. Non-conventional livestock production is expanding in crocodile and ostrich farming, and game cropping.

Dairy sub-sector

Kenya has one of the largest dairy sectors in sub-Saharan Africa, consisting of about 3.2 million dairy cows, which produce about 60 percent of Kenya's total milk production. The dairy herd is composed of genetically improved breeds, which include Friesians, Ayrshires, Guernseys, Jerseys and crosses. The mixed breeds form the bulk of the dairy herd, especially on smallholder farms. Smallholders account for about 80 percent of total milk production while medium and large-scale farmers account for the rest of the milk. Indigenous zebu cattle are estimated at between 8 and 10 million head and contribute significantly in providing milk, especially in pastoralist communities.

Dairy production is concentrated in Central, Rift Valley and Eastern (around Mt. Kenya region) provinces or high rainfall areas of the country. The geographical distribution of dairy cattle population in Kenya is summarized in Table 7.2. Milk production follows seasonal weather fluctuations and is based mainly on natural forages. However, concentrate feeds are given to animals in particular physiological phases such as at lactation time.

Co-operative societies play a key role in milk marketing and handle about 40 percent of the milk marketed through the formal market. There are about 250 dairy co-operatives countrywide, each with a dairy intake of about 20,000 liters and a total membership of about 200,000 farmers. Kenya produces about 2.5 million metric tons of milk annually which is disposed off through non-marketing channels that consist of family and calf consumption at the household level while the rest is marketed via various marketing channels. The milk marketing channels are both formal and informal. The formal market refers to milk that is handled through the official regulated channels consisting of the public-owned creameries and licensed private processors. The remainder of the milk is sold as non-processed milk whose channels include:

- direct milk sales to consumers by farm households;
- milk collected by dairy co-operative societies;
- self help groups; and
- individual milk traders/hawkers who sell either to consumers, private processors, or Kenya co-operative creameries (KCC).

Table 7.2   Dairy cattle population (thousands) by province

Province	1989	1991	1993	1995	1997	1999
Rift Valley	1,596.0	1,665.7	1,665.9	1,934.4	1,448.5	1,631.0
Central	755.1	829.7	808.9	808.3	851.6	833.0
Eastern	260.4	281.2	273.6	311.8	351.7	344.1
Nyanza	219.0	131.3	150.1	145.1	150.5	150.7
Western	90.0	114.5	101.1	105.3	102.1	127.3
Coast	28.3	31.2	45.4	68.4	86.9	69.3
Nairobi	–	11.4	13.8	13.7	15.5	15.6
North Eastern	8.7	0.2	0.2	0.15	0.15	0.15
Total	2,961.7	3,065.3	3,059.3	3,387.1	2,933.8	3,166.8

Source: Ministry of Agriculture (MoA), Nairobi, Kenya, Various years.

Many aspects of dairy production, processing and marketing have continued to change with the various economic and institutional reforms implemented in the country during the last several years. There is increased participation by private enterprises in processing and marketing of milk and milk products. The number of processors licensed by the Kenya Dairy Board (KDB) had increased to about 45 by 1998, including Meru co-operative dairy, Brookside in Kiambu, Delamere in Naivasha, Ilara in Nakuru, and Premier in Kericho. Most of the private processors operate in the range of 5,000–10,000 liters/day. Overall, trade in raw whole milk has drastically increased, although there are more than 1,000 traders in the industry. Although most of them are ailing, co-operative societies continue to play a key role in milk marketing and handle about 40 percent of the marketed milk. There are about 250 dairy co-operatives with a combined membership of more than 200,000 farmers.

Policy concerns.   Some major issues that need to be addressed in the dairy sector are:

- Access to veterinary services in disease management.
- Inadequate breeding services, including artificial insemination and bull schemes.
- High feed costs and suspect quality management.

- Limited credit and financial resources for investments.
- Poor sequencing and lack of popular participation in the liberalization process.
- Inappropriate (on-the-shelf) technologies, especially for smallholders.
- Inadequate research and extension services.
- Unavailable and unsuitable processing technology, especially for small operators.
- Narrow markets other than for liquid milk.
- Inefficient and inadequate regulatory systems (for example, a weak KDB).
- Anti-competitive practices such as dumping of imports and cartel-like tendencies.
- Effective management of strategic dairy reserves in a liberalizing economic environment and the costs of holding the stocks versus importation.
- Poor access to credit by the majority of smallholder farmers, especially women.

Policy suggestions. Policy must facilitate competition in input manufacture and milk processing. The various attendant legal provisions must be revised to permit efficient and legal operations in the industry. Policy must also review and legalize milk hawking to expand consumption and create employment. Informed stakeholder participation is crucial in institutionalizing participatory development and enhancing sectoral productivity.

Meat sub sector

Liberalization has widened opportunities for greater participation and competition in the meat sector. Except for swine and broilers, most of the meat animals and products are produced in the arid and semi-arid lands, under pastorals conditions. The environment in which pastoralists operate is characterized by hostile ecological conditions such as long dry seasons, low soil nutrients and high temperatures, that limit the productive capacity of livestock (Kariuki and Letitiya, 1996). This means that the major source of income to the pastoralists is limited by the agro-ecological conditions and their ability to exploit these assets in a sustainable manner is made worse by man-made conditions/factors (NOPA, 1992).

Policy concerns. Critical policy concerns impeding the development of an efficient, and perhaps self-sustaining meat sector include:
- Poor access to product and input markets. This is reflected in the generally poor state of infrastructure such as stock routes, transportation, water facilities, etc. This is made worse by the general exclusion of most pastoralists from access to public goods such as extension and animal health services, roads, energy, and communication systems;
- Weak or the non-participation of pastoralists in political processes in the country;

- Attenuated access to and control over land and natural resources;
- Insecurity and the cattle rustling menace;
- Poor breeding stock, largely due to inferior genetic potential; and
- High cost and frequent adulteration of inputs such as chemicals, fuel, etc., used in meat production.

Policy suggestions. Policy should focus on intervention, which takes into account the agro-ecological environment, social, and political empowerment of pastoralists, in order to improve service delivery and access to input and product markets.

In pastoral areas, water policies should avoid concentration of the human population and of livestock in restricted areas but aim to improve their distribution over extended pastoral areas. Development of new water points should account for ecological factors to avoid environmental degradation. Water sources should be developed and managed with the aim of optimizing grazing pressure geographically and seasonally. Pastoral associations should be the key actors in management of water systems but clear legislation is required for the establishment and management of water resources such as watering points, boreholes, streams, etc. Indeed, liberalization has widened opportunities for greater participation and competition but Kenya must improve her export capability while consolidating her hold onto niche markets through innovative marketing and quality control. There is also a need to facilitate contracting to avoid unnecessary duplication or competition. Domestic efforts to diversify eating habits will expand domestic consumption such as is happening with non-conventional livestock farming. While privatization will continue to provide an enabling environment, government must make concerted efforts to stem insecurity and cattle rustling, even within a regional context.

Poultry sub-sector

Chicken is the most important of the poultry types in Kenya. Relatively few turkeys, ducks and geese, ostrich and guinea fowls are kept. There are two basic categories of chicken farmers in Kenya, that is, those keeping indigenous birds and those with exotic commercial birds. Most of the indigenous birds are found in the Nyanza, Rift Valley, Eastern and Coast provinces while commercial birds, that is, layers and/or broilers, are reared near major urban centers as shown in Table 7.3.

Indigenous chicken production is characterized by small flock sizes per household that provide for animal-protein sources for rural households. Production is hindered by low productivity due to inbreeding, lack of selection and heavy losses, especially due to disease and predation. Commercial chicken production is based on purchase of day-old chicks from hatcheries. The major hatcheries are Kenchic and Muguku Poultry Farms but there are several other smaller hatcheries.

There are fluctuations in the number of day-old chicks produced from these hatcheries and Kenya discourages importation of commercial day-old chicks in order to control poultry diseases and stimulate domestic hatcheries. Production of layers and broilers is concentrated in peri-urban centers due to proximity to major consumer markets.

Table 7.3   Estimated poultry population by province, 1998

Province	Layers (eggs)	Broilers (meat)	Indigenous birds
Nyanza	224,540	19,490	5,638,690
Rift Valley	302,720	172,140	3,530,470
Eastern	95,580	40,100	2,901,010
Coast	315,350	141,050	2,739,810
Western	47,930	-	2,363,000
Central	752,900	207,300	1,164,200
Nairobi	123,820	166,100	50,060
North Eastern	1,200	600	28,000
Total	1,864,040	744,210	18,414,550

Source: MoA, Animal Production Division, 1998.

Poultry development is key to agricultural revitalization and the rural sector, especially for resource-constrained families such as widows, youth groups, etc. Poultry does not require high initial investment and can thus be a business option, especially for resource-constrained groups. This is especially true for egg production in arid and semi-arid areas and areas far removed from urban centers such as in parts of the Rift Valley, Nyanza, and Western Kenya.

Conclusion

The more liberalized macroeconomic environment, together with government fiscal constraints, has had a number of direct impacts on agriculture. Liberalization of prices, interest rate, trade and exchange rate regimes, has allowed the sector to more directly feel and respond to the incentives offered by a market economy. Liberalized marketing has found a number of producers and sectors not fully equipped to deal directly with market forces. A number of commodity boards are not responding to the new regime fast enough, resulting in conflicts and court battles between producers and management.

The agricultural sector is in a state of flux brought about by the change in orientation from government provided services and policy leadership, to one where groups of stakeholders are being called upon to provide both services and leadership for themselves. The ability of different groups of agricultural sector stakeholders to form workable institutional arrangements for solving some of their common problems, will be key to their future competitiveness and survival. Organizing ways of providing services no longer provided either by government, or the for-profit private sector, will be key in determining how well those sectors survive the globally competitive market environment of the next decade.

The Ministry of Agriculture has not been very visible in a number of important areas where it might play a leading role such as in setting the policy and regulatory framework within which the sector operates. An overall policy framework would help stakeholders to have some idea of the key elements of the policy environment that must be taken into account in determining their future roles. For the Ministry of Agriculture to take a lead in setting the policy framework for the sector it needs strengthening of its policy analysis capacity. Kenya needs centers of excellence in the collection, generation and analysis of policy relevant data in all agricultural commodities and services. This research-based information needs to be used to inform sector policymakers as well as stakeholders, and help all agricultural stakeholders develop common visions of the direction and actions needed for growth of the sector, commodity by commodity.

The specific issues to be addressed in revitalizing the agricultural sector include the following.

• Reducing the costs of production of agricultural commodities through low taxes on imported inputs such as machinery and chemicals.
• Enhancing the efficiency of production of the commodities through use of improved crop varieties and livestock breed and production technologies.
• Eliminating the bias on import duties on cereals (maize and wheat) and sugar that encourage inefficiencies in domestic production of these commodities.
• Ensuring that privatization of public organizations involved in processing agricultural commodities such as cotton ginneries and sugar factories is transparently done to encourage sound investments for efficient delivery of services to farmers.

- Clarifying the roles of public bodies such as the CBK, TBK, DBK, and others which are involved in the regulation of the sub-section. These organizations should deal with monitoring the activities in the respective industries and use appropriate laws to enforce contracts. They should not be involved in commercial activities such as delivery of marketing services to producers.
- Making certain that public bodies such as farmers' marketing boards and private organizations involved in processing and marketing are run efficiently to reduce costs of delivering services to farmers. These bodies or agencies should be monitored by independent regulatory agencies to ensure that they do not exploit farmers.
- Ensuring that the promotion of Kenyan exports (tea, coffee and horticulture) are given priority by the government to maintain existing markets or expand them into potential markets. Some of the other efforts required to promote exports involve reducing taxes on jet fuel to reduce freight costs of exports particularly, horticultural crops.
- Major efforts are required to improve the road infrastructure by the government. The funds from cess on export crops should be used exclusively and effectively for this purpose.
- Provision of animal health services by both the public and private sectors should be enhanced to increase livestock production. The public sector should play a leading role in the provision of these services for pastoral areas.
- Appropriate policies such as well-functioning laws for milk processing and marketing must be put in place to encourage competition in the dairy sector.
- Appropriate macroeconomic policies (interest rates and incentives for credit lending) to encourage credit availability from both public and private sectors to farmers should be developed to allow farmers to have access to credit for crop and livestock production.
- Appropriate infrastructure (livestock routes, transportation and water facilities) should be provided to pastoralists to encourage commercial livestock production for meat products.
- Poultry development should be encouraged through provision of better breeds and availability of quality feed to farmers.
- Irrigation infrastructure (dams and canals) should be developed by both the government and the private sector in semi-arid and arid areas where potential exists to increase crop and livestock production. The government should play a leading role in this area and also provide the private sector with appropriate incentives such as ownership of land in such areas to enable them to invest in irrigation programs.

References

Argwings-Kodhek, G. (1995), 'Liberalization of the Kenyan Cotton Industry', in *Proceedings of the Conference Toward 2000: Improving Agricultural Performance*, Policy Analysis Matrix, Egerton University: Nairobi, Kenya.

Evenson, R. E. and Mwabu, G. (1998), 'The Effects of Agricultural Extension on Farm Yields in Kenya', Paper presented at the *10th Anniversary Conference on Investment, Growth and Risk in Africa*, Center for the Study of African Economies, University of Oxford: Oxford, UK.

Gautam, M. and Anderson, J. (1998), *Returns to T7V Extension in Kenya: Some Alternative Findings*, The World Bank: Washington, DC & OCED: Paris.

GoK (1985, 1990, 1993, 1995, 1998), *Economic Surveys*, Government Printer: Nairobi, Kenya.

GoK (1997), *Industrial Transformation in the Year 2020: Sessional Paper No. 2*, Government Printer: Nairobi, Kenya.

GoK (1999), *National Poverty Eradication Plan 1999–2015*, Government Printer: Nairobi, Kenya.

GoK (2000), *Poverty Reduction Strategy Paper (Interim)*, Ministry of Finance and Planing, Nairobi.

Ikiara, G. K., Juma, M. A. and Amadi, J. O. (1993), 'Agricultural Decline, Politics and Structural Adjustment in Kenya', in Gibbons, P. (ed.), *Social Change and Economic Reform in Africa*, Nordiska Africaninstitutet: Uppsala.

Kariuki, D. P. and Letitiya, W. (1996), 'Livestock Production and Health Challenges in Pastoral Areas: Samburu Districk, Kenya', Kenya Agricultural Research Institute: Nairobi, Kenya.

Mose, L. O. (1998), 'The Influence of Gender and Cash Availability on Fertilizer Use in Maize', Paper presented during the Workshop on Strategies for Raising Smallholder Agricultural Productivity and Welfare, Tegemeo Institute of Agricultural Policy and Development, Egerton University: Nairobi, Kenya.

Mose, L. O., Nyangito, H. O. and Mugumieri, G. L. (1997), 'An Analysis of the Socio-Economic Factors Which Influence Chemical Fertilizer Use Among Smallholder Farmers in Western Kenya', in Ransom, et al. (eds.), *Maize Productivity Gains Through Research and Technology Dissemination, Proceedings of the Fifth Eastern and Southern African Regional Maize Conference, Arusha, Tanzania, June 3–7*, CIMMYT: Addis Ababa.

Mugumieri, G. L, Nyangito, H. O. and Mose, L. O. (1997), 'Agronomic and Socio-Economic Factors Determining Maize Yield Response to Fertilizers in Western Kenya', *African Crop Science Proceedings, Pretoria, January 13–17*, African Crop Science Society: Kampala, Uganda.

NOPA (1992), 'Pastoralists at a Crossroads: Survival and Development Issues in African Pastoralism', UNICEF/UNSO Project for Nomadic Pastoralists in Africa: Nairobi, Kenya.

Nyangito, H. O. (1998), *Agricultural Policy in Kenya: Reforms, Research Gaps and Options: IPAR Occasional Paper Series No. 2*, Institute of Policy Analysis and Research: Nairobi, Kenya.

Nyangito, H. O. (1999), 'Agricultural Sector Performance in a Changing Policy Environment', in Kimuyu, P., et al. (eds.), *Kenya's Strategic Policies for the 21st Century: Macroeconomic and Sectoral Choices*, Institute of Policy Analysis and Research: Nairobi, Kenya.

Nyangito, H. O. (2000), *Delivery of Services to Smallholder Coffee Farmers and Impacts on Production Under Liberalization: KIPPRA Discussion Paper Series No. 4*, KIPPRA: Nairobi, Kenya.

Nyangito, H. O. and Kimura, J. H. (1999), *Provision of Agricultural Services in a Liberalized Economy: The Case of the Smallholder Tea Sub-Sector: IPAR Discussion Paper Series No. 16*, Institute of Policy Analysis and Research: Nairobi, Kenya.

Nyangito, H. O. and Ndirangu, L. (1997), *Farmers' Response to Reforms in the Marketing of Maize in Kenya: A Case Study of Trans Nzoia District: IPAR Discussion Paper Series No. 3*, Institute of Policy Analysis and Research: Nairobi, Kenya.

Nyoro, J. (1996), 'Impact of Market Reform on Seed Development, Multiplication and Distribution', A paper presented at the *Workshop on Fine-Tuning Market Reforms for Improved Agricultural Performance*, June 27–30, Egerton University Policy Analysis Matrix: Nairobi, Kenya.

Nyoro, J., Kiiru, M. W. and Jayne, T. S. (1999), 'Evolution of Kenya's Maize Marketing Systems in the Post-Liberalization Era', Paper presented at the *4th Agricultural Transformation Workshop*, Tegemeo Agricultural Monitoring and Policy Analysis Project: Nairobi, Kenya.

Omiti, J. (2000), 'A Situational Analysis of the Livestock Sub-Sector in Kenya', Paper presented at a *Joint IFPRI/ILRI/IPAR Project Planning Workshop*, May 5–27, International Livestock Research Institute: Addis Ababa.

8

The Productivity and Competitiveness of the Kenyan Economy: A Survey of Selected Literature

AIDAN F. EYAKUZE

Introduction

A number of recent studies have shown that sound macroeconomic management, effective institutions, and policies that enhance competitiveness and productivity, are important in explaining differences in rates of economic growth and development across countries. Compared to the Asian economies, African economies have grown more slowly and have therefore been hard pressed to improve the general welfare of their populations.

During the last two decades, African governments have initiated structural reform programs in an effort to start and sustain economic growth as a means of achieving broad-based development. However, for a majority of African countries, official commitment to reform has proved difficult to sustain, resulting in continued structural problems and slow economic growth.

The chapter provides a brief review of selected theoretical, empirical and survey literature examining the productivity and competitiveness of Kenya's economy. The chapter begins by reviewing literature on the meaning of productivity and competitiveness, and identifies some of the major determinants of these concepts. The divergence between comparative advantage based on inherited factor endowments – land, labor, natural resources, versus a 'created' competitive advantage based on innovation, continuous improvement, upgrading of skills and technology, and the sophistication of firm strategies is touched on.

This chapter then turns to its central theme, a review of the performance of Kenya's productivity and competitiveness. The chapter provides a brief overview of macroeconomic performance and an assessment of Kenya's comparative advantage. It then reviews some survey literature focusing on the microeconomic environment and firm-level behavior. A summary of the evolution of Kenya's horticultural sector, especially the export of fresh produce and cut flowers, which has achieved significant international competitiveness, is provided. The final section looks at some of the critical policies that Kenya can adopt to restart and sustain high rates of economic growth through improved productivity and enhanced competitiveness.

Review of theory on productivity, competitiveness and growth

Productivity

Productivity describes the static level and dynamic rate of change in a nation's output per worker, or output per unit of a composite input combining labor, capital, and intermediate inputs (Hall and Jones, 1996). The productivity of an economy is measured by the value of the goods and services produced per unit of the nation's human, capital and physical resources (see, e.g., Porter, 1998). Porter (1998, p. 15) suggests that the concept of productivity must encompass both the value (prices) that a nation's products command in the marketplace and the efficiency with which standard units are produced. He argues further that the productivity of a nation's economy is linked directly to that of its firms, such that 'unless companies become more productive, an economy cannot become more productive'. Firm-level productivity rests on two interrelated areas; the sophistication of company operations and strategy, and; the quality of the microeconomic business environment – suppliers, human resources, marketing channels, and customer sophistication. In addition, sound legal, political and macroeconomic policies create the potential for productivity increases. Porter's fundamental argument is that 'improvements in national productivity and prosperity are a function of three interrelated influences; the political and macroeconomic context, microeconomic business environment and company operations, and strategy'. Harberger (1998, p. 4) examines the growth residual (Solow's residual) which represents 'technical change,' or 'total factor productivity (TFP) improvement' and which is the source of productivity growth. He recasts 'technical change' as 'real cost reduction (RCR)' in order to give the residual 'an address (the firm), and a face (the entrepreneur, the CEO, the production manager, etc.)'.

Harberger (1998) argues that real cost reduction is one of the five standard pillars of growth – the other four being the rate of increase of the labor force, the rate of increase in the stock of human capital, the increase in the capital stock, and the rate of return to capital. According to Harberger, the fundamental linkage between real cost reduction and economic growth is that strong real cost reductions and high rates of return create attractive investment opportunities. Harberger agrees with Porter (1998, p. 26) in suggesting that, because three of the five key elements of growth – rate of investment, rate of return, and real cost reduction, are also the critical elements in decision-making at the firm level, 'one cannot escape the conclusion that the great bulk of the action associated with the growth process takes place at the level of the firm'.

Competitiveness

While the concept of competitiveness is quite well understood at the firm level, it has been rather controversial when applied to national economies. Fagerberg (1988) defines competitiveness as, 'the ability of a country to realize central economic goals, especially growth in income and employment without running into balance of payments difficulties'. Castells (1996), on the other hand, defines competitiveness as 'the degree to which [a nation] can, under free and fair market conditions, produce goods and services that meet the test of international markets while simultaneously expanding the real incomes of its citizens'. Porter (1990, p. 73) suggests that competitiveness 'depends on the capacity of [a nation's] industry to innovate and upgrade'. *The Global Competitiveness Report* (1994) suggests that competitiveness derives from the combination of a country's assets, either inherited (for example, natural resources) or created (for example, infrastructure, and human capital) and the processes (for example, manufacturing) that transform them into goods and services, which are globally competitive in both price and quality.

The link between productivity and competitiveness was noted in a 1984 *Report of the President's Commission on Competitiveness* which stated that 'competitiveness at the national level is based on superior productivity performance.[1] This view is echoed by Porter (1990) who argues further that nations are competitive only when the firms based in these countries are competitive. In turn, firms' competitiveness is based almost exclusively on their success in the difficult task of innovating, which translates into competitive advantage.[2] The determinants of national competitive advantage are set out in Porter's (1990) famous diamond, showing the interaction between a nation's factor conditions, demand conditions, firm strategy, industry structure and rivalry, and related and supporting industries. As argued by Porter (1990, p. 83), '[a]t the broadest level, weaknesses in any one determinant will constrain an industry's potential for advancement and upgrading.' and the country's subsequent achievement of a sustained competitive advantage.

The importance of competitiveness for a nation's economy has been vigorously debated. In at least one article, Krugman (1994) argued that the concern with competitiveness was misplaced essentially because countries were not in competition with each other in the same manner as firms are. This view has been hotly contested by, among others, Prestowitz, 1994; Thurow, 1994; and Cohen, 1994. Thurow (1994, p. 190), for example, argues that:

> If the domestic economy is to succeed in moving to higher levels of productivity and income, it must first compete successfully in the global economy. Foreign competition simultaneously forces a faster pace of economic change at home and produces opportunities to learn new technologies and new management practices that can be used to improve domestic productivity. Put bluntly, those who don't compete abroad won't be productive at home.

The literature also reveals an interesting divergence between comparative and competitive advantage in explaining the economic performance of nations. Under the theory of comparative advantage, 'the success of nations in particular industries is based on so-called factors of production such as land, labor and natural resources' (Porter, 1990). In this view, 'a country is tied to what it has, not to what it can create. In contrast, competitive advantage is based on the ability of the people of a country to add value to the available resources (Doryan, 1993). The two views result in radically different implications for economic policy as Collier (1998) suggests in his analysis of the implications of globalization for Africa. He proposes a transactions cost argument to explain Africa's low level of manufactured exports relative to natural resource exports.

> On Woods thesis, Africa can forget about manufactures. There is nothing to be done. On the transactions costs thesis, there is everything to be done. Policymakers can, by reducing transactions costs to world levels, make Africa into the most competitive region in the world for labor-intensive manufactures because of Africa's low and relatively declining real incomes.

The economic success of natural-resource-poor countries such as Japan, Hong Kong (since 1997, a special administrative region of the People's Republic of China), Singapore, and the prevailing context of an increasingly knowledge-based, globalizing economy, tilts the argument in favor of created competitive advantage. The performance of Kenya's economy in productivity and competitiveness is reviewed against the background of this tension.

The productivity and competitiveness of Kenya's economy

This section begins with a brief overview of Kenya's recent economic performance. We then review four key studies that have investigated competitiveness in Kenya: Gerdin (1997); Kimuyu (1998); and Mwega and Ndung'u (1998). This macroeconomic analysis is followed by a closer look at the microeconomic environment and firm behavior drawing on an analysis by the Regional Program on Enterprise Development (R-PED) project.

Overview of Kenya's economic performance, 1981–1998

Kenya's economy grew by an average of 3.7 percent annually between 1981 and 1985 and maintained real growth rates above 4.5 percent annually from 1986 to 1990 (World Bank, 1992). However, the growth rate slowed from 4.3 percent in 1990 to 0.4 percent in 1992, the lowest growth rate recorded during the post-independence era. All major sectors experienced a sharp decline in 1992. Agriculture, excluding forestry and fishing, shrank by 4.2 percent; industrial growth fell from an average of 5.1 percent annual growth between 1986 and 1990 to 0.2 percent in 1992; growth in services shrank from 5.8 percent (1986–1990) to 3.0 percent in 1992 (World Bank, 1993). The year 1993 was the worst in Kenya's recent economic history in which a 0.2 percent GDP growth rate was recorded and per capita GDP shrank by 2.7 percent. Kenya experienced prolonged drought and the severe consequences of high inflation and a sharp depreciation of the shilling due in part to excessive growth in the money supply, with the latter linked with Kenya's first multi-party elections held in December 1992.

The economy performed better in 1994 and 1995, in large measure due to 'price decontrols, the removal of import licensing and exchange controls, as well as liberalization of trade and labor markets. Improved fiscal discipline reduced the deficit (excluding grants) from 6.3 percent in 1994 to 2.8 percent of GDP in 1996 (McPherson, 1997). In 1997, the growth rate for the economy slowed down again to 2.3 percent from 4.8 percent in 1996. Agriculture and manufacturing growth rates declined to 1.2 percent and 1.9 percent in 1997, from 4.4 percent and 3.7 percent in 1996 respectively. Growth in per capita GDP also contracted from 1.9 percent in 1996 to -0.3 percent in 1997 (GoK, 1998). Real GDP growth in 1998 was also sluggish at 1.6 percent (CBK, 1999).

The productivity of Kenya's economy

A comprehensive empirical analysis of Kenya's productivity performance between 1964 and 1994 was undertaken by Gerdin (1997) and this section borrows heavily from that analysis. Observations by Kimuyu (1998) are also included. Gerdin focuses on the determinants of growth following the neo-classical growth accounting tradition originated by Solow (1957) in which total factor productivity (TFP) growth is measured as a residual. Productivity growth is measured at the sectoral level based on sectoral production functions during the 1964–1994 period. This approach allows for an investigation of whether the observed behavior is common across all sectors or whether it is sector-specific. The sectors analyzed were agriculture, mining, manufacturing, wholesale and transport.

The empirical estimation found that agriculture, manufacturing and transport experienced positive productivity growth during the period. Productivity growth was neutral in the mining and wholesale sectors. The acceleration of productivity growth (defined as the rate of change of productivity growth with respect to time) was neutral in all sectors, except in transport where it was negative. The interpretation is that while productivity growth was positive, it did not accelerate over time in the four sectors and it in fact declined in the transport sector.

Labor (or capital) saving productivity occurs when productivity increases are associated with a reduction in the quantity of labor (or capital) input. Conversely, productivity growth declines with an increase in the quantity of labor (or capital). Productivity growth was labor-saving, that is, the rate of productivity growth declines with increases in labor, in all sectors except agriculture. In an attempt to reduce unemployment by promoting industrial employment, the government of Kenya had relied on wage guidelines as the basic strategy to hold down labor costs. However, the results suggest that productivity growth in manufacturing worked in the opposite direction. One explanation could be an overvalued currency, which made intermediate and capital inputs cheap compared to labor and other domestic inputs. An alternative explanation of labor-saving productivity growth might indicate low labor quality. The general level of education of the labor force might be a constraining factor to both labor promotion and productivity growth, and although there is a labor surplus, there might be a general shortage of sufficiently skilled labor.

In addition to being labor-saving, productivity growth in manufacturing was also capital saving, but intermediate input using. It is possible that the technology choice of multinational corporations, which were initially established after independence later, became a role model for newer firms. Technology promoting activities such as technology adaptation might have remained low due to policies which promoted the importation and installation of turnkey plants.

In agriculture, the positive productivity growth saved on intermediate inputs used capital and was neutral in labor. The acceleration of productivity growth was also neutral. A possible explanation for the intermediate input-saving observation was the policy bias towards industry which meant that scarce foreign currency was allocated to imported inputs for the manufacturing sector, constraining the country's ability to import essential inputs for agriculture.

In transport, productivity growth was positive but with a declining growth rate (negative acceleration). The initial large increase in paved roads mileage, followed by a significant deterioration in road quality in the 1980s and 1990s could explain this observation.

Output growth in the five sectors was due to growth in inputs and change in productivity. The average annual growth rate in overall output was 3.98 percent between 1964 and 1994, declining from 6.05 percent in the first decade to 2.12 percent in the 1984–1994 period. Annual productivity growth rates increased over time from 0.19 percent in 1964–1973 to 0.47 percent in 1984–1994. On average, productivity growth contributed about 0.37 percent to output growth.

Overall results, however, show productivity growth to have been the least significant source of output growth in Kenya. It accounted for about 9.30 percent of overall output growth compared to labor's 10.05 percent, capital's 30.65 percent and intermediate inputs' contribution of 50.25 percent.

The analysis estimated a mean rate of technical change (technological upgrading and innovation) of –0.18 percent and a mean total factor productivity (TFP) growth rate of –0.12 percent. Generally, TFP growth was negative throughout the period, except for an increase during the coffee boom years (1976–1978) during which there was an increase in the scale of production to meet the high demand brought about by the significant increase in export earnings.

Gerdin (1997) suggests that low productivity growth indicates the use of old or obsolete technology. Given the inward orientation and Kenya's small domestic market, there may not have been any major incentives for upgrading technology. Alternatively, utilization of such technology may have been constrained by lack of skilled manpower.

In summary, Gerdin's analysis suggests that over a period of 30 years, Kenya neither experienced productivity growth nor any level of technological advancement.

Kimuyu (1998) also observes that aggregate and sectoral data show that Kenya's total factor productivity growth has been varied, with periods of productivity growth being followed by periods of decline (see Table 8.1).

The productivity of capital in Kenya has also experienced significant deterioration. Kimuyu (1998) notes that estimates of the incremental capital output ratios (ICORs) increased from 5.3 in 1984–1989 to 13.9 in 1989–1994. He observes that:

> These ICORs are some of the highest recorded by any country in the world. Capital application in Kenya seems to suffer from inexplicably low productivity, casting doubts on the country's ability to achieve the high rates of economic growth projected in policy documents (Kimuyu, 1998, p. 12).

Table 8.1   Growth in total factor productivity in Kenya

Period	Total Factor Productivity Growth		
	Aggregate	*Agriculture*	*Manufacturing*
1961–1970	3.022	5.137	2.180
1971–1975	–5.619	–0.317	–1.228
1976–1979	0.168	–2.459	4.961
1980–1985	–0.467	–1.444	–0.840
1986–1990	1.780	1.633	0.619
1991–1996	–0.250	–1.790	–1.649
Overall Average	–0.198	0.109	0.578

Source: Kimuyu, P. (1998), 'Industrial Policies for the Twenty-First Century: Productivity, Competitiveness and Export Participation by Manufacturing Enterprises in Kenya', Paper prepared for presentation at the annual IPAR National Conference, Nairobi, Kenya, April 15–16.

The competitiveness of Kenya's manufacturing sector

In a preliminary study investigating manufacturing competitiveness in Kenya and Uganda, Siggel, Ikiara and Nganda (1999) used data on 78 Kenyan firms in 24 industries for 1984. These findings are compared with the analysis of more recent firm-level data on Kenyan manufacturing to assess how the sector's competitiveness evolved during the recent decade (also see Siggel, Ikiara, Nganda and Ssemogerere, 1999).

The analysis uses the microeconomic concept of competitiveness and more specifically, the concept of cost competitiveness in his analysis and notes that 'at the enterprise or industry level, producers are deemed to be competitive if their unit costs of production are inferior or equal to those of their competitors.' He also makes a distinction between competitive and comparative advantage, when he argues that. '[w]hereas competitiveness is understood as a cost advantage based on market prices and therefore various price distortions, subsidies and penalties, comparative advantage corresponds to a cost advantage at equilibrium (shadow) prices' (p. 3).

The analysis found that unit costs at shadow prices exceeded international prices by 15 percent. This suggests that Kenya had no comparative advantage in manufacturing in 1984. Unit costs at market prices also exceeded international prices by 10 percent so that Kenya's manufacturing sector as a whole also lacked a competitive advantage during that year. However, the analysis did find that plastic goods, beverages and spirits, miscellaneous food production, footwear and clothing, and petrochemicals and rubber industries were internationally competitive.[3] It also inferred that 'highly capital intensive industries tend to be less likely candidates for comparative advantage than labor- and input-intensive ones'.

The major conclusion from this analysis is that the Kenyan manufacturing sector as a whole lacked comparative advantage in 1984, most likely as a result of overly capital intensive production technologies; competitiveness at market prices was enhanced by the existing distortions in which positive rates of protection of output were significant. It is also suggested that, since price distortions in 1984 on the whole were only modestly important in Kenya, the liberalization that has occurred since then ought only to have slightly affected the competitiveness of industries.

An analysis of 1997 data shows that 'on the one hand, industries have gained somewhat in terms of comparative advantage, but have lost in terms of competitive advantage, due to increased distortions' (Siggel, Ikiara, Nganda and Ssemogerere, 1999). Unit costs at shadow prices were 8 percent higher than international prices (down from 15 percent). However, export competitiveness worsened, with unit costs exceeding international prices by 45 percent, up from 30 percent in 1984. The distortions to blame for the deteriorated competitiveness include higher interest rates, an overvalued exchange rate – overvalued in 1997 by 10 percent, compared to 1984, and an energy, transport and communications infrastructure which had declined in quality and was imposing excess costs on producers.

Siggel, Ikiara, Nganda and Ssemogerere's (1999) observations on the decline in Kenya's competitiveness are corroborated by the *Africa Competitiveness Report 2000/2001*. Based on the results of an Executive Survey, it shows that Kenya has dropped from 14th to 22nd place in a ranking of the overall competitiveness of 24 countries between 1997–1998 and 2000–2001. The ability of Kenyan firms to export was constrained by poor infrastructure services; including extremely poor roads, ports, and several forms of communications structures. At the same time, costs had increased and the legal system remain extremely unreliable, subjecting entrepreneurs to 'an average of 10 percent to 18 percent in additional or unofficial payments to secure a contract with the government' (p.137). Added to this was declining quality of primary and secondary education, as well as an increase in costs to the firm, of illness and disease, with negative effects on the quality of available labor.

Kenya's improvement index, which examined the direction of change of those factors which most affected economic growth during the three-year gap between the two reports, had worsened (-0.07). The Executive Survey respondents' optimism index also returned a negative outlook for 1999–2001 in terms of any improvement in key economic growth drivers.

The manufacturing sector is a key driver of Kenya's economic growth, and it is to this that the analysis turns next.

Kenya's manufactured exports

Mwega and Ndung'u (1998) assess the impact of exchange rate policy on Kenya's manufactured exports. The focus is on the influence of the real exchange rate and its misalignment, on the performance of manufactured exports. It is widely accepted that good manufactured export performance is predicated on stable and well-aligned exchange rates. Macroeconomic policies which lead to an appreciating and volatile exchange rate have an adverse effect on export performance by reducing the profitability and increasing the uncertainty of producing for export.

In the 1980s, manufactured exports accounted for 1.7 percent of total exports and 37 percent of non-traditional exports. In the 1990s, manufactured exports as a proportion of total merchandise exports rose to 30 percent. This has been attributed to the second round of trade liberalization, which started in 1987. However, it would seem that manufacturers are still producing for the domestic market. Manufactured exports as a proportion of manufacturing output increased from 2 percent in 1987 to 7 percent in 1995, but still remained below 10 percent.

Using regression analysis, Mwega and Ndung'u (1998, pp. 25–26) find that real exchange rate appreciation, volatility and (weakly) misalignment have negative influences on manufactured exports. Manufactured exports also increase with the capacity to produce, with an estimated output elasticity of exports ranging between 0.68 and 0.97. A one percent increase in real manufacturing GDP increases real manufactured exports by 0.68 percent to 0.97 percent.

Microeconomic analysis and firm behavior in Kenyan manufacturing

Productivity and technical efficiency in manufacturing

Lundvall, Ochoro, and Hjalmarsson (forthcoming) undertake a detailed analysis of productivity and technical efficiency in four manufacturing sectors – textile, wood, food and metal, based on data from a three-year (1993–1995) survey of 266 firms. The firms were interviewed at least once as part of a World Bank supported Regional Program on Enterprise Development (RPED) project.

In the RPED study, productivity was defined as the ratio of output to inputs, and technical efficiency as the ratio of actual output to the maximum output feasible, given a set of inputs. The set of maximum output levels corresponding to all positive input combinations forms the outer edge of the frontier production function.

The Productivity and Competitiveness of the Kenyan Economy   231

Productivity and efficiency were examined as they varied across sectors as well as between different categories of firms for the period 1992–1995. While corruption, infrastructural deficiencies, institutional inefficiency and low demand are likely to affect the overall level of performance, they were not expected to affect the indicators variation between firms. The partial factor productivity results are presented in Table 8.2.

Table 8.2   Partial factor productivity in Kenyan manufacturing

Firm Characteristics	Y/L (KShs worker)	Y/wL (KShs/ shilling in wages)	Y/K (KShs/ shilling of capital input)	K/L
Informal firms	72	5.05	4.30	15
Formal 1–5 employees	106	5.45	0.46	171
6–20 employees	195	7.78	1.38	181
21–75 employees	287	9.60	1.50	190
76–200 employees	405	9.31	1.42	333
500+ employees	187	8.63	0.82	260

Notes: From a sample of 625 (116 informal) observations on 266 (70 informal) in Kenyan manufacturing firms observed during 1993–1995.
Y: gross value of all output produced by the firm in a given year.
K: replacement value of machinery and equipment.
L: total number of full time workers including casuals involved in production during the year.

Table 8.2 shows that informal firms employ much less capital per worker, hence capital productivity is higher and labor productivity lower than for formal firms. Secondly, capital intensity of production generally increases with firm size. Given that all factors increase in productivity for firms in the 21–75 employee category, this could imply superior productivity for firms in this size bracket.

The inter-firm comparison of technical efficiency (within the same sectors) showed a strongly positive size-efficiency relationship up to and including firms with 75–149 workers. Efficiency declines for firms larger than this. Informal firms are less efficient than formal firms due to the former's small size and very low capital-labor ratio.

Comparisons across industry sectors were interpreted as productivity differences, rather than differences in technical efficiency. The results showed the food sector to be between 40 percent and 120 percent more productive than the wood and textile sectors. The metal sector was between 20 percent and 85 percent more productive than the wood and textile sectors. This ranking held even when the size categories were compared between sectors; that is, firms with 21–75 employees in the food sector were more productive than similar sized firms in all other sectors.

Determinants of firm-level productivity

Table 8.3 shows the results of estimated relationships between productivity and factors that might explain the differential performance between firms:

Implications of this analysis include the fact that overall sector productivity may increase with higher enterprise turnover, so that policy measures, which encourage the birth of new firms – rather than supporting the less productive ones facing financial problems, may be warranted. Secondly, access to credit seems to be more important to productivity and efficiency than export involvement and human capital. Government could prioritize reforms, which improve access to credit by the private sector.

Kimuyu (1998) uses the same data to analyze the input elasticity of output in Kenyan manufacturing by sub-sector. His major finding is that manufacturing output is more responsive to labor than to capital, regardless of firm size. Interestingly, Kimuyu's analysis seems to dispute the findings by Lundvall, Ochoro and Hjalmarsson (forthcoming) in Table 8.3 on the insignificance of export participation and foreign ownership on productivity. Kimuyu (1998, p. 15) notes that:

> ...enterprises with an outward look in terms of export participation and attraction of foreign equity are somewhat more productive than those that are inward looking. These results underscore the importance of ...encouraging enterprises to look beyond the domestic market and creating an environment that can attract foreign participation in local production.

He also finds that firms' technical efficiency is positively influenced by their participation in exports and access to foreign equity.

Table 8.3   Determinants of productivity

Determinant	Association with productivity
Sector	• Food was 70 percent more productive than wood and textiles, and 40 percent more productive than metal.
Location	• Nairobi and Mombasa had a positive and significant effect on productivity, suggesting that locating in the capital or the main trading port influence productivity positively. • However, textile firms in these two cities were significantly less productive, probably because they were hardest hit by imports of second-hand clothing.
Firm Age	• Yielded an insignificant relationship overall, except for a negative one in textiles.
Firm Growth	• Yielded a negative and significant effect in the pooled model, suggesting that positive growth may not be associated with productivity improvement. • Contraction of firms (negative growth of 3 percent or more) however has a negative relationship with productivity in the food and metal sectors.
Investment	• Positive and significant (at 10 percent) in the metal sector.
Capacity Utilization	• Positive and significant in the pooled and textile models.
Human Capital*	• Positive and strong relationship with productivity in the food sector.
Firm Owned by Africans	• Negative relationship to productivity in all models, but significant only in the pooled textiles models.
Access to Credit	• Positive and significant in all except wood and textile sectors.
Export Behavior	• Positive and significant in pooled and wood sectors. Magnitude is less than expected so does not lend strong support to efficiency arguments of export promotion.
Foreign Ownership	• Insignificant in all models.

Note: *Ratio of skilled workers to the total number of workers.
Source: Extracted from Lundvall, K., Ochoro, W. and Hjalmarsson, L. (forthcoming), 'Productivity and Technical Efficiency', in Bigsten, A. and Kimuyu, P. (eds.), Structure and Performance of Manufacturing in Kenya, Department of Economics, Goteborg University and Nairobi University.

Export behavior of Kenya's manufacturing firms

Graner and Isaksson (forthcoming) note that exports concentrate investments in the most efficient sectors of the economy, where a country has comparative advantage and specialization increases productivity. Access to larger foreign markets allows for larger scale operations and competition forces export industries to keep costs low and reduce technical inefficiency. Exporters also reduce inefficiencies through learning-by-exporting effects stemming from the recipients' technical expertise. The export sector can also have a stimulating influence on the productivity of the economy as a whole through spillover effects to other sectors.

The question that arises concerns, the determinants of a firm's decision and the amount to export. It is hypothesized that the decision on *whether to export* depends on three factors. First are the additional sunk costs of selling goods in the foreign market (Roberts and Tybout, 1995). These costs include establishing a distribution channel and modifying products to suit foreign tastes and requirements. Second, the decision to export is influenced by expected profitability of exporting. Profitability is in turn related to the degree of trade liberalization. Third, the decision to export is influenced by the relative efficiency of firms. This is due to the fact that low-cost producers can more effectively compete in international markets.

The decision on *how much to export* also depends on expected profitability, which is influenced by the real exchange rate. A real depreciation should increase the volume of exports and the share of output exported. In addition, the Heckscher-Ohlin model relates trade patterns to factor proportions in production, so that if a country is labor-abundant, firms engaged in labor-intensive production are more likely to be exporters.

Graner and Isaksson's analysis of Kenya's manufacturing firms showed that export participation increased from 26 percent to 36 percent of surveyed firms. The share of total production that was exported also increased from 24 percent to 28 percent with the metal and textile sectors doubling their mean export share. Technical efficiency was higher for exporters (compared to non-exporters) in all sectors except for textiles, but was statistically significant only for the food and wood sectors. Exporting firms were almost 6 times larger (using output volume as a proxy for size) than non-exporters and generally have higher capital and labor productivity and capital-labor ratios.

Empirical results also showed firm size and efficiency, which are related to future profitability, to be important determinants of the decision to export. Firm size was found to be irrelevant for the export share decision. Robert and Tybout (1995) conclude that the age of the firm has a negative effect on both the decision to export as well as the share of output to export. Younger firms using more recent technology may have an advantage over older ones that use relatively obsolete technology thus making them less competitive in the international market. Both the probability of exporting and the proportion of output exported was strongly influenced by labor. Robert and Tybout (1995, p. 189) note that this result is in line with the Heckscher-Ohlin theory of comparative advantage. Thus, to compete on the world market, Kenya should allocate resources towards labor-intensive industry production in order to reap the benefits of export-led growth.

Kimuyu's (1998) analysis 'confirms that labor intensive activities are not only more likely to export but also export a greater share of their production than other enterprises. This probably suggests that Kenya's comparative advantages presently lie in labor intensive manufacturing activities'. These conclusions echo Siggel's (1999) point on Kenya's apparent comparative advantage in labor-intensive manufactured goods.

Horticulture: Kenya's most competitive sector[4]

Overview of the sector

While the productivity growth of Kenya's economy as a whole has been shown by Gerdin (1997) to have been stagnant for three decades, and competitiveness seems to elude the manufacturing sector, the performance of horticultural exports is a good example of success in international competitiveness.

Over the past two decades, the horticultural export sub-sector has developed into an important component of the Kenyan economy, both as a major source of foreign exchange earnings and as a provider of substantial employment income opportunities. During this period, when Kenya's exports of many 'traditional' commodities (e.g., sisal, meat, and pyrethrum) either declined or fluctuated greatly from year-to-year (e.g., coffee and tea), the aggregate volume and value of horticultural exports increased substantially and consistently, mounting into double-digit rates most years. As Table 8.4 indicates, horticultural exports more than doubled in volume and increased by over 24 times in shilling value terms since 1984.

Trade expansion through the mid-1980s was broad-based. Survival in the increasingly competitive markets has been dependent upon the ability of producers to upgrade production through customized pre-packing for individual retail chains. The expansion of Kenya's fresh produce trade has been accompanied by, and is in many ways dependent on, the entry of many new participants, especially at the production level. In the case of vegetables, this expanded production came in response to a rapid increase in foreign demand during the 1970s and was stimulated by competitive pressures within Kenya, which led exporters to extend and diversify their sources of supply.

Table 8.4   Growth of Kenya's exports of fresh fruits, vegetables, and cut flowers

Year	Volume (000s Tons)	Value (KShs million)	Average Unit Value (KShs/Ton)
1984	31,298	416	13,291
1985	30,002	464	15,465
1986	36,211	630	17,398
1987	36,557	900	24,619
1988	65,119	1,328	20,393
1989	49,504	1,443	29.149
1990	49,147	1,678	34,142
1991	49,848	2,011	40,342
1992	57,363	2,516	40,348
1993	62,119	4,673	75,226
1994	65,178	4,972	76,283
1995	71,758	6,464	90,080
1996	84,824	7,701	90,788
1997	84,190	8,734	103,741
1998	80,722	10,109	125,232

Source: Horticultural Crops Development Authority, Nairobi, Kenya.

The production and trade of cut flowers has been one of the most dynamic components of Kenyan agriculture over the past two decades. This industry has experienced several new medium-to-large-scale investments, a secondary, yet substantial growth in small-holder production, and a considerable diversification in the mix of flower types produced and marketed.

Since 1973, participation in Kenya's horticultural export sub-sector has broadened considerably, with increasing numbers of small-holders and other producers providing commodities and raw materials and with increased entry into trade, especially for fresh produce exports. Over half of the leading firms are Asian-owned family companies or partnerships. Most had considerable experience in fruit and vegetable production and trade in the domestic market before entering the export trade. Most have their own wholesale and/or retail establishments and farms; some also have complementary interests in freight forwarding and transport. Several of the leading exporters benefit from having relatives in Europe with whom they conduct a significant proportion of their trade. These operating features have significantly reduced the risks and transaction costs that ordinarily characterize the market for highly perishable and heterogeneous horticultural commodities.

Some lessons from the success of horticulture

With the possible exception of South Africa, Kenya has developed the most diversified and competitive horticultural export trade within sub-Saharan Africa. In the processing industry, export success over an extended period has only been achieved by a limited number of firms which developed strong ties with major multinational corporations either through joint ownership or through long-term technical, management and marketing contracts. Strong long-term technical, managerial and marketing linkages between Kenyan and foreign firms have also been essential to the development of Kenya's cut flower export industry. In both industries, critical infant-industry support was provided by both colonial and post-independence governments during the 1950s and 1960s.

For African countries and entrepreneurs seeking to replicate aspects of Kenya's horticultural development experience, three lessons can be drawn: First, while many African countries share with Kenya some ecological, locational and labor cost advantages in the production of certain horticultural crops, few such countries are well endowed with the additional technical, financial, infrastructural, and managerial assets, which are critical for developing a competitive horticultural trade. In the absence of foreign investment or a considerable initial investment by government and/or the local private sector in horticultural research, training and marketing infrastructure, the development of horticultural exports will be a very slow process in Africa with a high incidence of failure among individual firms.

Second, the development of African trade in many horticultural commodities will require the attraction of foreign investment or at least the development of long-term technical and marketing contracts between domestic and foreign firms. This may be especially important in commodity lines requiring highly specialized knowledge and inputs, featuring rapid technical and market changes, and featuring highly concentrated international markets. Governments need to improve the incentives for foreign investment and the legal and informational infrastructure necessary to facilitate the development of complex contractual relations between local and foreign companies.

Finally, 'learning by doing' may no longer be a viable means of developing a horticultural export trade in light of the intensification of competition in European and other markets and the increased requirements for quality, supply continuity, and product variety in these markets. Prospective exporters would be advised to gain experience first in the domestic market, perhaps by developing crop procurement and distribution arrangements to supply high quality produce to restaurants, hotels and up-market retail outlets. In encouraging new entry into horticultural exports, attention should focus on private firms and co-operatives currently active in domestic fresh produce wholesaling, large individual growers, and firms or individuals which currently carry out exports of other agricultural or manufactured products and thus have market contacts and an understanding of the risks and mechanics of international trade.

Conclusions

This chapter presented a brief review of selected literature on productivity and competitiveness with specific reference to the Kenyan economy.

The literature shows that high and increasing levels of productivity are necessary conditions for national competitiveness, defined as the ability of an economy to produce goods and services which successfully meet the test of international markets while expanding the real incomes of its citizens. It also argues that the firm is the source of the technological innovation, which drives productivity improvements and enhances national competitiveness.

There is also an interesting divergence in the literature between a factor and resource-based comparative advantage, which is essentially inherited by nations, and a competitive advantage based ultimately on superior human capital and which must be created through continuous innovation. Rather different policy implications are proposed by this debate, ranging from economic growth based on primary commodity or natural resource exports, to economic growth based on the export of higher-valued manufactures.

Turning to Kenya, one study shows that the overall productivity of the economy has improved so marginally as to be imperceptible over the 30–year period ending in 1994. Technical change has also been insignificant. This is attributed in part to previously high levels of protection of domestic industry that removed the incentive for firms to innovate, and a labor force that has not been upgraded in terms of knowledge and skills and is thus unable to deliver strong productivity improvements.

Other analysis of the unit costs of Kenya's manufacturing sector found that, with the exception of a few industries, the sector lacked both comparative and competitive advantage in 1984. A 1997 update shows a slight improvement in the sector's comparative advantage, but a worsening of its competitive advantage. This was due to the overly capital-intensive production technology. Three studies reviewed conclude that Kenya's comparative advantage in manufacturing lies in labor intensive goods. An examination of the export behavior of Kenya's manufacturing firms also found labor to have a strong influence on both the decision to export and the proportion of output exported. Exporting firms were also larger and exhibited higher capital and labor productivity than non-exporters.

Kenya's horticulture sector has achieved international competitiveness and has risen to rival the importance of tea and coffee in export earnings. The success of this sector was based not only on the 'inherited' ecological, locational or labor cost advantages but more importantly on the 'created' technical, financial, infrastructural and managerial assets, which added significant value to the factor endowments. Foreign investment and long-term technical and marketing contracts between domestic and foreign firms played an important role in the dissemination of new technologies and techniques in production, post-harvest handling and marketing. Government's role in facilitating the contracts and investment was critical. Ultimately, the sector's competitiveness continues to be based on the success of individual firms which gained early experience in the domestic market, entered the export trade and have continued to innovate and upgrade to meet exacting international standards of quality, variety and delivery schedules.

While Kenya's institutional framework and macroeconomic climate will remain critical, improving the productivity and competitiveness of Kenya's industrial sector also depends to a significant extent on enterprises learning from the experience of the horticultural exporters and applying the lessons to their activities in the domestic and international marketplace.

Notes

1. Quoted by Cohen (1994).
2. Innovation is used in a broad sense that includes the introduction of new technologies and new ways of doing things.
3. The new RPED survey (1993–1995) confirms Kenya's international competitiveness in clothing. Despite a lower productivity level compared to India and China, the lower wages paid to Kenyan labor markets makes its shirts competitive on world markets. See World Bank Discussion Paper No. 346.
4. This section borrows from Jaffe (1995).

References

Bigsten, A. and Kimuyu, P. (eds.) (forthcoming), *Structure and Performance of Manufacturing in Kenya*, Department of Economics, Goteborg University and University of Nairobi: Goteborg, Sweden and Nairobi, Kenya.

Castells, M. (1996), *The Information Age: Economy, Society and Culture*, Blackwell Publishers: Cambridge, MA.

Central Bank of Kenya (CBK) (1999), *Monthly Economic Review*, April, Government Printer: Nairobi.

Cohen, S. S. (1994), 'Speaking Freely', Response to 'The Fight Over Competitiveness: A Zero-Sum Debate?', *Foreign Affairs*, Vol. 73, No. 4 (July/August), pp. 194–197.

Collier, P. (1998), 'Globalization: Implications for Africa', in Zubair, I. and Mohsin, S. K. (eds.), *Trade Reform and Regional Integration in Africa*, International Monetary Fund: Washington, DC.

Doryan, E.A. (1993), 'An Institutional Perspective of Competitiveness and Industrial Restructuring Policies in Developing Countries', *Journal of Economic Issues*, Vol. XXVII, No. 2, pp. 451–548.

Fagerberg, J. (1988), 'International Competitiveness', *The Economic Journal*, Vol. 98, pp. 355–374.

Gerdin, A. (1997), *On Productivity and Growth in Kenya, 1964–94*, Kompendiet: Goteborg, Sweden.

GoK (1998), *Economic Survey*, May, Government Printer: Nairobi.

Graner, M. and Isaksson, A. (forthcoming), 'Export Performance in the Kenyan Manufacturing Sector', in Bigsten, A. and Kimuyu, P. (eds.), *Structure and Performance of Manufacturing in Kenya*, Department of Economics, Goteborg University and University of Nairobi: Goteborg, Sweden and Nairobi, Kenya.

Hall, R. E. and Jones, C. L. (1996), *The Productivity of Nations*, National Bureau of Economic Research Working Paper No. 5812, NBER: New York.

Harberger, A. (1998), 'A Vision of the Growth Process', The *American Economic Review*, Vol. 88, No. 1, pp. 1–32.

Jaffee, S. (1995), 'The Many Faces of Success: The Development of Kenya's Horticultural Exports', in Jaffee, S. and Morton, J. (eds.), *Marketing Africa's High-Value Foods: Comparative Experiences of an Emergent Private Sector*, Kendall/Hunt Publishing Company: Dubuque, IA.

Kimuyu, P. (1998), 'Industrial Policies for the Twenty-First Century: Productivity, Competitiveness and Export Participation by Manufacturing Enterprises in Kenya', Paper prepared for presentation at the annual IPAR National Conference, April 15–16, Nairobi, Kenya.

Krugman, P. (1994), 'Proving My Point', Response to 'The Fight over Competitiveness: A Zero-Sum Debate?', *Foreign Affairs*, Vol. 73, No. 4 (July/August), pp. 198–203.

Lundvall, K., Ochoro, W. and Hjalmarsson, L. (forthcoming), 'Productivity and Technical Efficiency', in Bigsten, A. and Kimuyu, P. (eds.), *Structure and Performance of Manufacturing in Kenya*, Department of Economics, Goteborg University and University of Nairobi: Goteborg, Sweden and Nairobi, Kenya.

McPherson, M. F. (1997), *Exchange Rates and Economic Growth in Kenya*, Development Discussion Paper No. 607, Harvard Institute for International Development: Cambridge, MA.

Mwega, F. M. and Ndung'u, S. N. (1998), 'Exchange Rate Policy and Manufactured Exports Performance in Kenya in the 1980s and 90s', Paper prepared for an AERC/IMF/OECD Conference on Policies for Competitiveness in Manufacturing in sub-Saharan Africa, Johannesburg, November.

Porter, M. E. (1990), 'The Competitive Advantage of Nations', *Harvard Business Review*, Vol. 68, No. 2, pp. 73–93.

Porter, M. E. (1998), 'Porter's Microscope', *World Link*, July/August.

Prestowitz, C. V. (1994), 'Playing to Win', Response to 'The Fight over Competitiveness: A Zero-Sum Debate?', *Foreign Affairs*, Vol. 73, No. 4 (July/August), pp. 186–198.

Roberts, M. J. and Tybout, J. R. (1995), 'An Empirical Model of Sunk Costs and the Decision to Export', World Bank Working Paper No. 1436, March, The World Bank: Washington, DC.

Siggel, E., Ikiara, G., and Nganda, B. (1999), 'Industry Competitiveness, Trade Prospects and Growth in Kenya and Uganda: The Kenya Component and Comparisons with Uganda', Mimeo.

Siggel, E., Ikiara, G., Nganda, B. and Ssemogerere, G. (1999), 'Industry Competitiveness, Trade Prospects and Growth in Kenya and Uganda – Executive Summary', Paper presented at the *All Africa Conference – Africa in the Third Millennium: Trade and Growth with Equity*, October 18–20, Gaborone, Botswana.

Solow, R. M. (1957), 'Technical Change and the Aggregate Production Function', *Review of Economics and Statistics*, Vol. 39, No. 3, pp. 312–320.

Thurow, L. C. (1994), 'Microchips, Not Potato Chips', Response to 'The Fight Over Competitiveness: A Zero-Sum Debate?', Vol. 73, No. 4 (July/August), pp. 189–192.

World Bank (1992), 'Kenya – Reinvesting in Stabilization and Growth Through Public Sector Adjustment: A World Bank Country Study No. 11263', September, The World Bank: Washington, DC.

World Bank (1993), *Kenya Employment Growth for Poverty Alleviation*, Report No. 11650–KE, The World Bank: Washington, DC.

9

Policy Reforms, Competitiveness and Prospects of Kenya's Manufacturing Industries, 1984–1997, and Comparisons with Uganda

ECKHARD SIGGEL, GERRISHON K. IKIARA AND
BENJAMIN M. NGANDA

Introduction

Kenya and Uganda are at a critical stage of their economic development. After several years of trade policy and other reforms, Kenya's government predicts an important acceleration of industrial development with the hope of becoming a 'newly industrialized country' by the year 2020. But industrial growth in recent years does not seem to warrant such a prediction. Uganda, on the other hand, has recently experienced rapid economic growth and industrialization, but its manufacturing sector remains small in comparison to Kenya's, due to a long period of instability and de-industrialization. Kenya, Uganda, and Tanzania are engaged in a process of regional integration that will lead to free trade among them in the very near future. Industries in all three countries are also facing increased international competition due to past structural adjustments and an increasingly globalized world economy. International competitiveness is therefore a goal that industries must try to reach not only for further growth but also for survival. This does not mean that they can be expected to compete successfully under perfectly free trade. A certain level of protection against low-cost international competitors is likely to be maintained in the region, but it is not clear at this point what that level of protection should be.

The present study investigates the international competitiveness of manufacturing industries in Kenya and Uganda and attempts to derive conclusions on future trade flows and industrial growth in the two countries. It uses a method of analysis designed by Cockburn and Siggel (1995) and applied previously in another EAGER project in Mali and Côte d'Ivoire (Cockburn, Siggel, Coulibaly and Vézina, 1999) as well as with Indian data. This method is the result of a marriage between incentive measurement of standard trade theory and social cost benefit analysis. It consists of the computation of competitiveness indicators and their decomposition according to the major sources of competitiveness. The analysis is carried out with Kenyan data for 1984 and 1997 and Ugandan data for 1997. The Kenyan component of the study compares the competitiveness of 42 firms in 16 industries in 1997 with that of the same or similar firms in 1984. It is important to see how industries have adjusted to the various policy changes over a period of 13 years. The study also compares the present (1997) competitiveness with that experienced in eleven matching industries in Uganda.

The chapter is organized in the following manner. The first section examines the Kenyan policy environment focusing on policies that have affected the manufacturing sector. The second section explains the method and assumptions used in the analysis as well as issues concerning the database. The third section contains the sector-wide results of the analysis starting with the situation in the mid-eighties, then focusing on the changes between 1984 and 1997, and comparing Kenyan results with similar industries in Uganda. Each section examines the sources of competitiveness and comparative advantage, which is the specific contribution of our methodology. The final section concludes and derives various policy recommendations.

The manufacturing sector and its policy environment

Since the mid-1980s, Kenya has been under increasing pressure to strengthen its industrial competitiveness. This pressure can be attributed to a number of factors including the on-going economic globalization, the country's entry into various regional integration arrangements that require opening of the economy to the regional partners, and the general liberalization of the economy to enhance both foreign and domestic participation. In addition, the Government of Kenya (GoK) has declared its vision of turning Kenya into a newly industrialized country (NIC) by the year 2020. To achieve this goal, it is imperative to radically increase the country's competitiveness and to expand its export markets.

Kenya's industrialization process began at the start of this century under British colonial rule. The pace of industrialization was quickened after independence in 1963, as the country embraced an import-substitution strategy (IS) that was then popular in a number of developing countries. Since then, a number of incentives have been used to encourage manufacturing activities in the country, including protective tariff and non-tariff barriers, tax exemptions and, later, special schemes such as export compensation, manufacturing under bond (MUB) and export processing zones (EPZ).

The import-substituting industrialization strategy encouraged the establishment of industrial enterprises, which were dependent on heavy government protection through tariff and non-tariff measures. The government directly controlled pricing and other economic activities, the result of which was the creation of an industrial structure with many inefficient and non-competitive industries. The failure of many of the country's industries to be export-oriented was partly due to their lack of competitiveness in the international markets. Other factors that contributed to this lack of competitiveness were the weakness of the country's infrastructure, the failure of firms to effectively exploit and benefit from technological economies of scale, and the high cost of imported inputs (ADB, 1995, p. 67). The export promotion schemes mentioned above were introduced to counter this development, to create export-oriented enterprises, to generate employment, and to promote the transfer of technology.

Trends in industrial production

The inward-oriented strategy adopted at independence had served the country well in the first and second post-independence decades. From 1964–1973, Kenyan manufacturing grew at an annual average rate of 9.1 percent (compared to a growth rate of GDP of 6.6 percent) and between 1974–1979 at 10 percent (GDP grew at 5.2 percent). The policies adopted by the new Kenyan government resulted in better incentives and a more favorable economic structure than in most other sub-Saharan African (SSA) countries. Manufacturing's share in GDP grew from 10 percent in the 1960s to 12 percent in the late 1970s and 13 percent in the mid-1980s. In the second decade of independence, the economy experienced several major shocks, from the OPEC oil price increases of 1973 and 1979, a major drought in 1974/1975, the coffee boom of 1976/1977, to the collapse of the East African Community (EAC) in 1977. These and other factors led to an overall economic slowdown with average GDP growth of 4.8 percent in the 1980s and only 3 percent up to 1996. Since manufacturing growth had been fuelled mainly by demand growth (more than two thirds) and import substitution (slightly over one quarter), according to Sharpley and Lewis (1988), the slow-down affected the manufacturing sector not only by declining demand, but also by import substitution coming to a saturation point. The easy phase of import substitution in light manufacturing of consumer goods had come to an end, as in food, beverages, tobacco, textiles and clothing, most of the demand was being satisfied by domestic production. Further import substitution, in intermediate and capital goods was possible, but required heavy investments, new technologies, and higher skills. The 1980s, however, did not provide the necessary demand growth or the enabling environment for such projects. Manufacturing exports had contributed only about 5 percent of the sector's total growth, and the partial loss of the Ugandan and Tanzanian markets after the collapse of the EAC in 1977 meant a further decline of this potential source of growth. The realization of these constraints led the GoK to adopt the export promotion schemes mentioned earlier, but none of them was really successful in the circumstances. The sector remained essentially oriented towards the domestic market, with only a few industries producing for external and mainly regional markets.

Although the sector has always attracted more investments than its share in GDP, that share declined from 17 percent in 1970 to 14 percent in 1980 and to 13 percent in 1992, from where it started to rise only in the mid-1990s. The manufacturing growth of the 1980s was not driven by investment, but by fuller use of the existing capacities, and excess capacities that had been created, which is a well-known phenomenon under inward-oriented regimes. Another aspect of manufacturing growth also observed in Kenya was its low absorption of the labor force, which in view of strong population growth aggravated the problem of unemployment. Before dealing with the labor market in more detail, let us first review Kenya's industrial policies and their recent changes.

Kenya's industrial policies

Since the country inherited, at independence, one of the strongest industrial bases in the region, industrial development has been recognized as one of the key sectors of the economy for the whole of Kenya's post-independence period. This is well reflected in the official pronouncements on overall economic and industrial policy during the period. The policies that were pursued have largely reflected the dominant international viewpoint. Thus, the country's first development plan, 1966–1970, laid emphasis on import-substitution as the strategy for the country's industrialization (GoK, 1996). The strategy was to be implemented mainly through the protection of industries, using tariff and non-tariff barriers, exchange controls and import licensing. Other key elements of the country's industrial policy have been a liberal policy towards foreign investments, the promotion of labor-intensive technologies, greater focus on medium and large industries, and the pursuit of even geographical dispersal of industries, as well as Kenyanization (McCormick, 1998).

The government's policy statements of the early 1970s and 1980s started to emphasize the need to reduce protection of domestic industry in order to encourage efficiency and reduce the burden of industry on other sectors. Promotion of manufactured exports and encouragement of further import substitution featured as key policies for most of the period during 1963–1985. The former policy was especially promoted through the introduction of the export compensation scheme in 1974, a measure intended to assist manufacturers with cash subsidies to help them offset the protective effects of tariffs on imported inputs and the cascading effects of domestic excise and sales taxes. Import substitution was especially promoted through raising of the level of scheduled tariffs and the use of import licensing as a key element of macroeconomic management and protection for domestic manufacturing industries. Higher levels of protection were given to foreign private firms and parastatal enterprises than to locally owned firms (Sharpley and Lewis, 1988). The nature and incidence of trade policies will be examined in more detail in the next section.

Macroeconomic policies also affected industries in several ways. First in importance is economic stability, which is the basis for sound investment decisions. Fiscal and monetary policies, together with trade and exchange rate policies, were implemented to achieve high levels of employment and price stability. Price controls were also used extensively up to the mid-1980s as a key policy instrument. This, coupled with the extensive quantitative restrictions (QRs) on imports, reduced the incentives for firms to keep their costs down, and virtually stifled competition from imports. It also discouraged domestic firms from producing import substitutes and from seeking lower-priced or higher-quality inputs in international markets, resulting in high average unit costs. Price controls also had the effect of making producers shift to the production of commodities whose prices were not controlled. These negative effects of the price control policy on the incentives faced by local manufacturers were further exacerbated by exchange controls through import licensing.

In recognition of the burdens imposed on the economy by these policies, the government, in *Sessional Paper No. 1 of 1986*, proposed an industrial strategy that was to be driven by the private sector relying more on a market-based incentive structure. The new policy emphasized, among others, the need to reduce the importance of import licensing as a protective shield for local manufacturers and to gradually lower tariffs, in order to expose domestic firms to competition as a way of achieving greater efficiency.

In the 1989–1993 *National Development Plan*, industrial policy continued to emphasize the need to create incentives necessary for and capable of enhancing the emergence of a successful manufacturing sector, one not based merely on import substitution. The industrial development vision projected in the plan talked of adopting a strategy that would lead to the establishment of iron and steel, tool and die, a machinery industry, as well as a biotechnology and other high technology industries. Price liberalization, restructuring of the import and tariff regime, and the adoption of a realistic exchange rate were seen as crucial for increasing Kenya's competitiveness in world markets.

The early 1990s saw the beginning of dramatic liberalization of the economy and an even stronger focus on industrialization. In 1996, the government produced a key document on industrial policy called *Sessional Paper No. 2 of 1996 on the Industrial Transformation to the Year 2020*. The document highlighted some of the major constraints to industrial expansion and proposed a broad strategy for industrialization. The key elements of the strategy included the promotion of political and social stability, macroeconomic stability to build business confidence, more efficient and diversified primary production as a base for economic growth, increased investment in human resources, and rehabilitation of the physical infrastructure. It also included reform and development of the financial markets, formulation of trade and investment policies to transform the economy into an outward-looking one, increased co-operation and dialogue between the government and the private sector to foster greater and genuine partnerships, and an increase of the proportion of resources allocated to technology development and management (GoK, 1996).

Table 9.1   Effective rates of protection in Kenyan manufacturing, 1985, 1990, and 1992

	1985	1990	1992
Food preparations	111	51	44.1
Beverages	3	40.9	36.8
Textiles and garments	126	59.6	64.4
Textile raw materials	–	41.1	35.9
Garments	–	77.1	99.7
Leather and footwear	80	43	40.5
Paper and wood products	6	47.3	42.1
Chemicals	211	45.2	40.6
Rubber products	–	47.1	45.2
Paints and detergents	–	43.7	37.5
Non-metallic minerals	248	36.5	30.9
Metal products	312	46.9	40.4
Mean	107	47.9	44.5

Source: World Bank (1987), *Kenya: Industrial Policies for Investment and Export Growth*, The World Bank: Washington, DC.

Trade policy and its reforms

Trade policy is known to be the principal instrument affecting manufacturing industries and their incentive regime. As we have seen already, the strategy of import substitution entailed high and uneven tariff rates with frequent exemptions, QRs on imports, and import licensing. The liberalization of the trade regime from 1985 onwards had only weak effects in the first years, with frequent episodes of relapse; however, it became more effective after 1991. The average un-weighted tariff rate actually increased slightly from 40 percent in 1985 to 41.3 percent in 1989, but declined to 34 percent in 1992. The decline is even more visible for the import-weighted average tariff, which declined from 29.6 percent in 1988 to 20.4 percent in 1992. By 1994, the manufacturing sector was enjoying an average tariff of 28.5 percent, a figure that hides the wide dispersion of rates. Although maximum rates have declined substantially in the manufacturing sector, most of the reduction in the level of protection has occurred largely due to the reduction in the production coverage of quantitative import controls (Swamy, 1994). For example, whereas quantitative controls (Schedule IIIC) covered most manufacturing in 1986, the coverage fell to 79 percent in 1988, 45 percent in 1990, and 28 percent in 1991.

The QRs and high tariffs combined to provide high levels of effective protection to the manufacturing sector and a strong anti-export bias. In order to capture the effects of QRs on prices, it is necessary to make quality-adjusted comparisons between the prices of domestic producers and the border prices of corresponding imports. The resulting implicit nominal rates of protection have been used in several studies of effective protection, most of which have shown that the level of effective protection exceeded substantially the level of nominal protection, due to the cascading nature of the tariff and due to exemptions from tariffs on the input side. Also, it has been shown that import liberalization has failed to reduce the effective rate of protection (ERP) for Kenya's manufacturing sector, in spite of the decline in nominal rates (Sharpley and Lewis, 1988; Wignaraja and Ikiara, 1999). Estimates of the ERP by the World Bank, however, indicate that the average rate for manufacturing declined from 107 percent in 1985 to 47.9 percent in 1990 and to 44.5 percent in 1992. Some sub-sector rates are shown in Table 9.1. The figures show that trade liberalization started having some impact on the manufacturing sector only in the 1990s. Not only did the average rates decline, but also, and more importantly, the dispersion of rates among the industries was significantly reduced. The description of the trade regime would be incomplete without regard of the exchange rate. In inward-oriented trade regimes, high protection is often accompanied by an over-valued currency, where the effect of over-valuation is the opposite to that of protection. Let us see then how the GoK managed the foreign exchange market.

The foreign exchange market and the exchange rate

Up to the time the East African Currency Board broke up, the Kenyan shilling was nominally pegged to the British pound. After that, the peg was switched to the dollar and remained so up to 1974 when, following a series of devaluations precipitated by the oil crisis, the official peg was switched to the SDR. Between 1974 and 1981, the movement in the nominal exchange rate in relation to the US dollar was erratic and resulted in a depreciation of 14 percent. Further devaluations took place between 1980 and 1982, with the shilling depreciating by about 20 percent in real terms against the SDR. Towards the end of 1982 the exchange rate regime was changed to a crawling peg, which lasted until 1990, when a dual exchange rate system was adopted. That regime lasted only up to October 1993 when, after a series of devaluations, the official exchange rate was abolished. This led to the merging of the official exchange rate and market exchange rates. After an appreciation of 35 percent in 1994, the shilling depreciated slightly in 1995, which was more than offset by a similar appreciation in 1996. Since 1994, the government has continued to implement economic reforms in an attempt to rectify some of the major macroeconomic imbalances. The reforms included the abolition of exchange control regulations, abolition of import licensing, introduction of export retention schemes, and the removal of price controls.

Most observers agree that the Kenya shilling was not much over-valued in the 1960s. However, restrictive trade policies were actively applied in the 1970s when the economy started to experience large macroeconomic imbalances. Overall, the real exchange rate was fairly stable in the 1967–1975 period, but it registered more instability in the 1977–1982 period, when the shilling was subjected to a number of discretionary devaluations. Over the 1983–1991 period, during which the exchange rate was adjusted on a daily basis, the real exchange rate was relatively stable. Since 1991, the government has adopted a more market-based exchange rate regime, resulting in a massive depreciation in 1993, but which did not prevent renewed real appreciation in 1994–1995. Several observers have agreed that by 1997, the end of our study period, the shilling was again somewhat over-valued (Ndung'u, 1997, Mwega and Ndung'u, 1998).

The labor market

Although labor's share in total manufacturing costs is a relatively small fraction, usually no more than 10–15 percent, labor plays a much more important role as a potential source of comparative advantage. First, among all sources of competitiveness, labor is usually expected to be a prime source, but in reality often does not play this role, due to its low productivity. Second, the problem of a rapidly growing labor force, combined with constraints of employment creation in other sectors, places a huge burden of employment creation on manufacturers. Firms are expected to employ large numbers of workers, but they can do so only if labor remains cheap, in order to stay competitive. We shall examine now how government policy in Kenya has influenced manufacturing employment and the cost of labor.

The labor force in Kenya, estimated to consist of 14 million in 1998, is rapidly expanding at a rate of close to half a million new entrants per year largely due to continued high population growth and an age structure of more than two thirds being less than 40 years old (Tostensen, 1991, p. 298). The levels of unemployment and underemployment have remained high for most of the last two decades. Open unemployment is estimated to be about 25 percent, and underemployment is around 20 percent (GoK, 1996). Retrenchment and poor performance of the economy have aggravated the employment problem in the country in the 1990s, affecting workers in both the private and public sectors.

Manufacturing employment represents a proportion of 13.1 percent of total wage employment, and about 25 percent of private sector employment. Given the sector's higher-than-average wages, the proportion of wage earnings of total employment earnings is over 30 percent. In the 1990s, manufacturing employment grew at over 2 percent yearly, but its proportion of private sector employment decreased from 26 percent in 1991 to 23.6 percent in 1995, while its wage bill increased from 30.1 percent of total employment earnings to 36.7 percent, in the same period. These numbers reflect two tendencies, staff retrenchment as response to structural adjustment, and upward wage pressure supported by increasing labor productivity.

Generally, the Kenyan labor market has been characterized by relatively low wages, especially among unskilled and semi-skilled workers. Several factors have contributed to this situation. First, the government purposely pursued a policy of low wages aimed at making the country attractive to foreign investors. Second, the trade union movement in the country has been largely ineffective as an instrument for improving real wages, partly because of the government's close control over the affairs of trade unions, and partly because of high levels of unemployment, which made strikes risky for workers. Third, agriculture tended to subsidize industrial workers through remittances, so that workers were not wholly dependent on their industrial wages (Tostensen, 1991, p. 291).

For most of the last three decades, Kenya has had a highly regulated labor market. The wage guidelines, which have been in force since the 1970s, restricted wage awards that trade unions could negotiate with employers. The wage increase allowed by the wage guidelines was restricted below the rise in the cost of living index. As a result of these guidelines, the real wages declined substantially, so that the level of real wages in the early 1990s was below that in the mid-1980s. Through the mechanism of minimum wages and its wage setting in the large public sector, the government had significant influence on wage determination in the whole economy.

In the early 1990s, considerable liberalization of the labor market took place, largely as a result of the structural adjustment program the country was implementing. Some of the reforms that affected the labor market included the relaxation of wage guidelines, which allowed trade unions to negotiate for better wages with employer organizations largely based on labor productivity and performance of the enterprises. The redundancy laws, which made it difficult to declare workers redundant, were also amended, allowing employers now to declare workers redundant without having to obtain approval from the Ministry of Labor and Manpower Development. On the whole, these policy reforms are expected to assist the manufacturing industries in significantly improving their competitiveness.

The capital market

Capital costs are, as the present study shows, a decisive factor for competitiveness. In particular, the distortion of the market price, relative to the shadow price, of capital can either cause additional costs or can act as a subsidy. In Kenya, in the late 1990s, the distortion was both substantive and cost increasing. It is important, therefore to examine what caused the cost of capital to be exceedingly high.

Kenya has well-established financial and capital markets relative to the average sub-Saharan African country. By 1996, the country had about 40 commercial banks and non-bank financial institutions, 7 development finance companies, 5 representative offices of foreign banks, 40 insurance companies, about 1,500 co-operative savings and credit unions, and one of the oldest stock markets in Africa. The banking sector has been dominated by two multinational, and two government-owned, banks. The two government-owned banks have been gradually selling an increasing proportion of their shares to the public, although government influence and presence in the two institutions are still strongly felt.

The financial and capital markets have undergone considerable reforms in the 1990s, including liberalization of interest rates and foreign exchange markets. With regard to the Nairobi Stock Exchange, legislative measures have been taken to widen its base, to raise the level of competition and to facilitate greater inflow of external resources and investments in various sectors of the economy. A Capital Markets Authority was established in 1989 to guide the growth of the stock exchange market.

In spite of the relative depth that the financial sector has reached, it suffered a major banking crisis in 1985–1986, in which a number of financial institutions collapsed, with considerable adverse effects on locally owned and managed banking institutions. In 1991, the two quasi-government institutions suffered a crisis of failing confidence due to their heavy unsecured loans. In addition, the government financed deficits by borrowing from the banks. Together, these factors can be taken to explain why lending rates remained above 30 percent until the later part of 1998 and 1999, when most of the banks started to reduce their lending rates. It is worthwhile noting also that, there was a relatively stable and high nominal interest rate of above 30 percent and strongly fluctuating inflation rates of 28.8 percent in 1994, 1.6 percent in 1995 and 9.1 percent in 1996, the real interest rate also fluctuated strongly between 2 percent and over 30 percent during this period.

Another factor limiting access to credit facilities has been the high collateral requirement for gaining access to bank credit. Firms are often required to surrender to the bank collateral with more than double the value of the loan being sought. In the case of small-scale firms, they often do not have the required collateral, which in most cases is a land title deed.

Due to the problems associated with accessing bank credit facilities, a large proportion of the Kenyan firms rely more on self-financing in terms of retained earnings and supplier credit facilities, which attract low interest rates and do not require the type of collateral demanded by the banking institutions. According to a recent study, more than a third of the firms studied relied heavily on retained earnings, to the tune of almost 80 percent of their financing (RPED, 1996, p. 109). A study, sponsored by the Kenya Association of Manufacturers (KAM, 1992), examined the financing needs of manufacturing firms and found, in addition to the points made above, that currency depreciation, the external debt burden and lack of a conducive environment to attract new investment, were also factors responsible for the high cost of borrowing. The reforms carried out, especially in the last six years, have removed some of the above constraints, notably the shortage of foreign exchange and a host of government controls that were a disincentive to investors. But, most of the other constraints continue to be a source of concern for the Kenyan business community.

Fiscal policy and public expenditure

The inability to control government expenditures has been one of the major weaknesses in Kenya's fiscal management in the last decade. One writer on Kenya's fiscal policy commented that 'the heart of Kenya's fiscal problem is its inability to control expenditures, not its inability to generate sufficient revenues' (Swamy, 1994). Although the favorable policy environment prevailing in the first decade of the country's independence has been credited for having resulted in one of the dynamic economies in SSA in the 1960s and early 1970s, the fiscal policy pursued during the period resulted in the rapid expansion of the public sector. The Kenyanization of industry and the desire to industrialize rapidly created a large public sector, which spanned traditional activities such as utilities and transport, but also non-traditional areas such as distribution and manufacturing. Consequently, the budget deficit grew dramatically over the period, financed in part by domestic and external borrowing. Yet, the country followed relatively orthodox fiscal policies until the late 1970s. In the 1980s, however the fiscal responsibility and prudent monetary policy of the 1960s and 1970s was lost. Budgetary policy started to rely heavily on borrowing from commercial sources abroad, leading to unsustainable levels of external debt. In addition, domestic borrowing by the government remained a serious problem. By fiscal year 1979/1980, the public expenditure-to-GDP ratio had increased from its 1973/1974 level of 24 percent to more than 31 percent. The budget deficit increased from 3–4 percent in the early 1970s to around 10 percent by 1981. The inability of the Kenyan government to control expenditures was due in part to the structure and composition of public expenditures and partly due to lack of discipline in expenditure allocation and execution. The main consequence of this failure for the industrial sector and its competitiveness can be seen as twofold: a shortage of foreign exchange and its rationing through the licensing system, and the crowding out of private investment due to the rising cost of credit. Thus, whereas overall macroeconomic policy did not have much direct effects on the manufacturing sector, its effects came indirectly through its impact on the balance of payments, the direction of trade policy and the cost of capital.

Infrastructure

The final point of this review of the policy environment facing the industrial sector is one that is difficult to measure, but has created a lot of aggravation in the business community. Several recent studies, including the present one, show that inadequate and poorly maintained infrastructure has emerged as a major impediment to Kenya's industrial growth and other economic activities. A study, which covered more than 200 industrial enterprises in the country's main industrial towns, observes that 'the poor state of infrastructure continues to be a serious impediment to business activity and manufacturing' (RPED, 1996, p. 161). According to the firms interviewed during the study, the state of the country's infrastructure, especially with regard to electricity, water, freight transport, port-handling facilities, telephones, waste disposal, and security, had deteriorated substantially, compared with a few years earlier.

One of the consequences of the government's failure to effectively provide essential infrastructure is that a large proportion of the enterprises have been forced to engage in costly self-provision of various facilities, especially their own power generators, private telephone systems, etc. Of course, enterprises that have not been able to provide their own infrastructural services have usually failed to remain viable. Out of the 219 enterprises in the RPED study, 26 percent had their own generators, 20 percent had invested in own water supplies, such as wells or cisterns, 21 percent were providing own waste disposal, while almost 60 percent had increased expenses in security (RPED, 1996). This self-provision of essential facilities had raised the firms' operational costs, thereby reducing their overall competitiveness and in several cases, has forced some firms out of business.

A number of measures have been taken recently to improve the country's state of infrastructure. First, multilateral donor institutions like the World Bank have been approached to provide loan facilities to rehabilitate some of the dilapidated infrastructure. One of the ongoing activities in this regard is the World Bank funded urban roads project involving repair of roads in 26 towns in the country. Second, the government is restructuring parastatals and privatizing some of their activities, in areas such as power generation, transport and communication, railways and post and telecommunications. These efforts are expected to improve the country's state of infrastructure significantly in the coming years, but as we note in the present study, based on interviews with 42 manufacturing firms, much damage has already been done to the sector's competitiveness and its prospects for industrial growth.

The method of analysis and data base

Economists, politicians, and business leaders frequently use the concept of competitiveness, but there is little agreement about its precise meaning and even less about the methods of measuring it. While politicians and some economists tend to use the term in an economy-wide sense, we only use the microeconomic version of the concept, and more particularly the one involving *cost competitiveness*. At the enterprise or industry level, producers are deemed to be competitive if their unit costs of production are less or equal to those of their competitors. This can be the case in domestic as well as in international markets. International competitiveness is of particular importance when markets are open or being opened to international competition, such as is the case under trade liberalization. For a survey of the literature on competitiveness, the reader is referred to the proceedings of a recent symposium on *International Competitiveness* published in a special issue of the *Oxford Review of Economic Policy* in 1996, as well as a survey paper by Siggel (1997). Competitiveness in Kenya has been analyzed in several studies, in particular, RPED (1993 to 1995); KEDS (1993 and 1994a, 1994b); and Wignaraja and Ikiara (1999).

An indicator of competitiveness and its sources

The indicator of competitiveness used in the present study is a *unit cost ratio* (UC), defined as total cost (TC) divided by the value of output (VO), which in turn equals output quantity times the ex-factory price. For domestic sales, the ex-factory price is the domestic market price (Pd), which is typically higher than the international price of a similar imported product by a margin equal to the nominal rate of protection. For export sales, on the other hand, the ex-factory price is equal to the international (fob price (Pw)).

This particular definition of the unit cost ratio serves a double purpose. First, it helps to overcome the differences in product mix and quality that make inter-firm comparisons always problematic. We assume that the output price is usually proportionate to the quality attributes of products. Second, it makes the unit cost indicator independent of the data of an international competitor, whose cost we would otherwise need for comparison. We assume, therefore, that the international price (Pw) corresponds to the unit cost of a typical international best-practice producer. The fact that Pw is measured as the border price (cif) means that the benchmark for international comparison includes the transport cost to the border and therefore a margin of natural (geographic) protection. Our criterion for international competitiveness or export competitive advantage is then

$$UCx = TC/(Q\ Pw) = 1 \tag{1}$$

meaning that a firm is deemed to be competitive if its cost per unit of output is less or equal to the free-trade price of an equivalent import. This concept of cost competitiveness is multilateral, as opposed to a bilateral firm-to-firm or country-to-country comparison, but it allows bilateral comparison as well.

In addition to the notion of international competitiveness, we are also interested in domestic competitiveness, which means a cost advantage under protection. In this case, the denominator of unit cost is the output value at domestic prices (VOd = Q Pd), so that the criterion of domestic competitive advantage becomes:

$$CUd = TC/(Q\ Pd) = 1 \tag{2}$$

For those firms that export part of their output, Pd of the exported output equals Pw. This measure of competitiveness reflects the profitability of the firm. Since total cost includes the opportunity cost of capital, it exceeds one if the rate of return is lower than the interest rate, and it is less than one if the rate of return is higher. The most important distinction, however, and the hallmark of our method of analysis, is the one between competitiveness and comparative advantage. While competitiveness is understood as a cost advantage based on market prices including various price distortions, subsidies and penalties, comparative advantage corresponds to a cost advantage at equilibrium prices.[1] In order to measure comparative advantage we have to replace all prices, in output as well as all inputs, by shadow prices. A firm or industry then has comparative advantage if

$$UCs = TCs/(Q\ Ps) = 1 \tag{3}$$

where TCs is total cost in shadow prices and Ps is the shadow price of output. The latter is usually equal to the international price (Pw), but adjusted for any distortion of the exchange rate. TCs is the sum of all cost components adjusted for all price distortions and subsidies.

It is now evident that our concept of competitiveness differs from the one of comparative advantage only by including the sum of all price distortions. When CUd is smaller than UCs, the price distortions act as subsidies; when CUd exceeds UCs they act as penalties. Since price distortions exist on the input and output sides, appearing in the numerator and denominator, they have the opposite effect on the input and output sides. A tariff on output lowers unit costs, whereas a tariff on tradable inputs raises it. This shows that in the protected domestic market, a producer is more competitive than under free trade, as production tends to be more profitable under protection. But comparative advantage, which is the real core of competitiveness, is not affected by the price distortions. However, under protection and other distortions, input coefficients may be affected as well. In other words, cost-lowering price distortions may lead to lower efficiency.

Finally, total cost is broken down into four components, tradable inputs, non-tradable inputs, labor cost, and capital cost, and in each component the distortions are calculated and deducted from the costs at market-prices according to the following scheme:

VITs/Vos	(Shadow unit cost of tradable inputs)
+VINs/VOs	(Shadow unit cost of non-tradable inputs)
+LCs/VOs	(Shadow unit cost of labor inputs)
+KCs/VOs	(Shadow unit cost of capital inputs)

=TCs/VOs=UCs	(Total unit cost at shadow prices)
+dpe	(Exchange rate distortion of output)
+dpj	(Tradable input price distortion)
+dpje	(Exchange rate distortion of tradable inputs)
+dw	(Wage rate distortion)
+dpk	(Capital goods price distortion)
+dr	(Interest rate distortion)
+ds	(Direct subsidy, negative)

$=TCd/VOx=UCx$ (Total cost per unit of output at international prices)

$+dpp$ (Output price distortion)

$=TCd/VOd=CUd$ (Total unit cost at domestic prices)   (4)

In other words, total unit cost in shadow prices (indicator of comparative advantage) plus all cost distortions add up to unit cost per output value at free-trade prices (indicator of export competitiveness), plus the output price distortion add up to unit cost in domestic prices (indicator of domestic competitiveness). This accounting framework allows us to identify, with some limitations, the sources of competitiveness. The distortions are all expressed as proportions of unit cost so that the highest proportions indicate the strongest influence on unit costs. For the factors of production, on the other hand, this procedure is not applicable and is replaced by a statistical approach, as explained later in the chapter. While the cost components of tradable and non-tradable inputs are straightforward, the measurement of the distortions deserves special attention. Besides the distortion categories listed above, we also distinguish sub-categories such as energy cost distortions as part of the tradables, and transport and communications distortions as part of the non-tradables.

The measurement of distortions

In this study we are dealing with several kinds of distortions. The value of output is affected by the exchange rate distortion and the nominal rate of protection, which, in the absence of QRs, is normally equal to the tariff. Price margins stemming from monopoly power are unlikely to be substantial in a trade regime regulated only by the tariff. On the cost or input side, there are a number of distortions, in addition to that of input tariffs and the exchange rate, that need to be discussed, such as interest rate and wage distortions, energy distortions, and transport and communications distortions. The common characteristics of these distortions are that they are either directly policy-induced or they result from a regime that is, in turn, linked to government intervention. Energy, transport and communication fall into the latter category since the distortion results from the activities of state-owned utilities, if not from government spending and taxation directly.

Output price distortions

The domestic output price is assumed to depend on international prices of equivalent imports, tariff and non-tariff restrictions, and the exchange rate. While import restrictions are considered as distortions, the exchange rate may give rise to a distortion when it is misaligned. The total of all import restrictions is best measured by the implicit nominal rate of protection (NRP), which is the difference between the ex-factory price and the cif border or free-trade price of comparable imports, expressed as a proportion of the border price. In order to capture the output price distortion adequately, we have attempted to compare the prices of products with those of comparable imports. In praxis, this is a difficult exercise and requires the assistance of the producing firm, which knows best the exact composition of total output as well as the quality characteristics of the products. Unfortunately, in this attempt we were not fully successful since, in various industries, the estimated NRP did not seem to be reliable. Most often the quality differences between domestic products and imports were not sufficiently taken into account. In the end, therefore, we had to go back to the tariff, although in the data of 1984, the NRPs are based on price comparisons. In 1997, however, QRs were no longer of importance, so that the tariff seemed to capture more realistically and more consistently the existing price distortions. The only cases where the tariff is an insufficient measure of protection are in industries, where either smuggling erodes the protective effect of the tariff, or where dumping brings the import and domestic prices down to a level that is, possibly, below the true international price. In industries where smuggling is known to be significant, we have made adjustments to the tariff based on price comparisons that seemed to be reliable. Several firms in our sample have argued that there is dumping, but the term 'dumping' is not always used in its technically correct sense. So we are not totally sure about the correctness of dumping charges. In cases like textiles, where a lot of imports are allegedly entering the domestic market without duties and with values that are below the free-trade prices of comparable product that are officially imported, the question of dumping should be investigated more thoroughly.

Tradable input price distortions

Since the number of material inputs is usually large, it is difficult to deflate them one by one for distortions caused by tariffs and other policy-induced measures. Rather than estimating the price distortions of individual intermediate inputs, we have divided the total duty paid on imported inputs by their net value and taken this average rate as the distortion factor. Not all tradable inputs are imported, however. Many are purchased locally, in which case the users do not pay duties, nor do they know the implicit tariff. For these inputs we have taken the tariff rate as NRP if the nature of the input was known, or treated them as nearly non-distorted by applying only a small distortion factor reflecting their distorted transport cost and an average tariff rate of 5 percent.

Exchange rate misalignment

The existence of currency misalignment is difficult to justify and to measure when the exchange rate is flexible, as it has been the case in Kenya in recent years. It is known, nevertheless, that central banks can influence the exchange rate by various kinds of intervention that are sometimes referred to as 'leaning towards a higher or lower rate', depending on the nature of interventions. It can also be diverted from its purchasing power parity value by capital movements or strong fluctuations in the terms of trade. In Kenya, although the rate is market-determined, industry officials have argued that the going rate over-stated the value of the Kenyan shilling by an undefined margin. In particular, firms interested in exports argued that they felt penalized by the going exchange rate. We have examined this argument critically by using the purchasing power parity approach, and data on prices in Kenya and the OECD, and concluded that in 1997 the shilling was overvalued by about 10 percent. This rate is consistent with the studies by Elbadawi (1998) and Mwega and Ndung'u (1998).

The effect of this margin of over-valuation on our unit cost ratios is twofold. On the output side, it raises the shadow value of output above its value at international free-trade prices, and thereby lowers the unit cost ratio UCs. In other words, if the penalty of over-valuation did not exist, comparative advantage would be enhanced and comparative disadvantage diminished. On the input side, the opposite effect occurs for tradable inputs. The results show that the reported exchange rate distortion is the net effect on unit costs.

Energy costs

Utilities, consisting of electricity and water, have been treated, together with fuel, as tradable under the heading of energy costs, although at least water has the characteristics of a non-tradable service. Two kinds of distortions can be distinguished, price distortions and distortions in the quality of the service. For electricity and water, firms were asked to state not only the total expenditure and price per unit, but also to estimate by how much their costs exceed the 'normal' level. Abnormal costs have often been mentioned in the questionnaires and in interviews, and they usually take the form of service interruption forcing the firms to either rely on own generators or pumps in case of blackout, or to shut down the production process. For some industries, the irregular (interrupted) supply of electricity and water are a major cost factor impinging on their competitiveness. The average excess charge across all industries was in the order of 20 percent of the electricity and water bills. This may under-state the actual excess cost in some industries where shutdowns are especially costly.

Non-tradables

In the category of non-tradables the study distinguishes six kinds of services purchased by firms: repair, subcontracts, rents, transport, communication, and other services. The firms that were asked to estimate the excess cost relative to normal operation reported major distortions in the categories of transport and communication services. For transport services, the excess cost is generally attributed to the bad state of the roads, as well as to the unreliability of the rail services. For communications it was frequently reported that firms subscribe to multiple telephone lines in order to have one or two working. Frequently firms also use cellular telephones in order to secure services that are not available from the public telephone system for which they, nevertheless, pay. In these two categories, the individual firms' distortions vary according to the respondents' records and perceptions. The average cost distortion reported is 18 percent in transport and 19 percent in communications. All other categories of non-tradables are assumed to be free from major distortions.

Labor cost distortion

The wage and salary component in total cost is generally below 15 percent of the total due to the relatively low wages of unskilled workers, and in spite of the high cost of managers, especially expatriate ones. For all skilled occupations, we make the simplifying assumption that the paid wages or salaries reflect the social opportunity cost of these services. For unskilled labor, on the other hand, we discount the paid wages by 20 percent due to the severity of unemployment in this category, which includes casual (temporary) workers. This procedure is based on estimates of informal sector wages as well as the marginal product in agriculture. The resulting distortion component of labor payments is on average 0.3 percent and always under 3 percent of total costs.

Capital cost distortion

The cost of capital is measured by four components. First, the financial social opportunity cost is taken to equal the shadow interest rate applied to the total value of fixed and non-fixed assets at purchase prices. The shadow interest rate is computed as the mean of two estimates. Both are based on the assumption of strong international mobility of capital. The first is the international rate LIBOR (6.1 percent in 1997),[2] augmented by an inflation differential between Kenya and the OECD average of 10 percent,[3] resulting in 16.1 percent. This approach has been criticized as being unrealistic.[4] One can indeed argue that the shadow interest rate should include a margin that accounts for the underdeveloped state of the financial sector and low savings, implying costs and a risk factor that exceed those of high-income countries. Unfortunately, we were unable to find data measuring these factors. An alternative approach, based on the international interest parity condition, is to add to the LIBOR the expected rate of depreciation of the Kenya shilling. Using the actual exchange rate of 1998 as the expected one, we obtain an expected rate of depreciation of 2.9 percent and a shadow interest rate of 9 percent. We consider the rates of 9 percent and 16 percent as lower and upper bound (used in sensitivity analysis) and adopt the median rate of 14 percent as the shadow rate for our computations of the shadow cost of capital.

In contrast, the market opportunity cost of capital is equal to the capital stock times a market interest rate, which is taken to equal the average lending rate of 30 percent, based on IMF statistics (IFS, 1999). The difference between these two interest rates constitutes the main capital cost distortion and is the second component. The third component is the annual depreciation as reported by the firms, which is treated as undistorted for simplicity. The fourth component is a capital price distortion, due to the payment of import duties on imported capital goods. Only a few firms have reported this distortion, and even where reported, it represents a negligible proportion of total costs. We also do not attach much importance to this distortion, because we focus on present policy distortions. Duties on capital goods represent a policy distortion of the past; that is, of the time when major investments were made.

Data sources and coverage

The study is based on three data sets and additional information from various sources. The first set consists of the firm-specific data of 1984, which were collected by consultants for a study of protection and efficiency commissioned by the Government of Kenya (Jansen, et al., 1985). The second set consists of 1997 data from Kenyan firms, most of which are also members of the 1984 sample. The third set consists of 1997 data from a smaller sample of Ugandan firms, which are matched, as far as possible with the Kenyan sample of 1997. The latter two sets were collected by members of the present project team, 1998–1999.

The 1984 data

This data bank covers 78 firms in all major manufacturing industries and provides information on all costs and revenues. It also uses shadow prices, some of which were altered for the present study due to difficulties in justifying some of the consultant's assumptions. The product and firm-specific nominal rates of protection of outputs and tradable inputs are all adopted from this data bank. New estimates of the equilibrium exchange rate, the opportunity and social opportunity cost of capital, of the shadow wage of unskilled labor, and the treatment of non-tradable inputs are used here.

The opportunity cost of capital at market prices was taken to equal the average Kenyan lending rate of 14.4 percent (IFS, 1999). The shadow interest rate of 16.6 percent is based on the 1984 LIBOR of 11.8 percent plus an expected inflation differential of 4.8 percent estimated by comparing Kenya's and the OECD's consumer price index during the 1983–1984 period. The shadow cost of unskilled labor is estimated as 20 percent below the actually paid wages. This rate is based on the observation of substantial urban unemployment and estimates of the remuneration of unskilled workers in the informal sector. The potential misalignment of the Kenyan shilling (KShs) was estimated to have been zero in 1984. This is consistent with computations of Elbadawi (1998) and Mwega and Ndung'u (1998). The shadow prices of all tradable products and inputs are therefore equal to the world prices in KShs at the market exchange rate.

The data of 1997

The sample of firms in this data set was supposed to match the earlier sample of 1984, but it was, however, expected to be smaller, due to budget constraints. Thirty-three of the original 78 firms have supplied data, and nine new firms were added that had a similar output mix as the corresponding ones in the 1984 sample. A questionnaire and interviews were used to obtain the detailed cost and revenue data required for the computation of unit cost ratios. The firms were also asked to name what they saw as the main obstacles to competing successfully in the domestic and international markets. Furthermore, they were asked for an evaluation of excess costs of energy, water supply, transport and communication, that is, costs that may exceed what they would consider as normal under normal conditions of operation.

The firm-level data are supplemented by tariff data for industries where the price comparisons remained unsatisfactory, and also by interest rates and information on the exchange rate. The average lending rate was taken from IMF data (IFS, various years) as 30 percent. The shadow rate of interest and the shadow exchange rate were computed in the way described earlier.

The third data set of 21 Ugandan firms pertains also to 1997, although a few firms supplied data for 1998. The firms were selected to match the sample of industries in Kenya. As to the distortion analysis in Uganda, the computations needed to be adjusted for the border price differential between cif Mombasa and cif Ugandan border (Malaba), which corresponds to the transport cost through Kenya and is quite substantial for some products. The adjustment is described in detail in the Uganda component of this study (Siggel and Ssemogerere, 2000). The interest rates and exchange rates (market and shadow) were estimated in the same fashion as for Kenya with the average lending rate in Uganda being 21.5 percent and the shadow interest rate 16 percent. The Uganda shilling was found to be over valued by 20 percent in 1997.

Coverage

The number of firms in our sample (42) is small in comparison with the total number of firms in the manufacturing sector, even with the large ones with more than 50 employees, which the Central Bureau of Statistics estimates as about 630 in 1996 (GoK, 1996, p. 146). Since most of the firms in our sample are the largest in each industry, the coverage is substantially higher than the firm number suggests. Covering 16 out of 24 industries (defined at the 3-and 4-digit level of ISIC), we think of the sample as modestly representative of the manufacturing sector. The Ministry of Planning considered the sample of 78 firms in 1984 representative of the sector.

Sector-wide results of the data analysis

Since we are combining three different data sets in the analysis, a word on the presentation of results is appropriate. We first examine the situation in the mid-1980s based on the data set of 78 firms so as to use to a maximum the available data. We then use the new data set of 1997, which is a sub-sample of 42 firms of the earlier set, to analyze the changes in competitiveness and comparative advantage between 1984–1997. The next section compares Kenyan with Ugandan industries using the third data set based on 21 firms in Uganda. The analysis in the final section takes a general view of the manufacturing sector, without focusing on specific industries. More specific industry details are revealed only in the full-length report of the project (Siggel, Ikiara, and Nganda, 1999).

Competitiveness and comparative advantage in the mid-1980s

Based on the data provided by 78 firms, as well as the assumptions and shadow prices discussed above, the average shadow unit cost (UCs) was computed as 1.166, meaning that total shadow costs exceeded the respective international prices by 16.6 percent. To the extent that the sample is representative of the sector, this is interpreted as absence of comparative advantage for manufacturing as a whole. When the firm data are aggregated into 24 industries, only five of them have UCs smaller than one, as shown in Table 9.2. They are, starting with the lowest UCs (that is strongest comparative advantage), plastic goods (0.73), beverages and spirits (0.92), miscellaneous food products (0.93), footwear and leather (0.93), and petrochemicals and rubber (0.97). In five other industries (grain mills, fruit and vegetable canning, wood products, garment industry, and meat and dairy products), the UCs is less than 5 percent above unity, which means that firms may be able to realize comparative advantage with a modest amount of adjustment and cost cutting. All three unit cost ratios are shown in Table 9.2.

Table 9.2   Competitiveness (CUd) and (UCx) and comparative advantage (UCs) in Kenya's manufacturing industries in 1984

ISIC	Industry	CUd	UCx	UCs
3111/12	Meat and dairy	1.251	1.051	1.039
3113/15	Fruit and vegetqable processing	1.012	1.066	1.012
3116/17	Grain mills and bakeries	1.046	1.025	1.015
3118/19	Sugar and confectionery	1.421	1.842	1.450
3121/22	Miscell. Foods	0.857	0.917	0.927
3131–34	Beverages and spirits	0.923	1.001	0.916
3140	Tobacco products	1.213	1.302	1.249
3110	Cotton ginning	1.131	1.300	1.306
3111	Spinning, weaving and finishing	1.157	1.670	1.370
3212/13	Textile products	1.214	1.281	1.167
3219/20	Garments	1.098	1.600	1.033
3231–40	Footwear and leather	0.738	0.980	0.934
3311–20	Wood products	1.152	1.145	1.013
3411–20	Paper products	1.614	1.429	1.244
3511–14	Industrial chemicals	1.203	1.192	1.065
3521	Paints	1.021	1.491	1.248
3522	Pharmaceuticals	1.018	1.145	1.101
529/50	Petrochem. and rubber	0.848	1.110	0.969
3560	Plastics	0.705	0.867	0.730
3620–99	Non-metallic Minerals	1.175	1.337	1.575
3700	Basic metals	1.319	1.364	1.198
3811–19	Metal products	1.279	1.547	1.326
3843/44	Transport equipment	1.165	1.675	1.366
3900	Miscell. Manufactures	0.980	1.374	1.232
311–390	Average	1.125	1.252	1.166

As to the sources of comparative advantage, it is not possible to attribute low (high) shadow unit cost to a low (high) level of any of the four cost components, tradable and non-tradable inputs, labor, and capital. A labor-intensive technique can save capital, and high intermediate input costs may reflect a technique that uses highly transformed inputs as opposed to raw materials. Since our method of analysis excludes the analysis of a production function, the substitution possibilities between different factors are not considered. We can examine the question, however, whether one or the other cost component, tends to be particularly high or low whenever unit costs are low. We interpret a tendency of a factor to be heavily used whenever total costs are low, as evidence of this factor being a source of comparative advantage. Heavy use is taken to mean that the respective input coefficient is higher than average, which signifies that the trend line of input coefficients over UCs has a positive intercept.

For the four principal cost components, the linear trend lines have been estimated against UCs with the following results:

Capital costs:	$KCs = -0.31 + 0.49\ UCs$	$R^2 = 0.59$
Labor costs:	$LCs = 0.04 + 0.07\ UCs$	$R^2 = 0.12$
Tradable inputs:	$VITs = 0.21 + 0.34\ Ucs$	$R^2 = 0.29$
Non-tradable inputs:	$VINs = 0.06 + 0.10\ Uc$	$R^2 = 0.10$

where KCs, LCs, VITs and VINs are unit cost ratios of the respective cost components at shadow prices, as defined earlier. It appears from these regressions that capital cost is most strongly correlated with UCs. Its negative intercept suggests that low unit costs tend to be accompanied by lower than average capital costs and vice versa. In other words, firms tend to achieve comparative advantage most often when they use the least capital. All other components tend to be higher than average whenever UCs is low. Obviously, all four linear functions add up vertically to the 45° line, but the intermediate input and labor cost components are less strongly correlated with UCs. The size of the cost coefficients is of course a reflection of both the structure of transformation and the efficiency of factor use. We cannot separate these aspects unless we had numerous firm observations in a single industry with the same structure of transformation. But, one can nevertheless infer that highly capital-intensive industries tend to be less likely candidates for comparative advantage than labor and input-intensive ones.

Turning now to *domestic competitiveness*, the average unit cost ratio at domestic market prices (CUd) of the whole sample is 1.125, smaller than average UCs (1.166). This means that on average, the distortions sum up to an implicit subsidy, thereby lowering unit costs by about 4 percent. In 10 out of 24 industries, the distortions raised the unit costs, so that their profitability at market prices was lower than that at shadow prices. In 14 industries, CUd was lower than UCs that is, domestic competitiveness exceeded comparative advantage. It follows therefore that in the majority of industries—14 out of 24, further liberalization was likely to reduce competitiveness in the short run. In the longer run, they were however expected to become more competitive in real terms, by firms cutting costs or exiting the industry.

Finally, *export competitiveness*, as measured by UCx, indicates in column 3 of Table 9.2 that only 4 out of 24 industries had unit costs inferior to the free-trade value of their output. They are plastics, miscellaneous foods, footwear, and beverages/spirits. All of the aforementioned also had comparative advantage. Interestingly, only one of them (misc. food) exported a significant proportion of output. On the other hand, the three important exporting industries (meat, dairy, cement, and fruit and vegetable canning) were not export competitive, according to our data. This observation can be explained by the presence of various distortions such as still existing price controls at that time, export subsidies, and the fact that exporting to neighboring countries like Uganda was possible at higher than world market prices.

The breakdown of cost components and distortions suggests that the price incentives reflected by the NRP had the strongest impact on unit costs. In the normal case, where both output and input rates of protection are positive, the NRP on output reduces the unit cost ratio, thereby increasing domestic competitiveness, whereas positive NRPs on inputs have the opposite effect. In the presence of a cascading tariff, output protection exceeds input protection so that the net effect on unit costs is negative. This was the case in 14 industries, whereas in 6 industries the unit cost raising effect of input protection exceeded that of output protection. The latter case occurs usually in industries that export substantial proportions of their output. Some of those industries recuperated from these penalties through export compensation, but on average the subsidy had only a weak impact on unit cost ratios. One notable exception is the non-metallic minerals industry for exports of cement.

Another distortion of great importance is the one of the price of capital goods. In this matter, we rely entirely on the valuation supplied by firms in their interviews with the consultants. Nearly all industries suffered, in the mid-1980s, from positively distorted capital asset prices, normally a consequence of protective tariffs on imported capital goods. Their effect on unit costs ranged between minus 3 and plus 23 percent of output value.

The financial cost of capital, on the other hand, appears to have been subsidized, because the opportunity cost of capital was lower than the shadow interest rate. This follows from the fact that LIBOR was historically high in the early 1980s, reflecting the relatively high international rates of inflation, as well as the positive expected inflation differential in Kenya. The regulated market interest rate in Kenya therefore provided an implicit subsidy. Its effect on unit costs ranges between 0 and minus 7 percent of output value, and it is obviously most important in capital-intensive industries, such as the cement industry and sugar mills.

The smallest of all distortions is the one of labor cost, due to the assumption that most of the labor cost (that is, for skilled labor) is undistorted, and due to the relatively small proportion of labor payments in total costs, which is usually less than 15 percent.

Changes since 1984 and Kenya's competitive position in 1997

In light of the policy changes that have occurred in the 13-year period since 1984, we come to the main objective of this study now and examine whether Kenyan firms and industries have become more competitive, and whether comparative advantage has been strengthened as a consequence of more liberal trade policies. The comparison between unit cost ratios of 1984 and 1997 is made here at the firm level, in order to minimize the influence of differences in product mix. In other words, we are comparing the 1984 and 1997 performances of the same firms. However, in 10 out of 42 firms, the observations of the two years are not from the same enterprise, because either the firms of the earlier sample have gone out of business, or chosen not to collaborate in the study. In 8 cases, they were replaced by another firm with a similar output mix, sometimes a newcomer in the market, and in 2 cases, no match could be found. Here, we start with the unit cost ratio at domestic market prices (CUd), since this is the indicator that relies only on the cost and revenue data obtained from the firms, plus the average Kenyan lending rate, that is, it does not rely on assumptions about equilibrium or shadow prices.

Domestic competitiveness

As explained earlier, the indicator CUd reflects the profitability of firms, but uses a criterion that is stronger than that of the rate of return. Since total costs include the opportunity cost of capital, which is taken to equal the average lending rate times the purchase value of capital stock plus depreciation, a firm may earn a positive rate of return and still show up as non-competitive if its rate of return is lower than the lending rate. Competitiveness in this sense, therefore, means that the price covers full cost, including the full opportunity cost of capital, and is a long-run criterion.

The comparison is carried out in Table 9.3, which shows that the average unit cost ratio has increased by 12 percent, from 1.125 to 1.221. The number of firms with increases of this cost ratio (20) is the same as the number of unit cost declines, but the increases have been stronger than the declines. Table 9.3 also shows the main causes of the observed loss in domestic competitiveness.

The most important loss of domestic competitiveness is caused by the increase of the cost of borrowing. While in 1984 the market lending-rate was 3 points below the shadow interest rate, in 1997 it was 16 points above its shadow rate. This distortion in the price of credit has, on average, raised unit costs by about 22 percent across industries. The second most important factor is the re-appearance of currency misalignment. The estimated overvaluation of the Kenya shilling of 10 percent in 1997 adds on average 7.5 percent to the unit cost ratio. Tariff protection, on the other hand, has benefited the manufacturers, lowering their unit costs by about 8 percent—distortion increasing from -4.7 to -13.3 percent. This effect comes as a surprise, given the general lowering of trade barriers during the period 1984–1997. According to the data, the reason for this unexpected benefit is provided by firms whereby the tariff on imported inputs has declined more than the protective tariff on outputs. It is also evident that further cost increases have occurred in the costs of electricity, transport, and communications discussed in the next sub-section, but we have no exact data of these costs for 1984, so a comparative analysis is not possible.

The firms with the lowest unit cost ratios were found in rubber, metal products, and paints, which means that under the existing tariff protection, these industries offered the best opportunities for profitable production. The highest unit cost ratios were found in textiles, paper and cement. While in textiles this lack of competitiveness is largely a problem of pricing in the market, for the paper and cement industries, it is caused mainly by high capital intensity. More in-depth analysis of these conclusions is provided in the industry profiles included in the main report.

Export competitiveness

The loss of competitiveness observed in the domestic market makes it even more substantial in international export markets. The indicator UCx, it will be remembered, shows the firms' ability to export, selling at international border prices, while their costs are distorted as in the previous indicator. This unit cost ratio compares actual costs with the border prices of Mombasa, rather than export prices to neighboring countries, which may be higher, especially if the countries are land-locked like Uganda. Therefore, it measures the capacity to export internationally rather than within the region.

The comparison over time is shown in the first three columns of Table 9.4. The average unit cost ratio UCx has increased from 1.25 to 1.42, a decline of competitiveness of nearly 14 percent. For 24 firms, the cost ratio has increased and for only 16 it has declined. This means that it has become more difficult to export under present conditions than in the mid-eighties. It also means that with further declines in tariff protection, firms will find it more difficult to compete with imports in the domestic market.

Table 9.3   Unit cost ratio (CUd) and distortions in Kenyan firms, 1994 and 1997

| Industry or Firm | Unit Cost at market prices CUd | | | Main distortions | | | | | |
| | 1984 | Change | 1997 | Protection | | E-rate | Interest rate | |
				1984	1997	1997	1984	1997
Dairy A*	1.040	<	11.157	-0.003	-0.096	0.042	-0.002	0.146
Dairy B	–		11.094	–	-0.102	0.066	–	0.089
Fruit can. A	1.079	>	11.071	0.099	0.054	0.040	-0.025	0.074
Fish pack. A	–		11.145	–	0.036	0.044	–	0.09
Grain mill A	1.036	>	11.034	0.010	-0.028	0.037	-0.010	0.048
Bakery A	1.547	>	11.422	0.071	-0.072	0.071	0.058	0.229
Bakery B*	1.560	>	11.016	-0.095	-0.133	0.039	-0.061	0.057
Sugar/conf. A*	1.635	>	11.388	-0.298	-0.292	0.064	-0.085	0.204
Sugar/conf. B	1.157	>	0.914	0.006	-0.167	0.041	-0.023	0.075
Beverage A	0.934	<	11.312	0.017	-0.122	0.074	-0.031	0.199
Beverage B	1.036	>	0.963	0.100	-0.207	0.072	-0.006	0.054
Tobacco A	1.125	>	0.966	-0.088	-0.184	0.079	-0.024	0.109
Textiles A	1.078	<	11.569	-0.099	-0.226	0.099	-0.007	0.329
Textiles B	1.442	<	22.439	-0.259	-0.255	0.173	-0.042	0.800
Clothing A	1.165	>	11.161	0.025	-0.161	0.089	-0.021	0.158
Clothing B	1.140	>	11.026	0.104	-0.174	0.038	-0.013	0.056
Footwear A	0.698	<	11.054	-0.235	-0.178	0.074	-0.028	0.081
Wood prod. A	1.140	<	11.536	0.071	-0.125	0.102	-0.019	0.298
Paper A	1.591	>	11.238	-0.164	-0.063	0.071	-0.078	0.119
Paper B	1.697	<	22.113	0.248	-0.207	0.163	-0.059	0.680
Paper C*	0.888	<	11.008	0.121	-0.165	0.056	-0.010	0.115

Chem. Paint A	0.813	<	11.035	−0.122	−0.196	0.048	−0.011	0.079
Chem. Paint B*	1.149	>	11.032	−0.178	−0.206	0.060	−0.014	0.099
Chem. Paint C	1.056	>	0.890	−0.345	−0.160	0.042	−0.014	0.042
Ind. chem. A	1.278	>	0.967	−0.154	−0.203	0.092	−0.036	0.219
Ind. chem. B	1.185	<	11.259	0.190	−0.065	0.067	−0.004	0.193
Ind. chem. C	1.044	<	11.379	−0.386	−0.218	0.085	−0.056	0.234
Pharmaceut. A.	1.004	<	11.395	−0.124	−0.117	0.095	−0.027	0.269
Pharmaceut. B	0.951	<	1.562	−0.049	−0.241	0.106	−0.022	0.161
Plastics A	0.609	<	1.134	−0.155	−0.103	0.054	−0.027	0.062
Rubber A	0.850	<	0.871	−0.205	−0.158	0.057	−0.032	0.09
Cement A	1.190	<	1.768	0.058	−0.161	0.147	−0.074	0.452
Cement B	1.346	<	1.603	−0.393	−0.163	0.131	−0.070	0.481
Basic Metal A	1.373	<	1.940	0.133	−0.279	0.131	−0.026	0.517
Basic Metal B	1.194	>	1.090	−0.242	−0.141	0.027	−0.032	0.065
Metal prod A	0.980	>	0.884	−0.024	−0.185	0.044	−0.012	0.086
Metal prod B	1.263	>	1.084	0.028	−0.244	0.083	−0.016	0.293
Metal prod C	0.810	<	1.043	−0.050	−0.119	0.082	−0.018	0.131
Automotive A	1.019	>	0.961	−0.099	−0.258	0.070	−0.022	0.235
Automotive B	0.924	<	1.302	1.123	−0.259	0.107	−0.015	0.227
Automotive C	2.037	>	1.046	−0.536	−0.087	0.068	−0.076	0.096
Automotive D	1.170	>	0.965	−0.156	−0.109	0.035	−0.009	0.080
Average	1.125	<	1.22	−0.047	−0.133	0.075	−0.028	0.193

Note: The asterisk (*) indicates an industry in which the 1984 observation is taken from a different firm than that in 1997, because the latter was not included in the 1984 sample. The replacement was made only if the output mix was similar between the respondent firms in 1984 and 1997.

Table 9.4 Export competitiveness (UCx) and main distortions in 42 firms in Kenya, 1984 and 1997

| Industry/Firm | Export competitiveness (UCx) | | | Main distortions | | | | | |
| | | | | Input tariff | | Energy | Transp. cost | Total inputs | |
	1984	Change	1997	1984	1997	1997	1997	1984	1997
Dairy A*	1.04	1.296	<	0.051	0.043	0.006	0.014	0.009	0.232
Dairy B	–	1.222	>	–	0.026	0.005	0.027	–	0.215
Fruit can. A	1.078	1.071	>	0.098	0.054	0.012	0.010	0.068	0.182
Fish pack. A	–	1.145		–	0.036	0.008	0.010	–	0.0178
Grain mill A	1.006	1.66	<	-0.02	0.024	0.003	0.003	0.003	0.193
Bakery A	1.704	1.532	>	0.087	0.038	0.006	0.006	0.207	0.351
Bakery B*	1.722	1.270	>	0.067	0.121	0.012	0.015	0.197	0.226
Sugar/conf. A*	2.450	1.735	>	0.518	0.055	0.006	0.012	0.674	0.341
Sugar/conf. B	1.284	1.114	>	0.133	0.034	0.004	0.008	0.133	0.152
Beverage A	0.916	1.611	<	-0.001	0.177	0.002	0.002	-0.010	0.451
Beverage B	1.036	1.204	<	0.099	0.034	0.008	0.007	0.134	0.173
Tobacco A	1.302	1.174	>	-0.001	0.024	0.004	0.006	0.051	0.238
Textiles A	1.404	1.795	<	0.227	0.060	0.039	0.020	0.266	0.522
Textiles B	1.896	2.759	<	0.195	0.065	0.013	0.006	0.366	1.044
Clothing A	1.184	1.395	<	0.044	0.072	0.025	0.011	0.096	0.348
Clothing B	1.629	1.261	>	0.592	0.062	0.009	0.008	0.602	0.163
Footwear A	0.993	1.341	<	0.061	0.109	0.013	0.009	0.050	0.291
Wood prod. A	1.137	1.730	<	0.068	0.070	0.027	0.021	0.122	0.612
Paper A	1.768	1.420	>	0.013	0.123	0.108	0.018	-0.015	0.350

Paper B	1.493	2.141	<	-0.010	0.095	0.080	0.012	0.192	0.942
Paper C*	0.888	1.219	<	0.121	0.046	0.007	0.012	0.151	0.223
Chem. Paint A	1.195	1.293	<	0.260	0.063	0.005	0.004	0.279	0.194
Chem. Paint B*	1.655	1.283	>	0.328	0.046	0.004	0.014	0.339	0.221
Chem. Pain C	1.550	1.113	>	0.149	0.063	0.003	0.042	0.155	0.150
Ind. chem. A	1.483	1.203	>	0.050	0.034	0.022	0.011	0.281	0.362
Ind. chem. B	1.057	1.382	<	0.062	0.058	0.001	0.025	0.066	0.331
Ind. chem. C	1.639	1.670	<	0.209	0.073	0.003	0.042	0.280	0.412
Pharmac. A	1.159	1.612	<	0.031	0.100	0.007	0.012	0.032	0.481
Pharmac. B.	1.053	0.860	<	0.053	0.057	0.003	0.002	0.033	0.327
Plastics A	0.810	1.285	<	0.045	0.048	0.011	0.012	0.155	0.169
Rubber A	1.200	1.089	>	0.145	0.060	0.012	0.015	0.156	0.225
Cement A	1.249	1.972	<	0.117	0.043	0.003	0.031	-0.353	0.862
Cement B	1.713	1.844	<	-0.026	0.078	0.072	0.011	-0.090	0.706
Basic Metal A	1.525	2.263	<	0.286	0.044	0.008	0.008	0.321	0.783
Basic Metal B	1.584	1.285	>	0.148	0.054	0.010	0.021	0.259	0.174
Metal prod. A	1.075	1.135	<	0.072	0.067	0.005	0.008	0.102	0.228
Metal prod. B	1.323	1.139	>	0.088	0.062	0.011	0.022	0.126	0.452
Metal prod. C	0.937	1.207	<	0.077	0.045	0.009	0.017	0.107	0.275
Auto. A	1.165	1.250	<	0.047	0.031	0.003	0.007	0.047	0.339
Auto. B	1.154	1.601	<	0.108	0.041	0.008	0.002	0.127	0.400
Auto. C	2.669	1.200	>	0.096	0.068	0.005	0.006	0.045	0.236
Auto. D	1.679	1.140	>	0.353	0.067	0.006	0.015	0.309	0.182
Average	1.252	1.416	<	0.080	0.062	0.016	0.014	0.086	0.353

The main cost distortions are shown in Tables 9.3 and 9.4. The sum of all input distortions, that is, the difference between UCx and UCs, which excludes the tariff on the output price, is shown in Table 9.4. It has increased on average from 8.6 percent to 35.3 percent, which represents the loss of domestic profitability at market prices. The cost impact of the tariff on inputs has declined from an average of 8 percent to 6.2 percent, which is a benefit from trade liberalization. The main unit cost increases are caused by the interest rate distortion impact going from –2.8 percent to 19.3 percent, and the misalignment of the Kenya shilling, which accounts for 7.5 percent—from zero in 1984. Table 9.4 also shows the unit-cost impact of distortions in energy and transport and communications costs, which account for 1.6 percent and 1.4 percent, respectively. Their importance as a proportion of output value is surprisingly low, although their importance expressed by firm officials in interviews and on the questionnaire is much more substantial. The highest energy cost distortion is observed in the paper industry, where electricity failure and taxes on fuel amount to over 10 percent of output value. Even more constraining are the extra costs reported for transport of inputs and for communications, where firms cope with the deteriorating railway, roads and telephone system by increased costs that are likely to reflect less than the total cost including the cost of frustration of the mangers and agents directly involved. Since we do not have reliable estimates of these costs in 1984, we could not quantify them for comparison with 1997, but it is clear from the questionnaires that these cost categories are much higher now than they were in the mid-eighties.

The industries that appear to be most export-competitive in 1997 are fruit canning, paints (firm C) and confectionery, and the ones least competitive seem to be in the textile, paper, cement, and chemical industries. This observation raises the question of how the message of our indicator can be reconciled with the actual export performance. While fruit canning is actually an export industry, paints and confectionery are mainly produced for the domestic market, with only limited exports. On the other hand, cement and paper are exported to neighboring countries by Kenyan firms. This apparent contradiction can be explained by two factors. First, the neighboring countries import at prices that are substantially higher than the international border price (cif Mombasa), due to transport costs. Second, the unit cost ratio is an indicator biased against capital-intensive industries, as we have shown earlier, and both paper and cement have highly capital-intensive production processes.

Comparative advantage and its sources

The unit cost ratio UCs, in which all costs and revenues are based on shadow prices, informs us about comparative advantage, which is understood as competitiveness in real terms. Essentially, it reflects efficiency and factor abundance (cheapness). It is important to remember that since the indicator UCs compares manufacturing costs with international free-trade prices, the criterion, UCs=1, is a very demanding one. It shows not only which industries, under distortion-less conditions would be able to export, but also which of all industries is relatively strongest in this respect. In the best of all economic environments, only about half of all activities can be expected to have comparative advantage.

The indicator of comparative advantage is shown for 1984 and 1997 in columns 2 and 3 of Table 9.5 with 3 of the 4 cost components (tradable inputs, labor, and capital) in columns 4 to 9. The fourth component, non-tradable inputs can be obtained by deduction of the 3 others from UCs. Taking the average UCs of all firms in both years, it has declined from 1.67 to 1.06, or by about 10 percent. This means that the firms in the present sample have, on average, increased their comparative advantage. This finding is of great importance, as it is the expected outcome under trade liberalization. For Kenya, it means that in spite of increasing disincentives to manufacturers, and declining competitiveness at market prices, resources have been moved to activities with comparative advantage. The number of firms having gained comparative advantage (or diminished their disadvantage) is 22, compared with 18 firms experiencing the opposite development. However, on average, the gains exceed the losses of comparative advantage by a significant margin.

As to the cost components, which can be seen as the sources of comparative advantage, one must remember that without a cost function analysis, we cannot derive definite conclusions. Only changes in the average can be observed. The most notable change is the reduction of the share of capital costs by 24 percent, from 27.8 percent to 22.2 percent of the output value. It is important to stress that this reduction is not due to the shadow interest rate, which was nearly the same in 1997 (14 percent) as in 1984 (14.4 percent). Rather, it reflects an improvement in the utilization rate of capital, which has been reported by the responding firms. The change in the average share of tradable inputs from 67.3 percent to 59.1 percent is evidence of rationalization in the use of inputs. The share of non-tradable, however, has increased from 12.9 percent to 14.9 percent, reflecting increases in the costs of transport and communications. Labor costs have increased from 8.6 percent to 10.2 percent.

The industries with the greatest comparative advantage seem to be rubber products, fruit canning, tobacco products and some chemicals, whereas textiles, paper and pharmaceuticals seem to have the least comparative advantage. This conclusion also holds some surprises because among the leaders in comparative advantage at least one is not an important exporter, whereas within the laggards we find at least one exporter. In other words, as long as industries function in price-distorted environments, they may find it more profitable to cater to the domestic market than to the export one in spite of comparative advantage, and firms with a comparative

Table 9.5   Unit cost ratios (UCs, VITs, LCs) of 42 firms in Kenya, 1984 and 1997

Industry/Firm	UCs		Cost components						Δ (**) in comp. advantage
			Tradable inputs		Labor		Capital		
	1984	1997	1984	1997	1984	1997	1984	1997	
Dairy A*	1.031	1.063	0.801	0.837	0.103	0.027	0.025	0.145	∨
Dairy B	–	1.007	–	0.504	–	0.096	–	0.115	
Fruit can. A	1.010	0.889	0.573	0.634	0.125	0.116	0.238	0.104	∧
Fish pack A	–	0.967	–	0.659	–	0.042	–	0.120	
Grain mill A	1.004	0.973	0.856	0.757	0.027	0.020	0.098	0.061	∧
Bakery A	1.497	1.181	0.746	0.751	0.106	0.095	0.569	0.237	∧
Bakery B*	1.525	1.044	0.660	0.841	0.060	0.046	0.601	0.081	∧
Sugar/conf. A*	1.777	1.393	0.472	1.031	0.249	0.070	0.812	0.280	∧
Sugar/conf. B	1.151	0.963	0.509	0.664	0.130	0.190	0.212	0.099	∧
Beverage A	0.925	1.160	0.454	0.801	0.147	0.096	0.255	0.218	∨
Beverage B	0.902	1.031	0.566	0.415	0.091	0.118	0.067	0.093	∨
Tobacco A	1.251	0.936	0.740	0.307	0.165	0.216	0.240	0.138	∧
Textiles A	1.139	1.273	0.627	0.649	0.201	0.173	0.061	0.453	∨
Textiles B	1.560	1.715	0.700	0.870	0.199	0.069	0.427	0.765	∨
Clothing A	1.089	1.047	0.560	0.422	0.150	0.219	0.209	0.166	∨
Clothing B	1.027	1.098	0.744	0.842	0.113	0.083	0.117	0.155	∨
Ft.wear A	0.943	1.050	0.254	0.530	0.179	0.233	0.258	0.098	∨
Woodprod. A	1.015	1.119	0.569	0.610	0.085	0.126	0.188	0.351	∨
Paper A	1.783	1.074	0.431	0.644	0.207	0.159	0.702	0.138	∧
Paper B	1.248	1.472	0.467	0.626	0.062	0.076	0.615	0.681	∨

Paper C*	0.738	0.996	0.464	0.604	0.103	0.128	0.103	0.163	<
Chem. Paint A	0.916	1.100	0.623	0.770	0.095	0.090	0.106	0.094	<
Chem. Paint B*	1.316	1.062	0.812	0.628	0.151	0.119	0.128	0.113	>
Chem. Paint C	1.394	0.962	0.609	0.655	0.184	0.104	0.125	0.049	>
Indi. chem. A	1.202	0.841	0.232	0.195	0.133	0.160	0.464	0.354	>
Ind. chem. B	0.992	1.051	0.799	0.645	0.068	0.114	0.041	0.197	<
Ind. chem. C	1.359	1.258	0.655	0.741	0.075	0.140	0.522	0.286	>
Pharm. A	1.127	1.131	0.728	0.573	0.090	0.193	0.243	0.256	<
Pharm. B*	1.020	1.533	0.343	0.700	0.244	0.149	0.200	0.178	<
Plastics A	0.655	1.116	0.192	0.691	0.103	0.151	0.280	0.161	<
Rubber A	1.043	0.064	0.508	0.470	0.107	0.096	0.322	0.116	>
Cement A	1.602	1.110	0.653	0.368	0.108	0.116	0.718	0.520	>
Cement B	1.802	1.138	0.770	0.407	0.004	0.148	0.743	0.558	>
Basic met. A	1.204	1.480	0.821	0.829	0.056	0.065	0.257	0.563	>
Basic met. B	1.325	1.111	0.888	0.995	0.024	0.024	0.332	0.075	>
Metal prod. A	0.973	0.907	0.695	0.650	0.085	0.083	0.112	0.114	>
Metal prod. B*	1.197	0.938	0.834	0.485	0.095	0.076	0.155	0.343	>
Metal prod. C*	0.830	0.932	0.364	0.309	0.165	0.120	0.175	0.166	<
Auto. A*	1.118	0.911	0.626	0.478	0.148	0.116	0.206	0.254	>
Auto. B	1.027	1.201	0.682	0.432	0.073	0.150	0.140	0.214	<
Auto. C	2.624	0.964	1.693	0.451	0.097	0.224	0.636	0.102	>
Auto. D	1.370	0.958	1.140	0.760	0.084	0.032	0.116	0.087	>
Average	1.166	1.063	0.673	0.591	0.086	0.102	0.278	0.222	>

Note: Asterisks indicate (*) firms as preceding tables and (**) increase (>) and decrease (<) in comparative advantage. ? = change.

disadvantage may be able to export under distorted market prices. The explanations of this phenomenon are similar to those given under export competitiveness.

As to the sources of comparative advantage from a more general point of view, we saw in the analysis of 1984 that there was a bias against capital-intensive industries. Firms were more likely to be non-competitive (UCs>1), when their capital cost was particularly high. In the 1997 sample of firms, the bias is less significant, due to the smaller sample size. The highest correlation (R^2=0.44) exists again between UCs and capital, which has a negative intercept, implying that the use of capital is still a source of disadvantage. The firms with lowest unit costs tend to use the least capital. The equations for the trend lines of all four factors are as follows:

VITs = 0.106 + 0.475 CUs	with R^2 = 0.232
VINs = 0.183 - 0.048 CUs	with R^2 = 0.006
LCs = 0.154 - 0.034 CUs	with R^2 = 0.014
KCs = -0.443 + 0.607 UCs	with R^2 = 0.441,

where VITs, VINs, LCs and KCs are the unit cost ratios of traded and non-traded inputs, total labor and total capital, respectively. In 1984 the bias could be attributed to low capacity utilization, but in 1997, it is attributable to the high price of capital, since capacity utilization rates were generally higher. The analysis also shows that the strongest bias is in favor of traded inputs. Firms may be able to achieve lower unit costs by using more transformed tradable inputs, a phenomenon well known as specialization in more industrialized countries.

Industry-level analysis and comparisons with industries in Uganda

The aggregation of data from 42 firms to 16 industries, defined at the four-digit level of the International Standard Industrial Classification (ISIC), makes the presentation of results easier and hides firm-specific details in the interest of confidentiality, but it also hides particular insights one gets from working at the firm level. The aggregated data do not permit us to infer to what extent firm-specific factors influence the industries' unit costs. When firm-level data are being used, one can easily find industries in which one firm does extremely well and another extremely badly. It is then interesting to investigate the reasons for different performance, separating market and policy-induced factors from firm-specific ones, such as managerial efficiency or inefficiency. Since in the present context we focus on policy-induced effects rather than intra-firm characteristics, it is useful to move to the aggregated results, although there are some problems of comparability between the samples of Kenyan and Ugandan industries. The sample of 21 Ugandan firms is aggregated to 12 industries, 11 of which have a counterpart in Kenya. In one industry, animal feed, we could not obtain any data from a Kenyan firm. For details about the Ugandan industries and policy environment, the reader is referred to the Uganda component of the present study.

Competitiveness and comparative advantage

Starting again with the indicator of domestic competitiveness (CUd), that is, under the full influence of distortions, the comparison with Uganda leads us to a surprise. The Ugandan firms in our sample are, on average, more profitable and in that sense more competitive than the Kenyan firms. This conclusion is reached not only by use of the unit cost ratio, but is also counter-checked against the gross rate of return as computed from the cost and revenue data. The difference is in the order of 13 percent (based on the weighted average of CUd as obtained from aggregation and shown in the bottom line of Table 9.6, which is substantial. Given the fears frequently expressed by Ugandan industry officials, of Kenyan industrial superiority, the observation comes as a surprise.

Table 9.6 shows that, out of 11 industries with comparable but not fully equal product mix, 6 Ugandan industries have a lower CUd than their Kenyan competitors. The reverse is true in only 4 Kenyan industries, while 1 industry is on equal footing. One could explain this finding by possibly higher protection in Uganda, but the opposite is the case. As we shall see in the discussion of distortions, the total impact of tariff protection is lower, and that of the exchange rate higher, than in Kenya. Therefore, the higher Kenyan unit cost ratio must be a consequence of additional or higher cost factors.

With regard to export competitiveness, the situation is similar, but less pronounced: Kenyan industries appear to be less competitive (average UCx = 1.416) than Ugandan industries (UCx = 1.332). Since UCx differs from CUd only by the output tariff and, in Uganda's case, by the border price differential, the answer is clear: the combined protective effect of the output tariff and the border price differential is smaller than the unit cost differential. In other words, if the border price differential was zero and the output tariff equal in both countries, the unit cost differential would be even greater and to the disadvantage of Kenya.

The data in Table 9.6 show that, in terms of comparative advantage, based on the unit cost ratio at shadow prices, the situation is reversed: Kenyan industries are, on average, more competitive in real terms than their Ugandan counterparts. The conclusion also holds for 7 out of 11 individual industries. On a one-by-one basis, the reversal (from CUd and UCx) occurs only in 2 industries, bakeries and cement. Their distortions are stronger penalties than those in Uganda. In all other industries, the unit cost superiority or inferiority runs in the same direction for all 3 indicators.

Given the importance of the distortions for policy purposes, let us now see how they differ between the two countries.

Table 9.6   Unit cost ratios in Kenyan and Ugandan industries, 1997

Industry	Unit cost rations					
	CUd		**UCx**		**UCs**	
	Kenya	*Uganda*	*Kenya*	*Uganda*	*Kenya*	*Uganda*
Dairy products	1.096	1.172	1.224	1.359	1.008	1.080
Fruit/Fish process.	1.080	0.996	1.080	0.996	0.886	0.878
Grain mills	1.034	1.090	1.166	1.277	0.973	1.117
Bakery prod.	1.287	1.066	1.454	1.386	1.132	1.190
Sugar/Conf.	1.160	–	1.437	–	1.170	–
Bever/Tobacco	0.990	–	1.215	–	0.982	–
Text./Clothing	1.408	2.365	1.660	2.991	1.199	2.099
Footwear	1.054	0.885	1.341	1.132	1.050	0.967
Wood/Paper	1.738	1.500	2.005	1.334	1.276	1.152
Chem: Paint	0.992	1.078	1.236	1.324	1.039	1.143
Industr. chem.	1.178	–	1.347	–	0.998	–
Pharmaceut.	1.538	–	1.824	–	1.458	–
Plastic/Rubber	0.879	–	1.095	–	0.828	–
Cement	1.721	0.961	1.936	1.539	1.139	1.257
Metal prod.	1.099	1.099	1.326	1.418	1.063	1.157
Automotive	0.985	0.728	1.171	0.947	0.963	0.839
Average	1,221	1.089	1.416	1.332	1.063	1.115

Distortion analysis

The distortions with the greatest impact on unit costs are, in the order of magnitude, the interest rate distortion, tariff protection and the exchange rate distortion. Table 9.7 shows them at the industry level in both countries. The total effect of the tariff regime, including output and input tariffs, is shown in columns 1 and 2. The average impact on unit costs is 13.8 percent in Kenya and 4 percent in Uganda, both being negative, since the protective effect on output is stronger than that of the tariff on imported inputs, due to the cascading tariff.

The currency misalignment, which is estimated to be 10 percent in Kenya and 20 percent in Uganda, has an average unit-cost impact of 7.5 percent in Kenya and of 9.5 percent in Uganda. The interest rate distortion is much more important in Kenya due to the high lending rate of 30 percent, while in Uganda it is only 21.5 percent. In addition, the shadow rate used in Kenya (14 percent) is lower than that used in Uganda (16 percent), which can be seen as a reflection of a more developed financial sector.

The average interest rate distortion, therefore, adds 19.3 percent to unit costs in Kenya, but only 5.6 percent in Uganda. The other distortions, in labor costs, capital goods, prices, and non-tradables, are of similar magnitudes and small in both countries. The transport cost distortion on input costs is the only one that is significantly bigger in Uganda, due to its landlocked geography and major problems in the transport link between the seaport of Mombasa and the Ugandan border. The communications cost distortion, on the other hand, is smaller in Uganda, since its telephone system is reported to be more reliable.

Table 9.7   Main distortions in unit costs in Kenya and Ugandan industries, 1997

Industry	Main distortions					
	Tariff protection		Exchange rate		Interest rate	
	Kenya	*Uganda*	*Kenya*	*Uganda*	*Kenya*	*Uganda*
Dairy prod.	−0.101	−0.004	0.065	0.111	0.091	0.043
Fruit/Fish packing	0.043	0.053	0.040	0.047	0.076	0.014
Grain mill	−0.028	−0.001	0.037	0.081	0.048	0.028
Bakery prod.	−0.099	−0.168	0.062	0.088	0.178	0.040
Sugar/Confect.	−0.230	–	0.049	–	0.158	–
Bev./Tobacco	−0.185	–	0.077	–	0.098	–
Text/Clothing	−0.184	−0.267	0.097	0.398	0.272	0.319
Footwear	−0.178	−0.131	0.074	0.091	0.081	0.015
Wood/Paper	−0.190	−0.007	0.126	0.102	0.456	0.029
Chem: Paint	−0.192	−0.041	0.054	0.071	0.081	0.040
Ind. chem.	−0.112	–	0.075	–	0.202	–
Pharmaceut.	−0.207	–	0.106	–	0.176	–
Plastic/Rubber	−0.121	–	0.060	–	0.089	–
Cement	−0.164	−0.102	0.142	0.153	0.481	0.167
Metal prod.	−0.149	−0.052	0.045	0.125	0.114	0.052
Automotive	−0.115	−0.074	0.041	0.083	0.094	0.035
Average	−0.133	−0.040	0.075	0.095	0.193	0.056

For the energy distortion, the computed rate appears to be higher in Uganda, but this may be the result of evaluating it differently. While in Kenya it is based on the firms' own evaluation of the cost differential between actual and 'normal' operation, in Uganda, it is based on the finding of another study (UMA, 1996). In both countries, firms have regularly reported electricity blackouts, but it is not clear whether they are more or less important, cost-wise, in either country.

In conclusion of the comparison between Kenyan and Ugandan industries, it appears that Kenya has an edge over Ugandan manufacturers in terms of comparative advantage, but this edge is cancelled out by the sum of all distortions. At present prices and rates of protection, Ugandan firms are more profitable, and thereby have a reserve to use when competition heats up under further regional integration. On the other hand, the landlocked position of Uganda, which raises most of its prices above those in Kenya and provides some natural protection to Uganda's industries, makes it also more difficult to envisage exports towards Kenya by Ugandan industries, even if some of them may have a slight comparative advantage vis-à-vis Kenya.

Sensitivity analysis for the indicators of the Kenyan sample of firms

The sensitivity of our findings to changes in some of the key variables is being explored by simulating the indicators. We examine how the indicators are affected by different assumptions about the shadow prices. This approach attempts to overcome the uncertainty about finding and using the most accurate estimates of true scarcity prices. It leads us to determine the maxima and minima of UCs that determine the ranges of greater certainty and possible error in our evaluation. Obviously, these simulations do not affect the values of CUd and UCx, and only the findings about comparative advantage are being modified.

As we have shown in the preceding section, the price distortion with the strongest impact on unit costs is that of the interest rate. This follows from our assumption of international mobility of capital and the choice of a shadow interest rate that equals the international rate in the form of LIBOR, adjusted only for differential inflation. This assumption may be, and has been, criticized as being unrealistic.[5] One can argue that the scarcity price of capital in a country like Uganda must include certain real costs that are due to the underdeveloped state of the financial sector and to low domestic savings. Unfortunately, we do not possess reliable data on these factors. On the other hand, we also see the average lending rate as a rate that includes elements, which we would clearly label as distortions, such as the impact of insufficient enforcement of banking regulations. The sensitivity of the unit cost ratios to variations in the shadow interest rate (rs) is therefore examined by calculating a lower and an upper bound of it. An alternative rate based on the interest rate parity condition can be computed as LIBOR plus the expected rate of currency depreciation. Taking the actual exchange rate of t+1, one obtains an expected rate of depreciation in Kenya's case of 3 percent, implying a shadow interest rate of 9 percent. Under purchasing power parity, this rate should be the same as the one based on the inflation differential. The fact that it is lower suggests that investors may have expected some appreciation of the Kenya shilling in real terms. This is unlikely, however, given the weakness of foreign capital inflows. If one takes the total rate of overvaluation as the expected rate of depreciation, that is 10 percent, one obtains an interest rate of 16.6 percent, which we consider as the upper bound, while the rate of 9 percent is taken as the lower bound, and the median rate of 14 percent is used in the computations as the most likely value.

As to the misalignment of the exchange rate, we had argued earlier that by 1997 the Kenya shilling had appreciated in real terms and we estimated the rate of overvaluation as 10 percent. For simulation purposes we are using a lower bound of zero and an upper bound of 20 percent. The latter rate is a conservative estimate, based on the fact that the shilling had depreciated very strongly in 1993, which one could consider as a year of equilibrium (with possibly some degree of over-shooting) and that the real exchange rate vis-à-vis the US$ appreciated by at least 20 percent between 1993 and 1997. Based on these estimates of upper and lower bounds of the shadow interest rate (rs) and exchange rate overvaluation (Reo), the data in Table 9.8 show the unit cost ratios at shadow prices of the total sample of firms (weighted average).

Table 9.8 Comparative advantage (UCs) under varying assumptions about the shadow interest rate (rs) and currency overvaluation (Reo)

	Shadow interest rate (rs)		
Reo (percent)	9.000	14.000	16.6
0	1.044	1.111	1.145
10	1.003	1.063	1.095
20	0.970	1.025	1.054

The analysis suggests that for our sample of industries, the unit cost ratio at shadow prices may vary between a minimum of 0.97 and a maximum of 1.15, depending on what values of rs and Reo we assume to be most realistic. Since the interest rate and the exchange rate are related, and since the maximum of one is not compatible with the minimum of the other, the median value of each appears to be the safest estimate. A unit cost ratio of 1.06, taken as a sector average, means comparative disadvantage vis-à-vis the rest of the world, but a slight comparative advantage vis-à-vis Ugandan manufacturing, where the comparable rate was computed as 1.12. We have concluded in the detailed industry analysis only presented in the full-length report of the project (Siggel, Ikiara, Nganda, 1999), that there are several industries in which Ugandan firms may become suppliers of Kenyan demand or, at least, Kenyan exporters may lose their competitive advantage relative to Ugandan producers under further regional integration and adjustments by the firms.

Conclusions

The analysis reveals that, in the Kenyan manufacturing sector, only very few industries had comparative advantage and were internationally competitive in the mid-1980s. This situation has not improved, but instead seems to have deteriorated, in spite of over 10 years of structural adjustment and trade policy changes. If this was only true for profitability and as a consequence of decreased protection, then one could consider this as normal for such a transition period. But since it is not even clear that actual protection, as measured by comparison of domestic and international prices, has declined as one would expect, the declining competitiveness must be attributed to increased costs, and we have substantial evidence of this. Competitiveness in the protected domestic market is also weakened due to these cost increases. At present, using the tariff instead of the implicit NRP in about half of the cases, it appears that on average, protection is not reduced in comparison to the mid-1980s.

Although price distortions may have diminished somewhat, new kinds of cost distortions have been added. Generally speaking, we may call them distortions of public service deficiencies, such as the extra cost resulting from the deterioration of infrastructure, especially transport and communication, but also energy and water supply. The biggest additional cost, however, is caused by the inefficiency of the financial sector, which makes borrowing for investment prohibitive. Finally, the exchange rate also contributes to competitive weakness by showing signs of overvaluation.

Judging from the responses of the participating firms and from the quantitative analysis of their data, we conclude that in order to accelerate industrialization, the Government of Kenya must make fundamental policy changes. It is not sufficient to plunge a still adolescent industrial sector into partially or even fully liberated international trade, hoping that the invisible hand will do the rest. What is needed is an industrial strategy in which the government plays an active role in creating the enabling environment. It would appear that in Kenya the environment for business has been rather disabled than enabled in recent years, in spite of the existence of very well intentioned policy documents. If the present downward trend is not drastically reversed, the goal of industrial maturity in the year 2020 is more like wishful thinking.

Policy recommendations

Given the national goal of transforming Kenya into a Newly Industrialized Country (NIC) by the year 2020, and given the environment of globalization and liberalized trade, it is clear that increased competitiveness must become a major objective and challenge for all industries. This is true in international as well as in regional markets.

The study shows that some of the macroeconomic policies and variables are of crucial importance for the attainment of competitiveness by industries. In particular, low cost of borrowing, a stable and well-aligned exchange rate, as well as a sound infrastructure in transport, communications, energy and water supply, are a pre-condition for industrial growth.

We recognize the benefits of liberalized trade, but we also observe that opening up of the economy is not sufficient to achieve the goals of increased competitiveness and industrial growth. What is needed is a cautious progression of trade liberalization combined with an industrial strategy that recognizes the importance of the pace at which industries can adjust to the changing environment.

The study clearly shows that the enactment of a liberal trade policy is not sufficient, but must be accompanied by effective enforcement of the trade regime. The recent changes in the trade regime seem to be sufficient to create a level playing field for competing firms, but only if the respective laws are effectively enforced. This pertains particularly to the customs administration. We observe that several sectors have been adversely affected by the failure to enforce the existing trade policies.

The recent trend of declining interest rates is a step in the right direction, but it needs to be further pursued by sound fiscal policies, in order to bring the cost of borrowing to a level that permits industries to make new investments for increased competitiveness.

We also recognize that the recent depreciation of the currency has reduced the observed misalignment and often-heard complaint of over-valuation that hurts competitors in international markets. A cautious approach to currency depreciation is, however, necessary to prevent new inflationary pressure, which would cancel the gains in competitiveness.

Transport and communications are two areas in which industries suffer from substantial extra costs that inhibit their competitive strength. We recognize that some steps are being taken to reduce these problems, but it is urgent to accelerate the pace of such renewal. In addition to improvements in the road infrastructure, it seems urgent to further the pace toward privatization of the railways in order to make them again fully functional.

There seems to be an urgent need for more stringent quality controls and the enforcement of standards, in order to assure that Kenyan producers can compete in export markets. This is particularly important in the food industries and especially urgent in fish processing, where the ban of exports from East Africa to the European Union has badly hurt the sector.

Some sectors require political support, as well as regional co-operation, in order to allow industries to exploit their natural comparative advantage. Regional integration tends to be successful when intra-industry trade flourishes. The study provided us with some preliminary evidence of superior competitiveness in some fast growing industries in Uganda. Some Kenyan producers may see this as a threat to their traditional export perspectives. It can, however, also be seen as an opportunity to develop intra-industry trade between the countries of the East Africa region, which would benefit their economic growth.

Notes

1. This proposition is demonstrated in Siggel (1993) and originally established in Dornbusch, Fisher and Samuelson (1979).
2. IMF, IFS Yearbook (1999, p. 106), LIBOR on one year US$ deposits.
3. Based on consumer price indices of Kenya (12 percent) and industrial countries (2 percent). IFS Yearbook (1999).
4. Comments by Mr. Tumusiime Mutebile, Secretary of the Treasury, Government of Uganda.
5. Comments by Mr. Tumusiime Mutebile, Secretary of the Treasury, Government of Uganda.

References

ADB (African Development Bank) (1995), *African Development Report, 1995*, ADB: Abidjan, Côte d'Ivoire.

Cockburn, J. and Siggel, E. (1995), 'Une méthode d'analyse de la compétivité', Fiche technique #6, *Réseau sur les politique industrielles*, CODESRIA: Dakar, Senegal.

Cockburn, J., Siggel, E. Coulibaly, M. and Vézina, S. (1999), 'Measuring Competitiveness and Its Sources: The Case of Mali's Manufacturing Sector', *Canadian Journal of Development Studies*, Vol. 20, No. 3, pp. 491=519.

Dlamini, A. T. (1987), 'Management of Foreign Exchange Reserves Through Quantitative Controls: The Kenyan Experience', MBA Research Paper, University of Nairobi: Nairobi, Kenya.

Dornbusch, R, Fischer, S. and Samuelson, P. A. (1977), 'Comparative Advantage, Trade and Payments in a Ricardian Model With a Continuum of Goods', *American Economic Review*, Vol. 67, No. 5 (December), pp. 823–839.

Elbadawi, I. A. (1998), 'Real Exchange Rate Policy and Non-Traditional Exports in Developing Countries', AERC Mimeo: Nairobi, Kenya.

GoK (1986), *Sessional Paper No. 1 on Economic Management for Renewed Growth*, Government Printer: Nairobi, Kenya.

GoK (1996), *Sessional Paper No. 2 on Industrial Transformation to the Year 2020*, Government Printer: Nairobi, Kenya.

GoK (1996, 1997, 1999), *Economic Survey*, Government Printer: Nairobi, Kenya.

Jansen, D. J., et al. (1985), 'Preliminary Protection and Efficiency Indicators for the Kenyan Manufacturing Sector', Ministry of Planning and National Development & Ministry of Commerce: Nairobi, Kenya.

KAM (1992), 'The Financing Needs of Kenya's Manufacturing Sector', Kenya Association of Manufacturers, Nairobi, Kenya, Mimeo.

KEDS (1993), 'Kenya Export Policy Baseline Study', Kenya Export Development Support Project, Development Alternatives, Inc. and The Services Group, Inc., Mimeo.

KEDS (1994a), *Export Competitiveness Study, Vol. I: Comparative Analysis*, The Services Group, Inc., Mimeo.

KEDS (1994b), *Export Competitiveness Study, Vol. II: Policy Measures to Improve Competitiveness*, The Services Group, Inc., Mimeo.

McCormick, D. (1998), 'Policies Affecting Kenyan Industrialization: 1964–1994', in Ng'ethe, N. and Owino, W. (eds.), *From Sessional Paper No. 10 to Structural Adjustment: Towards Indigenizing the Policy Debate*, Institute of Policy Analysis and Research: Nairobi, Kenya.

Mwega, F. M. and Ndung'u, N. S. (1998), 'Macroeconomic Policies and Exchange Rate Management in African Economies', AERC and Economics Department, University of Nairobi:: Nairobi, Kenya.

Ndung'u, N. S. (1997), 'Active Exchange Rate Management: The Case of Botswana and Kenya—A Contrasting Example of Managing Booms With a Stabilizing Instrument', Paper presented at the *Commonwealth Secretariat Training on Economic Reform and Management for the Africa Region*, June 2–20, Nairobi, Kenya.

RPED (1996), 'Regional Program on Enterprise Development: Report on Round 3 of the Kenya Survey', Department of Economics, University of Nairobi & Department of Economics, University of Gotenborg: Nairobi, Kenya and Gotenborg, Sweden.

Sharpley, J. and Lewis, S. (1988), 'Kenya's Industrialization, 1964–84', IDS Discussion Paper No. 242, Institute of Development Studies: Sussex, UK.

Siggel, E. (1991), 'Recent Industrial Growth and Development in Kenya: Constraints and Prospects for the Future', in Dasgupta, P. (ed.), *Issues in Contemporary Economics: Proceedings of the 9th World Congress*, International Economic Association and Macmillan: London.

Siggel, E. (1993), 'International Competitiveness, Comparative Advantage and Incentives: Interrelationships and Measurements', Discussion Paper Series, DP 9314, Department of Economics, Concordia University: Montreal, Canada.

Siggel, E. (1997), 'Les concepts, measures et sources de la compétitivité internationale: une revue de la litérature', *Resau de politiques industrielles*, Mimeo, Dakar, Senegal.

Siggel, E., Ikiara, G. K. and Nganda, B. (1999), 'Industry Competitiveness, Trade Prospects and Growth in Kenya and Uganda: The Kenya Component and Comparisons With Uganda', Mimeo.

Siggel, E. and Ssemogerere, G. (2000), 'Uganda's Policy Reforms, Industry Competitiveness and Regional Integration: A Comparison with Kenya', EAGER Discussion Paper No. 4.

Swamy, G. (1994), 'Kenya: Patchy, Intermittent Commitment', in Husain, I. and Faruquee, R. (eds.), *Adjustment in Africa: Lessons from Country Case Studies*, The World Bank: Washington, DC.

Tostensen, A. (1991), 'Between Shamba and Factory: Industrial Labor Migration', in Coughlin, P. and Ikiara, G. K. (eds.), *Kenya's Industrialization Dilemma*, Heinemann: Nairobi, Kenya.

Wignaraja, G. and Ikiara, G. K. (1999), 'Adjustment, Technological Capabilities and Enterprise Dynamics in Kenya', in Lall, S. (ed.), *The Technological Response to Import Liberalization in sub-Saharan Africa*, Macmillan: London.

Index